John L. Sullivan

John L. Sullivan

The Career of the First Gloved Heavyweight Champion

ADAM J. POLLACK

McFarland & Company, Inc., Publishers

Jefferson, North Carolina, and London

LIBRARY OF CONGRESS CATALOGUING-IN-PUBLICATION DATA

Pollack, Adam J.
John L. Sullivan : the career of the first gloved heavyweight champion / Adam J. Pollack.
p.   cm.
Includes bibliographical references and index.

ISBN-13: 978-0-7864-2558-7
ISBN-10: 0-7864-2558-X
(softcover : 50# alkaline paper) ∞

1. Sullivan, John Lawrence, 1858–1918.
2. Boxers (Sports)—United States—Biography.
3. Boxing—United States—History.   I. Title.
GV1132.S95P65   2006   796.83092—dc22   2006022232

British Library cataloguing data are available

Cover photograph © 2004 Brand X Pictures

Manufactured in the United States of America

*McFarland & Company, Inc., Publishers
Box 611, Jefferson, North Carolina 28640
www.mcfarlandpub.com*

For my parents.
You were always in my corner.

Acknowledgments

I would like to thank all of the fantastic folks who have been of help to me:

The University of Iowa Interlibrary Loan Services: You have been an integral part of this process, and your wonderful assistance has made my dream of writing this book come true. In particular, I want to thank Randy Essing, whose time, assistance, support and wisdom has been invaluable. You are awesome. Christine Klein, it is always good to see you and you have been a huge help to me. Thank you also to Cheryl Huyck (who makes the best brownies); you have been quite kind to me and are always so helpful. Debra Lee, Amy Kohlstedt, Gina Peterson, and Aaron Burnett, all of whom do great work at the university and help foster a wonderful environment.

The University of Iowa Media Services: I always look forward to seeing all of you as I conduct countless hours of research. In particular, thanks to Pamela Barta-Kacena, who has always been very supportive. Julita Potter, Allyson Herman, Mischa Andersen, Eric Earhart, Mark Anthony, Colin McGellit, Rich McWilliams and Mark Huelsbeck, you have been so helpful, and do a wonderful job of maintaining important historic microfilms and microfilm machines.

The University of Iowa is an excellent place to learn and grow, and to develop meaningful projects.

All the folks at Cyberboxingzone.com and Boxrec.com: You have created and supported two fantastic boxing Web sites that are devoted to improving knowledge about the sport, and whose contributions are invaluable to boxing history. I am in awe of you. Stephen Gordon, I appreciate all your kind words of encouragement over the years.

Clay Moyle: You maintain a wonderful collection of historic boxing books and memorabilia. You are a really nice guy and your generosity in providing me with primary resources and photographs was amazing. Folks, look out for his upcoming book on Sam Langford.

Connor Wittman: Thanks for your assistance with photo scanning.

Iowa Historical Society: Thank you for maintaining such rare and important historical documents.

Sean Curtin: You are a true historian and I always enjoy conversing with you. Thank you for generously providing me with those *Ring* magazines.

The State Library of New South Wales, Michael Pascoe of W & F Pascoe Pty Ltd. (www.pascoe.com.au), and Robert Archer of Gosford Micrographics Pty Ltd., (www.gosmicro.com.au): You kindly provided me with Australian primary source information, and I hope that you will continue to maintain and archive these valuable resources.

Wes Kelm: You are a great teacher and friend. Your lesson about citing and analyzing sources remains with me today.

Will Toomey, Steve Coughlin and Derek Mays: You are the best boxing buddies a guy could have. Thanks for always being so supportive, insightful, and fun.

Thank you to all those that have supported the Iowa City/Coralville Boxing Club as well as other boxing gyms across the country. You help make dreams come true.

Brian Allen: Thanks for believing in my club when others might not have.

Jeff Nehring: Thank you so much for taking an interest in me and for believing in me in all things. As a boxing coach, you have been amongst a special fraternity of selfless volunteers who really make the world a better place. Your words of wisdom are indelibly imprinted upon me.

Cindy Parsons and Gary Klinefelter: Thanks for always being so supportive. You have a fantastic family, and I am thrilled to be a part of it.

Katy Klinefelter: Thanks for being kind enough to review a draft of my work, and, for being so dedicated to boxing. Katy is my first national champion.

Emily Klinefelter: You are a unique and brilliant person, as well as one heck of a fighter.

Grandma Elsie: You are with me still. Grandpa and Grandma: I'll never forget from where I came.

Carlye: Thanks for always being such a great sister, no matter what.

And most importantly, Mom and Dad: Thank you for accepting and supporting my interest in what many consider to be an odd sport. You provided me with the strong educational background that enabled me to write this book, and to live my life as I desire. Without you, I would not be who I am today. You've done well as caring and supportive parents and I love you for it.

Contents

Preface: Why I Undertook This Project and Why You Should Read It

Before reading this book you should ask yourself why you are willing to invest your valuable time in it as opposed to many others that you could select.

I have written a book that is unique among boxing books. It is not going to give the same facts and stories that other books continually regurgitate and steal from each other, adding nothing further to history. It will be revealing and informative even to seasoned historians, for it is the most thoroughly researched and detailed accounting of legendary champion John L. Sullivan's career. This book

1. Presents facts and analysis that no other book has presented. My research reveals previously unknown historical details and addresses many unsolved mysteries.
2. Provides multiple local and national primary source fight accountings to highlight differences in what was said at the time (the 1870s through the early 1890s), rather than simply put forth one version of events. I have extensively researched primary source accountings of significant bouts and cite those sources.
3. Discusses opponents' careers so that the significance of the bouts can be analyzed. The opponents are more than just names on paper.
4. Describes Sullivan's skill development and provides critiques of his abilities over the course of his career. Very few boxing fans know much about Sullivan's skill level, or the types of techniques that he utilized. Boxing books rarely chart over the course of a fighter's career how the press and experts changed their views regarding that boxer's skills and abilities.
5. Provides sociological, legal, and historic context. Readers will further understand what happened inside the ring by learning about what was going on outside the ring. This includes a discussion of how anti–prize fight laws prevented or affected fights, as well as an in-depth and frank analysis of the color line and Peter Jackson's career. Even Australian primary sources are used, giving the perspective of Jackson's home country.

This book is distinguishable from other books written on Sullivan (including his autobiography) in that it is more thorough, corrects mistakes, adds missing information, further develops and highlights factual discrepancies, relies on local primary sources, provides multiple perspectives, and supplies greater detail and analysis regarding the fights and opponents. One thing this book won't do that many others do is focus on every detail of fighters' personal lives, unless those facts have some significant bearing upon their careers. I'm writing about boxers and their boxing lives.

Also in this book, I bring to life the era's boxing scene, to assist readers in understanding the period and who these fighters were and what their relative merits were. I consider who they fought, why they were important, what their bouts meant for the sport and society, and whether boxers were worthy contenders and champions. Facts regarding how boxers performed against different and common opponents are provided so that readers can make comparisons and assess their careers. I describe what other fighters, champions, and future champions were doing at the same time to provide context. These are the types of things that I have found to be lacking in boxing books.

Boxing history also demonstrates how history gets recorded and how different people can witness the same event and provide different perspectives regarding what occurred. It is the history of reporting, of human perception, memory, discourse and its variations. From a historian's perspective, boxing is fascinating because its history is extensive and traceable. Even with that said, many holes in boxing history remain, and sources often differ in their accountings of facts or lack citations to support their assertions. I call attention to these differences and issues in this book.

Two things that I have learned in writing about boxing history and which explain the way that I have written this book are (1) never trust a book that doesn't cite its sources (unfortunately, this is very commonplace when it comes to boxing) and (2) the most complete and accurate understanding of an event is usually derived from referring to more than one local source. Too many boxing books cannot support their assertions, or over-rely on non-local or secondary sources, or fail to give multiple views of a fight, leading to questions about their accuracy and completeness. Even today, one fight can often have multiple perspectives and analysis. Therefore, it is important to review historic bouts through more than one viewpoint.

The sport's significant controversies, mysteries and debates are addressed using mostly primary but also secondary sources. Without the benefit of film, and being able to actually watch a bout from Sullivan's time, it is difficult to determine the accuracy of written accounts. This is why I often present different versions of fights, particularly ones with some controversy—to emphasize the difficulty in determining exactly what happened, and to provide readers with an overall feel for what was said about what occurred. Boxing books generally fail to do this. This book better discusses Sullivan's fights and provides many of the details that other books on Sullivan do not. It also corrects and addresses many of the factual inaccuracies put forth by many secondary sources.

Usually, when more sources are reviewed, more is learned about an event, at times unraveling a mystery, and at times further highlighting the factual confusion which existed. Again, many boxing books fail in this respect, as they simply present their version as the gospel truth. It is difficult for authors not to do that, and I may at times inject my opinion or slant my comments based on my review of the accounts, but I also try to present different versions of an event.

The varying shades of old-time bout accountings highlight another difficulty in attempting to recount boxing history. Newspaper and written accounts of bouts are quite often inaccurate. Even discounting the failings of sight, memory, and the inability of non-fight people to understand what goes on in a bout without the benefit of instant replay, newsmen often took liberties with their accountings, either to boost sales or as the result of bribes. Sometimes, reporters or periodicals allowed personal feelings towards certain fighters, either positive or negative, to influence their coverage. Periodicals could even have their own financial reasons to promote or attack certain fights or fighters because of their own financial ties to them. Sometimes, fighters themselves or their managers would tell vastly different stories than those reported in order to boost their own reputations or to gain momentum for a match or rematch. Writers would at times rely on the fighters for their facts, so the veracity of reports could depend on the truthfulness of the fighters.

History is also about the process of selecting which facts to discuss. Differences could be the result of one writer including facts that another did not, with both rendering truthful but incomplete stories. Many fight reports were based on one or more telegraphs, and could be an amalgamation of multiple accounts by a writer who may or may not have witnessed the bout. This is why it is so important that more boxing books provide multiple fight accountings and citations to sources, as this book does. When not utilizing multiple sources, I usually tried to rely on a local source, because most often it is those sources that are the most accurate and thorough, and the bout most likely was actually viewed by the writer. That said, those accounts are not necessarily always the final word, because sometimes non-local reporters were more interested in a fight than were the locals.

Another fascinating aspect of boxing is that it often interacted with the law and world events, having national, social, and racial symbolism. Its champions were national figures whose lives were often extensively followed by the media. Their careers can be a useful way to track world history. Sociological and legal analysis of boxing provides further insight into what occurred or was allowed to occur inside the ring, but sociology books usually neglect the in-the-ring occurrences. This book provides social and legal background where it has a significant impact on the sport or the analysis of a champion's reign, but not at the expense of the actual in-the-ring occurrences.

In conclusion, by combining factual results, well-researched analysis of primary and secondary sources, and history, sociology, and law with critical views of the bouts, I have told the story of this champion in a unique way so that readers may obtain a new perspective about John L. Sullivan.

Adam J. Pollack
Summer 2006

CHAPTER 1

Understanding the System Under Which They Fought

> Honored stranger, come and test yourself in competition ... for there is no greater glory
> for a man than that which he wins with his own hands and feet.
> —Homer, *The Odyssey*, book VIII

To view the beginning of gloved boxing through the prism of today's understanding of the sport is to completely misunderstand the sport as it was performed at the time. To appreciate the fighting style and techniques of early gloved bouts, one must understand the bareknuckle style and rules from which gloved bouts arose, as well as the early rules of gloved bouts. Many historians and analysts criticize the techniques of early boxers. While some of the criticisms are meritorious given that the sport's techniques were developing, some of those analyses are misguided, failing to consider the specific rules criteria under which those techniques were developed and employed. Fighters developed the techniques best suited for success under the rules by which they competed.

Boxing as it began as a sport was almost completely different from the sport as we know it today. Although there was boxing in ancient Rome, Greece, Egypt, and even Ethiopia, it disappeared for many centuries, and truly began its evolution with bareknuckle fights dating back to the 1600s in England. Early bareknuckle fights had few rules and only some skill. In style and ferocity, they probably more closely resembled some of our modern no-holds-barred fights combined with some stand-up wrestling (and lacking the ability to fight on the ground). The fights were often essentially brutal street brawls with only a modicum of civility.

England's James Figg in 1719 is the first recognized bareknuckle world champion, and he was quite popular in England. Of course, at that time, England was the world of boxing. In 1743, then-champion Jack Broughton published the first code of rules. He also invented boxing gloves, known as mufflers, which were used only for exhibitions, not actual fights. Broughton's rules were used for about 95 years, from 1743 to 1838, when the London Prize Ring Rules (mostly the same but with some additional safety) were adopted.

For well over 150 years, longer than gloved fighting has existed, fights took place without gloves. Fighters not only had to suffer the impact of being struck by bare fists, but also had to endure the pain and damage inflicted upon the human hand when striking their opponent's skull. This meant that they had to be careful about how and where they struck.

Rounds were not timed in the manner that they are today. Today's three-minute round with one minute of rest did not exist. Rounds only ended when someone was knocked or wrestled down. Yes, wrestling moves to throw an opponent down were legal. Because a round only ended when someone hit the ground, a round could last an hour or just a few seconds. Duration of the bout was of little concern, as most fights were of unlimited duration. Sometimes fights lasted many hours.

After a boxer was knocked down, he did not have to almost immediately rise or present himself ready to fight as became the case in the gloved era. The 10-count did not exist. Under Broughton's rules, a knocked down boxer would have 30 seconds to be revived by his handlers (who were able to carry him to the corner) and to again present himself ready to engage in battle. Cornermen (and sometimes stools) often remained inside the ring during the round so that a fighter could quickly be brought to the corner to be revived. Under the later London Prize Ring Rules, after the rest from a knockdown, in order to signal the ability or willingness to continue, a boxer would "toe the line," which meant that he would walk to the scratch line in the center of the ring. After the 30 seconds time was called, the fighter then had another 8 seconds to arrive at the scratch to fight. Thus, a fighter could obtain a great deal of rest or limit the damage done simply by going down often or quickly from blows. Technically, it was illegal to go down voluntarily, but this rule could be abused. Even a fighter knocked unconscious could usually be sufficiently revived to continue after such a lengthy rest. This rest period and the ability to obtain it every time a fighter went down could immensely extend a bout's length.

Fights were contests of submission, decided according to which boxer could render the opponent unwilling or unable to continue, or declared a draw because no end could be achieved (typically, because both fighters were too tired, or the fight was stopped by darkness). Outcomes were not subjective, as there were no points decisions rendered. Whether one looked good or seemed to be doing better was irrelevant. There were no limits to the number of times someone could be knocked or thrown down. The rest periods and no limitation on knockdowns essentially meant that fights, particularly championship bouts, were often wars of attrition where mere temporary unconsciousness or loss of control over one's legs were not enough to terminate a bout. Conversely, because they were bareknuckle and brutal due to few rules, fights could also be extremely short. A superior fighter was one who could administer and absorb punishment over potentially lengthy periods of time, to continue fighting and see to it that his opponent was unable to do so.

These fights were not merely about punching. Under Broughton's rules, wrestling above the waist, holding and hitting, head butting, hair and ear pulling, and hurling an opponent to the ground (and often falling on him) were accepted, commonly used tactics. Combatants often shaved their heads so that their hair could not be grabbed. The bouts could be quite brutal.

However, Broughton's rules forbade gouging, hitting a downed fighter, hitting or grabbing below the waist, and kicking. That said, attention to the rules was not amongst the sport's stronger points, for they were not always strictly enforced by officials. These were fights with the barest of rules and civility. As a result, the techniques of bareknuckle boxing were reflective of the needs of a lengthy battle of attrition with limited rules and rule enforcement.

Early boxing did not have the type of rings used today, and often did not have rings at all. They simply fought in designated spaces. The fights were usually held on stages or platforms in amphitheaters, or outside on soil, surrounded by a crowd. Sometimes they were held in the middle of a room, or even on ships. There was no canvas floor padding. Thus, the impact to the head or body upon being knocked or thrown to the ground could be great.

Once the London Prize Ring Rules came about in the late 1830s, rings were usually 24

Typical prizefight scene, from the October 30, 1858 issue of *Frank Leslie's Illustrated Newspaper* (Library of Congress, Prints and Photographs Division).

feet square, much larger than today's typical 18- to 20-foot ring. This gave combatants more room to move and elude. Ring posts did not have soft padding like today, and there were usually eight posts, one on each corner and one in the middle of each side. Boxers' heads or hands could be damaged when striking these hard, usually wooden posts. Some fighters even strategically stood next to a post and moved away when their opponent struck so that he would injure his hand on it. Boxers could be hurled into these posts. Even when there were ropes, there were only one or two at most, so it was easy to knock or throw an opponent through or over them onto the floor below (when the rings were elevated on stages or platforms, as was often the case).

These rules and objectives made the sport in many ways fundamentally different from what boxing has become. Brute strength, wrestling skills, ability to absorb or evade punishment, ability to administer effective punishment, and endurance were the most necessary qualities. These qualities are important today, but not to the extent that they were at that time.

Early boxing mostly took place in Great Britain, but it also developed in the American colonies, which on July 4, 1776, 33 years after Broughton published his rules, declared independence from Britain, leading to the lengthy American Revolutionary War. Not surprisingly, the best boxers were generally from the British Isles or America.

Fighting wars was acceptable, but prizefights were usually illegal. A fighter could be charged with murder if an opponent died. Bareknuckle championship bouts were at times sporadic because fighters risked lengthy prison sentences if caught engaging in these bouts, and also because of their brutality, requiring greater recovery periods between fights. This also meant that sufficient prize money had to be on the line in order for a fighter to be willing to risk the pain and potential prison sentence.

Gambling was generally attendant on the sport and bets between the combatants and their financial backers were one of the primary ways that money was earned or lost. In order to secure a championship bout, a fighter had to be good enough to convince financial backers to risk their money on him by putting up stakes money and side bets. Even then, some fights were alleged to be fixed, which, amongst other reasons, impeded boxing from flourishing as a sport.

There are a whole host of good fighters from the bareknuckle era, each with varying degrees of skill. In about 1794, Daniel Mendoza, a Spanish Jewish fighter, was credited as being amongst the first champions to pay some attention to defense and bring the science of boxing to a new level. He utilized agility and speed rather than only brute strength. However, opportunities to utilize what one may call skill as we know it today were limited under the rules of a game that lent itself to sheer brutality.

In America, slaves and ex-slaves often competed. Tom Molineaux, a former slave from Virginia, gained some notoriety. In 1810 in England, Britain's Tom Cribb defeated Molineaux in the first title fight between a white champion and black challenger.

The London Prize Ring Rules were generally adopted by 1838. They required a 24-foot ring, usually on turf, with two ropes. Downed fighters had a total of 38 seconds to toe the line. These rules added further safety to Broughton's rules, making head butting, rabbit punches (hitting behind the head), kidney punches (to the back), and falling on an opponent all fouls. Things like low blows, eye gouging, kicking, tearing at the flesh with the fingers and biting remained fouls. Violation of these rules, especially those regarding low blows and hitting a downed opponent, was grounds for immediate disqualification. However, despite its additional rules increasing safety, holding and hitting as well as wrestling tactics such as throwing an opponent to the ground and twisting his head were still allowed. The fights remained quite brutal and many referees continued to allow almost anything to occur.

Fighting didn't just take place in the ring. In 1846, the Mexican-American War began, as the United States under President James K. Polk declared war on Mexico when it refused to sell western territories. When the United States won, by early 1848, Mexico recognized Texas as part of the U.S. and ceded territory that would become the future states of California, Nevada, and Utah, almost all of New Mexico and Arizona, and parts of Colorado and Wyoming.

In about 1866–1867 (post–U.S. Civil War), John Sholto Douglas, then the Marquis of Queensberry, helped publish a set of boxing rules (written by John Graham Chambers) which are the foundation of today's rules. However, the Queensberry rules only gradually gained notoriety and acceptance because they created some major differences from the accepted form of fighting which the world had been accustomed to for over a century. Thus, it would require the advocacy of a star, in conjunction with legal circumstances, to really make the Queensberry rules become popular.

The Marquis of Queensberry rules prescribed that boxing matches would be fought with gloves (usually ranging from 2 to 8 ounces, but typically on the lower end of that range, sometimes padded, sometimes just hard leather), as opposed to bare fists. Boxers liked the gloves in part because it saved their hands from being destroyed. Rounds were three minutes in length (as opposed to continuous, until someone went down), with one-minute rests in between rounds. Wrestling and holding were made illegal, although this rule left some room for interpretation and was at first little enforced. Many of the grappling tactics of the bareknuckle era still remained, but their use or overuse could be grounds for disqualification. When a boxer was knocked down, he had only 10 seconds to rise on his own (unassisted by his handlers) and the bout continued immediately after the boxer rose (as opposed to the optional 30- to 38-second recovery period). There was no neutral corner rule, which meant that a fighter could hover near his fallen foe, and as soon as he rose, he could be struck. Fights could still be to the finish (until someone was stopped) or a draw was agreed upon, but under these rules, decisions were also allowed. Decisions were usually rendered only by the referee. Other safety rules remained the same.

There were no rules regarding ring apparel. Combatants often wore tights, as opposed to the boxing trunks of today. The tights could be of various colors, even pink, a color which at that time had masculine, not feminine associations. However, they could also wear shorts or pants. Shirts were optional, and they could be of any type.

Purses were usually divided ⅔ to the winner and ⅓ to the loser, but generally this split was simply of the gate receipts. There would often be a large side bet put up by both sides that went only to the winner. Sometimes, the fights were winner take all. These compensation standards made the incentive to win, or at least to receive a draw (wherein the money was equally divided), quite high. Fighters were not merely being paid to entertain, but their pay depended upon success, motivating their efforts. This made them fight hard and be less willing to quit. However, ironically, this also made many bouts dull, because some fighters became risk averse, employing tactics designed for lengthy, slow paced fights that were snoozers, but winning efforts (or at least not losing—in the case of a draw).

The gloves and new rules allowed greater room for the development of today's skills. The gloves were very small, allowing punches to be extremely powerful. Given the power that the small gloves yielded, fighters would often attempt to quickly administer debilitating blows before their opponents could do so. However, because some bouts were to the finish, the sport still required boxers to have immense endurance and the ability to pace themselves. Boxers had to develop and utilize techniques and styles to ensure that they were economical with their energy so that they could last indefinitely, but this was coupled with the need to both administer and avoid punishment that would have a debilitating effect. This created an internal dilemma that allowed for the development of multiple styles and techniques, and allowed for varying bout tempos.

Boxing was illegal in most of the United States, but these new Queensberry rules gave it some semblance of civility, and helped begin the path for boxing to very gradually become more socially acceptable and legalized. Ironically, a strong minority believed that Queensberry rules were more brutal, because fighters could punch even harder due to the protection of the hands, and because the rests after knockdowns were shorter, forcing boxers to recover and fight again more quickly. Generally, though, Queensberry rules were looked upon much more favorably than London rules. Despite the more civilized image these Queensberry rules brought the sport, boxing had an odd relationship with the law for quite some time, and legal acceptance lagged far behind social acceptance. This book is about the career of the man who brought the Queensberry rules to prominence and made gloved boxing the norm rather than the exception.[1]

CHAPTER 2

Sullivan's World

John L. Sullivan represents the transition from bareknuckle era fights under the London Prize Ring Rules to the gloved era bouts of the Marquis of Queensberry rules with which today's boxing fans are familiar. Some of John L. Sullivan's bouts were bareknuckle fights which continued indefinitely until someone was knocked out or a draw was declared. However, most of his bouts were with gloves and of a limited, pre-determined duration, where the referee would render a decision if there was no knockout. Sullivan was essentially the last of the bareknuckle heavyweight champions, but he was also the first heavyweight champion to fight under more modern boxing rules with gloves. Few realize that he really was more of a gloved fighter than a bareknuckle fighter, and was actually the main reason that gloved fighting achieved acceptance when it did.

Sullivan's immense popularity gave rise to the popularity and social and semi-legal acceptance of the sport of Queensberry rules gloved boxing, which at the time was considered the anomaly, as opposed to the bareknuckle London rules norm. Boxing was considered to be a fringe sport with only a small following, but Sullivan gained it national and international popularity. Bareknuckle prize fights had been known for primarily attracting undesirable and less than reputable criminal elements, but with the ascendancy of Sullivan, newspapers would increasingly note that a wide cross section of society attended his bouts, including what they would often term the best members of society. His stardom had transcendent power.

Sullivan arrived at a time when the world of bareknuckle boxing, a.k.a. "the prize ring," was at a low point. Even as late as 1883, one Australian newspaper wrote that

> An attempt is being made to revive public interest in the departed glories of the prize ring.... We have not the slightest sympathy with the prize ring. Its surroundings have invariably been of the lowest kind.... Had pugilism possessed a little of the advantages claimed by its advocates it would never have lost its popularity, but its demoralizing influence has always proved too much even for those interested in its maintenance. It is a sport best left alone.[1]

Boxing demonstrated an internal social conflict. John L. Sullivan's bouts were often technically illegal. Despite its illegality, boxing was nevertheless quite popular during his career, attended by all social classes, and usually well covered by the news media. Boxers could be convicted criminals for engaging in their professions and simultaneously be public heroes. Those arrested and charged with illegal prizefighting could be fined, serve jail terms, or escape punishment via jury nullification (juries wouldn't convict).

The law generally allowed bouts to occur if they were mere gloved "exhibitions of skill" or "sparring" rather than fights. Sometimes these really were semi-competitive, friendly sparring exhibitions. However, the reality is that they were often serious, competitive battles under the guise of being something less in order to avoid the law.

Technically, the police could stop the bouts if they believed that the fighters were slugging or throwing punches designed to injure and no longer giving a mere exhibition of skill. Often, the police would not consider the boxers to be slugging until one was on the verge of being knocked out. They would usually stop fights when one boxer was badly hurt, essentially making themselves secondary referees. However, because the law was left open to interpretation, the police had a great deal of discretion, and what action or lack of action they took often was a reflection of their own feelings about the sport or the fighters, or a result of the local political climate. They could stop the bouts and either arrest the combatants or let them go, or allow the slugging to continue until someone was knocked out and arrest them for it afterwards, or they could do nothing. In many jurisdictions, as long as the men were boxing with gloves according to the Queensberry rules, they did not offend the law against prizefighting.

Sullivan was a reflection of the era from which he emerged. He grew up in post–Civil War America, being born just before the war began. After Abraham Lincoln was elected president in 1860 on a platform expressing the need to limit slavery, Southern states seceded from the union of 33 states. The ensuing civil war, from the early to mid-1860s, was one of the bloodiest wars in history. More Americans lost their lives in the Civil War than in any other war to the present date. Its casualties were massive, as an estimated 558,000–620,000 died from combat, disease, privation, and accidents.[2] This was in a country that only had 34.3 million people (as opposed to well over 281 million as of the 2000 U.S. Census). On April 14, 1865, President Lincoln was shot by John Wilkes Booth. He died the following day.

Violence and the willingness to fight to the bitter end were essential parts of the American and world culture, as was the desire to achieve dominion over others. Dominion over one's foe has traditionally been an admired quality in all nations throughout history, and helps explain the popularity of and fascination with dominant boxing champions like Sullivan. Fighting is an inherent human trait. As one newspaper wrote in 1883, "Do what we will with him, man is naturally a fighting animal."[3] Even after the Civil War, the U.S. Indian Wars continued against Native Americans over the next several decades. Fighting and war were omnipresent realities. Therefore, it cannot be a surprise that a great fighter such as Sullivan would emerge from such a culture. The American sport that most directly reflected the culture of battle and domination was boxing. Therefore, boxing's illegality was ironic, and revealed the world's hypocrisy and internal conflict with itself.

President Lincoln had issued emancipation proclamations abolishing slavery on September 22, 1862, and January 1, 1863, but slavery was not officially abolished until December 18, 1865, after the Civil War was over. Despite slavery's abolition, and perhaps because of it, the racial prejudice that had developed during slavery did not disappear, but in many ways only increased in post–Civil War America. 1865 was the year that the Ku Klux Klan emerged. Reactionary attempts to reassert white supremacy in the absence of slavery led to hundreds of lynchings in subsequent years, and eventually, to a legalized caste system that enforced separation of the races and dominion of the white race over the black race. The Civil War technically ended slavery, but many in both the North and South were determined to ensure that was all it did.

The abolition of slavery did little to change the historic racial divide in America, and if anything, served to intensify racial tensions and divisions, even in sport. Boxing is social history; the two are intertwined. As a post–Civil War American, Sullivan reflects the racial tone and views of the time, which affected the way the sport was conducted in and out of the ring, and would do so for much, if not all, of its history.

The late 1800s were a paradoxical time of violence and growth, destruction and innovation. 1876 was the year of the last major Indian victory over U.S. military forces when General Custer and 250 soldiers were wiped out by the Sioux. The Indian Wars would sporadically continue until 1890, when the final band of Sioux was trapped and destroyed by the U.S. Army in the Battle of Wounded Knee. Despite the destruction of the Indian population, by 1880, the U.S. had grown to 38 states and 49,371,340 persons. New York was the biggest state, with 5,082,971. California only had 864,694 people. Of the total population, 6,518,372 were black.

Thomas Edison invented the light bulb in 1879, which later made it easier for boxing exhibitions to take place at night; something Sullivan took full advantage of. Fifteen years later, after inventing the movie camera, Edison would make boxing one of his first money making subjects. Edison was a boxing fan who had seen Sullivan fight.

Sports were just becoming part of the American scene. American football, which used no pads or helmets, was first invented and played at the college level just after the Civil War and would not become a professional sport until 1895. There was no basketball until its invention in 1891. Baseball was popular, but was pitched underhanded until 1884, and they didn't even use gloves.

The development of the railroad contributed to the rise of sports stars. Although the first U.S. railroad began in 1826, it was not used or developed on a massive scale until much later. On July 1, 1862, President Lincoln signed the Pacific Railway Act, authorizing construction and subsidizing with land and loans the first transcontinental railroad. This project would eventually link the entire country by rail, making travel easier and more rapid. (The automobile wasn't even invented until 1887.) On May 10, 1869, the Central Pacific and Union Pacific railroads met in Utah, linking the East and West coasts. This set the stage for boxers like John L. Sullivan to be able to easily tour the country and allowed most of the nation to see them in action. An act in part motivated by war had helped make this possible.

Like the railroad, the telegraph gradually developed into an interstate system, and contributed to Sullivan's stardom. Although Samuel Morse conceived the telegraph in 1832, it was not until 1861 that the two coasts were linked by the telegraph. (The telephone was not invented by Alexander Graham Bell until 1876, and its use was limited for quite some time.) This nationwide telegraph system allowed reports to quickly be communicated throughout the country. What fight reporters saw in one town could easily be reported the next day by newspapers throughout the country. Consistent press also fostered the development of a star like Sullivan. The telegraph and railroad allowed Sullivan to be seen or read about by the entire nation.

Although there have been many bareknuckle heavyweight champions since the 1700s (mostly British), John L. Sullivan's ferocious, hard punching style and lengthy reign through the 1880s made him the first American sports hero. Although Sullivan's vicious slugging was the most illegal style, it made him the world's most popular and financially successful sports figure. Sullivan was phenomenally talented, very fast and strong, entertaining, and willing to back up his claim to being the best with money and deeds. He took boxing to new heights.

CHAPTER 3

The Local Rise
of the Boston Strongboy

John L. Sullivan was an Irish-American born on October 15, 1858, in the Boston, Massachusetts, area.[1] He began his fighting career somewhere around 1877 or 1878, when he was about 19 years old, although there are some indications that he started informally fighting as early as age 16.[2] Sullivan said that when he was 16 years old, he lasted only six months in a Catholic institution in Boston. His father had hoped that he would become a priest. However, even at that point, John "had already begun to pound the boys."[3]

Sullivan also said that at about age 16 or 17, he had an affinity for athletic sports, and learned that he could make $30 or $40 per week playing baseball. He took up the profession and left school. From baseball he eventually drifted into boxing. At one time, he even ran a saloon.[4]

Sullivan later claimed that his first real fistfight was when he was 17 years old, when he was working in a tin factory. Even at that point, he weighed about 200 pounds. He played baseball during his lunch break, and came back to work a bit late. A harsh and often violent foreman kicked John. Sullivan hit him back with a right thrown as hard as he could. "I caught him under the chin and lifted him through the glass window into the yard." John did not want to allow him to recover, so he went after him with more punches and took all the fight out of him. This would become Sullivan's signature finishing style. "After that everybody in my neighborhood called me the 'strong boy.' I think it was this affair that really made me turn to boxing in earnest."[5] Sullivan had learned early on that being a good fighter earned him respect.

Sullivan said that he "drifted into the occupation of a boxer" at about age 19. His first fight with a boxing glove was at a variety entertainment show against someone named Scannell. Scannell was supposed to box someone who failed to shown up, so the master of ceremonies asked Sullivan to fill in, because John had a local reputation for being able to hold his own with anyone. After some cajoling, Sullivan agreed.

Scannell attacked him ferociously and put John on the defensive, against the ropes. Sullivan dodged and moved about. Eventually, he timed the attacking Scannell on the way in and landed a right thrown as hard as he could, sending Scannell through the ropes and off the stage, landing on a piano.[6]

According to Sullivan, he was self taught, learning from observation and experience. It was later reported that Sullivan was once taught boxing by Professor Bailey, a black man who was a 6 foot, 200-pound instructor at Harvard for years. Trainer Tom O'Rourke claimed to have, along with Sullivan, taken classes taught by Bailey in Boston.[7] Sullivan in his 1892 autobiography denied the claim, saying, "Some one has said that old Prof. Bailey claimed the credit of teaching me, but he was wrong in the assertion, as I never took a boxing lesson in my life, having a natural ambition for the business."[8] Sullivan was consistent throughout his career in his claim that he learned through experience and observation. In 1882, Sullivan said, "When I was between 19 and 20 ... I first began sparring, but I have taken no course of lessons. I seemed to acquire the art naturally, and whatever styles I have adopted I picked up from exhibitions between famous boxers."[9]

Known as the Boston Strongboy, John L. Sullivan was not generally considered a scientific boxer (at least initially), but a vicious slugger with huge power and very good speed. That said, there is a little appreciated science to hitting and knocking out one's opponents while avoiding their blows. Sullivan knew how to land his punches, and land them well. He had an underrated ability to avoid being hit, and absorbed the blows he did receive very well. He could hurt his opponents, and no one could hurt him.

Although on one hand the bareknuckle style suited Sullivan's strength and ferocity, he nevertheless preferred gloved Queensberry bouts. This was in part due to the protection gloves afforded the hands. It was also because of the shorter duration of time a downed boxer had to recover and continue after a knockdown, which favored his puncher's style. Because there was no neutral corner rule, Sullivan was very good at immediately pouncing upon his opponents and finishing them off as soon as they rose from a knockdown. Also, the Queensberry rules limited a fighter's ability to simply wrestle to the ground in order to end the round and get a long rest. Some felt that a smaller boxer could take advantage of the London rules by going down often to obtain lengthy rests, to extend the length of a bout and tire out a larger and stronger fighter. Another perhaps more important reason gloved bouts were favored was that the law was more likely to overlook anti–prize fight laws when gloves were used, because they could more easily be sold as exhibitions of skill rather than as fights. Fights were bareknuckle; exhibitions were not. Sullivan actually fought mostly gloved bouts and very few bareknuckle ones.

After having some unrecorded fights, Sullivan began developing a local Boston reputation. One secondary source claims that Sullivan's March 14, 1879, KO5 over John "Cocky" Woods was the first that the newspapers took any notice of.[10]

Actually, the 20-year-old Sullivan fought twice on March 14, 1879. Sullivan had another fight earlier that day that has previously not been listed on his record, but it was reported by the local newspaper. Really, it was a late night show on March 13 that went into the early morning hours of March 14. Sullivan fought Jack Curley of Philadelphia for $250. The 6'1" Curley weighed 193 pounds to the 5'10" Sullivan's 196 pounds. The bout took place between one and two o'clock a.m.[11]

Not much is known about Curley, but he was no novice; rather an older, more experienced fighter. A decade earlier, on February 18, 1869, in a bareknuckle bout, he had been stopped by Charley Gallagher in 18 rounds lasting 18 minutes.[12]

The local paper said of the Sullivan-Curley fight that

Both men appeared stripped to the waist, and both were bent on their work. After a hard-fought battle of 1 hour and 14 minutes Sullivan was declared the winner. It is the opinion of the sporting fraternity that Sullivan is the coming man, and it is understood that he will be backed by a well-known sporting man of this city for from $500 to $1000 against any heavy-weight pugilist in the prize ring.[13]

The great length of the bout demonstrates something heretofore unknown about a young Sullivan: that he had endurance as well as great speed and strength. It is unclear as to whether this was a bareknuckle or gloved bout.

Another report that same day said that later in the evening on the 14th the "strong boy" Sullivan boxed with gloves against John Woods, who was "well known a dozen years ago among the patrons of the manly art in Boston." All that was said of the Sullivan-Woods bout was that the "encounter gave the spectators great pleasure."[14] This has generally been reported by secondary sources as a KO5 win for Sullivan. Sullivan in his autobiography only said that Woods was a noted man of reputation whom he soon disposed of.[15] The Curley, Woods, and subsequent bouts demonstrate that a young Sullivan was not afraid of and could defeat more experienced opponents.

The fact that Sullivan fought both Curley and Woods during the same calendar day is not all that odd. During his career, it was not uncommon for Sullivan to box multiple times in one day or evening. One of the ways that he would later make money was by giving sparring exhibitions with one or more boxers as part of a larger exhibition show. He would eventually go on tour throughout America with a combination of boxing buddies, and they would give sparring exhibitions before paying audiences. The boxers would do somewhat of a round robin, each boxing with each other and with Sullivan. Essentially, he was getting paid by the public to watch him and others train. Sometimes, a local fighter would try to win money that Sullivan offered to anyone who could last 4 rounds with him, and Sullivan would step up the intensity. After knocking them out, he would spar with other members of his troupe.

But initially, Sullivan made his name as a local fighter in gloved exhibitions. According to secondary sources, in 1879 Sullivan had a KO3 Dan Dwyer, W4 Tommy Chandler, and W4 John "Patsy" Hogan.[16] It is unclear as to what the actual results of these bouts were.

Sullivan gave the impression in his autobiography that these bouts took place after his match with Woods. Sullivan said that he fought Dwyer in 1879 (after Woods), that Dan was considered a strong boxer and the Massachusetts champion. To the surprise of many, Sullivan "had the best of the encounter."[17] One 1884 report said, "The first pugilist who met Sullivan was Dan Dwyer, whom he whipped in two blows."[18] However, an earlier, 1882 report said that Sullivan's first appearance as a boxer was against Woods and that Chandler and Dwyer followed.[19]

Sullivan provided no details of his victory over Tommy Chandler, whom he called one of the "old timers," but who was not the Chandler of the Pacific Coast fame. It is unclear whether this is the correct fighter, but a *National Police Gazette* report said that Chandler had been born in Ireland in 1842 (making him about 36 or 37 years old), stood 5'8", and weighed anywhere from 136 to 160 pounds. As a London rules fighter, his first fight was in 1862 when he fought a 64-round draw over 1 hour and 24 minutes. He won an 1865 bout in 19 rounds. An 1866 fight went 69 rounds and was stopped due to darkness, but Chandler won when the following day his opponent failed to appear to complete the fight. In 1867, he won a 23 round bout, and then retired. This may have been the Pacific Coast Chandler (not the man Sullivan fought) because a photo caption called him the middleweight champion of California, although his record is consistent with his being called an old timer. William Burns claimed to have seen Tommy Chandler fight Johnny Files for the middleweight championship in Chicago in 1878. Under Queensberry rules, both knocked each other out with right hands in the 18th round, but Chandler came to first and was given the decision.[20]

Sullivan said that Jack Hogan also "shared the fate of those mentioned." It is unclear whether this was the same "Patsy" Hogan who had been a lightweight, born in 1852 (making him about 27 years old), standing 5'7½", and who had been boxing since the early 1870s. Hogan lost an 1872 17-round bout lasting 58 minutes, but won an 1874 fight lasting 23 minutes. He had retired in about 1876, but was said to be willing to assist first class pugilists.[21]

Mike Donovan. From Billy Edwards, *The Portrait Gallery of Pugilists of England, America, Australia* (Chicago: Athletic Publishing Co., 1894). Clay Moyle, www.prizefighting books.com.

Sullivan also said that at a benefit in Boston, he boxed the experienced Professor Mike Donovan, a future occasional sparring partner, for 3 rounds. Donovan many years later said that he and Sullivan had sparred 4 rounds in Boston in 1880 (possibly February). Donovan had been boxing since the 1860s and said that he was a middleweight champion.

Donovan observed that Sullivan was "quick as a cat and very strong," rushing at him "like a panther." He was quite impressed. "In fact he was the strongest man I had ever met, and I had boxed nearly every big man of reputation up to that time, Paddy Ryan included, and was considered the cleverest man in the ring." Mike had to do everything that he could and call upon all his experience to last, and felt exhausted at the end. "[N]ever in my life did I have to do such clever ducking and side-stepping." Donovan also said, "He hit me on top of the head several times, and his blows made me see stars of different colors." He at that time con-

cluded, "I had just fought the coming champion of the prize-ring."[22] An 1882 report said that the bout was exciting, but that "Donovan was forced to lower his colors."[23]

Briefly venturing out of the Boston area for the first time, in New York on March 6, 1880, according to the local *New York Clipper*, Sullivan exhibited with Jerry Murphy as part of an exhibition show in which many bouts took place.[24] In a report some years later, *The National Police Gazette* called "Johnny" Murphy a Sullivan "side partner." Of Sullivan, it said that "[e]very time he appeared improvement was noted in him."[25]

CHAPTER 4

The World's Best ... but with Gloves

American bareknuckle champion Joe Goss was an aging veteran of the game who was past his prime, having had his toughest battles back in the 1850s and 1860s in his native England. Goss had fought many bareknuckle bouts (at least 14, losing only twice) that lasted one, two, and even three hours.

In the late 1850s, Goss fought Jack Richson over 3 hours before the fight was stopped by the police. In 1859, he won a fight that lasted 64 rounds, in 1 hour and 40 minutes. After winning some other bouts, in July 1860 Goss defeated Dan Crutchley in 120 rounds, in 3 hours and 29 minutes. In 1861, Bill Ryan or Ryall was defeated in 37 rounds over 2 hours and 30 minutes. They fought a rematch draw that lasted 3 hours and 18 minutes.

Amongst his many bouts, in the 1860s, Goss fought England's world bareknuckle champion Jem Mace three times, being beaten in 19 rounds lasting 1 hour and 55 minutes (1863), fighting him to a 1-hour and 5-minute draw (1866), and losing a 21 rounder lasting 31 minutes (1867). Goss also fought fellow Brit Tom Allen to a 1-hour, 52-minute, 31-round draw (1866). These and many other short and lengthy battles all took place in England throughout the 1860s.

Goss came to America in 1876 and in a rematch defeated Tom Allen on a foul in a 21 rounder that lasted 48 or 52 minutes for a bet of $2,000 or $2,500 (sources vary). Allen too had been defeated by 41-year-old Mace six years earlier in America, in 1870, in a 10 rounder lasting 44 minutes. Although both Allen and Goss were British, their bout was for the American championship. Afterwards, both men were arrested for violating Kentucky's anti–prize fight laws. Allen jumped bail and returned to England. Goss was sentenced to six months' imprisonment and a $250 fine.[1] Such was the state of bareknuckle prizefighting.

In 1880, Joe Goss was matched to fight Paddy Ryan in a London rules bout for $1,000 a side and the championship. In preparation, both Goss and Ryan gave exhibitions. Goss, "widely known as one of the most accomplished of sparrers and gamest of fighters," was advertised by *The New York Clipper* as set to give a Boston exhibition against Sullivan, "the coming man."[2]

On April 6, 1880, in Boston, approximately 190-pound 21-year-old-Sullivan, listed between 5'10¼" and 5'10½", took on American bareknuckle champion Joe Goss in a 3-round gloved exhibition. The 5'10" Goss was an elderly 42 years old and weighed about 170 pounds.[3] Still, his immense experience and respected reputation made him Sullivan's first serious test against a then nationally recognized championship fighter.

In this gloved exhibition, to the surprise of many, Sullivan had the better of it and clearly hurt and dropped Goss in the 2nd round. Goss was out of it, but was allowed to recover and agreed to continue when Sullivan promised to spar lightly with him for another round.[4]

A local primary source, *The Boston Daily Globe*, said that 1,800 people observed the exhibition. It called Goss the world's champion. Years later, *The National Police Gazette* (which liked to minimize Sullivan's accomplishments) asserted that Goss was not the world champion because he had been defeated by Jem Mace.[5] Interestingly, though, when it backed Paddy Ryan against Goss, it occasionally described the fight as being for the world championship. Also, the 49-year-old Mace was basically retired and had not fought in many years. Most of the great bareknucklers were aging and inactive. Thus, it was open to argument as to whether there was a recognized world champion and who it was.

The local account said that the 1st round of the Goss-Sullivan bout was a surprise, as Sullivan exhibited more skill than was expected and "planted blow after blow with his left on the face of the champion." Goss occasionally landed, but was countered by Sullivan.

In the 2nd round, after several rapid exchanges, Sullivan landed "no less than four sledge-hammer-like blows upon the right ear of Goss, and the latter went reeling to the floor. He was assisted to his feet by the master of ceremonies, who, thinking that the champion had only slipped, left him to get to a seat upon the stage." However, without that assistance, "Goss went reeling like a drunken man about the stage, and the danger of his falling among the audience was so great that the master of ceremonies at last realizing his situation, at once caught him and assisted him to a sitting on the platform." The audience was quite excited. The two boxed one more round after Goss recovered.[6]

Even at this early stage in his career, John had proven that he was the best boxer in America, and perhaps the world. However, he was not considered the champion because he had boxed Goss with gloves in a Queensberry rules (sort of) exhibition, which was not considered a real prizefight at that time. A recognized fight was a bareknuckle London Prize Ring Rules contest. However, this performance made the national press take further notice of Sullivan.

Goss and John L. became friends and would later box each other in short exhibitions. During his career, Sullivan quite often had short, usually 3- or 4-round sparring exhibitions in front of paying audiences.

About two months after meeting Sullivan, on June 1, 1880, Goss was defeated by Paddy Ryan after 87 rounds lasting 1 hour and 24 minutes, for the American bareknuckle championship under London Prize Ring Rules. Supposedly, it was only Ryan's first or second official bout, but that only meant bareknuckle fights.[7] Ryan did have experience in gloved exhibitions, having sparred men such as Steve Taylor and William Miller.[8] Record keeping at that time was poor, so it is unclear just how experienced many fighters were. It is also unclear as to what they weighed because they rarely had official weigh-ins as they do today, and the fighters or their trainers often self reported weights.

Although Ryan became the American champion with his victory over Goss, Sullivan had already clearly bested his result; but with gloves. Ryan had won the title in a prizefight, the accepted version of a true championship test. However, given that John L. had taken Goss out much more quickly and easily, really, even at that point, he was the best fighter in America, if not the world. Furthermore, before Sullivan had taken on Goss, Ryan had refused to spar Sullivan, telling him to go and get a reputation first. That he certainly did.

In June 1880, it was advertised in *The National Police Gazette* that Sullivan was willing to fight anyone in America, with or without gloves, for $500. John L. was listed as weighing 200 pounds and was called a pugilist "of no mean pretensions."[9]

On June 28, 1880, in Boston, Sullivan took on George Rooke, who since 1867 had claimed the American middleweight championship. He was born in England in 1843, but came to New York at an early age. He stood 5'11", was about 37 years of age and weighed only 150–160 pounds in condition.[10] He had boxed in both England and America. It was said that Rooke was "one of the finest sparrers in the country, as well as the cleverest of fighters that ever came to America. His victories in the mother country have been legion." Rooke was giving local boxing lessons.[11]

According to *The National Police Gazette*, in this Queensberry rules bout, Sullivan made a "shuttle-cock" of Rooke. He dropped him three times in the 1st round, and continued pounding on him for two more rounds that "were a repetition of the first," until Rooke was knocked out in the 3rd round.[12] It is clear that this New York based paper took its report from a local source or sources, as it often did. However, it left something out: The local *Boston Daily Globe* called Sullivan the "Highland boy," referencing the area which John was from. It said that Sullivan was "large, even larger than expected." The audience included "first-class citizens" and sporting men who were lovers of the "manly art."

Of the bout, it said that the manner in which Sullivan handled Rooke was "truly ludicrous," in part because

> [I]t was plain to be seen that Rooke had been imbibing something stronger than soda water. In fact, when both men put up their hands he staggered, and during the first round Sullivan knocked him down three times. The following two rounds was but a repetition of the first, when the friends of the New York man took him to his room. The cry among the audience was "Drunk-Drunk-Drunk."[13]

The Police Gazette failed to mention that Rooke was drunk.

Sullivan said that he subsequently gave several exhibitions with Dan Dwyer.[14] A secondary source said that in November 1880, Sullivan sparred with John Kenny in New York.[15]

"Professor" John Donaldson. From Billy Edwards, *The Portrait Gallery of Pugilists of England, America, Aus tralia* (Chicago: Athletic Publishing Co., 1894). Clay Moyle, www.prizefightingbooks.com.

Sullivan was invited to come to Cincinnati, Ohio, by *The Cincinnati Daily Enquirer*, which offered him $150 plus expenses to box with middleweight sized "Professor" John Donaldson. This demonstrates the symbiotic relationship that newspapers sometimes had with boxing.[16]

Donaldson was said to have previously met in his career four good men in the ring, having defeated them all. Those four bouts were bareknuckle prize ring bouts, as the term "ring" implied back then. He had stopped Dan Carr in 7 rounds requiring 23 minutes, Bryan Campbell in 3 rounds lasting 11 minutes, Bluett Boyd in 2 minutes and 45 seconds of the 1st round (May 1880), and Jim Taylor in 5 rounds occupying 6 minutes (August 1880). He probably had more gym experience, because he was a boxing instructor; hence his designation as "Professor." Donaldson only weighed about 160 pounds and stood 5'10½", but had a reputation for being a clever boxer and had displayed some good power in his bouts.[17]

Secondary sources generally say that Sullivan and Donaldson boxed on December 20, 1880, but they are incorrect. Sullivan and Donaldson actually boxed on December 11, 1880, at Robinson's Opera House. The local *Cincinnati Commercial* announced the exhibition the week before and had a next day report. The 212-pound Sullivan was listed as "the hero of many sparring exhibitions, and is considered by the Bostonians as the best boxer living."[18]

Both men had sculpted Herculean frames. They wore sleeveless athletic shirts and went to work, "making exchanges and parries with a rapidity that could scarcely be followed. Not a blow was wasted or misdirected, as they danced around the stage as light as feathers." Sullivan soon showed his superiority. In the 1st round, Donaldson went down on a slip and a hit, and became defensive thereafter, using his splendid science to save himself.

In the 2nd round, Sullivan was fresh, while Donaldson seemed a bit fatigued. They feinted often, as Sullivan was "self possessed and determined, showing an entire absence of the novice." However, the round ended slightly in Donaldson's favor.

In the 3rd, which was called the "wind-up," Sullivan led well with his left and they made "rattling exchanges." A right nearly knocked Donaldson out, and the round ended with Donaldson's head under Sully's arm. There was apparently one more round: "They, on being recalled, gave one more bout, and the entertainment was over." The exhibition was called very satisfactory and worth traveling miles to see. Sullivan was said to be willing to fight any man in the world for $2,500 a side.[19]

Without providing a date, *The National Police Gazette* gave its accounting of this encounter. Sullivan exhibited "extraordinary strength and wonderful quickness" in attacking Donaldson. Donaldson attempted to keep away, but Sullivan's right eventually landed and dropped him. The Professor essentially had enough after 3 rounds and initially retired, pulling off his gloves. He said that he was sick and not in condition to spar. However, he was encouraged to continue and eventually agreed. This perhaps explains the local account's reporting that they were "recalled" after the 3rd round for another round. In the 4th, "Sullivan went at him again like a flash and had it all his own way to the end." After the round, Donaldson said that he wanted another try at Sullivan at another time, in a fight with hard gloves for $500.[20]

Almost two weeks later, on December 24, 1880, they fought again. For their rematch, although they fought with hard gloves, London Prize Ring Rules were otherwise used, so wrestling was legal, the round ended when someone went down, and the 30–38 second rests after falls and knockdowns were longer than the 10-second rests (although shorter if you consider that there were no one-minute between-rounds rest periods).

Early gloved bouts were fought with either hard or soft gloves, depending on the agreement. Hard gloves were essentially the next closest thing to being bareknuckle. They were hard leather gloves with no padding, just as driving or riding gloves have little or no padding. Soft gloves were mittens that contained padding such as hair or cotton, more like today's gloves, but they were usually quite small. Thus, the hard gloves that Sullivan and Donaldson used provided a bare minimum of protection.

The local *Cincinnati Daily Enquirer* questioned whether Donaldson really wanted to fight Sullivan again. It felt that he merely made the match to counteract the poor impression that he had made from his previous set-to with Sullivan at Robinson's Opera House, but did not really intend to go through with it. The fight was to have taken place the day before, on the 23rd, but Donaldson's backers attempted to obtain a license for the match, giving away the location, and the mayor through the police force prevented it. Although gloved, it was a prizefight to the finish and therefore illegal. Donaldson's courage was then questioned in the press, which probably motivated the match taking place the following night in a more secret locale.

Only about thirty persons witnessed the battle because fear of police interference caused information about it to have limited dissemination. The purse amounted to less than $100. They fought in a room in a space about twenty feet square, the surrounding crowd partly constituting the ring (along with the walls), and several trunks being utilized for the men and their seconds to sit. Donaldson supplied the hard gloves. Both men wore knit shirts and shoes made of rubber soles.

The *Cincinnati Daily Enquirer* (CDE) and *Cincinnati Commercial* (CC), two local primary sources, provided their slightly differing accounts of the fight:

1st Round

CDE: Sullivan charged Donaldson "like a mad bull" sending in lefts and rights until a right to the neck "knocked him over against the wall." Sullivan continued to punch until Donaldson went down in a heap. Already it was seen that Donaldson had no chance.

CC: No effective blows were landed and Donaldson was thrown down.

2nd Round

CDE: A left drew blood from the Professor's mouth. Donaldson attempted to move, duck and dodge, but he eventually went down from "a little clip" "in a very suspicious manner to avoid further punishment," meaning that he may have voluntarily gone down to get a rest or avoid blows, which was illegal.

CC: Donaldson grabbed Sullivan by the leg (illegally), trying to lift him to no avail. He moved about the ring, chased by Sullivan, and went down to avoid punishment (also illegal).

3rd Round

CDE: Donaldson tried to fight back, but Sullivan "rushed him back over a pile of rubbish, and eventually knocked him down over a couple of trunks." Obviously, these were not ideal fighting conditions.

CC: Sullivan landed a telling uppercut, the first good square blow. Donaldson fought back hard, but was knocked over a trunk. He regained his feet and continued fighting until dropped near a straw heap and kicked by Sullivan. A claim of foul was not allowed.

4th Round

CDE: Donaldson was again sent to the wall, and slipped down. Sullivan was unable to restrain himself and hit him while he was down, but it appeared to be accidental, so the claim of foul was not allowed. The spectators agreed that it was accidental.

CC: Donaldson tried to keep John away by extending his guard out, but a hard right dropped Donaldson, whose lip was bloody.

5th Round

CDE: Donaldson wanted his second to give up for him, but he would not. The Professor attempted to elude Sullivan by running around, but was again fought down "over the trunks."

CC: Donaldson missed two blows. A smash to the jaw discouraged Donaldson, who went down to avoid another punch.

6th Round

CDE: The essentially beaten Donaldson ducked and ran away until he slipped down from a light punch.

CC: The short round ended by a sledge-hammer blow dropping Donaldson. Sullivan was laughing.

7th Round

CDE: Donaldson slipped down against the wall without being struck. Sullivan's seconds claimed the fight on the foul and a war of words ensued. After a couple of minutes, the referee said that the fight must go on.

CC: Sullivan landed two rights in quick succession. Donaldson went down and while there, was struck on the head. The cries of foul were not allowed.

8th Round

CDE: The Professor hit John L. in the nose but went down over the trunks again when Sullivan rushed him.

CC: Donaldson dropped down on the planks without fighting.

9th Round

CDE: Sullivan "knocked him about like an old sack," sending him down.

CC: Donaldson went down as quickly as possible.

10th Round

CDE: 20 seconds into the round, Donaldson was again sent to the floor from rights and lefts. After being dragged to his corner, he informed his seconds that he would not continue, stating that he was overmatched. It had lasted almost 22 minutes.

CC: Donaldson grabbed with his left around Sullivan's neck, but Sullivan kept swinging and landing rights. Donaldson finally went down. When time was again called, Donaldson walked up to Sullivan and said that he was satisfied. It was apparent to all that Donaldson had no chance to win, and so no one criticized him for retiring.

Afterwards, Sullivan seemed upset that it had taken him so long to "do" his man. "But what could I do ... he wouldn't stand up and fight, but would run away and even throw himself on the floor." Donaldson said that Sullivan was too big and strong. "I knew that I couldn't lick him, but I was tired of being called a coward."

Sullivan was highly complimented by the press as "a man who has probably no equal in the prize-ring today." The locals also opined, "If the days of the prize ring were not gone by, Sullivan would stand at the head and front of the fraternity."[21] That was how impressive he had been. *The National Police Gazette* said that although Donaldson put up a "plucky fight," the 212-pound Sullivan was too much for him from the beginning, proving that he was "the best man in America."[22] Thus, even at that point, John L. was viewed as America's best fighter, if not the world's best, despite lacking an official title.

Years later, when discussing the fight, Sullivan claimed that he had to chase Donaldson all around before he could get to him to knock him out. Donaldson's version was that he should have won the fight several times on a foul and that the fight was stopped by the police, possibly a bit of revisionism.[23]

The day after the fight, the two fighters were arrested and charged with engaging in a prizefight, which was illegal in Ohio, but were released two days later when no witnesses could be found who would substantiate that they had fought. When asked if he had seen a fight, one witness said, "No; I've seen a foot race." When asked, "Who was ahead?" the witness replied, "Donaldson, and Mr. Sullivan was running after him but could not catch him."[24] Having to deal with the law would become an occasional theme in Sullivan's career.

Sullivan was even beginning to gain international recognition. *The Australian Sportsman* noted,

> The American ring is characteristically represented by John Sullivan, who is stated to be a remarkable specimen of humanity. He is 22 years of age, stands six feet in height, and weighs 212 pounds. He has met all the heavyweight pugilists so far that dared meet him with the gloves in his native city, Boston, and made short work of them. He was recently sent for by McCormick, of the *Enquirer*, Cincinnati, to fight Donaldson.... In this battle Sullivan demonstrated that he was a clever two-handed fighter and a terrific hitter.[25]

Sullivan was quite active in 1881 and became renowned for quickly hurting and stopping his opponents. His growing popularity allowed him to fight often, which enabled him to gain valuable experience and improve as a fighter, which further fueled his popularity. By fighting so often, he made good money, enabling him to make boxing his primary source of income, something no fighter had previously been able to do.

Just ten days after the Donaldson fight, on January 3, 1881, back in Boston, Sullivan took on Jack Stewart, who was billed as the Canadian champion. Stewart was listed as 28 years old (born in 1852), 6'1" and 205 pounds, and had recently been sparring with former

Sullivan opponents Joe Goss and George Rooke. Called the Scotch giant of Glasgow, the Scottish born Stewart had been fighting since at least 1869, when he won a London rules bout in 17 rounds. Stewart had fought a draw with Tom Allen. Following an 1870 bout stopped by the police in the 10th round, Stewart fled to Canada to avoid arrest. He had won an 1880 gloved fight against Lon Wright.[26] One March 1880 report said a James Stewart of Glasgow (possibly the same) was defeated by Alf Greenfield on a foul in 20 rounds lasting 1 hour and 20 minutes.[27] However, that Stewart was listed as being about 37 years old.[28]

It was said by the local paper that the Sullivan-Stewart bout "attracted an audience such as has never before attended an exhibition of the kind in this city, and the hall was crowded to its utmost capacity." Sullivan was a big attraction. His bout was part of a larger exhibition benefit in which many bouts took place, including one that featured a future regular Sullivan sparring partner, lightweight/middleweight Pete McCoy.

Most secondary source records report that Sullivan scored a KO2 over Stewart, perhaps based on Sullivan's claim that he ran him off the stage in 2 rounds.[29] However, it is unclear whether he did knock him out, or if so, when. The local Boston Herald said that Sullivan did not knock him out. "Sullivan, it was anticipated, was going to 'knock someone out,' but he did not." It said that the closest he came to it was when Stewart "had his back turned toward him, not expecting blows. Sullivan appeared vicious, and, after hitting Stewart two cowardly blows, from which the latter sustained a black eye, he realized his mistake and was greeted with hisses." Sullivan then worked with Joe Goss in a tamer manner. "His bout with Goss was altogether uninteresting." On the whole, though, it was said to have been the best exhibition show given in the city for some time.[30]

However, another local paper, The Boston Daily Globe, said of the bout that Sullivan "managed to cross counter almost every blow from Stewart, in fact, in the first round, he knocked Stewart out of time. The second and third rounds were the same, Sullivan just playing with Stewart as a cat does with a mouse." Thus, this version gives the impression that Sullivan knocked him out in the 1st round, as well as each subsequent round, but that he was allowed to recover (perhaps in London rules fashion) and Sullivan to a certain extent carried him through 3 rounds. Therefore, this appears to have been a 3-round exhibition bout. This makes sense, because at exhibition benefits, the sparring was generally supposed to be of a friendlier nature. This perhaps explains why Sullivan might be hissed at for taking it to Stewart too hard and not working with him.

The "Boston boy" followed the Stewart bout with a "grand wind-up" with Goss, who was called the "champion boxer of England." Overall, the exhibition show was said to have been as orderly as ever given (countering the anti-boxing claim that these bouts only led to disorder and riots).[31]

Providing some insight into the state of boxing in the world at that time, The Australian Sportsman said,

> Boxing is a sport which has lost much of its olden popularity, principally by reason of the low character of many of its professors, although it still retains a place in the list of athletic amusements in colleges and other institutions where physical training is encouraged.... In America, however, it is otherwise. In that country, boxing matches are extremely numerous.[32]

In America, gloved exhibitions were gaining increased popularity.

On March 21, 1881, in Boston, Sullivan sparred 3 exhibition rounds with middleweight Mike Donovan, with whom he had sparred the previous year. Sullivan was said to weigh about 212 pounds.

The non-local *New York Clipper* said that Donovan was cautious, but did the best he could. Sullivan tried to knock him out during the 3 rounder, but Donovan's cleverness and quickness in dodging saved him. John was unable to land many of the "pile drivers which he sent out so savagely, while Donovan's steadiness and superior science enabled him to plant some hard facers; but they made no impression whatever on the solid Bostonian." Sullivan was hissed at for trying to take advantage of his smaller foe.[33]

The local *Boston Daily Globe* said that it was an exhibition benefit in which a number of exhibitions took place, amongst them being one between Joe Goss and Jack Stewart. Sullivan was called the strongest man in the profession and "the coming champion." His brutality and lack of mercy were immediately noticed:

> A well-directed blow from him has, seemingly, force enough to lay low a full grown Texas steer, and when he gets upon the stage he considers that it is the proper caper for him to immediately throw all the brutal force within him into his arm and launch it forth at his opponent.

Sullivan attacked the scientific "middleweight champion" Donovan, who coolly dodged his blows. There were 3 intense and exciting rounds in which John L. was unable to land a solid punch. Donovan, however, landed some clean blows to the face. "The affair was not at all satisfactory, the conduct of Sullivan being of such a brutal description as to invoke the hearty disapproval of the audience, who gave vent to their displeasure by prolonged hissing."[34] Again, because it was a benefit, the boxers were supposed to work with each other in a friendly manner and not try to take each other's heads off. Apparently, Sullivan was not in the mood to work with someone. Still, there was no ill will. Donovan and Sullivan would occasionally spar in the future.

Ten days after this exhibition, on March 31, 1881, in New York, John L. took on Steve Taylor (whose original name was John Mahan). Remember that name, because Taylor would eventually become one of Sullivan's chief sparring partners. Taylor wanted to earn the $50 Sullivan had just offered to anyone who could manage to box 4 Queensberry rules rounds with him and not be knocked out. This became a Sullivan signature. As John L. said, "This was the first time that anything of this kind had been offered."[35] He would offer increasingly larger amounts to anyone who could merely last 4 rounds with him, let alone defeat him. Such an offer and the ability to successfully knock out within 4 rounds those who attempted to win the money served to make Sullivan even more famous. Talk about confidence.

Taylor had some good experience, amongst his bouts having an 1876 L17 Billy Edwards and W18 Charles McDonald, and 1877 L15 John Dwyer.[36] Some papers years later called Taylor the ex–heavyweight champion of America.[37] Sullivan claimed that Taylor had fought Dwyer to an 1876 draw. He said that Taylor had trained Paddy Ryan for Ryan's fight with Goss (meaning that he was his sparring partner), and had also sparred with Jem Mace all over the country. John described him as a "six footer, of very powerful build, and as agile as a cat."[38]

Sullivan was listed as at least 212 pounds. From later descriptions, Taylor was probably close to 200 pounds. Steve was described as soft and puffy, with many pounds of superfluous flesh. John had a look of confidence "that bordered on contempt."[39]

The fight took place at Harry Hill's theater. *The New York Herald* and *National Police Gazette* said that Taylor began by assuming a defensive position, while Sullivan "held his hands very low." John immediately attacked Taylor, delivering heavy rights and lefts, "and so rapidly were they delivered that parrying them was an impossibility, and Taylor was knocked up against the wall, and there he stood taking hit after hit ... without returning. He was knocked down three times, and fell without a blow twice." Of the two times that he went down voluntarily, Taylor's second told him to drop without being hit, and then yelled "foul" as if Sullivan had fouled, but in reality it was Taylor who had committed the foul by going down voluntarily without a blow.

The New York Clipper said that the result of the fight was foregone in a few moments. In the 1st round, Sullivan landed rights and lefts to the head in rapid succession, sending

Steve Taylor. From Billy Edwards, *The Portrait Gallery of Pugilists of England, America, Australia* (Chicago: Athletic Publishing Co., 1894). Clay Moyle, www.prizefightingbooks.com.

Taylor to his knees. After rising, a swinging left to the right ear dropped him to the stage again. He was assisted to his feet (in London rules fashion—although it was a Queensberry rules bout), but the fight had been knocked out of him. "The severity of Sully's hitting had dazed him and caused him to forget all he knew about sparring. ... he suffered himself to be made a defenseless chopping block until the three minutes were up, and he had been hit to the floor."

The Herald said that in the 2nd round, Sullivan rushed at him, and three or four blows had Taylor against the "scenery" again. While there, after Sullivan struck him multiple times, Taylor's second threw up his handkerchief to retire him.

The New York Clipper said that in the 2nd round, Taylor was knocked down repeatedly. As soon as Steve was on his feet, Sullivan was at him with both hands. Taylor was fought against the scenery, whose support was the only thing which enabled him to remain upon his feet. However, a well-placed right to the head sent him down, and the sponge was thrown up. Sullivan did not lose his $50, but gave Taylor a present of $5.

It too noted that Taylor "in each round tried to get the verdict on a claim of foul, based on his being hit when on his knees, but, as the referee held that he went down without a blow, the claims were disallowed."

Sullivan was critiqued as a powerful hitter, but as throwing mostly "round handed" blows. *The Herald* felt that he would not do as well with a good straight hitter, but said, "As it is he is the champion." Even then, some considered Sullivan the champion.

The Clipper's critique was similar:

Sullivan maintained the reputation he gained in former encounters of being a tremendously hard and punishing hitter and a quick fighter ... but on the score of science he is not the equal of Taylor.... Unless a man is quick on his feet, coolheaded and possessed of good heart, the science of any man would not prevail against the batteries of so strong and earnest a fighter as Sullivan.[40]

Sullivan and Taylor became friends and would go on to give many sparring exhibitions together for years to come.

A month and a half later, on May 16, 1881, in Yonkers, New York, according to a secondary source, a 196-pound Sullivan fought 197-pound John Flood in a bout where London Prize Ring Rules were used, but it was fought with gloves. It said that the fight was held on a barge six miles up the Hudson River (a good way to escape the law) and it lasted 8 rounds totaling 16 minutes. Flood was knocked down or thrown down (with Sullivan sometimes illegally falling on top of him) to end the rounds. In the 8th round, a right knocked Flood out, who lost when he failed to come to the scratch after the 30-second rest.[41]

John Flood. From Billy Edwards, *The Portrait Gallery of Pugilists of England, America, Australia* (Chicago: Athletic Publishing Co., 1894). Clay Moyle, www.prizefightingbooks.com.

It is likely that the men were smaller than has been reported by secondary sources. *The New York Herald* said the 22-year-old Sullivan weighed 180 pounds to the 33-year-old, 5'11½" Flood's 185 pounds. *The New York Clipper* agreed that Sullivan had trained down 20 pounds from his usual weight of 203 pounds and was 5 pounds smaller than Flood (which would be 183 Sullivan, 188 Flood). Generally, fighters intentionally trained down in weight for London Prize Ring fights because the fights could last indefinitely. Boxers wanted to be lean and efficient. Also, the long hours of endurance training naturally caused them to lose weight.

The Herald claimed that Flood had never before fought a prize fight. That did not necessarily mean that he had never fought at all, because a prize fight in the parlance of the time was a London rules bout. *The Clipper* said that Flood had a local reputation for "rough and tumble fistic engagements" without rules. Sullivan said that they fought for a purse of $1,000, of which the winner was to receive $750. They wore small, hard gloves.[42]

The Herald summarized the London rules rounds:

1st round: The two hit away in close with half arm rights and lefts for about two minutes until Flood went down. "This was the fiercest round ever seen in so short a time."

2nd round: In a clinch, both hit rapidly with both hands "in the roughest and most unscientific manner until Flood again went down."

3rd round: They fought give and take in close for a minute until Flood was dropped.

4th round: As in prior rounds, they were clinched and throwing half arm blows for about 30 seconds, until Flood went down.

5th round: Flood butted Sullivan, who then landed a swinging right to Flood's head, dropping him in a heap.

6th round: In a clinch, Flood was dropped from a few short shots. He was bleeding from his mouth.

7th round: After a few moments of half-arm work, "Flood went down completely used up."

8th round: Flood was immediately dropped at the start of the round with a right to the side of the head. He was unable to rise at the call of time and his corner said that he would fight no more. It had lasted 16 minutes total.

The National Police Gazette noted that the first blow that Sullivan had landed left Flood "groggy and no good from that moment."[43] *The Clipper* agreed that Sullivan lost no time, dashing at Flood with both hands and quickly knocking him down with severe blows, "the effects of which he failed to shake off" for the duration of the bout. Sullivan had him at his mercy throughout and administered severe punishment, while receiving little. Every round ended with Flood being either knocked down, fought down, or thrown down. Flood was dropped with a "jaw breaker" to end the 8th round and his backer threw in the towel after 16 minutes had elapsed.

The Herald was critical of both fighters, stating that neither "seemed to understand the first rudiments of the art of self-defense. It was all pull and haul and hitting at close quarters. Nothing but 'slugging' from the call of time to the end, Sullivan had the best of the fight from the start to the finish." However, *The Clipper* said of Sullivan, "What he lacks in science is fully made up by his tremendous strength and hitting power, coupled with a quickness of action not often found in big men."[44]

Almost a month later, on June 13, 1881, in New York, Sullivan and Flood sparred in a friendly 3-round exhibition that "was highly unsatisfactory to those who looked for anything but a very mild bout."[45] These types of friendly exhibitions were customary follow ups to serious bouts, financially assisting the losing combatant.

Discussing the state of boxing, in Australia it was reported that

[o]ur English and American files furnish abundant testimony of the wholesale revival of boxing and pugilism in the two countries, the glove fighting being practically a modified form of pugilism, gloves of such thinness being used that the force of the fists is but slightly deadened. In England, however, the police authorities are unremitting in their attempts to suppress pugilistic displays, and one result of this is that the leading English pugilists are rapidly finding their way to the United States.[46]

In Philadelphia on July 11, 1881, Sullivan took on one of those Englishmen: Fred Crossley. The local *Philadelphia Press* said that Crossley was 6'1" and 200 pounds. Sullivan was weighing 196 pounds. John had offered $25 to anyone who would box him 4 rounds, but Crossley said that he would take up the challenge without financial inducement.

John L. began aggressively and "landed two sledge-hammer blows rapidly in succession on Crossley's head and face, and knocked him down." The Englishman rose and attempted a punch, but his blow was "warded off with the greatest ease, and he received a stinging blow in the face, which set his nose bleeding. Crossley showed the white feather at once." He went to his corner and asked to have the gloves removed, but was persuaded to continue. "Again did Sullivan deliver his powerful shoulder blows, and the discomfited Englishman was forced to acknowledge that he was no match for his scientific opponent."

The crowd howled in disappointment at how quickly Crossley had quit in the 1st round. To satisfy them, Sullivan said that he would spar with "Johnny Madden", but the "greater part of the audience dispersed without waiting to see its conclusion."[47] This was likely Billy Madden, Sullivan's then trainer and manager.

The *Philadelphia Record*'s version said that in about a minute from the time that the fight started, Sullivan pressed the

BILLY MADDEN,

MANAGER AND TRAINER OF THE CHAMPION, JOHN L. SULLIVAN.

Billy Madden. From Richard K. Fox, *John L. Sullivan, Champion Pugilist of the World* (New York: Richard K. Fox, 1882). Clay Moyle, www.prizefightingbooks.com.

taller Frederick Crossley to the ropes and landed a left to the nose that made the blood flow, and Crossley said that he had had enough. Sullivan and Madden then wound things up in a pleasing exhibition, despite their size disparity.[48]

The non-local *New York Clipper* said that the Crossley bout had lasted but one minute. A smash to the nose dropped him and took all the fight out of him. Billy Madden then took the stage with Sullivan, who did not try to knock him out.[49]

Still in Philadelphia, Sullivan and Madden sparred nightly over the next week.[50]

Secondary sources generally say that a mere ten days after the Crossley bout, on July 21, 1881, again in Philadelphia, Sullivan scored a 1st-round knockout over Dan McCarthy (or McCarty).[51] *The New York Clipper* and *National Police Gazette* said that Sullivan had fought Dan McCarthy of Baltimore. *The Gazette* said that McCarthy stood 5'9" and weighed 175 pounds. Both agreed that in the 1st round, Sullivan dropped him with a left to the head. Upon rising, he was hit by the right, which knocked him out. One said that the bout lasted 40 seconds, while the other simply said that it required less than a minute. *The Gazette* noted that it took a few minutes before McCarthy was resuscitated.[52]

However, one local source does not confirm the opponent's name of McCarthy. *The Philadelphia Press* said that Sullivan boxed John Buckley, a blacksmith, who was the only one who accepted the offer to try to last 4 rounds of sparring for $50.

After about four seconds, Sullivan landed a left fired from the shoulder and "Buckley dropped like a lump of lead on the floor. He fell all in a heap and instantly gave a convulsive shudder and stretched himself out like a dead man." He was unconscious for a number of minutes, despite the application of restoratives. After being taken to the dressing room, he finally regained consciousness. "This incident brought the exhibition to a close, as no one else had courage enough to stand up before the pugilist from the Hub."[53]

Yet another local paper, *The Philadelphia Record*, said that the fighter was identified as Dan McCarty of Baltimore. *The Gazette* and *Clipper* appear to have taken their reports from this paper. The 5'11½" Sullivan weighed about 190 pounds to the 5'9" McCarty's approximately 175 pounds. Sullivan went right to work driving McCarty back, and with a left to the face dropped him. As soon as he rose, Sullivan dropped him again with a tremendous right to the neck. McCarty was out cold. The combat had lasted just 40 seconds. "For a few minutes there were grave doubts about resuscitating the defeated pugilist," but he eventually recovered. Sullivan once again had immensely impressed observers. One was quoted as saying, "Well, I have seen all from Hyer down to the present day, but none could have beaten that young fellow Sullivan."[54]

It is unclear whether this opponent was Dan McCarthy/McCarty or John Buckley. Sullivan was a few years later quoted as saying, "In my present tour only one amateur has faced me—a man named Buckley, a rough and tumble fellow from the rolling mills in Philadelphia. He cried for quarters inside of thirty seconds."[55] Yet, in his autobiography, Sullivan quoted a Philadelphia paper (name and date not provided, but likely *The Philadelphia Record*) in discussing the bout, and called the opponent McCarty. Sullivan did not address the issue of the name discrepancy.[56]

The Clipper said that during the next week in Philadelphia, Sullivan and Billy Madden sparred nightly, and planned to do so again in a week or so, when Sullivan would increase his offer to $100 for anyone who could last 4 rounds with him.[57]

About three weeks after the Buckley/McCarty bout, Sullivan traveled to Chicago, Illinois, to take on 28-year-old "Captain" James Dalton. Dalton had some experience, including a victory over former Sullivan opponent Professor Donaldson. He was known for his skill, and one paper said that he was the best man in the West. A local paper said that Dalton had fought "some of the crack ring men of the country." Sullivan cited a report that said that "Dalton had successfully downed John Dwyer, Ryan, Donaldson, Chandler, and others."[58]

Dalton was listed by *The National Police Gazette* as being 5'11½" and 185 pounds, but the same periodical listed him two months later as 5'10½" and 172 pounds when untrained and 154 pounds when trained, again demonstrating the uncertainty regarding many of boxing's facts.[59] Two local papers listed Dalton as 175 pounds to Sullivan's 190 pounds.[60] Dalton was trying to win $50 for lasting 4 rounds against Sullivan.

Of this August 13, 1881, bout held in Chicago, *The Chicago Tribune* wrote that although Dalton did well for 2 rounds, in the 3rd Sullivan "smashed him viciously a few times," and in the 4th round, Sullivan "knocked him so stiff" that Dalton was unable to beat the ten count.[61]

The Chicago Herald said that the preliminary featured a match between "Abe Williams, colored, and Thomas Coglin for a silver cup, which the darkey won in three rounds." The main event featured Dalton, of the tug *Ingram*, and Sullivan. Dalton worked and hit hard, and even managed to land one or two good punches, but Sullivan did not seem to mind them. Dalton took a terrible pounding in the 3rd round before he was eventually knocked out in the 4th. "Sullivan proved that he is capable of tackling the best in the ring. He stated that he is ready to meet any man in the ring, either in this country or England."[62]

The Chicago Times provided additional details. This was the first Chicago exhibition of boxing in two years, and at least 3,000 people were in attendance. Some preliminary bouts took place, but the crowd began shouting for Sullivan until he and Dalton appeared.

The 1st round opened up cautiously, each sizing the other up. After about 30 seconds, Dalton landed a right and evaded a counter left. They exchanged some lively blows and a few clinches. In the 2nd round, Dalton forced matters and occasionally landed "a blow that would have knocked down an ordinary man, but which did not appear to effect [sic] Sullivan in the least." Whenever Sullivan got going, Dalton would rush in and clinch, doing so five times.

Sullivan began forcing the pace in the 3rd round and appeared to understand Dalton's tactics. After two minutes, Sully landed a right to the temple that knocked the Captain flat on the ground, "as though struck with a trip-hammer." Dalton struggled to his feet, clung to Sullivan, and even managed to throw him (in London rules fashion).

It appeared that Dalton was done for, for he seemed groggy and dazed. However, he again entered the action in round 4. The round was all in Sullivan's favor, as he knocked Dalton out before one minute had expired.

Sullivan gave Dalton the $50 anyway, because he considered him the best man that he had ever met. This satisfied the crowd, which sympathized with Dalton. "A good many people in Chicago were inclined to think him too much a talker; but he showed on last evening an extraordinary talent for hard hitting, as well."[63] *The Police Gazette* said that Sullivan gave him $25.[64]

Less than a month later, on September 3, 1881, again in Chicago, Sullivan met 29-year-old Jack Burns (sometimes called Byrne or Byrnes), a large, 6'3", 215-pound Canadian-born Englishman (now hailing from Michigan) who was said to have fought numerous prize fights.[65] He too was attempting to win $50 if he could last 4 rounds.

The Chicago Tribune said that Sullivan sent Burns down to the stage within the first 20 seconds. Jack had just risen when a right hand immediately dropped him again (boxers could stand over their fallen opponents), sending him off the stage into the audience. Burns declined to continue. It said that it lasted less than a minute.

Because of the bout's short duration, in order to provide further entertainment that evening, Sullivan's opponent from the previous month, Captain Dalton, entered the stage, and they engaged in "a friendly sparring match" of 4 rounds.[66]

The Chicago Herald said that Sullivan "pounded Burns with sledge-hammer effect, and so completely demoralized" him, scoring three knockdowns in two minutes, once knocking him off the stage, that Burns retired. Sullivan and Dalton then engaged in a friendly bout.[67]

The Chicago Times said that Sullivan quickly decked Burns with a right to the jaw. Burns rose and dashed forward with his head down, but was met with an uppercut to the chin that lifted him off the stage into the audience. He climbed back up, but was groggy on his legs and was met with a hurricane of blows. Jack's arms waved around in the air attempting to defend, but to no avail. In less than a minute the fight was over. It took the dazed Burns half an hour "again to get fairly acquainted with himself," and even then he didn't quite know where he was.[68]

The Daily Inter Ocean said there were fully 2,000 people in the hall. Despite Burns' size and reputation, within the first 15 seconds, he "was sprawling near the foot-lights, and an instant later he was knocked a distance of twenty feet, going over the stage into the audience." He was helped back up to the stage, but was groggy. A half dozen blows ended him. "The audience was frantic with delight, the more so because the affair was something of a surprise. Later, a friendly set-to between Sullivan and Captain Dalton demonstrated that Sullivan is as scientific as he is powerful."[69]

On July 2, 1881, U.S. President James A. Garfield was shot in the back by Charles Guiteau, a disappointed office-seeker. Garfield died on September 19, 1881, and the following day, Chester A. Arthur became president. Sullivan, fond of criminal celebrities, actually went to visit Guiteau while he was being held on the assassination charge.[70]

The men with whom Sullivan sparred in 1881 included Joe Goss, middleweight Mike Donovan, John Flood, Billy Madden, Steve Taylor, and lightweight Pete McCoy. These and various others that Sullivan fought would often eventually become members of his sparring troupe. Their sparring sessions had varying intensities, but generally Sullivan worked with them and did not show his full power against these men. In this way, Sullivan could maintain his conditioning, work on his skills, and get paid for it by audiences who sought entertainment.

In New York sometime during October 1881, Sullivan offered $50 to anyone who could last 4 rounds with him. No one took up the offer, so a crowd of 2,000 watched him spar Steve Taylor in a tame set-to. Sullivan upped the offer to $250, but still no one accepted. It was said that his next exhibition would be in Philadelphia.[71]

Sullivan sparred with Billy Madden on November 5 in New York. It was said that he was headed to Boston, but would be back to spar in Buffalo on November 16. He and his sparring partners were then set to go on the road.[72]

On November 28, 1881, in Cincinnati, Ohio, John L. sparred Pete McCoy and Madden. Sullivan first sparred with McCoy, the agile middleweight. Sullivan's comparatively immense bulk made it an unequal contest. The wind-up was between Sullivan and Madden. It was a clever exhibition, but quite tame, for it was opined that they could have been more vigorous without anyone being hurt.

Sullivan was called the heavyweight champion by the local press, which complimented his progress as a fighter. "Since Sullivan was here in December last his improvement has been something wonderful." He had back then done terrific work in his display of round arm hitting against Donaldson, but the knowing ones felt that his roundhouse blows were a waste of time and force. Since working with Billy Madden as his trainer, Sullivan had corrected his amateur habits and had become a "skilled man in straight hitting." "He has acquired a great deal of 'science,' and he already had an almost unlimited quantity of strength and stay."[73]

All of Sullivan's 1880 and 1881 bouts, except for the Donaldson and Flood fights, were fought under the Queensberry rules, but all of them were fought with gloves.

CHAPTER 5

A "Real" Fight

John L. Sullivan and bareknuckle champion Paddy Ryan agreed to fight in a bareknuckle prizefight set for early February 1882. Sullivan went into training in December 1881 under the direction of Billy Madden. Sullivan said that he gave exhibitions with Madden, Pete McCoy, and Bob Farrell (a lightweight) on the way to New Orleans, in preparation for the match.[1]

Ryan was backed by Richard K. Fox, publisher of *The National Police Gazette*, a successful weekly paper which did more to promote boxing than any other publication, having reports on the sport in every issue. It billed Ryan as the world champion (although at times it merely called him the American champion). It was unclear at that time who really was the world champion, so it all depends on perspective. Former bareknuckle champion Jem Mace had been retired and inactive for quite some time, and was about 50 years old, so Ryan could be considered the champion.

Ryan had won the bareknuckle championship in June 1880 by knocking out Joe Goss with a right, ending the 87th round after 1 hour and 27 minutes of London rules fighting.[2] It was reportedly Ryan's first prize ring fight. In it, he proved that he was "a game man and a hard hitter, and one of the best fighters and wrestlers of his time." One writer said that it was something for Paddy "to lick the old man, though he's not what he was, for Goss is tricky."[3] Ryan had also engaged in a number of sparring exhibitions, including some against Steve Taylor.

The Sullivan-Ryan fight was a hot topic of conversation, and there was a great difference of opinion as to who would win. Betting in New York favored Ryan, while Sullivan was the favorite in Chicago. One observer who had seen Ryan spar during the past few months said that he had "wonderfully improved in the use of his hands, and may now be called a clever man." Ryan backers liked the fact that he had proven himself in a lengthy London rules fight. Some questioned whether Sullivan's bare hands would be able to stand the hard blows that he could strike. One sporting man said, "I consider Ryan a wonderful man. I saw him when he fought Goss, and his abilities as a wrestler and in fighting are immense. I don't know why I think so, but I am inclined to believe that if Sullivan gets a hot-facer he will have a fit of the sulks." A New Yorker said, "Ryan will fight cautiously from the start, and will not allow Sullivan to hit him. He is longer in the reach and can fight him at long range for a time. This will break Sullivan up, and then, when he loses his temper and rushes in, Ryan will cross him and get the best of it."

One Sullivan supporter said that betting on John was like finding money in the street. A Chicago man said,

> Sullivan will down Ryan as sure as you live. I have seen a good many fighters, and I give you my word that I have never seen a man that I considered his equal. I saw him when he knocked Dalton out in Chicago, and his blows are like those struck with a sledge-hammer. He is a terrible hitter, and I believe he will stand to the scratch just as long as the other man will.

Another said that Sullivan "is a tremendous hitter and the most perfectly built man that I ever saw. I regard him as a wonder and think that he will out fight Ryan from the start." Joe Goss, who had fought both, when asked what he thought of Ryan, who had given an exhibition on the last day of January, said, "He looked very well, I thought, and has improved wonderfully in his sparring, but my man will lick him sure." Although the masses generally supported Sullivan, most of the leading sporting men believed that Ryan would win, and bet their money that way.[4]

When asked if he was at all scared or nervous, Sullivan replied, "No, sir; not a bit. There ain't a man in the world that I am the least bit afraid of, nor one that I wouldn't fight." In training, Sullivan did 100-yard sprints in 11 or 11.5 seconds. In the morning, Sullivan would go on walks. In the afternoon he would go for a run and fight the ball attached to a rope, doing his work "with machine-like regularity."

Ryan too was confident. One observer said, "I think I shall have to walk home if Ryan is whipped, but I know he won't be. I have just seen him, and he is as quiet and confident as a man can be. Nothing worries him, and it would take tonight a man with a club to beat him. Put that in your diary."[5]

Five days before the fight, on February 2, 1882, in New Orleans, Sullivan sparred 3 short rounds with Joe Goss. The local *Daily Picayune* said that Sullivan was looking much thinner than he had before entering training, and against Goss appeared "quick and graceful and did not exert himself, getting in his blows and warding off those of his adversary with ease. Goss showed that he had lost none of that science for which he has so long been justly celebrated."[6]

Another local paper, *The Times-Democrat*, said 800 people came to see the "Boston Wonder." This paper was not as impressed with Sullivan, saying that Goss had the best of it all the way through.

> The Boston Boy's habit of ducking his head and shutting his eyes was very unfavorably commented upon by the sports present, and many stated that compared with Ryan, the Troy man is the better sparer of the two, being cooler in his judgment, quicker with both hands and fully as agile as his opponent. The friends of Sullivan were rather disappointed at the showing that he made and admitted that while he was a harder hitter than Ryan, yet the latter was the more scientific man of the two.[7]

A sporting man said that it would never do for Sullivan "to turn his head when he strikes at Ryan, as he did when boxing with Goss, for if he does he'll get hurt. People say that Sullivan is a wonder, but I can't see it."[8] It is likely that so close to the fight, John was just taking it easy. Another possibility is that in order to secure better betting odds for his backers, Sullivan did not want to look too good.

On the morning of the fight, February 7, the ring was pitched at 11 a.m. in front of a Mississippi City, Mississippi, hotel, about 100 miles north of New Orleans, Louisiana. A train took the spectators and principals there.

There had been some question as to where the fight's location would be. Mississippi governor Robert Lowry issued an edict that the fight would not be allowed to take place in his state, ordering sheriffs of all counties to prevent it.[9] It took place in Mississippi anyhow. Apparently, the local sheriff had business in Biloxi that day (wink, wink).[10] Technically, though, there was no Mississippi law against prizefighting. Governor Lowry would subsequently redouble his efforts, get an anti–prize fight law passed, and seven years later, would figure prominently in another Sullivan fight.

On February 7, 1882, in Mississippi City, Mississippi, a 23-year-old, 175–182 pound

RICHARD K. FOX.
Editor and Proprietor of the "Police Gazette" and "Fox's
Illustrated Weekly."

Richard K. Fox. From Richard K. Fox, *Life and Battles of John L. Sullivan Ex Champion Pugilist of the World* (New York: Richard K. Fox, 1891). Clay Moyle, www.prizefightingbooks.com.

Sullivan took on 190–195 pound, 29-year-old champion Paddy Ryan for the American bareknuckle heavyweight championship, if not the world championship, under London Prize Ring Rules.[11] This was likely Sullivan's first bareknuckle prizefight, although he had twice before fought under London rules with gloves. Sullivan's reported weight range seems much lower than typical for John, who usually weighed around 200 pounds, but it is likely that he brought himself down in weight as a result of his intense endurance training, or in part because it was believed that being heavy was a detriment in a potentially lengthy finish fight. Even Ryan trained down.

The Police Gazette listed John as being 175 pounds when in condition, but just after the fight listed him as 182 pounds.[12] Six days before the fight, Sullivan told the local press that he was weighing 177 pounds.[13] Five days before the fight, *The Boston Daily Globe* listed Sullivan as being 178 pounds.[14] *The Police Gazette* listed Ryan as 6'½" and as normally weighing 221 pounds, but shortly after the fight listed him as 190 pounds.[15] *The New York Herald* said that the shorter Sullivan was 180 pounds, but was more muscular than the 190-pound Ryan.[16] The more local New Orleans based *Daily Picayune* said Ryan stood 6'2½" and weighed 193 pounds. It listed Sullivan's fighting weight as being about 178 pounds. A Mississippi paper said Ryan was 6'2½" and 190 pounds, while Sullivan was 5'10½" and 175 pounds.[17]

Ryan wore white drawers and stockings with spiked shoes, while Sullivan wore green drawers and stockings. Sullivan's handkerchief had a green border with Irish and Confederate flags in the corners. John also wore a "white kid plaster" protector, which concealed the small of his back and loins. There were about 2,000 spectators present.

They fought for $2,500 per side, with an additional $1,000 bet put up by Ryan's backer Fox just before the fight, which Sullivan accepted. Thus, the winner stood to make $3,500, a sizable amount of cash in 1882. The annual real per capita gross domestic product for that year was $3,550. The purchase power of the dollar at that time was almost eighteen times greater than its 2003 value.[18] This would be the equivalent of financial backers today being willing to part with more than $62,619 on the result of one fight.

Pursuant to the bareknuckle London rules, Sullivan and Ryan fought in a 24-foot ring on soil, with eight stakes or posts, one on each corner, and one in the middle of each side, with two ropes. When downed by a blow or throw, a fighter had 30 seconds of rest, and then another 8 seconds to come to the scratch and resume again.

The fight began at 1 p.m. and lasted 9 rounds. *The New York Times* reported that Sullivan exhibited "remarkable skill as a two-handed fighter," from the beginning acting on the offensive, attacking with ferocity, and following his attack with clinching and wrestling, as allowed by the London bareknuckle rules. It was a fairly easy victory. Each round only lasted between 4 and 30 seconds, most being only about 20 seconds long.

The New York Herald said that it was evident from the 1st round that Sullivan was superior. Ryan's blows "appeared weak for a man of his great size. It was clear that the first blow he got in the neck dazed him." After being knocked about, Ryan mostly resorted to wrestling tactics. Sullivan was too fast and Ryan weakened quickly.

The Daily Picayune and *Times-Democrat*, the most local New Orleans based papers, had reporters on the scene. According to the *Picayune*, Sullivan from the beginning was fierce and aggressive, rushing in and delivering multiple blows in rapid succession, following up by clinching or fighting at close quarters. Sullivan did not retreat or feint but attempted to quickly crush his opponent, leaving Ryan no time to rally. Paddy never did recover from Sullivan's rights. The 9-round fight only lasted 11 minutes total.

The Times-Democrat called it the greatest fistic battle of the past 20 years and complimented Sullivan's skills and abilities:

> It was short, sharp, and decisive.... [I]t is generally conceded that the Boston Boy is a wonder. His hitting powers are terrific, and against his sledge-hammer fists the naked arms of a man are but poor defense. He forced the fighting from the start and knocked his opponent about as though he were a football, receiving himself but little punishment in return. Ryan was dazed after the first round.... Nothing but his gameness kept him in the ring from that time on....

> [Sullivan's] style of fighting differed from that of any pugilist that has entered the ring of late years.... He is a rusher, and it is this quality and his tremendous hitting powers that really make him a great pugilist. Beside, he is a skillful wrestler and a good in-fighter, quick to dodge and always on the alert for any opening that an opponent may leave.

The fight by rounds:

1st Round

Daily Picayune (DP): The men sparred, Ryan threw a hard punch which fell short and Sullivan landed a right that almost staggered Paddy, who closed in. John landed several more rights in close and knocked Ryan down in less than a minute. Paddy was able to walk back to his corner.

Times-Democrat (TD): Ryan's guard was low and from the beginning he was on the defensive, wary of Sullivan's right. "Sullivan's guard was good, and his left hand was in constant motion as he moved around his adversary." Ryan missed a right and was countered by a left on the mouth and nose that started the "claret" flowing. Before Ryan could recover, Sullivan "swung his right like a sledge-hammer, catching Ryan under the ear and knocking him down."

The New York Herald (NYH) said the round lasted only 30 seconds.

PADDY RYAN.

OF TROY, N. Y., BACKED BY THE "POLICE GAZETTE" OF NEW YORK, IN THE GREAT
PRIZE FIGHT.

Paddy Ryan. From Richard K. Fox, *John L. Sullivan, Champion Pugilist of the World* (New York: Richard K. Fox, 1882). Clay Moyle, www.prizefightingbooks.com.

2nd Round

DP: Sullivan forced the fighting and landed several blows. Ryan closed in and used his wrestling skills. After wrestling fairly evenly, Ryan managed to throw Sullivan down on his back.

TD: Blood trickled from Ryan's nose and mouth. Sullivan followed him and attacked, landing a couple blows before being countered. Ryan closed in and wrestled. They hit each other in close, but Ryan's blows lacked steam. With some effort, Paddy managed to whirl John around and trip him, falling heavily on Sullivan. Both men were carried to their corners by their seconds.

The NYH added that the round only lasted 25 seconds, and although Ryan threw and fell heavily on Sullivan, "the fatigue that the effort cost him seemed greatly to impair his strength."

3rd Round

DP: After several feints by both, Sullivan dropped Ryan with a right to the mouth, drawing first blood.

TD: The round was quite short. Ryan was cautious and tried to keep away, but Sullivan made a few lightning attacks, rushing towards him. He finally landed a right over the left eye, causing Paddy to stagger and fall heavily on his back.

4th Round

DP: They countered one another, but Sullivan's blows were far more frequent. John followed him about the ring punching all the time until Ryan fell in the corner, the round only lasting 30 seconds.

TD: Ryan appeared to be suffering, bleeding from his mouth and a cut on the nose. He was wary and watchful, but "it appeared impossible for him to win, Sullivan's tremendous battering powers being more than Ryan could stand." Sully landed a right to the head but was countered with a blow to the neck. Sharp infighting followed until Ryan retreated. Sullivan landed body shots until clinched. "Ryan tried to back-heel Sullivan, when the latter forced him to the ropes and both fell, Ryan being the most damaged by the fall."

5th Round

DP: Sullivan again forced and followed Ryan about the ring, administering blows all the time. Ryan finally clinched and Sullivan fell on his back.

TD: The men fought desperately, but Ryan's neck swelled and the blood was sent flying from his mouth. Ryan landed a couple rights and clinched until Sullivan back-heeled and threw him heavily. Paddy "was suffering terribly from the blows that no pugilist in the world but Sullivan can deliver, while it was plain to be seen he was gradually failing. Sullivan, on the other hand, was just as fresh as when he commenced the battle about six minutes before."

NYH: They struck each other in the face before a wrestle down ended the round. Some said Ryan wrestled John down, while others said that Sullivan threw Ryan.

6th Round

DP: Ryan was bleeding profusely from the nose and mouth. Sullivan rushed in striking away with both hands until Ryan staggered and went down. The round lasted a little over 30 seconds.

TD: The men feinted and exchanged blows. While in close, Ryan landed a nice uppercut. Sullivan took it without flinching and landed the same blow right back with telling effect. Ryan staggered, and before he could recover, was beaten down.

7th Round

DP: Sullivan forced the fighting, avoided Paddy's blows, and landed his blows in rapid succession. They came to a clinch and Sullivan threw him down easily.

TD: "A close fibbing, and Ryan down at the end, tells the story of the round."

NYH: They hit for just a short while, with Ryan going to the grass "a wreck." Another version said that Paddy landed a right "which made Sullivan put down his hands for a moment and look at Ryan in a bewildered way." A few moments later, John knocked him about with rights and lefts until Paddy went down.

8th Round

DP: Sullivan dropped Ryan by another one of his rushes. Ryan rose and continued, but John punished him and then threw him to the turf.

TD: Blows were rapidly exchanged. Sullivan showed no fear for Ryan's punches, while Paddy was powerless to resist the incoming volley. After almost being knocked over the ropes, Ryan closed in and struggled for several seconds until he went to one knee. Sullivan

released him and they were both about to return to their corners, but as a result of the urg-
ing their seconds, continued. They clinched and struggled until both went down together.

9th Round

Most papers said Ryan went down senseless after being struck by a right under the ear.
However, *The New York Herald* said that Sullivan "delivered several telling righthanders on
Ryan's jaw and temple which knocked him about without his being able to return the blows
and sent poor Ryan down all in a heap." This version indicated that a series of rights (as
opposed to one blow) sent Ryan down. Sullivan's version of the conclusion agreed, stating,
"On the last round I fought him down. He fell all in a heap from a succession of blows on
his head, not from any particular one of them. His strength was overcome and exhausted."
Ryan failed to regain consciousness and come to the scratch for the 10th round. The sponge
was thrown up by his seconds, signaling defeat.

The Daily Picayune was a mixture, saying that Sullivan pounded on him until the final
devastating punch was landed. First, Sullivan landed a heavy right to the chest that could
be heard all over. Sullivan then followed up, administering blows as Ryan staggered back.
Paddy continued, but John L. finally landed a settler that dropped him. Ryan was carried
to his corner in a poor condition. When time was called, Sullivan walked to the center, but
Paddy could not rise. His second threw up the sponge. It had lasted 11 minutes. Ryan had
to be carried to his quarters.

The other semi-local paper, *Times-Democrat*, said that Ryan struggled to make it to the
scratch on time to begin the 9th round. He closed in a couple times but was twice pushed
off. After the second time, Sullivan followed up with a left on the neck which sent Ryan
down almost senseless. At the call of time for the 10th round, the sponge was thrown up,
after 11 minutes had elapsed.

Some said that it had only lasted about 10½ minutes total. The NYH said the actual
fighting time, excluding the rests, was about 6 minutes.

It had been a slugging match, but Sullivan's hammering powers were too much from
the beginning, having clearly established his mastery. Ryan admitted that he had been fairly
defeated. The NYH said that Paddy's jaw had been broken in two places. The DP said that
Sullivan only had a slight swelling above the left eye. Ryan had gashed lips, a cut across the
nose and a large swelling on the left side of his neck. The TD also added that Ryan had
suffered a slight cut near the left eye and had contusions on his chest.[19]

Of Sullivan, Ryan said,

> I never faced a man who could begin to hit as hard, and I don't believe there is another man
> like him in the country. One thing is certain, any man that Sullivan can hit he can whip.... I
> have heard it said dozens of times that he can't box. It is true that he is not what could be fairly
> called a brilliant boxer, but on the whole he spars about as well as the general run of pugilists ...
> and he can hit hard enough to break down any man's guard that I know of.[20]

Boxing men were very impressed. One said, "I have seen all the big fighters in the ring,
not alone in this country, but also in England, but never in my life saw such a hitter as Sullivan. So far as science is concerned, he has improved wonderfully in the past year." Another
said, "I have seen Tom Hyer in his best days, Morrissey and others in the ring; all, as you
know, were good ones, but I am satisfied that Sullivan could lick any of them." Others noted
that science was not Sullivan's strong point, but that he rushed in and forced matters, and

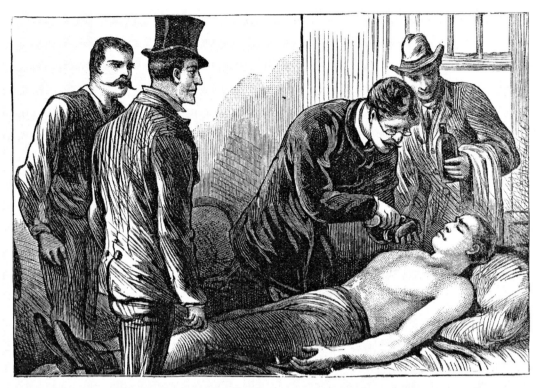

RYAN AFTER THE FIGHT.

Paddy Ryan after the fight. From Richard K. Fox, *John L. Sullivan, Champion Pugilist of the World* (New York: Richard K. Fox, 1882). Clay Moyle, www.prizefighting books.com.

all he needed was to be able to hit his opponent.[21] "The result of this fight must undoubtedly give Sullivan the highest place as the hardest hitter that is now to be found upon the American continent."[22]

Despite the many accolades for Sullivan, some criticized prizefighting itself, saying that it was "nothing more or less than an exhibition of brute force in its most repellant form.... If the encounter yesterday is a sample of the latter-day prize fight, then the sooner the prize ring is abolished and the whole race of modern prize fighters swept out of existence the better."[23]

Sullivan quoted a later *Times-Democrat* report as saying,

It is amusing to observe the style in which the newspapers now speak of the Sullivan-Ryan fight. They describe it contemptuously as a mere brutal hammering ... one would suppose that Ryan was a helpless, old imbecile.... The fact is, however, that previous to the battle, nine tenths of the sporting men in the country looked upon Sullivan's pretensions with open derision.... Ryan was lauded as a Hercules and a hero; a man who could endure any amount of punishment; who was a magnificent boxer and invincible wrestler,—in a word, a winner.... Experienced sports ... bet their money on Ryan.... You must have thought the backers of Sullivan the most besotted fools upon the globe....

Sullivan won the fight by virtue of superior science and irresistible strength.... He cared nothing for Ryan's blows, and his own hitting is so tremendous that it seems beyond the power of man to recover from the shock of one of his hands let out from the shoulder.[24]

There is no doubt that Sullivan was phenomenally talented. Although he had little or no formal boxing training, he was able to learn the game and improve his skills through

John L. Sullivan. From Richard K. Fox, *John L. Sullivan, Champion Pugilist of the World* (New York: Richard K. Fox, 1882). Clay Moyle, www.prizefightingbooks.com.

experience, fighting and sparring quite often. This combined with his natural fighting instincts and superior speed and strength enabled him to easily defeat more experienced fighters.

At that point, some sporting men felt that the only man who could stand up to Sullivan was England's Alfred Greenfield.[25] However, Greenfield had in 1881 fought a 28-round draw with a fellow Englishman named Tug Wilson, whom many felt had the better of it. Sullivan would meet Wilson before 1882 was through. Sullivan and Greenfield would meet almost three years later.

Although the Sullivan-Ryan fight was technically for the American championship, many Americans considered Sullivan to be the world champion at this point, as Ryan had been promoted by *The National Police Gazette* as the world champion. After the fight, it called Sullivan the champion of the world.[26] However, *The New York Times* and others billed the fight as being for the American championship. If Sullivan was not the world champion, it was unclear as to who was, for most of the former great bareknuckle champions had not fought in many years, essentially being retired. Sullivan was clearly the best fighter in the world.

CHAPTER 6

Now They'll Have to Do It My Fashion

The 1882 Ryan fight was Sullivan's first bareknuckle prizefight, and he would not fight without gloves again until 1888, six years later, so really, Sullivan was more of a first gloved world champion than a last bareknuckle champion. Sullivan preferred gloves, saying, "They said that I was only a glove-fighter, and that I was afraid of the bare knuckles. For that reason I consented to fight Ryan as I did. I think I have proved that I can fight with my knuckles, and now anyone who wants to tackle me will have to do it my fashion."[1] That meant future opponents would have to fight him with gloves under Queensberry rules. Many old school boxing people did not consider him to be champion because of the fact that he fought with gloves and not under the London rules.[2] However, he had proven his mettle against Ryan using the traditional system, which legitimized him as a champion in the eyes of many. Still, critical purists remained and eventually in the late 1880s, Sullivan gave in to them by engaging in two bareknuckle prizefights.

In addition to his numerous sparring exhibitions, Sullivan fought at least eight times in 1882, all with gloves except for the Ryan fight. Over the next few years, Sullivan boxed quite often.

Sullivan said that after the Ryan fight, he, Madden, Goss, McCoy, and Bob Farrell exhibited in Chicago, Detroit, Cleveland, Pittsburgh, Philadelphia, and New York.[3]

In Boston on March 23, 1882, Sullivan said that he was willing to meet any man in the country for $5,000 per side. He would fight with gloves, and his opponent could use gloves or fight bareknuckle. "I will not fight again with the bare knuckles, as I do not wish to put myself in a position amenable to the law."[4]

On March 27, 1882, in New York, John L. gave two 3-round sparring exhibitions, one with a blacksmith named Joseph Douglas and the other with Billy Madden. Douglas was "evidently a novice in the science of self-defense" who asked Sullivan to take it easy on him and to not knock him out. Sullivan played with him over 3 short rounds, striking him to the head and body without return, only once landing a right with any power, which turned Douglas around and nearly knocked him down. At that point, Douglas wanted to quit, but was convinced to continue, and Sullivan handled him lightly. Sullivan easily blocked the novice's awkward blows.

John then sparred Madden, and his display of skill provoked favorable comment.

[Sullivan's] quickness in hitting, the activity he displayed, and the improvement shown in his style of sparring, surprised the spectators, many of whom changed their previously unfavorable opinion regarding his scientific attainments after seeing him set to subsequently with Billy Madden, the pair making a very pretty and interesting display, wherein the champion held his punishing powers in reserve.... In hitting, guarding and evasive tactics, Sullivan displayed decided skill.

This changed the minds of many who had previously simply regarded Sullivan "as a bull like rusher, hitting round and at random."[5] Sullivan claimed that 6,000–8,000 had witnessed the exhibition.[6]

The following day, on March 28 in New Jersey, Sullivan sparred 3 rounds with Steve Taylor.[7]

On April 15, 1882, Sullivan sparred Pete McCoy in a friendly exhibition.[8]

Sullivan's first real match after defeating Paddy Ryan in early February was in Rochester, New York, on April 20, 1882. All of the local and semi-local newspapers agreed that he was scheduled to meet a black fighter named Johnson. The day of the fight, Sullivan said, "There are a great many boxers who are anxious to cope with me, but when they come to put the gloves on they seem to weaken. I hope Johnson will be on hand tonight, for I am anxious to give him a few points."[9] However, that evening, despite the crowd's calling his name, Johnson did not appear, apparently too afraid. "A darky named Johnson had agreed to undertake the job, but when the pinch came he weakened." One said that Johnson refused to appear when he learned that it would not be a friendly contest.

Was Sullivan actually going to take on a black fighter? Many years later, Sullivan would become known for his refusal to take on Peter Jackson, a black fighter, due to his race. A question many historians have asked was whether Sullivan simply used the color line as an excuse to avoid Jackson. He certainly did not mention it in regard to Johnson.

The opera house "never saw a greater throng of men," as 1,800 men and boys were on hand to watch Sullivan spar. Because Johnson failed to show, John was instead just going to work with a member of his combination, but a local fireman named John McDermott stepped up and said that he would attempt to win the $100 offered for standing up against Sullivan for 4 rounds. Listed at either 147 or 140 pounds, McDermott was obviously much smaller than the 200-pound Sullivan. Yet, Mac proved himself to be agile and strong.

According to *The New York Herald*, in the 1st round, McDermott escaped all of Sullivan's blows with scientific dodging and moving around the stage. In the 2nd round, Sullivan "clipped him twice, which sent him to the floor." Sullivan dropped him three times in the 3rd, and then knocked McDermott into the stage scenery. He rose, still lively, but a sweeping left "used McDermott up, and he withdrew."[10]

The New York Clipper said that McDermott was not clever with his hands, but quick on his feet and adept at ducking. With his movement, he managed to avoid being taken out in the 1st round. In the 2nd, "he caught some pepper," and in the 3rd round, "he was repeatedly floored and gave up the unequal struggle."

The sympathy of the crowd was with the underdog McDermott, and it hissed and jeered at Sullivan during and after the bout. Sullivan was supposed to wind up the exhibition by sparring Billy Madden, but he was hurt by the crowd's ill treatment, and did not entertain them again.[11]

According to the local papers, Sullivan wore a light gauze shirt and green silk knee pants, and was called "the model of physical beauty." McDermott wore a blue flannel shirt and other heavy clothing. Although he did not claim to be a fighter, he showed that he had knowledge of the art of sparring.

The Rochester papers appeared biased in favor of their local man, highlighting his strong points and overlooking and minimizing much of Sullivan's work:

1st Round

Rochester Morning Herald (RMH): McDermott slipped once and went to his knees, but was at it again in an instant. The crowd urged on the local man. Neither won a fall in the round.

Rochester Democrat and Chronicle (RDC): "McDermott sent the champion to the wings with two palpable hits and thoroughly out of breath."

Rochester Daily Union and Advertiser (RUA): Mac showed a good deal of skill and greater liveliness than Sullivan, delivering some telling blows, one of which nearly floored the champion.

2nd Round

RMH: Sullivan struck sledge-hammer blows, but McDermott with surprising agility ducked and countered. Mac occasionally slipped to the ground, but recovered himself each time until he was finally knocked down.

RDC: "It was announced that the set-to was to be governed by the Marquis of Somebody's rules which limited the rounds to three minutes ... [but the] master of ceremonies allowed the round to last 4½ minutes ... and the reputation of the champion was saved."

RUA: The round winded both considerably.

3rd Round

RMH: Both were tired, and toward the end of the round, McDermott gave up, but "had not been touched in the face during any of the rounds."

RDC: Sullivan struck him a terrible blow in the face with the heel of this hand and sent him out among the scenery. Mac came to time, "and it was necessary for the Bostonian to jump around and hit him in the back of the head with one of his sledge-hammer blows to send him to the floor."

RUA: Before the round was over, McDermott had enough.

The local papers were not impressed with Sullivan. "Sullivan showed nothing at all but brute force, and the assemblage was quite disgusted." Another said that if Johnson had appeared, he would have knocked out "the so called champion" in the 1st round. "This man from Boston may be a mechanic in the pugilistic art ... but if so, he did not give any evidence of it.... [Sullivan] could probably break a lamp-post with his fist if he got a fair blow at it, but it would be a clumsy lamp-post that did not dodge his blows." Of course, if McDermott was doing so well, why wouldn't he have finished the fight and earned the $100?

The crowd's anti-Sullivan feeling "was intensified by a few words of his nauseating bombast." With his "characteristic conceit," Sullivan made a speech in which he said that despite opportunities to do so, he did not take advantage of the man he called a novice. He claimed to have carried him. In response, the crowd jeered at Sullivan, one saying, "You big duffer, you got all you wanted any how." It was said that Sullivan in private spoke highly of Mac's boxing skills. Sullivan's share of the receipts was $852. He was said to be headed back to Boston.[12]

On July 4, 1882 in Brooklyn, New York, Sullivan took on an over 20-year London rules veteran named Jimmy Elliott. A native of Ireland, Elliott was 37 years old and had begun his fighting career in America in about 1861, when he won a fight after 34 rounds lasting 1 hour. In 1862, he fought Hen Winkle in a 99-round bareknuckle draw that lasted 2 hours and 15 minutes. In 1864, he served about one year of a two-year prison sentence for engaging in an illegal 1863 prizefight. In 1867, Elliott knocked out Bill Davis in 9 rounds. In 1868, he defeated Charley Gallagher in 23 or 24 grueling and foul laden rounds that lasted 1 hour and 17 minutes. In 1869, Elliott knocked out British champion Tom Allen in the 2nd round after just three minutes of fighting.[13] Elliott was the American champion, but in 1870, was convicted of robbery and assault with intent to kill, and was imprisoned until 1879.[14]

In May 1879, Elliott lost to American Joe Dwyer in a 10- or 12-round bareknuckle bout that lasted 12 minutes.[15] Prior to that fight, Elliott was listed as 6'1" and 175 pounds. Revealing the lack of championship clarity at the time, the Elliott-Dwyer fight was described as being for the heavyweight championship of America.[16] Apparently, Dwyer claimed the crown owing to Joe Goss' inactivity.[17] Following the loss to Dwyer, Elliott left the ring for two years.

However, on May 1, 1882, Elliott defeated Dick Eagan (or Egan), "the Troy terror," which again put him on the map. Elliott weighed 179 pounds to Egan's 205, but Elliott stopped him in the 4th round with a right uppercut.[18]

For the Sullivan-Elliott match, the ring was a wood platform of 24 feet square, elevated about five feet from the ground. About 100 policemen were in attendance. Elliott wore white tights and stockings, but was naked from the waist up. Sullivan wore blue stockings, green tights and a white sleeveless undershirt.[19] John L. said that over 5,000 persons were present and they fought with hard gloves, as was Elliott's desire.[20]

Sullivan had offered $500 to Elliott if he could last 4 rounds under Queensberry rules. For this bout, the 6'1" Elliot weighed about 185 pounds, although during his career he was listed as weighing as little as 171 pounds and as much as 210 pounds.

A secondary source said that the 195-pound Sullivan dropped Elliot twice in the 1st round, once in the 2nd, and once in the 3rd round, a blow to the neck knocking him out.[21]

Local primary sources differed slightly in their accountings of the number of times that Elliot went down in each round, and in the amount of detail provided.

1st Round

The New York Times (NYT) and New York Daily Tribune (NYDT): Sullivan immediately attacked with heavy blows that kept Jim on the defensive. Elliott went down a number of times in the round, sometimes slipping on the wet boards.

The New York Herald (NYH): Sullivan forced the fighting and quickly dodged Elliott's blows. Elliott was partially knocked down, but recovering, clinched. He was knocked down into his corner, and grabbed John L.'s legs as he got up. He was again knocked down (for the third time) and the fall against the ropes and post stripped skin off his back.

2nd Round

NYT/NYDT: Jimmy attempted some offense to no avail, as Sullivan "rained down upon him, and before the round was concluded, Elliott's breast, shoulders and face were almost as red as blood. In this round also Elliott was knocked down a number of times."

NYH: Sullivan's blows forced Elliott to the ropes. Elliott was "choking from blood flowing inwardly from his nose." When Elliott stepped forward, he slipped and fell as John stepped back. When he rose, a terrible blow on the neck knocked him to his corner. "Another rally was followed by a crusher from Sullivan that compelled his second to help Elliott to his chair."

3rd Round

NYT/NYDT: The round only lasted 20 seconds, as a Sullivan right to the neck sent Elliott down, and he was unable to rise.

NYH: Before the round began, "Johnny Roche finding the blood in the nose interfered with his principal's breathing placed his mouth to that organ, sucked it clear and spit the blood so obtained upon the floor of the platform ring." Talk about the lengths that some seconds were willing to go to in order to assist their man.

Sullivan almost ran across the ring to begin the 3rd round. After a few passes and exchanges

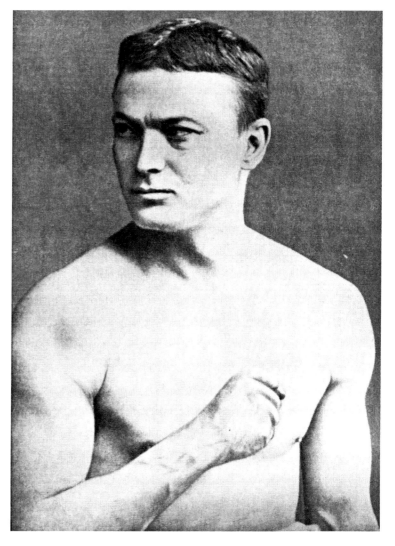

Jimmy Elliott. From Billy Edwards, *The Portrait Gallery of Pugilists of England, America, Australia* (Chicago: Athletic Publishing Co., 1894). Clay Moyle, www.prizefighting books.com.

a blow to the neck "sent Elliott off his feet flying into his corner senseless. He was unable to speak or to move and lay limp and lifeless." Sullivan made Elliott a present of $50 for his suffering. Yet another veteran of the game had been easily crushed by John L.

The descriptions of the fight give the impression that hybrid rules were used, using three-minute rounds, but only 30-second rest periods. *The Times* and *Tribune* said that only 30-second rests were given between rounds and that the fight lasted 7 minutes and 20 seconds, which would be the equivalent of two 3-minute rounds, two 30-second rests after the first 2 rounds, and the 20-second 3rd round.[22]

However, it is possible that the rounds were also short because they might have ended in semi–London rules fashion. The NYH did mention Elliott's cornerman bringing him to a chair after a knockdown in the 2nd round, usually done only in a London rules fight.

Elliott and his cornermen were likely more used to the London rules. *The National Police Gazette* said the rounds were 2 minutes, 3 minutes, and 2 minutes, with two one-minute rest periods, making the actual fighting time 7 minutes and 20 seconds. However, its calculation of the fight length seems to be off. It failed to account for the 20 seconds, and its calculation would have the total time as being 9 minutes. Clearly, though, this was not a true Queensberry rules fight.[23]

The most local paper, *The Brooklyn Daily Eagle*, didn't even have a report on the fight. A few days before, it lamented the fact that since the Sullivan-Ryan fight, "the country has suffered an epidemic of prize fighting."[24]

Just under two weeks after the Elliott fight, on July 17, 1882, at New York's Madison Square Garden before a huge crowd of more than 10,000 people, a 23-year-old, 190-pound Sullivan fought a 160-pound, 34-year-old, 5'8½" Englishman, Joe "Tug" Wilson (whose real name was Joe Collins).[25] Wilson was somewhat experienced, having begun his career in 1866, although he had an 11-year hiatus beginning in 1868, coming back in 1879.

In 1881, Wilson fought fellow Englishman Alf Greenfield in a prizefight. Both weighed 165 pounds. Wilson had shown that he was the superior man over 28 rounds lasting 1 hour and 45 minutes, when Greenfield's friends broke into the ring and stopped the fight. It was technically declared a draw.[26]

The New York Times reported, "It was agreed that there should be a sparring match between Mr. Wilson and Mr. Sullivan before any arrangements for a prize-fight should be made."[27] Apparently, in order to warrant a lengthier prizefight under London rules, Wilson had to do well in a 4-round gloved bout.

Actually, a great number of Sullivan's fights were scheduled for 4 rounds of "sparring" for legal purposes, in order to not be considered serious fights. However, it was a legal fiction as John L. usually succeeded in knocking out his opponents prior to a bout's conclusion. Sullivan had offered Wilson $1,000 and half the gate receipts if he could last 4 rounds of sparring, so almost everyone knew that his real intention was to score a knockout. Boxers could sometimes operate under the facade that a gloved fight was civilized and tame compared to the bareknuckle prizefight, perceived as brutal.[28]

The New York Herald noted that it was really a fight rather than mere sparring, and that the "pretence of calling it a glove contest was as thin as the gloves the men were expected to wear and deceived no one." This was necessary, though, in order to avoid its being considered an illegal fight.

The Herald called Sullivan the American champion and Wilson the English champion, something echoed by *The New York Daily Tribune*. *The National Police Gazette* backed Wilson and called him the champion English pugilist. Thus, in some sense, this was a world championship bout, if there was such a thing as a gloved champion.

They fought with gloves weighing approximately 2–4 ounces, which were "very small and almost as hard as wood."[29] From the beginning, it was clear that Wilson's plan was merely to survive. He incessantly went down, both intentionally and otherwise, in order to kill time, and also wrestled and moved about to avoid being knocked out. Wilson was technically entitled to the $1,000 and half the gate receipts because he lasted the 4-round distance, but it was clear that Sullivan was the superior fighter. Fighters like Wilson were not fighting Sullivan to defeat him, but only to survive in any way possible, even if it meant disgracing themselves and abusing the rules to the utmost.

The Herald indicated that in the 1st round, as Sullivan threw his right, Wilson stepped in and hit him with a left. Sullivan then dropped Wilson with a right. Wilson rose and hit

Sullivan with a left, but received several blows in return, staggering him, until a right dropped him again. After rising, Wilson went down from the subsequent onslaught. Tug continued fighting, but went down yet again. The pattern of the fight was that Wilson landed an occasional good blow, but would inevitably go down again. "In this manner, without the slightest display of science on Sullivan's part, he made his rush and downed Wilson every few seconds until at the ninth knockdown," the 1st round ended.

Wilson began the 2nd round smiling, but was continually either knocked down or "went down easily to kill time.... Tug took advantage of the hit, no matter how light it might be, to go down." Sullivan was described as wild, sometimes even grabbing Tug around the neck and illegally hitting the back of his head. Wilson went down eight times in the 2nd round.

Tug hit John twice to begin the 3rd round. Wilson kept close so that Sullivan's swings could not land, and Tug began laughing. John's blows seemed to have lost some of their force. After wrestling, Sullivan threw Wilson and fell on top of him, which was technically illegal, giving the bout a bareknuckle flavor. Shortly thereafter, "Tug went down rather suspiciously to avoid punishment and to kill time, and as he did so he took hold of Sullivan's leg and tried to pull him down." Going down suspiciously meant that he went down voluntarily without being hit, or when he did not really need to go down. That was technically against the rules, as was grabbing the leg. After avoiding some blows, Wilson managed to strike John twice more. Despite John L.'s appearance of fatigue, he still dropped Wilson two more times.

They wrestled and fell twice to begin the 4th, Sullivan engaging in his tactic of falling on top of his opponent. Wilson was hit by some weak rights, and dropped to avoid another. Both went down during Sullivan's next rush. Wilson then went down from a push. He would go down the moment he was hit, knowing that time was on his side. He was thrown towards the end, with John again falling on top of him. When time was called, Tug was the winner only because Sullivan had failed to knock him out within 4 rounds.[30]

The New York Times' next day report was not quite as glowing towards Sullivan. It reported that Wilson came out quickly and struck John L. on the neck. Sullivan attacked with a nonstop series of blows, trying to take him out quickly. Wilson escaped and hit Sullivan in the body. Sullivan pushed him back until Wilson hit the ropes and fell. After striking Wilson several hard blows, he fell again. This report said that ten times during the 1st round Wilson was either pushed down or fell down, but was not knocked down. Often throughout the bout, Sullivan "took an unfair advantage ... by striking him before he was fully on his feet." It indicated that Sullivan made little attempt to display "science," and that the crowd agreed that he was a "slugger."

In the 2nd round, Sullivan again attacked, and the Englishman was crowded to the ropes and pushed down six times. Both struck "heavy blows." In the 3rd round, when they clinched, several times they fell to the ground. Wilson either evaded or took Sullivan's blows well. They again clinched and fell in the 4th round as Sullivan continued to try to stop him. Sullivan was clearly fatigued and Wilson lasted the 4-round distance.

This account tends to give the impression that Sullivan's pushing, swinging, mauling, and fouling tactics were the cause of Wilson's hitting the ground so often. Sullivan's own brand of swarming power science made it difficult for boxers like Wilson to exhibit their skill. However, *The Times'* view of things appears to be the in the minority.[31]

The New York Daily Tribune described the crowd of all classes as numbering 12,000, and said that the building was not nearly big enough to hold all those who purchased tickets.

The ring was a square platform of 24 feet, raised 6 feet from the floor, with a post at every corner and one on each side's midpoint, with two ropes.

It essentially mirrored *The Herald's* accounting, consistent with the story that Wilson was doing everything that he could to last the distance:

Tug Wilson. From Billy Edwards, *The Portrait Gallery of Pugilists of England, America, Australia* (Chicago: Athletic Publishing Co., 1894). Clay Moyle, www.prizefightingbooks.com.

Sullivan forced the fighting in tremendous style, raining crushing blows on Wilson's neck and head, and knocking him all about the platform, against the ropes and upon the floor. Wilson was down almost as much as he was up. The thundering strokes which he received again and again seemed enough to knock a dozen men senseless.

John knocked him down quite often with "avalanches" of "thumps," but Wilson continued rising. "Very rarely in a prize-ring or out of it has a man been knocked down so often and got up again so many times in so few minutes. Sullivan could knock down Wilson easily enough, but he could not knock him out."

The Tribune observed the difference between bareknuckle and gloved fighting, saying that the "bare knuckles cut and bruise but the hard gloves shock and stagger fearfully." Of Sullivan, it was said that his "short career in the ring had been so remarkable that it was generally believed that few if any of the past champions were his equals."[32]

Secondary sources indicate that Wilson totaled 21 to 24 incessant knockdowns.[33] Sullivan said that it could hardly be called a fight, for Wilson was only interested in "floor-crawling and hugging." Ex-senator Tim McCarthy said, "Wilson went in merely for the money, and he got it by sticking to Sullivan as long as he could, and when he went to grass he took the full benefit of his knockdown." Sullivan said that a later scheduled rematch with Wilson was prevented by the authorities.[34]

Tug Wilson's style of fighting in this fight, in being purely interested in surviving, constantly going down no matter what the blow, was forever how he would be remembered. Subsequently, in describing other fighters' survival techniques when fighting Sullivan, newspapers would often refer to them as using Tug Wilson tactics. Apparently, these were commonly used tactics of the London rules prize ring, which partially explains why so many of those bouts lasted so long.

It was clear that momentum had been gathering for boxing's legalization, but it was a back and forth debate for many decades. *The New York Times* wrote, "In view of the prevailing public sentiment in regard to prize-fighting, it is surely time that the nearly obsolete law against this manly sport should be repealed." It noted that those in the crowd witnessing the Sullivan-Wilson bout "were by no means the lowest elements of our population." It also called attention to the fact that usually no attempts were made to enforce the law against fighting:

> Now, when a man can thus violate ... the law which forbids any person to set on foot or to promote a prize-fight, and when prize-fights ... can take place in the heart of our City under the protection of a platoon of Police, and in the presence of thousands of people, why should we any longer retain in the statute-book any part of the law against prize-fighting?[35]

About four or five weeks after Sullivan had easily knocked out Jimmy Elliott, Jimmy posted a monetary forfeit and issued a challenge to fight Sullivan according to the London Prize Ring Rules. Sullivan did not accept and Elliott claimed the American championship. No one recognized this claim other than *The National Police Gazette*, which backed Tug Wilson, who not surprisingly was then set to meet Elliott for the championship.[36]

This was in part a reflection of the traditional view that a true championship test was a London rules fight. Gloved boxing and bareknuckle fighting were practically two separate sports. A victory in one did not necessarily mean a victory in the other. Sullivan's general avoidance of bareknuckle bouts further confirmed that he was more of a gloved champion than a bareknuckle one. Of course, Sullivan was clearly better than both Elliott and Wilson, so the public did not recognize Elliott. The Elliott-Wilson fight never took place, as Tug went back to England and did not return to the U.S.

There are a number of reasons why *The National Police Gazette* tried to have Sullivan defeated or stripped of the title. The NPG not only reported on the fight scene, but it actually backed fighters, who usually coveted its valuable publicity and economic strength. *The Gazette* had a financial incentive to be the backer of the "champion." Quite naturally, because of its financial stake in certain fighters, it was quick to (in today's terms) "strip" Sullivan of the title.

In addition, for whatever reason, Sullivan and NPG owner Richard K. Fox, two big egos, took a dislike to one another. (Legends vary as to why.) Thus, although the NPG's circulation benefited by Sullivan's popular status and it reported on his fights, it would also build up his opponents, back them, and sometimes minimize Sullivan's successes against them when he won. It was usually the first to lodge criticisms of Sullivan. That said, overall, it was not necessarily unfair to Sullivan, and often presented multiple perspectives. The NPG's search for someone to defeat Sullivan ironically helped make both it and Sullivan quite popular.

A month after the Wilson bout, on August 19, 1882, in North Adams, Massachusetts, Sullivan and former American champion Joe Goss gave one of their exhibitions. The men were met at the train depot by a large crowd of nearly a thousand people who cheered themselves hoarse. Sullivan and Goss began sparring at 5:30 p.m. in the middle of a picnic grove. One semi-local paper said the crowd numbered 6,000, while another said it contained between 7,000 and 8,000 men, women, and children.

JOHN L. SULLIVAN. Library of Congress, Prints & Photographs Division.

John had the advantage in the 1st round, between feints landing some heavy blows to the eye and nose, perhaps too heavy, because the round was ended after only two minutes and three seconds. Rounds were often ended early by a master of ceremonies if the sparring was too severe. Another reason it might have ended early was because the police were experiencing great difficulty in holding back the surging crowd, which was actually entering onto the rope-less platform on the ground, making the sparring space smaller. The 2nd round was prematurely ended because about a dozen crowding spectators around the stage began fighting. The police used billy-clubs for five to ten minutes to restore order. Fearing a riot, the police stopped the exhibition.

However, the sparring was resumed at 9:30 p.m. in a local hall. One report said that not much happened in the 3rd round, while another said that Sullivan landed a severe blow to the left eye and it was a short round, neither having much of an advantage. In the 4th round, "Goss struck Sullivan in the left eye, nearly closing that member." They punished each other severely in the round. In the 5th round, "Sullivan punished Goss badly, the latter being nearly exhausted by his exertions." All of the rounds were short, likely ended early by the master of ceremonies as a result of their intensity. Although the reports called the 1st round of the subsequent exhibition the 3rd round, treating it as a resumption of the earlier sparring, really, it was just another 3-round exhibition given after the 2 rounds had been fought and terminated hours earlier.[37]

Sullivan in his autobiography said that his company signed an agreement to spar six nights a week for twenty weeks at $500 per night, beginning September 4.[38] As part of the sparring exhibition show in Newark, New Jersey, on September 4, Sullivan sparred with Billy Madden. It was called a "grand affair."[39] The combination exhibited on September 9 in Philadelphia, on the 11th at Pittston, the 12th at Scranton, and on the 13th at Wilkes-Barre.[40] Of the Wilkes-Barre exhibition, it was said that Sullivan and Madden gave a "decidedly tame" and short exhibition.[41]

Sullivan also exhibited with Madden on September 22, 1882, in Buffalo, New York. The Buffalo Courier said that "Sullivan made many expert passes and showed remarkable quickness in dodging blows with his head."[42] John L. often exhibited his defensive prowess in these exhibitions.

The following evening, on September 23, 1882, still in Buffalo, Sullivan scored a KO3 over 194-pound Henry Higgins.[43] The New York Clipper said that Higgins was no match, and "a plaything" in Sullivan's hands.[44] The National Police Gazette said that a tremendous right took him out in the 3rd, and Higgins was unconscious for 20 minutes.[45] The Buffalo Courier said that Higgins was from Buffalo and was trying to down the champion within 4 rounds. Higgins made one or two good passes to the applause of the crowd, but was no match. It was "simply a question of mercifulness on Sullivan's part. The third round winded him badly and time was called."[46] This report did not give the impression of a brutal ending that the others did, but of course it failed to say exactly how the fight ended.

On October 16, 1882, at Fort Wayne, Indiana, Sullivan knocked out the burly and taller 180-pound S.P. Stockton. The Police Gazette said that Sullivan measured him in the 1st round, and in the 2nd round, "the champion knocked Stockton clean off his feet and he lay like a log on the stage."[47] A semi-local source, The Indianapolis Sentinel, said that Stockton was an amateur boxer blacksmith who weighed 175 pounds. He was done up in 2 rounds, but showed "great grit."[48]

The Sullivan combination of sparrers appeared in Chicago on October 30, 1882. As usual, Sullivan said that he would spar any man in the city 4 rounds. A short, chunky man named Charles O'Donnell, who was from Cleveland, took up the challenge. One local paper simply said that Sullivan pounded him about the stage.[49]

The Chicago *Daily Inter Ocean* said that just as Sullivan and the much smaller regular troupe member Pete McCoy were about to spar, O'Donnell stepped up and said that he wanted to meet Sullivan. O'Donnell wore black pants, calico shirt, and cotton handkerchief tied around his waist for a belt, while Sullivan wore a scarlet costume.

The *Chicago Herald* said that O'Donnell was knocked down a half dozen times, or as often as he got onto his feet. It was a total mismatch as O'Donnell displayed no science and did not make it out of the 1st round. *The Daily Inter Ocean* said that using his left only, Sullivan dropped him five times, until Charley said that he wanted no more. Sullivan then sparred with McCoy in mere play, but "it showed to advantage the matchless form of Sullivan and the cat-like agility of McCoy."[50]

The exhibition was repeated the following evening, October 31, but no takers could be found for Sullivan's challenge, so the "champion of the world" sparred in a friendly 3-round bout with McCoy before a small crowd composed mostly of the city's tough element.[51]

On November 17, 1882, in Washington, D.C., Sullivan took on P.J. Rentzler. According to *The New York Clipper*, the show drew a crowd of 2,000, and the "house was packed to suffocation and many were turned away." Rentzler wanted to try to win the $500 offered to anyone who could last 4 rounds.[52]

The local *Washington Post* called him Rensler, but *The Washington Evening Star* called him P.J. Rentzler, a Georgetown blacksmith. *The Post* estimated that he weighed a muscular 190 pounds, stood 5 feet tall, and was 30 years old. *The Star* described him as a well-built, muscular man of 27 or 28 years of age, and about 180 pounds. P.J. claimed that he had only donned the gloves once before. It is unclear as to whether he had any bareknuckle experience. He wore a white knit shirt and plush colored tights. Sullivan wore a complete suit of sleeveless blue tights with gaiters.

The Washington Post said that after shaking hands, on the call of time, Rensler tried to hit Sullivan with the left, but was countered by a right to the face, dropping him to his knees against the scenery. Sullivan stepped back, but when Rensler rose, John "sprang savagely forward" and dropped Rensler again. "This brutal display continued until Rensler was knocked down eleven times, not having once struck Sullivan a blow, and a more sickening spectacle of brutality was never witnessed here before." He was out of it by the eleventh knockdown, bleeding from his mouth and nose. The crowd called upon the police to stop it, which they did.

Some in the audience had hissed at Sullivan, but he denounced them as mules. He announced that he could knock out the best that they had, having knocked out Rensler in 1 minute and 33 seconds of the 1st round. This local paper opined that no man from the District of Columbia would ever again be willing to stand up against "Slugger Sullivan, the champion heavy weight."

The Evening Star said that wearing medium soft gloves, Rentzler put up his fists in "approved attitude" and began to make a pass at the champion but was sent to the floor from a single blow. After that, P.J. only held up his arms, ineffectually attempting to block. He was dropped six times, and upon rising the last time, Sullivan landed a punch to the nose which drew blood. At that point, the police interfered and ended it, after only a minute and a half had elapsed. Sullivan closed the performance by sparring McCoy 3 rounds.

According to *The Post*, Sullivan said that he had not used his greatest force in the fight because he knew that Rensler was no match. It opined that "Rensler, like many others, though, had evidently sought the glory of standing up before the champion of the world." According to *The Star*, John said that he did not hit him as hard as he could because of the scenery standing about the stage, which interfered with Rentzler's free movement. P.J. felt that he could have kept going and wanted to meet Sullivan again the following night. However, given the police action, the manager was not going to allow it.[53]

It was said that the Sullivan combination of sparrers would be in Cincinnati during Thanksgiving week.

Sullivan said they appeared in Chicago on December 10, 1882. Sullivan was supposed to meet Jimmy Elliott in a rematch on the 22nd, undertaking to stop him in 4 rounds, but the authorities prevented it.[54] Elliott was coming off a late November 46-second knockout over former Sullivan opponent Captain James Dalton.[55]

A new member of the sparring troupe was former American bareknuckle champion Joe Coburn. The 47-year-old Coburn's fight career had begun back in 1856. In 1863, he defeated Mike McCoole in a 67-round bout that lasted 1 hour and 10 minutes. In 1871, he

fought world champion Jem Mace to a 12-round draw that lasted 3 hours and 48 minutes. Coburn subsequently served a prison term for assault with intent to kill a policeman and had been out of the ring for 10 years. He was released on December 7, 1882.[56] Sullivan was probably sympathetic to the old fighter and he made him one of his sparring mates. They engaged in a number of friendly 3-round exhibitions.

The first of those exhibitions took place in New York on December 28, 1882. The local *New York Herald's* press release stated, "This encounter will be strictly a scientific one, as neither intends to go in for rough work."[57] Still, 3,000 people from all walks of life came to Madison Square Garden to witness the exhibition. The platform was raised a few feet from the ground and draped with some old canvas. A single rope was drawn around it.

In the 1st round, Sullivan danced about the stage and sent in leads to the head as Coburn was mostly defensive,

Sullivan in 1882. An almost identical line art version of this shot appeared in *The National Police Gazette*, November 11, 1882. Sullivan was called the "Champion Pugilist of the World" (Library of Congress, Prints and Photographs Division).

parrying. The crowd got a little boisterous and encouraged the men to let each other have it. *The New York Herald* reported,

> The men upon the platform seemed a trifle annoyed, ceased sparring, and then both stopped and advanced to the rope, while Pop Whittaker raised his voice.
> "You will remember, gentlemen, that this is a friendly exhibition with the gloves and that Mr. Sullivan has kindly come here to spar for Mr. Coburn's benefit."
> There was a moment's silence when Sullivan brushed past the speaker and sent this reminder ringing over the house:—
> "I came here to box with Mr. Coburn in a friendly wind-up. This is no knocking out business. On some future occasion I'll kill a man for you."
> There was an outburst of applause and the exchange of fisticuffs was interrupted no more.

Thereafter, Sullivan danced about hitting lightly and showing great dexterity as Coburn was on the defensive or attempting counters. The audience cheered after the 3 rounds of sparring was over.[58]

Sullivan occasionally had these types of exhibitions with his sparring pals. He would spar lightly and develop his skills, but at the same time earn money by charging the public to watch what were essentially training sessions.

24-year-old John L. was again quite active in 1883, having at least seven official bouts, but possibly many more against unknowns throughout America.

The Sullivan combination gave an exhibition in Buffalo, New York, on January 20, 1883, before a crowd of 2,000. Sullivan sparred Coburn in a lively and exciting bout.[59]

On January 23, 1883, the combination appeared in Toronto, Ontario, Canada. The Toronto papers said that the hall was so packed that even standing room was at a premium. A number of sparring exhibitions took place, the wind up being between Sullivan and Coburn. Joe Coburn wasn't what he once was, but had not forgotten his science. That said, their bout was not very satisfactory, as it was called a case of "mutual forbearance."

Because Sullivan had gone easy, it was difficult for the local reporter to judge his ability. "It is a very sure thing that light sparring is not his forte." However, that is what he had to do with Coburn. "Of course Coburn is not a man who would care to stand up night after night and take the sledge hammer blows of Sullivan even with the soft gloves."[60]

About that time, a *National Police Gazette* writer said of Sullivan's ability and skill,

> One thing is certain, and that is that neither Mace or Sayers ever encountered so hard or so quick a hitter as is John L. Sullivan.... It was the writer's fortune to see the fight between Heenan and Morrissey, and had Sullivan been on the boards that day as big, as capable, and as in as good condition as when he fought Paddy Ryan, it is my opinion that he could have whipped both of them, one after another. Those who think that he is not a thoroughly scienced man, are somewhat mistaken. He has a far better knowledge of the fistic art than either Heenan or Morrissey possessed. He is stronger than either, and unquestionably he is the hardest hitter known to the records of the ring.[61]

Secondary sources report that on January 25, 1883, in Toronto, Sullivan scored a KO3 over Canada's Harry Gilman. However, the local sources did not report this bout, so it is unclear whether this fight took place, or if so, when. Sullivan did not mention it in his autobiography, although he omitted some known bouts.[62] William Burns said that a Harry Gilmour was the lightweight champion of Canada.[63] The local Toronto papers only mentioned that the mayor of Troy, New York, was refusing to allow the scheduled January 29 sparring between Sullivan and Coburn.[64] They sparred in Troy anyway.[65] Sullivan arrived in Utica, New York, on January 30 from Troy, and announced that he would fight contender

Herbert "the Maori" Slade in a prizefight, but after that would never enter the ring again.[66] By "the ring," Sullivan meant the prize ring or the bareknuckle London rules format.

Jem Mace had brought his pupil Slade over from Australia. He said that Slade stood 6'2" and weighed over 200 pounds. Mace called Slade the hardest hitter that he had ever seen and a wonderful wrestler who threw Professor Miller (a top Australian wrestler and fighter) like a baby. He could withstand punishment and was active as a cat.

Although 52 years of age, Mace said that he too would be willing to take on Sullivan. However, John L. said that he would rather take on Slade because there would be more credit in it. "I care nothing for the title of champion of the world which Mace claims, but am satisfied with that of champion of America."[67] There actually had been some intermittent discussions of a Sullivan-Mace bout, but later, after Mace saw Sullivan, he changed his tune.

There were legal complications in arranging the Sullivan-Slade prizefight. Merely for arranging sparring between Slade and Mace, the two boxers and *National Police Gazette* publisher Richard K. Fox were arrested in New York on a warrant charging them with a violation of the penal code for planning to participate in and promoting and aiding a prize fight.[68] However, a judge ruled that the arranged sparring was not a violation of the law. *The Police Gazette* called it a victory over "bigots and sneaks."[69] Certainly though, with the law clamping down, it meant that the eventual Sullivan-Slade match would have to be fought under the Queensberry rules.

Around that time, in February, Sullivan and Coburn gave another one of their exhibitions in Rochester, New York. Coburn was said to have retained a great deal of his scientific skill, but was "no match for his youthful opponent's ponderous muscles." Coburn said that he was 48 years of age and had retired from the ring.[70]

On February 22, 1883, in Boston, Sullivan boxed combination member and "middleweight champion" Pete McCoy in 3 exhibition rounds. *The Boston Herald* said, "Both men were in fine condition and gave a magnificent display of the science of boxing. Heavy blows and lightning-like parries and counters were the order of exhibition between them, and elicited frequent rounds of applause."[71]

On March 1, 1883, in New York's Madison Square Garden, Sullivan took part of an exhibition arranged by Professor John Laflin, "a well known athlete of this City," to benefit recent Ohio Valley flood survivors. Sullivan's presence "was sufficient to arouse the greatest excitement among the spectators. The applause was terrific." Sully sparred with Laflin in the feature of the evening. *The New York Daily Tribune* said,

> Both are finely-formed men, and both spar well, but Sullivan forced the fighting and got decidedly the best of the first two rounds. In the third round, however, Laflin rallied and held his own. Sullivan was received with great cheering. As he left the stage, he exclaimed savagely: "If that was only the Maori, I'd show you more!"

The New York Times said that the audience could not have been better satisfied, for the exhibition was sufficiently exhilarating to satisfy the most eager of spectators. "Mr. Sullivan rapped the Professor on the nose, forehead, ears, and mouth, but the Professor never flinched." There was prolonged loud cheering afterwards, and "Hail to the Chief" was played.[72] One year and eight months later, Sullivan and Laflin would box in a more serious bout.

The same day as the Sullivan-Laflin exhibition, in Chicago Jimmy Elliott was shot and killed by Jerry Dunn. The two had a running feud, resulting from Dunn's casting aspersions upon Elliott's courage in regard to his willingness to box Sullivan. A gun fight had ensued.[73]

On March 19, 1883, back in Boston, the active Sullivan even had three separate 3-round sparring sessions on the same day, with Steve Taylor (his former opponent and now sparring buddy), Joe Coburn, and Mike Cleary. The 5'8½" Cleary was born in Ireland one year before Sullivan and weighed around 175 pounds. He was known for his scientific abilities and good power, having in 1882 knocked out former Sullivan opponent George Rooke in 3 rounds.[74] Cleary became another one of Sullivan's favorite sparring exhibition mates.

12,000 people witnessed the exhibition. Every seat in the house was filled, the standing room was packed, and thousands more were unable to gain admittance. Tickets were being scalped by spectators for $4 and $5 with no problem. It was "the largest assemblage of people ever gathered together to witness a sparring exhibition in Boston." Sullivan was "looked upon as the champion of all champions." It was clear that Sullivan could pack a house even for friendly sparring sessions.

World champion pugilist (as he was called) Sullivan told the crowd that it would be a scientific exhibition with no knocking out. They boxed on a platform five feet high with a double row of ropes and stakes. Police were stationed at each corner of the 24-foot ring and at the mid-point of each side.

First up for Sullivan was Steve Taylor. Sullivan wore light orange tights and a white shirt. Taylor wore bright pink tights and a white shirt trimmed with blue. Sullivan and Taylor exchanged blows for 3 rounds. Taylor did most of the leading in the 1st round. They both picked it up in the 2nd. The 3rd round was fairly even.

Some other exhibitions followed, including one between Pete McCoy and Jake Kilrain. "Some very scientific sparring was shown, and the boxers proved themselves very proficient in the science of self-defense." The first 2 rounds were close, but Kilrain had the advantage in the 3rd with some short arm hitting. Jake Kilrain would years later become a major contender for Sullivan's crown. Before their eventual championship match, it was reported that Sullivan had years earlier bested Kilrain in a couple of exhibitions, possibly in 1880 and 1882.

Second up for Sullivan was Coburn. Despite his age, Joe nevertheless "exhibited considerable strength and agility." They boxed evenly and well for 3 rounds. However, the article later said that "Sullivan could have made a fool of old Joe Coburn, but he used his 'left' only." A non-local source said that Sullivan and Coburn "made one of the most enjoyable displays ever witnessed in Boston." Sullivan drove him around in the 1st round, but Joe showed good defense and got in a few light taps. Both were more aggressive in the 2nd and 3rd rounds, but Sullivan was "clearly the master of Joe in strength."

After more exhibitions, Sullivan and Cleary wound things up. Because Cleary was suffering from a bad hand, they sparred lightly. The non-local source said that it was a friendly but exciting bout in which many light blows were exchanged. "Sullivan maintained the manifest superiority he had shown in the two other meets."[75] This became the typical pattern for many of Sullivan's exhibitions; sparring multiple times in between other exhibitions.

A well-known Sullivan vice was alcohol. In April, while in Boston, Sullivan's drinking problem caught up with him. After he had been on a lengthy binge, he began coughing up blood and was unconscious for a day. Many feared for his life. However, John recovered.[76]

CHAPTER 7

The Game Little Englishman and the Maori

24-year-old Sullivan fought in at least six confirmed bouts in 1883. His most famous fight of the year was on May 14, 1883, in New York's Madison Square Garden, against Englishman Charley (or Charlie) Mitchell in a gloved Marquis of Queensberry rules bout, scheduled for 4 rounds. The 22-year-old Mitchell had been fighting in England since 1878 at age 16, and had many fights under his belt, including victories over much larger men. Amongst those bouts, weighing only 132 pounds in 1879, he stopped a 176-pound black fighter named Baily Gray in 1 bareknuckle round of 11 minutes. In February 1881, he won a 4-round gloved fight against 224-pound Caryadoff, the Continental champion. In June 1881, he fought a bareknuckle 25-round draw against fellow Brit Jack Burke in a bout that lasted 1 hour and 17 minutes, being stopped as a result of darkness. Both were sentenced to six weeks' imprisonment for their competition.

In late December 1882, Mitchell won an all-comers tournament in England. According to a secondary source, Mitchell possibly also had exhibition wins over Tug Wilson and Alf Greenfield. Burke, Greenfield, and Wilson were all top English fighters.

In America in April 1883, Mitchell defeated top middleweight and Sullivan sparring partner Mike Cleary, pounding on him and dropping him until the police stopped the fight in the 3rd round.[1]

The New York Clipper said that Mitchell was the champion of England by virtue of his victory in the all-comers tournament held in London. Sullivan was called the "technical champion of America and virtual champion of the world." He was generally described by the local press as the American champion and Mitchell as the English champion. *The National Police Gazette* agreed that Mitchell was the champion pugilist of England.

The local papers said that the 5'7½" Mitchell weighed only about 150–154 pounds. He was also listed as 151 pounds, "but he may have been a few pounds heavier." Mitchell was spotting the 5'10½", 202-pound Sullivan some 40–50 pounds, but he was a clever and strong boxer, comfortable fighting larger men. One local source said that Sullivan "probably weighed not more than 200 pounds." *The Boston Herald* listed Mitchell as 5'8½" and weighing 154 to Sullivan's 194 pounds.[2] *The National Police Gazette* said Sullivan was 190 to Mitchell's 150 pounds.[3]

The fight was huge. The newspapers reported that no soft glove sparring exhibition had ever attracted so much public attention. At least 10,000 people packed Madison Square Garden "to its utmost limits." Everyone was there—politicians, judges, members of the sporting fraternity, and the police. Even ex–U.S. senator Roscoe Conkling, who had once been a bareknuckle fighter, was present. The cosmopolitan group had come from all over the country. "The event was the biggest of its kind."

The boxers were supposed to be engaging in a "friendly spar of four rounds. Probably all present would have been disappointed had they been assured that the contest was in truth to be a 'friendly' one." They all knew that it was not a friendly exhibition but a fight. It was merely being called that for legal purposes.

The police captain checked the gloves to make sure that they were indeed soft. John wore no shirt and salmon colored drawers, while Mitchell wore white drawers and a gauze sleeveless shirt. Referencing Sullivan's hard drinking and resultant illness the month before, it was said that John looked "none the worse for his reported illness and hard living." Sullivan said, "I haven't touched a drop today."

Summarizing the primary sources, in the 1st round, Sullivan knocked down Mitchell one or more times, but was then dropped himself in a flash knockdown. Sullivan immediately rose and attacked until the bell rang. In the 2nd round, Sullivan pounded on Mitchell, again knocking him down one to four times (depending on the source), once over or through the ropes off the stage. In the 3rd round, Mitchell was knocked down anywhere from one to five times, again depending on the source, until the police stopped the bout to save Mitchell from further punishment.

The New York Times, New York Tribune, New York Herald, and New York Clipper provided versions that differed. The New York Times reported that Mitchell came out and hit Sullivan, but John L. responded by dropping him. The New York Herald said that Mitchell was knocked down when Sullivan let fly his left and right on the run, catching Charley on the sides of the head. The Clipper agreed with this. The National Police Gazette said that Mitchell landed his stiff left quite often, but was knocked down several times.

Charlie Mitchell. From Billy Edwards, *The Portrait Gallery of Pugilists of England, America, Australia* (Chicago: Athletic Publishing Co., 1894). Clay Moyle, www.prizefightingbooks.com.

The New York Tribune merely said that Mitchell slipped and fell when dodging a blow in the 1st round.

They went on to say that the fighters engaged in lively hitting. *The Herald* also mentioned that Sullivan subsequently "rushed in so desperately at Mitchell that he drove the latter to the ropes and by a left hander knocked him over them." The others did not mention that occurrence.

Mitchell scored his own knockdown of Sullivan in the 1st round, but each account had its own version of how this occurred. *The Times* said that after a clinch, Mitchell backed and Sullivan followed:

> Suddenly however, the little man stopped, and making a quick stroke upward, caught his opponent a square blow in the face which knocked him clean off his feet.... Sullivan was on his feet again in an instant, and again the two clinched and Mitchell was borne down to the ropes, the heavy form of his opponent pressing against him. This ended the round.

There is some discrepancy amongst sources regarding whether a left or a right dropped Sullivan, but most said it was a right.[4] This description gave the impression that it was somewhat of an uppercut, but the other sources gave the impression that it was a straight right. It may have been a straight right thrown in a slight upward fashion.

Of Mitchell's 1st-round knockdown of Sullivan, *The Tribune* said that as they worked towards the ropes, Mitchell "cross-countered and put in a left and right which sent Sullivan to the floor fairly on his back." Of this knockdown, *The Herald* said that Sullivan landed a right which staggered Mitchell over to the corner, but when John followed up, Mitchell hit him with "a terrific right-hander on the chin, which floored him as if he had been hit with a pole-axe. This seemed to enrage the Bostonian, for when he got on his pins again he dashed after the wily Englishman." *The Clipper* version said, "Mitchell planted his right straight and squarely on the chin, fairly knocking Sullivan onto his seat." Sullivan instantly picked himself up and rushed at Mitchell, who retreated. They continued to exchange hard blows, Mitchell landing well and showing some good defense on the retreat, but receiving most of the punishment inflicted.

Sullivan in his autobiography claimed that he was standing with his feet close together and that he was "set down" as a result of being off balance. He quoted a writer as reporting, "Sullivan says his legs got crossed, and Mitchell hitting him knocked him down as you would knock over a chair." John immediately got up and went at Mitchell like a bull.[5]

According to *The Times*, the 2nd round was clearly Sullivan's, as Mitchell only landed a solid body shot. Sullivan knocked him against the ropes three times, and then hit "him a blow which sent him entirely over. Mitchell fell head-foremost to the floor, and would have sustained severe injuries had his fall not been lightened by the hands of his friends."

The Tribune said Sullivan came out furiously in the 2nd round, delivering sledge-hammer blows that drove Mitchell against the ropes multiple times. Mitchell did land a left to the mouth that made a smacking sound heard throughout the building. John's temper was up and he demonstrated his brute strength, landing a tremendous body blow that "nearly winded the little Englishman, who was pushed gradually to the ropes, and finally pushed clean over, falling head over heels into the crowd below." *The Times* and *Tribune* only mentioned this one knockdown in this round.

The Herald's description of the 2nd round was a bit different, accounting for four knockdowns. It said that a Sullivan left and right knocked Mitchell down. A succession of three rights dropped him again. Mitchell was sent down for the third time in the round by two lefts and a right to the head. When Mitchell rose, a right knocked him through the ropes, and he fell head first off the stage.

The *Clipper* observed three 2nd-round knockdowns. After Sullivan landed a right to the jaw, he was clinched, but then "fought his man down at the ropes. The moment Mitchell got up Sullivan sprang at him again." There was an exchange of blows and clinches. Sullivan ran at him and landed both hands on the head, a right knocking Charley down for the second time in the round. Mitchell looked weak and dazed upon arising. Sullivan rushed him and landed a right to the jaw that knocked him clear off the stage. The bell rang before he was assisted back up.

The *National Police Gazette* simply said that Sullivan knocked him around and down *à la* Tug Wilson. Mitchell fell over the ropes off the stage and injured his back.

Of the 3rd round, *The New York Times* said that Sullivan dropped Mitchell five times in the round. "He was dazed, and it was evident that he could not sustain the unequal contest much longer." The police captain entered the ring and asked Mitchell "if he was satisfied, and the Englishman said that he was.... The opinion was freely expressed on all sides that had Mitchell been allowed to enter the fourth round, he would have been knocked senseless before it was concluded."

The common practice was for the police to inject themselves and terminate a bout when one boxer was being outclassed or about to be knocked out and they deemed it to no longer be a mere exhibition of skill. In this case, *The Times* reported, "As it was, Sullivan, with his trip-hammer blows, succeeded in dazing Mitchell so completely that he was quite willing, and even thankful, to have the fight stopped, and the Boston prize-fighter was declared the winner of the match."

Charlie Mitchell. From Billy Edwards, *The Portrait Gallery of Pugilists of England, America, Australia* (Chicago: Athletic Publishing Co., 1894). Clay Moyle, www.prizefightingbooks.com.

The Tribune differed a bit, saying that when Mitchell slipped early in the 3rd and fell against the rope, Sullivan attempted to throw him over, but Charley managed to escape. Mitchell landed a good body blow, but John knocked him "clean across the ring, and he fell in a gasping heap against the ropes. Within the ten seconds, however, he was on his feet again, only to be confronted by Captain Williams, who held up a warning hand. The match was over."

The police captain said that he had stopped the match because he thought Mitchell was completely done for and that any further display would merely have been punishment. The captain did note that Mitchell was on his feet within the ten seconds, but felt that he would have just been knocked down again, which would have been no sparring match. In this version, Mitchell said that he was ready to go on if the police had not interfered. "The general impression among 'sporting' men was that though Mitchell had shown his superior science, Sullivan was much too heavy and powerful an opponent for him to meet with bare knuckles."

The Herald said Mitchell moved about in the 3rd round, with Sullivan chasing. After a clinch, John hit him in the face twice with his left, and then a heavy right knocked Mitchell down. At that point, the police captain jumped on the stage and told the men that they had to stop. "The referee, who saw that Mitchell was beaten, declared that Sullivan had won the fight." It appeared to be a good stoppage though. "It was remarked that this is the first occasion on which police interference with a fight has not been hissed.... Every one admired the pluck of the Englishman, while they understood it was of no avail and were glad to see him exposed to no further punishment." Sullivan received 60 percent of the proceeds, while Mitchell received 40 percent.

The Clipper gave its version of the 3rd round and conclusion. It said that it was clear that Mitchell was shaky and that "he had undertaken a task he was physically incapable of accomplishing." He was game though. A left and right sent Mitchell down. A right dropped him again. Charley rose once more, but, "it being apparent to all that he was not able to longer continue the unequal conflict, Captain Williams mounted the stage and informed the men that the bout could proceed no further." Sullivan wanted to finish him and Mitchell was willing to continue, but

> the action taken by Capt. Williams was probably best for all concerned, and no fault was found with it by the spectators, usually so strenuously opposed to any interference with their amuse-ments, but who on this occasion recognized that to prolong the affair would only cause needless punishment to be inflicted upon a game man whose power to fight had gone.[6]

The National Police Gazette said that Sullivan floored the overmatched Mitchell several times in the 3rd. Sullivan fought him down at the ropes and fell on top of him. Although Mitchell was dazed upon rising and was going to continue, the police captain stopped it.[7]

The Brooklyn Daily Eagle's summary was that "but for the intervention of the police, Mitchell would unquestionably have been 'knocked out.'"[8]

Sullivan and Mitchell both provided commentary afterwards. Sullivan said that Mitchell was "a very game little man. There is no Tug Wilson about him. He stands up and takes his punishment well." He also said that Mitchell "is a good little man, but too small for me."[9] Although Mitchell reportedly told the police captain that he was satisfied before the bout was stopped, Mitchell was less than satisfied in the days following the fight:

> I was not hurt at all, and felt as well at the finish as I did at the start.... I was never knocked down, but was borne under by the superior weight of my opponent and the slipperiness of the

stage.... I am sure had the rounds continued, he could not have knocked me out ... but I must say, in justice to Sullivan, he is the strongest man, if not the cleverest, that I have ever met.... But I don't think he will be over-anxious to meet me again.[10]

It was Mitchell's position that he had been willing to continue. This position was backed by *The National Police Gazette*.[11] He might well have been willing, but the primary sources clearly questioned his ability to do so without being knocked cold. It should also be noted that even Mitchell mentioned that Sullivan was clever, an aspect of his fighting often overlooked because of his powerful punching.

Sullivan in his autobiography said that he had Mitchell on the ropes helpless and completely at his mercy when it was stopped. He wanted to finish him off, but the police captain thought that he would be killed. "When Mitchell recovered, he made all sorts of bluffs, and Capt. Williams said:—'You go to your dressing-room. You are a lucky individual that I stepped in and saved Sullivan from killing you.'" He quoted ex–U.S. senator Roscoe Conkling as saying, "Mitchell is a very good man, but he met another who is his superior all the way around.... Mitchell was unquestionably overmatched."[12]

As can be seen from these multiple accounts, it is not always easy to determine exactly what happened in boxing matches back then, particularly without the benefit of film to help settle matters. However, the overall gist of these accounts is that although Mitchell had a few bright moments, Sullivan was the superior man, having decked and hurt Mitchell multiple times, and was about to put him out when it was stopped.

John L. Sullivan, as he appeared in 1883. An almost identical line art drawing appeared in *The National Police Gazette*, May 26, 1883. Mike Donovan, *The Roosevelt That I Know* (New York: B.W. Dodge and Co., 1909). Clay Moyle, www.prizefightingbooks.com.

Mitchell might have been willing to continue taking punishment, but most agreed that he was quite done for and it would have been to no avail, and that it was a good stoppage.

Sullivan should be considered the world champion no later than this point, because he had defeated the best of America, Canada, and England, and he did it easily. Really, there was no definitive starting point for Sullivan's world championship career, for there was no active champion for Sullivan to dethrone. Certainly there was no gloved champion. He claimed to be the best and proved it against anyone willing to take him on. He was probably the best fighter in the world even after he defeated Goss in 1880. After defeating Ryan, many called him the world champion, though some called him that even earlier. Those who withheld the championship designation did so because Sullivan rarely fought under London Prize Ring Rules, which they considered necessary for a true championship fight. Some were slow to recognize the legitimacy of the first gloved Queensberry rules champion.

About that time, a black fighter named C.A.C. Smith, who stood about 6' and 210 pounds untrained and 180 pounds in first class condition, challenged Sullivan, "but the champion objected to meeting Smith on account of his color." *The National Police Gazette* said, "We do not see why Sullivan should refuse to arrange a match with Smith merely because he is a colored man. Bob Travers, the great pugilist, was a colored man, and he arranged matches with and fought some of the best pugilists in England."[13] However, on August 16, 1883, Jack Stewart, who had been bested by Sullivan in an exhibition, easily knocked out Smith in six minutes.[14] Naturally, discussion of a Sullivan-Smith bout was short-lived, but this was an early indication that Sullivan would draw the color line.

The Police Gazette position was actually the minority viewpoint. 1883 was the year that the United States Supreme Court held that race discrimination in public accommodations such as inns, hotels, theaters and railroad cars was perfectly legal and that Congress had no power to create legislation requiring equal treatment. Discrimination and separation of the races was the order of the day.

Many thought that Sullivan's next real test would come from a large New Zealander named Herbert "the Maori" Slade. Some later sources report that in 1881 in New Zealand, Slade had been stopped in 2 rounds by future champion Bob Fitzsimmons, who was then just a middleweight. However, some have said that Fitz actually stopped Slade's brother. Slade's trainer and manager Jem Mace said that Slade was undefeated. In 1883, no one mentioned any Slade-Fitzsimmons bout.

In early 1883, a 222-pound Slade gave 4-round gloved exhibitions with Mace. In these exhibitions, both fighters were reported to look strong and clever in their boxing skills, but of course, the report came from *The National Police Gazette*, which had an interest in promoting Slade.[15] There were some reports by that paper only *after* the Slade-Sullivan fight that Slade previously had been bested in exhibitions with Joe Coburn and George Robinson.[16]

A report of a January 8, 1883, exhibition between Mace and Slade in San Francisco said that the general opinion expressed about Slade was that Sullivan would find him "to be a harder man than he has met yet." Mace said that the 6'2" Slade had whipped every man he had faced at "rough-and-tumble fighting." "He can outbox, outwrestle, and outjump any man in the world, and he ain't 28 years old."

Mace also said, "I wish I was 40 instead of 50, so that I could enter the lists for the championship." It was later reported that Mace was willing to spar Sullivan, but only if John L. would promise to not knock him out, which John would not do.[17] Pupil Slade had to be his substitute.

One report of a San Francisco exhibition between Slade and George Robinson was critical of Herbert:

[Slade's] sparring was neither as scientific nor as satisfactory as that of his opponent. Slade was not quick to counter and he missed almost every opportunity for cross-countering.... The action of Slade gives rise to the suspicion that his success in the prize-ring will depend upon his ability as a wrestler. He certainly has failed to show any marked ability as a boxer.[18]

However, Mace and Slade later countered this by saying that a promise had been made to Robinson to play lightly, which of course Robinson later denied.[19]

Sullivan took on Slade using Queensberry rules on August 6, 1883, again at New York's Madison Square Garden, in a fight scheduled for 4 rounds. Sullivan was approximately 193–205 pounds to Slade's 195, 201, or 220 pounds (depending on the source).

The New York Times called Sullivan the heavyweight champion of the world and Slade the "half-breed Maori." The Maori were the native people of New Zealand, believed to have migrated there from Tahiti or Polynesia.

The New York Herald listed Slade as 220 pounds to Sullivan's 197 pounds, and two or three inches taller than Sullivan, but some accounts, like *The National Police Gazette*, indicated that Slade had slimmed down to as low as 195.

Herbert "the Maori" Slade. From Billy Edwards, *The Portrait Gallery of Pugilists of England, America, Australia* (Chicago: Athletic Publishing Co., 1894). Clay Moyle, www.prizefightingbooks.com.

This was another very big Sullivan fight. There was a

crowd above 13,000 at the Garden, which was, according to *The Times*, the "largest crowd that ever gathered there." The crowd included U.S. senators and representatives, the U.S. attorney general, physicians, brokers, lawyers, and businessmen, amongst others.

The New York Herald said that it was a sold out house. "The oldest timers at fairs, shows and walking matches admitted they had never seen the like of it." The crowd had paid from $1 up to $25 per ticket. "Over $20,000 were taken in. When it is remembered that the President of the United States is paid at the rate of about $270 a day ... the transcendent abilities of the two performers of last night can be appreciated." Actually, U.S. president Chester A. Arthur's annual salary was at that time a whopping $50,000, which would not be exceeded until 1909. The vice-president only made $10,000 per year, with senators following at $5,000.[20]

The ring was 24 feet with an 18-inch extension beyond the ropes to help prevent a pugilist from going over the ropes and onto the floor. Sullivan wore a white shirt and pink trunks. Slade wore all white. They removed their shirts before the bout.

Slade was easily bested by Sullivan, who knocked him down at least twice in each of the first 2 rounds before he was taken out in the 3rd round. Primary sources such as *The New York Times* (NYT), *New York Herald* (NYH), and *New York Clipper* (NYC) had fairly similar accountings of the bout, but with the usual slight variations.

The NYT said that Sullivan began in usual fashion by attacking savagely, utilizing his "irresistible rushes," while Slade found it difficult to hit him. They exchanged some blows and clinched. Sullivan's mouth was bloody at the corners. The NYH did not mention Sullivan being bloody, but rather said that a Sullivan left to Slade's nose drew blood. The NYC said that Sullivan's blows were more numerous and effective.

The NYT went on to say that John rushed Slade and knocked him backward to the floor with a clean hit under the ear. The NYC said it was from a right to the eye. The NYH agreed that a right dropped Slade. It then described another knockdown not mentioned by the other two sources, saying that a left to the nose followed by a right dropped Slade again.

The NYT said that subsequent to the first knockdown, with a right, Sullivan knocked Slade either over or through the ropes, with Herbert falling below to the floor. The round ended shortly after Slade reentered the ring. The NYH said of this sequence that a left turned Slade half around, and then a swinging right at the back of his head knocked him head first through the ropes and onto the floor below. The NYC said that after Slade rose from the first knockdown, Sullivan delivered numerous furious blows that sent Slade to the ropes. Slade turned and ran across the stage, pursued by Sullivan, who threw as he ran after him. A hard right to the body knocked Slade through the ropes off the stage backwards. It took him more than ten seconds to get back into the ring, but this was understandable under the circumstances. They resumed fighting until time was called ending the 1st round.

The NYT said that Slade fought hard in the 2nd round, countering Sullivan's "shower of sledge-hammer blows." They hit each other's bodies. Sullivan knocked him down, possibly by a blow to the side of the neck, although *The National Police Gazette* said it was a right to the jaw. The NYH said it was a right to the nose that sent Slade down on the seat of his pants. The NYC said Sullivan began the 2nd tapping gently, but then made a rush and drove Slade back with a succession of blows. After some sparring, Sullivan made another rush and fought Slade down. Slade got up quickly and continued fighting.

The papers all mentioned a second knockdown in this round. One indicated that it was the result of a right coming out of a clinch. Another said that Sullivan followed Slade, who turned his back and ran away. As he did so, John hit Herb with a left and right that knocked him off the stage. The third said that Slade failed to ward off the fusillade and was simply knocked down. The fourth paper also mentioned this second knockdown, saying that Sullivan hit him with two rights and a right uppercut, and dropped him with a right to the face. Slade was bloody and bruised, while Sullivan was unmarked.

Although the NYH and NYC did not mention it, *The Gazette* said that a third knockdown occurred in the 2nd round, by a right after the two men had been wrestling. It noted that Slade was at times assisted to his feet after being knocked down, and that there were some wrestling tactics engaged in by Herb. This perhaps reflects the transitional hybrid quality of the bout between London and Queensberry rules. Given where Slade was from, he and his seconds were probably more accustomed to bareknuckle rules, which allowed wrestling, and let seconds assist their man in rising after being downed and to bring him to the corner.

The NYT said that in the 3rd round, a right to either the cheek or nose turned Slade partly around. Sullivan followed with an onslaught that staggered him backward. A right dropped Herb heavily to the floor in a heap. "Slade fell like an ox knocked down with a butcher's axe, and he lay bleeding from the ear, mouth and nose, beaten and helpless." The police captain entered the ring and Slade was assisted to his corner by his seconds, too weak to continue.

The NYH said of the finish that Sullivan hurt him with a left to the body and right to the head. He again hurt him with a right to the body and right to the head. Seeing that the "game was up" with Slade, the police captain mounted the stage, but a few more blows were delivered by each man, after which Sullivan landed a heavy right to the face that dropped Slade. "When lifted up and taken to his corner he was quite stupid, and being unfit to face Sullivan again, Harry Montague gave up for him, and Barney Aaron, the referee, declared Sullivan the winner of the fight amid the uproarious cheers of the crowd."

The NYC said that Slade mostly attempted to escape "the succession of blows showered on him." Slade ran across the stage. Sullivan pursued, repeatedly throwing his right, until the final punch caught him on the back of the head and neck, sending Slade "sprawling upon the floor, face downwards, under the ropes." He got to a sitting posture, but was dazed. One of his seconds helped him to his feet and led him to the corner. Slade was down ten seconds, but Sullivan was still willing to allow him to continue. However, neither Slade nor his backers wanted any more. This version did not mention the police stopping it.[21]

The Brooklyn Daily Eagle summarized that it was not a fight at all but a brutal beating administered by the greatest pugilist in the world. It was disguised as a "friendly set to with gloves," but the "gloves are put on merely to evade the statute against pugilism."[22]

No one even came close to being able to compete with Sullivan, let alone defeat him. Sullivan quoted John Boyle O'Reilly's assessment of his skills:

The superiority of Sullivan lies in his extraordinary nervous force and his altogether incomparable skill as a boxer.

In what does his extraordinary skill consist? In hitting as straight and almost as rapid as light; in the variety and readiness of his blows; in standing firmly on his feet and driving his whole weight and nervous force at the end of his fist,—a very rare and a very high quality in a boxer; in movements as quick and purposeful as the leap of a lion. He can "duck" lower than any featherweight boxer in America; he can strike more heavy blows in ten seconds than any other man in a minute, and he watches his opponent with a self-possession and calculation that do not flurry with excitement, but only flame into a ravening intensity to beat him down....

Other boxers begin by sparring; he begins by fighting—and he never ceases to fight. But from the first instant of the fight, Sullivan is as fierce, relentless, tireless as a cataract.... He does not waste ten seconds of the three minutes of each round.

And look at the odds he offers, and offers to all the world! ... Observe, he will not only defeat all comers, but he will defeat them in four rounds—in twelve minutes! ...

The American champion, Sullivan, has done more than attempt to defeat all pugilists ... he has made a manly and most creditable effort to establish the practice not only of sparring, but of fighting with large gloves. The adoption of gloves for all contests will do more to preserve the practice of boxing than any other conceivable means. It will give pugilism new life, not only as a professional boxer's art, but as general exercise.[23]

CHAPTER 8

The Tour: 1883

John L. Sullivan's skilled aggressive ferocity and punching power made him an American icon. Some have even said it was an honor to shake the hand that shook the hand of John L. Sullivan.[1] Sullivan was the first real American sports hero, and his dominance made him world renowned. He was willing to back up his claims of prowess with significant cash, available to whomever might accept his challenge.

Sullivan had already in 1881 and 1882 established his successful pattern of traveling to various cities and issuing his challenge to anyone who was willing to try to last 4 rounds with him. If no one could be found willing to fight him, John would simply work with various members of his traveling sparring combination before a paying audience.

From late 1883 to early 1884, this touring style intensified and came to its zenith. Sullivan traveled across the entire country taking on just about anyone who would fight him, boxing almost nightly. Because Sullivan eventually made the lucrative offer of $1,000 to anyone who could last 4 rounds with him under Queensberry rules, many were willing to attempt the feat, but almost none had the ability to do so. It did not matter whether they were novices or experienced boxers, small or large, for there were no regulations. All they required was the courage to step into the ring with Sullivan, to test themselves against the best. Sullivan fought often, and usually quickly dispatched his foes. John L. claimed that he fought 59 men during this tour.[2]

Generally, Sullivan would spar before a paying audience in a more or less controlled manner with one or more members of his sparring troupe, who would also spar with each other. If a local boxer wanted to accept his offer to win the money if he could last 4 rounds, Sullivan would turn up the heat on that poor person and show what he could really do. It was typical for the tour to remain in one spot for a day, a few days, or a week, probably depending on business, and then to move on to another town. The company traveled across the country, allowing the public and the media to see just how good Sullivan really was. This caused his popularity to rise even further.

Sullivan would often spar two or three times per exhibition, 3 or 4 rounds each time. This helped him to remain in shape, and also to further develop his skills. The fact that Sullivan was able to spar so many times in one day or evening and to keep doing it day after day for approximately eight months is a further testament to his skills. Without defense, it would be quite debilitating to spar as much as Sullivan did.

One newspaper in September 1883 reported that the tour across America was to begin in Washington, D.C., and Baltimore, then continue to Pennsylvania, West Virginia, Ohio, Indiana, Kentucky, Missouri, Illinois, Wisconsin, Minnesota, Kansas, Nebraska, Nevada, Montana, Utah and California. On the return trip places including Michigan, New York, and Boston would be visited. There were also some plans for Sullivan to visit England,

Ireland, Scotland, and possibly Paris. The recently vanquished Herbert Slade had accepted an offer to join the tour.[3]

The combination consisted of Slade, former Sullivan opponent Steve Taylor, Mike Gillespie, and Pete McCoy, amongst others. Sullivan's itinerary listed Baltimore, Maryland, as the tour's starting point, and it appears that this is where they began.[4]

Of their Baltimore exhibition on September 28, 1883, the local papers said that 2,000 people were delighted by the man who had "succeeded in securing to himself the name of being invincible in a fight." After various tour members sparred, Sullivan appeared with Herbert Slade. The exhibition was not in earnest, as they just worked with each other in a pretty but imaginary fashion. Slade showed cleverness with counters and parries. Sullivan's "shoulder blades were worked up and down like the walking-beam of a steamboat." Sully did not really let himself out, allowing Slade to demonstrate his skill. In the last round, when the audience called for him to knock out Slade, John "sailed in, delivering his blows with right and left alternately, knocking Slade back to the footlights and very nearly over them. Then he smiled and turned his back to the Maori." John briefly showed what he could do if he wanted to, but then backed off. This was typical for these exhibitions.[5]

On the 29th, they repeated their performance twice—a matinee and evening show. Sullivan said that he was weighing 222 pounds. So popular was Sullivan that it was suggested that he could run for public office and make things interesting.

John said that the prize ring business (bareknuckle fighting) was not doing very well, but that "glove contests are growing more popular, and a set-to with the mittens, no matter how lively, is not often interrupted."[6] One newspaper opined, "All decent people will be glad that prize fighting has rushed to a swift degeneration."[7]

At first, no one took up Sullivan's offer, so the tour members just sparred with each other. Sullivan said that they were headed for Richmond, Norfolk, and Petersburg, Virginia, over the next week, and would be in Washington, D.C., by the following Saturday.[8] They appeared in Richmond, Virginia, on October 1.[9] The itinerary showed them set to be in Petersburg on the 2nd, Norfolk on the 4th, Washington, D.C., on the 6th (twice), Harrisburg, Pennsylvania, on the 8th, Reading on the 9th, and Lancaster on the 10th.[10] On October 11, they appeared in Pottsville, Pennsylvania.[11] The itinerary said they would be in Wilkes-Barre on the 12th, Scranton the 13th, York the 15th, and Altoona on the 16th.[12]

On October 17 or 18, 1883, in McKeesport, Pennsylvania, Sullivan scored a KO1 over 27-year-old, 160-pound James McCoy, the first man who took up Sullivan's challenge on this tour.[13] One newspaper said that McCoy had previously defeated 15 men.[14] Without identifying McCoy, The New York Clipper said that on the 18th a young fellow was knocked senseless in half a minute.[15]

A later report of this fight said that Jim McCoy had for some years prided himself on his science and grit, and recently had defeated a local pugilist named Callahan after 9 rounds. Because he was at least 50 pounds smaller than Sullivan, McCoy was advised to take on another member of the combination, but he wanted to win the $250 offered for standing before Sullivan for 4 rounds.

After a "few gentle taps, and futile efforts by McCoy to protect himself, Sullivan landed a left-hander on the poor fellow's mug; the blow felled him and he refused to again face the champion. The round lasted twenty seconds." Sullivan said, "I didn't want to slaughter a duck like that.... I only tapped him lightly. I would have broken his jaw had I struck hard." McCoy's lower lip was badly cut. He said, "Well, I can say what few men can, that I fought the champion of the world." Of Sullivan's power, Jim said, "Holy murder!"[16]

McCoy in December of that year made a name for himself by fighting Pat Moran 114 rounds lasting 1 hour and 36 minutes with a broken wrist before losing.[17] It was like that though. Many of the fighters whom Sullivan handled easily and who might be considered poor fighters based on their performance against him were either previously or subsequently noted for their good abilities and grit against other opponents. Sullivan was in another league.

On October 19 in Allegheny City, Pennsylvania, the combination entertained 3,000–4,000 people who so packed the coliseum that it was almost a solid mass of humanity. Members of all walks of life attended, from the bullies and toughs to lawyers and doctors, all under the glare of the electric light. "Merchants and manufacturers worth their hundreds of thousands sat in the same row of chairs with the $7-a-week clerks." One woman was in attendance.

After a number of exhibitions, the "champion of the world" boxed with Steve Taylor, who had earlier sparred Mike Gillespie. John wore yellow tights and white stockings, and was bare-chested. He was "beyond doubt one of the finest specimens of physical manhood that ever faced an audience." The crowd "howled and stamped with delight," giving John an ovation as he bowed. He and Taylor looked like "twin gladiators." During their sparring, a Sullivan blow to the neck "sounded all over the house," momentarily staggering Taylor.

> For the space of two minutes there was a display of science that took the crowd off its feet. As Sullivan warmed to the exercise every movement of his body developed a wonderful suppleness. He rarely let out that powerful right arm, but when he did it counted. Taylor, who is a scienced boxer and athlete, brought great skill into play, but Sullivan was more than his match.

McCoy and Gillespie then sparred, and then Sullivan and Slade provided the wind-up. Slade had earlier sparred with Pete McCoy, before Sullivan worked with Taylor. Against Slade, Sullivan "sprang into the air like a cat" and landed a right to the cheek. He repeated this and staggered Slade. Twice in the round Sullivan beat down his guard with a rush. Slade took the blows and defended some, and slugged back as well as he could, but Sullivan demonstrated his superiority. Another local account said that Slade battered John's body, delivering blows in quick succession.[18]

On October 20, they exhibited in Alleghany again before 1,000 folks in the afternoon, and 3,000 more in the evening. They were set to be headed to West Virginia, New Jersey, Ohio, Kentucky, and Indiana, all before the month was out.[19]

Sullivan said that boxing was something that every man should be skilled in and was cognizant of its growing popularity, although he was also aware of what the public generally thought of pugilists:

> I am aware of the fact that they are regarded as a set of brutes and a degraded class generally. The public might be right to a certain extent, but I maintain that there are gentlemen in the profession.... The public forget that John Morrissey [a former bareknuckle fighter] was a member of Congress.... Why is it that people raise such a cry against boxers ... when there is not a college in the country of any standing that does not encourage their students in boxing, fencing, and rowing? ...
>
> Aristocratic gentlemen of Europe, and sometimes in this country, go out with a couple of friends and try to kill each other with swords or revolvers at 20 paces. Why don't they settle the question with their fists? There would be no loss of life, and it would be equally as effective in determining who is the better man....
>
> I tell you that this science of self-defense is growing in favor. There is hardly a city or town that does not have its class of gentlemen who are under instructions. Look at the audience last night at the Coliseum. It was as orderly and intelligent an assemblage of men as I ever saw.[20]

Sullivan also told a story of being approached by Baptist preachers while in Altoona, and being asked if he did not see the error of his ways.

> I listened to them, and when through I said I thought my way of robbing the people about as clever as theirs, and on the whole it didn't make much difference. They didn't bother me the balance of the time I spent in Altoona. Fanaticism prompts some men, you know, to step beyond what is right, and I looked at it in that light.[21]

Their itinerary listed the troupe as being in Wheeling, West Virginia, on the 22nd, Steubenville, Ohio, on the 23rd, Newark, Ohio, on the 24th, Columbus on the 25th, and Dayton on the 26th and 27th.[22]

The combination was in Cincinnati, Ohio, on October 28, 1883, filling the house during both afternoon and evening exhibitions.[23]

After arriving in Louisville, Kentucky, on October 29, Sullivan spoke to a local reporter, who found him in a bar, drinking bourbon, about dealing with fame.

> No matter where I go there is a multitude of people who seem to know me, and always a certain portion of the rabble and gutter duffers who consider it an honor to shake my hand. I am gazed at by everybody, and at first this was calculated to overawe me, but I have well gotten used to it. It is an innocent request to satisfy and I don't mind them a bit.

Sullivan said that he would fight anyone in the world who put up $10,000, but insisted that he would not fight in the ring again, meaning in a bareknuckle fight. "I would not fight a ring fight and make myself amenable to the laws for a bloody $10,000. Fist-fighting days are over with me. I have introduced the new rules of the fight into this country, and I intend to stand by them." He believed that he could hit just as hard with gloves as with his bare fists.

Sullivan felt that the *Police Gazette* had "never done him justice, and that a strictly correct account of his life and battles had never been written."[24]

That evening in Louisville, "Each event consisted of three rounds and a wind-up." Sullivan first sparred Steve Taylor, who had earlier sparred 135-pound Mike Gillespie. John and Steve "went to work and gave and took blows that seemed hard enough to fell an ox, for three rounds and a wind-up. The crowd went wild with delight." Sullivan hit hard, but kept in reserve a level of power that was even greater, for he had already proven himself in his 1881 2nd-round stoppage of Taylor. Sullivan knew how to work with his sparring partners and give an entertaining exhibition, but usually tried not to hurt them too badly.

After another intervening exhibition, Sullivan sparred Slade for the grand wind-up. Slade had earlier sparred Pete McCoy. John and Herbert went at it in "good earnest, and, though there was no 'slugging,' the blows were hard enough and fast enough to satisfy any one." A few times, Sullivan, "with surprising agility, sprang three or four feet in the air, raining down terrific blows on Slade's exposed face during this short fight."[25]

One source shortly thereafter noted that in an exhibition in Louisville, Sullivan had hurt his right arm landing on the elbow of his opponent.[26] *The National Police Gazette* confirmed that Sullivan had strained the tendon of his right arm on Steve Taylor's elbow.[27] However, he continued exhibiting.

Sullivan said that the tour was next headed to Indianapolis.[28] The itinerary said that they were to be in Indianapolis on the 30th, Terre Haute on the 31st, Lafayette, Indiana, on November 1, and then Danville, Illinois, on November 2.[29]

On November 3, 1883, the tour was in East St. Louis, Missouri. The local press said that world champion Sullivan arrived in St. Louis on the 3rd and was set to pitch in a baseball game the following day.[30]

The evening of November 3, Sullivan fought James Miles, who was otherwise known as Gypsy Brady. It was clear that Miles wanted the glory of having stood before Sullivan. The Gypsy was only 140 pounds, but refused the offer of Al Smith (Sullivan's then-manager) to win $200 to box the 155-pound McCoy for 2 rounds. Miles wanted no one but Sullivan, and so he took up the modified offer to be paid $50 if he could merely last two minutes with Sullivan.

The St. Louis based *Missouri Republican* said that John L. weighed 224 pounds, and it was "at once evident that he does not allow any superfluous flesh to accumulate on the upper portion of his body." He was said to stand just over 5'11". The weight difference was 84 pounds. First, some preliminary sparring bouts between members of Sullivan's combination took place. Then came Sullivan v. Miles.

As soon as Miles put up his hands, Sullivan landed a powerful left that sent Jim spinning half way across the stage. Miles struck at Sullivan but John didn't even try to stop the blows, for Miles "might has well have struck the water tower, for all the effect it produced." Sullivan landed his left to the side of the head and knocked Miles to his knees. The Gypsy rose and was immediately dropped again, falling against John, grabbing his legs. The blood flowed in streams from his nose and mouth. The audience shouted for it to stop.

The police entered the stage and picked Gypsy Brady up and ordered him to quit. However, he wanted more, and was allowed to go on. A lead left to the mouth dropped him for the third time, and Miles fell against Sullivan, who pushed him off the stage. The police again stepped in and ordered it to stop. After taking a few seconds to recover, Brady wanted more, but was sent home. The fighting had lasted only 30 seconds.[31]

Another local paper, *The St. Louis Daily Globe-Democrat*, said that Miles was about 135 pounds and stood 5'7". The Gypsy went at Sullivan, but the first blow sent him to the floor. He rose and staggered, then struck out wildly. Sullivan pounded him unmercifully. Within four seconds he was down again, the blood streaming from his nose and face. The crowd yelled for John not to hit him anymore. The police chief entered the stage and separated them. Miles asked the timekeeper if it had been two minutes, but it had been only twenty seconds. So Miles made a lunge at Sullivan, who landed a blow under the chin and knocked Miles off the stage into the left wing, where his head struck between the rounds of a ladder. Although "about half dead from the pummeling," Miles was still game and would have come up for more, but was held back.[32]

To provide further entertainment, Sullivan and Steve Taylor, listed as the ex–heavyweight champion, sparred in an exciting bout. Taylor had earlier sparred Mike Gillespie. After Sullivan and Taylor boxed, Pete McCoy and Gillespie sparred. Finally, Sullivan and Slade, who had earlier sparred McCoy, boxed in another exciting bout "which lasted some time." Slade did well, landing forcefully to the nose several times, but Sullivan was better, demonstrating "his usual style, and all the spectators left with the conviction that he was indeed, the best man in the world."[33]

One local paper said the Gypsy was the 45th man to lose to Sullivan, but only the second man to face him since the company started out on the season. The first man was said to have been Sullivan's opponent in McKeesport, Pennsylvania (James McCoy), who was finished in the same time as Miles, which was just 30 seconds. Sullivan later said that he did not hit Miles hard, though the crowd and Miles felt that the blows were quite vicious.[34]

The National Police Gazette claimed that Sullivan had injured or strained his arm in knocking out Miles, the local St. Louis pugilist.[35] It is unclear as to whether Sullivan hurt his arm on Miles or Taylor, both, or at all. Obviously, it was not hurt that badly because he continued using it regularly, both to pitch and to punch.

Sullivan pitched 6 innings in a baseball game the following evening, but was called a poor ballplayer by the press, neither his hitting nor his pitching impressing anyone. Still, 3,500 people, according to one paper, and between 4,000 and 5,000, according to another, paid to see him play ball.[36] The public liked seeing stars, even if they weren't doing what made them famous. Sullivan and subsequent champions later capitalized on this fact.

Still in St. Louis, the Sullivan combination sparred before Governor Crittenden on November 5, 1883. The crowd filled the house to the doors. After sparring took place between other members of the combination, Sullivan, "champion of the world," as he was announced, appeared with Taylor for 4 rounds. As usual, Taylor had earlier sparred Gillespie.

At the end of the 1st round, Taylor received a left to the right side of his head that sent him staggering into the second right entrance. Steve fought vigorously and landed several strong blows, but he was overmatched. Sullivan looked to be holding back, but still administered some punishing blows.

One local paper complimented Sullivan:

Judging from his appearance last night it is safe to say that he is fully entitled to all that has been said of his wonderful muscular powers. He is a fine specimen of physical manhood, quick in his movements, and delivering his blows with good judgment.

Another local paper said,

The secret of the champion's prowess was apparent.... He carries his strongly-muscled shoulders forward. The consequence is that when he delivers a blow he doesn't have to bring the upper part of the body forward in the delivery. The arm straightens out and the blow is in with a suddenness which seems paralyzing to the spectator, to say nothing of the man in front of him. There are no recoil movements in Sullivan's fighting. He stands with one foot well behind and his body pressing forward. The first round closed with a blow that sent Taylor staggering backward. Moran ran up as Taylor took a chair and said: "Sullivan stepped on your heel, didn't he?" "No," said Taylor grimly. "He stepped on my head with his big foot."

After Sullivan and Taylor concluded their 4 rounds, another exhibition followed, and then Sullivan sparred Slade, who had earlier sparred McCoy, as was typical. John and Herbert sparred 2 rounds. Sullivan picked it up more because it appeared that he felt that he had a worthier opponent in front of him. Although they both fought well, one writer said that Slade "was recoiling when he ought to have been getting in his best blows. Once the champion brought down a round of applause by springing to the air and coming down over Slade's guard with a hot one on the top of the head." The pleased audience rose to their feet and cheered vigorously when the curtain fell.[37]

They sparred again in St. Louis on November 6. Sullivan and Taylor were said to have made a wretched showing, for Taylor was not in condition for an appearance in public and was too groggy on his feet, tripping and falling over. The implication was that Taylor was drunk, although the article did not come out and say it. However, Taylor had earlier sparred Mike Gillespie in a give and take affair in which Taylor had the advantage. So perhaps it was just lack of condition or that Sullivan caught him with a good one that made him groggy. Sullivan took it easy on Steve and "showed a better left hand than was expected."

Sullivan later sparred with Slade, and they engaged in rapid exchanges. John L. "proved himself a two-handed boxer ... [and] essayed dodging to an unexpected extent." The writer opined that the Maori was often awkward with his footwork and position, but was otherwise clever. The bout was worth the price of admission. The tour was said to be headed to Quincy, Illinois, the following day.[38]

When preparing to leave St. Louis on November 7, Sullivan and Taylor were arrested on warrants charging them with having violated the law with their sparring exhibitions on the 5th and 6th. This was ironic given that one of those exhibitions had been attended by the state's governor. They posted bonds for their appearance and left town. They did not show up for their hearing set for November 16.[39]

Sullivan was reportedly heading to Chicago, then Omaha, Oregon, and on to Texas.[40] Their itinerary said that they would be in Keokuk, Iowa, on November 8 and Burlington, Iowa, on the 9th, and then the following Illinois towns: Peoria on the 10th, Galesburg on the 12th, Mendota on the 13th, and Streator on the 14th.[41]

The tour was in Chicago from November 15 to 18, 1883.[42] On November 16, seats were sold for $.50 and $1.00. A huge crowd of 9,000 people attended the exhibition show. Multiple sparring sessions took place.

Sullivan first sparred Steve Taylor, who had earlier worked with Gillespie. John was said to be weighing 225 pounds and looking less than in condition. They cleverly exhibited their science. "There is no child's play about Sullivan's sparring. His is a sharp stand-up fight, first, last, and all the time." Although the stipulation was that there would be no knocking out, the punishment was as severe as could be under the circumstances.

Time was called ending the 1st round after Sullivan landed a "few telegraph poles on Taylor's neck and shoulders." Sullivan had the advantage in the 2nd round and landed eight effective blows to four by Taylor. Occasionally the master of ceremonies ordered them to walk around in order to prevent Sullivan from doing too much damage. Apparently John was letting himself out a bit too much. John was again superior in the 3rd, when he staggered Taylor with two lefts to the neck. Taylor managed to counter, but Sullivan forced him to the ropes. Both hit hard in the 4th round, and Taylor rushed in several times. After a clinch, they whirled about, and John could have hit him when Steve was momentarily without guard and his back was turned, but Sully refrained.

Other exhibitions followed, and there is some suggestion in a poem that Sullivan boxed a man from Indiana, who was only called the Hoosier. It is unclear as to whether the bout with the Hoosier took place on that night or at another time. The accounting said that John touched him lightly, but that even his lightest touch was like a ton. He hit the Hoosier's nose and dropped him. He rose and attempted a blow, but John sent him down again. Time was called for round 3 and the Hoosier was during that round knocked completely out. The impression from the description was that possibly each round ended when he was dropped, in London rules fashion, because it only describes the Hoosier being dropped twice and then states that the 3rd round began after he was dropped the first two times. This remains unclear.

Sullivan closed the show by sparring with Slade, who as usual had earlier sparred McCoy. Slade tried as hard as he could, and hit Sullivan's nose. The angered champion sprang at him. "Jumping from the floor as if to leap over the Maori, he made a feint with his right, and as Slade ducked to dodge it, Sullivan's left described a half-circle and landed with the motion of an upper cut on the Maori's under jaw." It paralyzed Slade.

Sullivan leapt into the air several times in the 2nd round. "At each leap he would curve his arm over his opponent's head and come under with his left. He jumps viciously and hits hard. Moran called time as soon as it became evident that Sullivan's punishment of Slade was becoming too severe to be strictly hippodrome." A hippodrome was a contest in which the fighters were merely working with one another and not putting up a serious fight. It could also be a contest with a predetermined winner. Many of Sullivan's exhibition rounds had to be cut short due to his becoming a bit too fierce.

In the 3rd round, Slade mixed it up well on the inside in a number of exchanges. The round ended with Sullivan stepping away and then returning a second later in the air as usual, driving Slade to the ropes. They sparred for one more round, but nothing in particular was mentioned about round 4.[43]

The combination gave another Chicago exhibition the following day, on November 17.[44] Sullivan claimed that they made between $18,000 and $19,000 in two nights.[45]

Known for his excessive drinking and occasionally getting into bar brawls, Sullivan said that any story of his giving up drinking for a year was "bosh." He said, "I don't drink much, say five or six glasses of ale a day and a bottle for dinner, if I feel like it."[46]

Their itinerary listed them as being in Wisconsin over the next week: Racine on the 19th, Milwaukee on the 20th, Fond-du-Lac on the 21st, Oshkosh on the 22nd, and Eau Claire on the 23rd.[47]

The local *Eau Claire Daily Leader* said that the exhibition there on November 23 was a hippodrome, as the boxers exerted themselves little and threw few hard blows. That said, Sullivan was described "as powerful as a Clydesdale, and about as graceful."[48] An assessment of Sullivan by *The Eau Claire News* a couple weeks later said that Sullivan was "probably the hardest hitter in the world, though inferior to many in pugilistic science."[49]

After Eau Claire, they were next set to tour throughout Minnesota, exhibiting in Stillwater on the 24th.[50]

On November 26, 1883, in St. Paul, Minnesota, Sullivan sparred with members of his tour and also took on 195-pound Morris Hafey or Hefey (the two local papers spelled it differently).

It was advertised the day before that Sullivan's great combination of boxers included Sullivan, "Champion of the Word," as he was called by two local papers, the recently vanquished Herbert Slade (who still sported a black eye from their encounter), Steve Taylor, and Pete McCoy, who was billed as the American lightweight champion, as well as Frank Moran, Mike Gillespie, and T. Munzigner/Jake Munsinger.[51]

The local *St. Paul and Minneapolis Pioneer Press* called Sullivan "the best man with his fists on the face of the earth." "So far he has met in the prize ring, or upon the stage, fifty-two men, and all have succumbed to his wonderful strength and science as a sparrer.... His style of boxing is peculiarly his own, and has not been learned by book."[52]

The St. Paul Daily Globe said that

Sullivan is a man of Herculean proportions, his massive frame giving evidence of the muscular might which enables him to withstand the assaults of the most scientific pugilists, and when he chooses, to break down his opponent's guard and close the contest by dint of the crushing force of his irresistible blows.... Probably no man has yet presented himself in the prize ring in America who could withstand the impact of Sullivan's fist when it shoots out from the shoulder with the intent of doing harm.[53]

The local papers confirmed that Sullivan offered $1,000 to anyone who could stand up to him for 4 rounds without being knocked out.

For the bouts that evening, Sullivan wore pink tights and white stockings and gaiters. John was listed as weighing 226 pounds but looking good.

As seen later in the evening, he was as swift and supple on his feet as a squirrel, striking always from the shoulder, the blades of which gyrate with a rotary movement, and at times you could hang your hat on them. His blows are always aggressive and they beat like hail on the neck of his antagonist.

St. Paul's Morris Hafey or Hefey was described as standing 6 feet high and weighing a muscular 195 pounds. He was a stationary engineer by profession. One paper said that he had a local reputation as a "vigorous and plucky man with his fists.... Hefey has some little skill, and is a powerful man among average men."

First, Steve Taylor sparred with Mike Gillespie. Next up was Sullivan and the local man. One local paper said that as soon as time was called, Sullivan dropped Hafey. He rose and John "knocked him silly." At first it looked as if he had fallen asleep. However, Hafey rose and leaned weakly against the scenery. "All of this did not occupy over fifteen or twenty seconds." It was obvious though that he had had enough.

The other local paper said of the bout that Sullivan's dash made Hefey fall heavily against the back of the stage. He rose and advanced and even landed on John's neck, but the champion again sprang forward and Hefey was dropped so heavily into a corner that many thought that he was seriously hurt. He rose, reeled and staggered like a sick man, but was knocked down again. At that point, he was willing to quit. Hefey said afterward, "If you want to know what it is to be struck by lightning, just face Sullivan one second."

Slade and McCoy then followed with their 4-round sparring session, and then Steve Taylor and former Sullivan foe Professor John Donaldson, who had come to St. Paul from Minneapolis, fought a bit. Taylor dropped Donaldson twice, who then quit, saying that he wasn't there to slug. Apparently Taylor was either getting revenge for a claim by Donaldson that he had once made Taylor quit, or he put it on him because Donaldson had said that he was going to stop Taylor, or "do him up," as they said then.

Right after boxing Donaldson, Taylor sparred with Sullivan, which was Taylor's third time up that evening.

Sullivan was magnificent; he tapped Taylor on the neck, the blows falling with the precision of clock-work. The latter showed great sand and took the punishment in fine shape. It was evident that Taylor is no slouch himself, but although very "gamey," he was not equal to the corkers of the wonderful man who stood before him.

Sullivan and Taylor sparred 4 rounds. "At times Sullivan would change his attitude and fairly spring upon his antagonist, indicating the wonderful amount of reserved strength there is tied up in his anatomy and before which it is safe to say, no man could face and live."

Pete McCoy and Gillespie then sparred 4 rounds. Following this, Sullivan gave a splendid exhibition for the third time, this time with the strong looking Slade. Although "in prowess Slade is no match for the champion," Herb put up a fair resistance. However, "it was a picnic for the giant and his blows fell with crushing force on Slade's neck." They too sparred 4 rounds. That concluded the evening's exhibitions.[54]

This was the typical style for these exhibitions. Sullivan alternately sparred with one or more of his mates in between their sparring with each other, and knocked out any local tough willing to try to last 4 rounds.

It was said that Sullivan would be continuing on to other places in the Northwest, including Minneapolis, then to Kansas City and Omaha, and a trip along the Union Pacific to Ogden, Utah, then to Montana, and then along the coast.[55]

The following evening, in Minneapolis on November 27, 1883, a number of sparring bouts took place, the final one being between Sullivan and Slade. "The New Zealander was a little the worse for liquor. The exhibition was not brutal enough for one half of the audience, and there was not enough good sparring for the other half."[56]

Sullivan's itinerary reflected that they would be in Winona, Minnesota, on the 28th and La Crosse, Wisconsin, on the 29th (but they in fact did not show up there), and then tour Iowa, including McGregor on the 30th, Dubuque on the 1st and 2nd of December, and Clinton on the 3rd.[57]

According to *The National Police Gazette*, on December 4, 1883, in Davenport, Iowa, Sullivan knocked out a 190-pound Iowan named Mike Sheehan in 1 minute and 30 seconds of the 1st round.[58] Two local sources gave their version of events.

The Davenport Daily Gazette said that over a thousand persons of all classes packed the opera house. First Taylor sparred Gillespie. Then Sullivan took on the local man, Mike Shean (at another time spelt Shehan), a local iron worker, who was evidently a powerful man.

> As Shean put up his hands he seemed dazed, or stage struck. In an instant more something else struck him as with a movement inconceivably swift for so burly a man, Sullivan lengthened out like a leaping panther and smacked the blacksmith a facer, while the building shook with yells and inextinguishable laughter. Shehan evidently had enough, but was persuaded to again "scratch," getting another "biff on the smeller" so sudden and solid that he stayed no longer, and hurriedly tore off the gloves after consuming exactly three seconds of John's valuable time.

Steve Taylor then sparred with champion Sullivan and looked clever. "In science they were not so unequal." Slade then sparred McCoy, and then McCoy worked with Gillespie. In the finale, Sullivan sparred Slade and "showed during several close encounters what vicious work he could do."[59]

The Davenport Democrat was a bit more detailed. It said 1,197 men and 3 women attended the world champion's exhibition. It was not brutal, but "a display of the wonderful quickness of movement, litheness, nimbleness and agile activity which men can attain by training."

Davenport's 35-year-old Mike Sheehan took up the offer to spar 4 rounds to win $250. Mike wore pants with bare body above. Sullivan wore flesh colored tights and was "stripped to the buff."

> Sheehan put up his fists; Sullivan pushed down those fists with his right, and with his left tunked Sheehan on the right side of his nose—and the latter threw his two hands to his face and looked at Sullivan in perfect amazement! It was pitiable, but very laughable. After a little loss of time, Sheehan approached the champion again—down went his guard again, and a light blow fell upon his left cheek and turned him partly around, and quick as lightning a cuff under the left jaw fairly sent him spinning towards the rear of the stage. The $250 was no object now—and Sheehan went to pulling off his gloves and walking toward the north wings, behind which he disappeared feeling of his nose the while. Mr. Sheehan is a very powerful man ... but he lacks training as a boxer. Had he got in one on Sullivan, the latter would have felt it, surely.

Sullivan and Taylor then engaged in some heavy work. After two more exhibitions, Sullivan and Slade stepped forth. As Sullivan sparred Slade, Sheehan appeared at one of the wings, and the crowd began hissing at him and telling him to go back and hide himself. This poor treatment of Sheehan angered Sullivan, who turned and said to the crowd, "If any of you fellows who are hollering and hissing, think it is fun, come up here and I will give you some." The crowd then began hissing at Sullivan, calling him a bully. The round was ended. They hissed during the following round. When time for the 3rd round was called, Sullivan stepped forth and said:

> Gentlemen: I wish to say that when I made the remark I did in the other round, I didn't mean it as an insult to the whole house, I only meant it for those that were hissing and hollering. I am no speech maker. We are traveling in the country giving exhibitions of what can be done in the art of boxing. Two of these gentlemen fought me in New York and I done 'em up—but they are my friends now and I am their friend. We do no fighting though we hit hard; we are simply giving these exhibitions that the people may see something of the art of boxing.... I challenge any man in the world to box with me, and I'll back up what I say with money—that's the kind of man I am.

Then he resumed sparring Slade, and their "fearful, heavy hitting, avoiding, and close, exciting slugging, stalled the audience as if they were in church." The audience cheered tremendously after the bout's conclusion.[60]

Another Davenport exhibition was given the following day, on December 5, but the crowd only numbered about 600. Amongst the exhibitions, Sullivan sparred Slade. The audience was highly interested and frequently excited. The exhibitions demonstrated their "power of great endurance and most wonderful agility and quickness of movement." The blows seemed tremendous. Sullivan was asked if they hurt. He replied,

> Well ... not often. Such blows would hurt any person whose training of flesh and muscle had not made him ready. ... though we hit hard ... we suffer no injury.... Slade got a black-eye once, and was laid up a couple of days by a body blow, since we started out, but those were accidents; ... We know what we are about, what we have to endure; it keeps us in practice and in good form, besides putting money in our pockets, and we like it. Why, man ... do you think if it hurt that we could endure these blows night after night? ... Sometimes they sting like fury, but it doesn't last long.... But it would be terrible punishment if a novice had to take it ... and that's why I just merely cuffed Sheehan last evening.

They were said to be exhibiting in Muscatine, Iowa, on the 6th.[61] A report said the combination was scheduled to appear in Kansas on December 18, Missouri on the 19th and 20th, Kansas again on the 22nd, and then would head to Denver, Colorado.[62]

The itinerary, which may not be entirely accurate and was more of a blueprint, said they were to be in Marshalltown on December 7, Oskaloosa on the 8th, Ottumwa on the 9th and 10th, and Des Moines on the 11th. From Iowa, they were to go to Lincoln, Nebraska, on the 12th, and Omaha on the 13th, before coming back to Iowa on the 14th to exhibit in Council Bluffs. They then were set to be in St. Joseph, Missouri, on the 15th and 16th. Kansas was next, in such places as Atchison on the 17th, Leavenworth on the 18th, Lawrence on the 19th, Topeka on the 20th, and Wyandotte on the 21st. Kansas City, Missouri, was to be visited on December 22. Although the itinerary said they were to be in Pueblo, Colorado, on the 26th, they in fact wound up in Denver on that date.[63]

On December 26, 1883, in Denver, Colorado, Sullivan sparred Steve Taylor and was reported to have fractured Taylor's jaw. Taylor said that Sullivan had been unusually vigorous in his work. Early on, a right to the jaw hurt him. Every blow thereafter hurt, and he had to end the sparring before it was half over. A doctor said that the jaw had received a bad fracture.[64] However, it is unlikely that Taylor actually broke his jaw, because he was back sparring again in early January. Sullivan hit him so hard that it probably felt that way and his jaw might have swelled, giving the impression that it was broken.

The troupe was in Leadville, Colorado, from December 27 to the 30th, and Sullivan said that they were given a grand reception.[65] One report said that after an exhibition on the 29th in Leadville, Sullivan and Pete McCoy got into an argument, and when John went to strike him, Pete picked up a chair and broke it over his head. McCoy ran away and Sullivan threw a lamp that missed. The police marshal stepped in to stop the fray, but Sullivan told him to go away or he'd knock him out. The marshal replied by drawing his revolver and saying that if he came near him, he would put a bullet through him. Sullivan calmed down.[66]

Another report said that while in Denver, Colorado, Slade had a free fight with a local celebrity in front of a saloon. They were all drunk. "An officer interfered, but was soon done up. Others came to the rescue and the belligerents were all jailed." It said that Sullivan demanded and tried to grab a revolver from the saloon proprietor.[67]

However, another report said that the recent stories against Sullivan were completely false.[68] Sullivan in his autobiography denied ever having anyone threaten him or attempt to shoot him, and said that the stories were the result of over-zealous reporters looking for some sensational news.[69]

CHAPTER 9

The Tour Continues: 1884

Sullivan had at least ten confirmed bouts in 1884.

The Sullivan itinerary reflected that they would be in Denver on January 1, in Cheyenne, Laramie City, and Rawlins, Wyoming, on the 2nd through 4th, Salt Lake City on the 5th and 6th, and Ogden, Utah, on the 7th.[1]

Sullivan told a Helena, Montana, reporter, "Oh, the days of prize fighting are over. There never will be any more big prize fights in this country. The gentlemanly sport of sparring has supplanted it, and I think in some respects, wisely, too."[2]

A grand reception was tended to Sullivan when he arrived in Butte, Montana, on January 8. The sidewalks were lined with people and the city band was there to help form the procession.[3] The combination exhibited there on the 9th. One local Butte writer analyzed Sullivan's huge popularity:

> The problem of why a successful pugilist should excite in the public mind such a furor as has been created by the fistic successes of John L. Sullivan is difficult to solve, but it probably rests upon that subtle influence, which exists in every human composition to admire everything in which the mind recognizes great superiority, whether it be in the achievements of the intellect or victories of muscle. It is said that Champion Sullivan has vanquished no less than forty-five adversaries, ten of whom were recognized champions.... Wherever he has appeared the largest assembly rooms obtainable have been packed to their utmost capacity.... The champion is accompanied by ten pugilists of scarcely less renown.[4]

The "Champion of the World" and his combination then headed to Helena, Montana.[5] The first Helena exhibition took place on January 10, 1884. Admission was $2 per seat, which was double the usual rate for first-class entertainments; $2.50 for reserved seats; upper boxes $15 and lower boxes $18. Consistent with their typical pattern, first, Steve Taylor sparred Gillespie 4 rounds. Slade then sparred McCoy.

Next, Sullivan sparred Taylor 3 rounds. Sullivan was called "a model of strength and agility." "His blows ... were sudden, straight from the shoulder, and quickly followed up, and fell with staggering force upon his opponent, Taylor often narrowly escaping a fall. He did fall once."

McCoy and Gillespie then sparred 3 rounds, after which Sullivan met Slade in the finale.

> This was the most animated bout of the evening, both men apparently going in for all they were worth. But Sullivan's superiority was plainly apparent. His eye was quick to detect an opening, and he let no such opportunity pass without taking advantage of it—and a blow once in was quickly followed by several others, each of them seemingly heavy enough to knock an ox down. Slade, however, stood up unflinchingly, and although not able to give his antagonist blow for blow, he got in a number of good ones.

The combination again performed the following night, on January 11th, in the same location. The price of admission was reduced to $1.50 because it had been a bit too expensive. "These exhibitions are not for the purpose of 'slugging,' but only to show the skill which training will give, and are consequently unobjectionable."[6]

For the exhibitions on the 11th, the "order of business was the same as on the previous night, with perhaps a little more vim thrown into the wind-up of each encounter." Afterwards, Sullivan said that he was 25 years and four months old, and was weighing 219½ pounds, one half pound larger than Slade.

For the first time, Sullivan gave the indication that he was getting burnt out. "He is now tired of prize fighting and intends retiring from it after another year." They had been exhibiting almost nightly for over three months, and would continue doing so. The combination was said to be leaving for Butte to exhibit there again, after which they would continue on to the Pacific coast.[7]

The National Police Gazette reported that on January 14, 1884 (an incorrect date), in Butte, Montana, before a crowd of 2,000, the 225-pound Sullivan took out 153-pound Fred Robinson in 2 rounds. They had a weight difference of 72 pounds. Robinson was from Texas, and was attempting to win $1,000 for lasting 4 rounds.

Robinson went down seven times in the 1st, and was dropped eight more times in the 2nd round. Still, he was aggressive and showed a great deal of pluck. Despite being knocked down numerous times, he kept rising quickly and showed good conditioning. He was knocked through the ropes once in each round, but each time got right back into the ring. He took his punishment and tried, but there was only so much a man could take from John L. "As he was unable to stand Sullivan's batteries any longer, Sullivan was declared the winner."[8]

The local *Butte Daily Miner* reported that an immense crowd of over 1,700 paid $2 each to witness the exhibition, which actually took place on January 12, 1884. It essentially mirrored the above-referenced report, but with a few more details and some slight variations.

Before the boxing began, Sullivan announced to the audience that the contest was not of his own seeking, but had been requested by Robinson, who desired to win the $1,000 for lasting 4 rounds. Sullivan did not want to be perceived as a bully taking advantage of a much smaller man.

Despite the weight difference of 225 vs. 153, Robinson showed more pluck and endurance than had ever before been seen from a man of that size. Robinson from the beginning was aggressive and defensive, showing that he was comfortable and likely experienced in the fighting business. Sullivan knocked him down seven times in the 1st round, but each time he rose quickly and was ready for more. Once he was knocked through the ropes off the stage, but quickly got to his feet and ran up the steps to the platform stage again.

In the 2nd round, Robinson fought hard, but was dropped six times, and then on the seventh knockdown was again knocked through the ropes to the floor. He again reentered the ring. He was dropped for the eighth time, and then upon rising was sent down for the ninth knockdown.

> Just here is where there seems to be a diversity of opinion. One party claiming that time had been called before the "Boy" rose to his feet, and the other that it was not called until after he was knocked down the last time..... The fight, however, was awarded to Sullivan.

It is unclear exactly what was meant by this. He might have been counted out.

Although Robinson was no match for Sullivan, everyone admired the fact that he was the only man in Montana with the courage to face John L., and also that he fought him with gallant style. Even Sullivan said that he was one of the toughest men that he had met in a while.

Sullivan and Slade wound up the exhibition with their sparring, and John L. "showed his superior skill in the manly art."[9]

They exhibited in Butte again the following evening, on January 13. At least 2,000 people attended. McCoy knocked out Dave Cusick, who retired after the 2nd round. The other sparring contests between combination members were the same as on the previous evening.[10]

Sullivan again seemed to be contemplating retirement. "I am going around the world now, and am prepared to meet any man living. After this trip is over I am done with the ring."[11]

The itinerary reflected that they would be in Salt Lake City on January 15, and then in Nevada towns including Reno on the 17th, Carson City on the 18th and 19th, and Virginia City, Nevada, on the 20th.[12]

Sullivan's tour wasn't always a huge success. When there was criticism, it was that the sparring was too tame, too short, or the prices too high. The combination was in Nevada City, California, on Monday, January 21, Sacramento on Tuesday, January 22, Stockton on the 23rd, and San Jose, California, on Thursday, January 24. The sparring on those occasions was said to be too tame and unsatisfactory, with only a little dodging done. When one spectator asked if their program was being cut too short, he was invited to "come up here and we'll make it as long as you want."[13]

They exhibited in San Francisco on Friday, January 25, 1884. So great was Sullivan's popularity that between 5,000 and 7,000 people waited at the docks for his ferry to arrive. They rushed and swarmed him and shouted themselves hoarse chanting his name. The band played "Hail to the Chief." 2,500 assembled in the courtyard outside his hotel, and John L. appeared at the balcony and took a bow.

A black fighter named Bill Williams wanted to attempt to last 4 rounds with Sullivan for the $1,000. When asked if he had seen the challenge, Sullivan responded,

> Yes; but I have never sparred with a colored man in public and never will. However, if he or any of his friends have money and will bring five of his friends and allow me to take five of my friends into a private room I will give him all the Marquis of Queensbury he wants.

Sullivan's stance did not elicit any criticism.

The exhibition admission prices were $2, $1.50, and $1, but ticket speculators drove the prices up even more, up to $5, which was said to be the reason why only 3,500 turned up for the exhibition when the pavilion could have accommodated 6,000. During the show, Sullivan through master of ceremonies Moran announced that the ticket prices would be lowered the following evening to $1 for all locations, first come first served.

A grand jury was in attendance, likely there to determine whether legal charges should be brought if the exhibition was too rough. This may explain why the sparring was fairly dull. First, Taylor held back and played for 4 one-minute rounds with Gillespie. Slade and the much smaller McCoy sparred 3 rounds and did nothing to enthuse the spectators. Some locals then boxed.

By the time the champion of the world was introduced to spar with Taylor, the audience was indifferent to it all. Sullivan too mostly held back. *The San Francisco Daily Examiner* said of John L.,

He is as lithe as a panther, and his rush is like an avalanche. His fists flash through the air like bolts of lightning, and his every movement is the perfection of grace. The trouble was that he simply showed what he could do. His exhibition with Taylor was nothing more or less than a farce.... The disparity between the men was too great.... All that Taylor did was to try to keep out of Sullivan's way, and the latter extended his hearty sympathy by allowing him to do so. Once Sullivan struck Steve on the forehead with his right, knocking his head back, and was following it up with a blow on the jugular as the throat lay bare, when Taylor threw up his hands in a pitiful way and John's hands fell to his side.... Sullivan darted around jumped up and lunged out in splendid style, but refrained from touching Steve. As a matter of fact, Sullivan acted as though he was fighting an imaginary foe, with neither life nor substance.

Another local paper, *The San Francisco Chronicle*, gave the impression of a more rigorous exhibition, saying,

What was most noticeable about Sullivan's performance was the lightning quickness with which he stretched out his shapely arms at the touch of which Taylor recoiled like a rubber ball. The force with which the blows, some times re-enforced by a rush and jump, in which the whole body was thrown forward, were delivered was tremendous, and more than once Taylor, only a target, was forced to look for protection near the ropes and in the corners. Sullivan either forgot himself or his antagonist, much to the latter's damage to chest and head. They boxed three rounds, in which Sullivan fully succeeded in convincing everybody that the reports of his strength and agility have not been exaggerated.

Sullivan threw lightning-like blows from his long arms of steel, which had the force of a mule kick, driving Taylor around the ring, causing Steve to several times throw up his arms in the air to remind Sullivan that it was not a knocking out contest.

A couple other exhibitions followed, and then Sullivan wound things up with Slade for 3 one-minute rounds. *The Examiner* said that "[Slade] could no more resist the onslaught of the champion than can the soft earth the sharp edge of the plow. He was a babe in Sullivan's hands. Although he made a show of resistance, it was evident to all observers that he is no match for the Boston boy."

The Chronicle said of Sullivan's exhibition with Slade,

Here again Sullivan showed how terrific is the force with which he delivers his blows, jumping forward on his right leg at the same time, apparently throwing the weight of his whole massive body into his arms. The movement is executed with lightning-like rapidity, and it certainly seems that no man can stand up against it.

The spectators were disappointed with the show overall, but not with Sullivan.[14]

The audience was no more enthused the following evening, on January 26. An even smaller audience turned up this time, numbering about 1,600. It was again too tame. Sullivan sparred Taylor and the audience hissed because every time John got warmed up and became too vicious, the referee called time, making the rounds only last about 30 seconds.

A non-local report said that the audience applauded liberally at first, as Sullivan and Taylor sparred rapidly and engaged in hard hitting. However, the master of ceremonies cut the rounds short because he saw that Sullivan was not holding back, making the 1st round only 35 seconds, and the 2nd and 3rd rounds only 30 seconds. The audience enjoyed what they did see, but were upset that it was so short, and hissed. Even in the short period of time that they did spar, Taylor's mouth started bleeding and he had his eye darkened. As he left the stage, Taylor said to the audience, "If any of you fellows want to see some more, get up in front of Sullivan yourselves."

The local newspaper said that the hissing upset the sensitive Sullivan, who addressed the audience, saying, "Gentlemen, this hissing is all uncalled for. I am sparring in a friendly set to with Mr. Taylor. I am not obliged to kill him. If the law allowed me to knock out somebody I would be willing to accommodate any or all of you." He also said, "[T]hose who hissed are loafers. ... if any of them fellers that hissed would come up and tell me, I'd slap 'im in their jawah [sic]."

The non-local source reported that an upset Sullivan had said,

> You fellows ain't got no right to hiss. I did the best I dared. If I did all I knew these exhibitions would stop right here. Them as hissed are a lot of loafers, they are; and any man as hissed and dares say so, I'll give him a slap in the jaw. I'm sorry I can't give every gent here the pleasure of seeing me knock out someone, but there ain't no one to knock out, and the police won't allow it.

Other exhibitions followed, and Sullivan wound things up with Slade, before which he gave another speech in a more conciliatory tone. Slade suffered punishment because Sullivan was out of humor and eager to please the crowd.[15]

Sullivan said that he would appear in Oakland on Monday and Tuesday, January 28 and 29, then go to Oregon on Wednesday, and then return to San Francisco.[16] After exhibiting in Oakland, one paper said that Sullivan intended to exhibit in Astoria and Portland, Oregon; New Tacoma and Seattle, Washington; and Victoria, British Columbia before returning to San Francisco.[17] Another paper said the tour would then head to Texas and New Orleans.[18]

It was reported that Sullivan's tour had made between $18,000 and $19,000 in Chicago in two days; $10,220 in Pittsburg in two nights; $5,040 in Dayton, Ohio, in two days; $4,900 in one day in Cincinnati; $3,000 in one day in St. Paul; and $3,007 the next day at Minneapolis. "It would not be an exaggerated estimate to put down the clear profits of the tour at $150,000, or about one hundred times as much as a brainy homunculus would earn in the same time."

Amongst those Sullivan was said to have defeated included James McCoy, who this paper said had defeated 15 men, Hefey of St. Paul, the local champion of Davenport Iowa, "The Gypsy" of St. Louis, a lumberman of Eau Claire, Wisconsin (though the Eau Claire press did not mention this bout when Sullivan was there), and the champion of Butte City, Montana.[19]

On February 1, 1884, "The Champion's Triumphal Tour Across the Continent" was in Astoria, Oregon. As usual, Sullivan was billed as the "Champion of the World."[20] Admission was $1.50.

The National Police Gazette reported that the huge Sylvester Le Gouriff, a 300-pounder, was stopped in just 20 seconds of the 1st round. Sullivan feinted, staggered him with a left, and then knocked him out with a right to the neck. Demonstrating report inconsistency, an earlier account by The New York Clipper said that Sullivan had defeated "Le Gowriff" in 12 seconds, "during which time he was thrice knocked down, and then he beat a retreat."[21]

The local Daily Astorian said that Sullivan stood about 5'10" and weighed about 190 pounds. Frenchman Sylvester La Gouriff's weight was not provided. He was attempting to win $1,000 for lasting 4 rounds.

After Sylvester put up his fists, Sullivan made one or two feints and then landed a powerful blow to the cheek that staggered him. Sylvester advanced but Sullivan bounded toward him and "sent him sprawling on the stage." Sylvester rose but was dropped for the second time. La Gouriff removed his gloves, shook his head, and withdrew. The local paper said it lasted about 30 seconds.

Sullivan next sparred Steve Taylor 3 rounds. Sullivan's form and style were complimented. "Whatever has been said in praise of Sullivan is not exaggerated."

> He is about the most restless piece of humanity that we ever saw in the shape of a man. His every move conveys the idea of restlessness. He strikes to count, and fights to win. He goes at his opponent with a dash, hits out right and left, recovers his guard and strikes another smashing blow, then, jumping from the ground he rushes at his antagonist and follows him up, shooting out terrific blows and recovering himself with lighting rapidity.

Slade and McCoy then sparred, followed by Gillespie and McCoy. The final bout of the evening was between Sullivan and Slade. Sullivan was obviously not trying to hurt his opponent, as every now and then when he was about to unload, he checked himself, while Slade acted mostly on the defensive.

Their abilities were admired. "Both are heavy weights but display the most wonderful activity in ducking and dodging." Slade was good enough to be a "holy terror" to the ordinary citizen, but had more than his match with Sullivan. The writer called it an evening of excellent boxing containing an extraordinary display of science.[22]

Years later, Sullivan said that the Frenchman had weighed 340 pounds. When before the bout Sullivan was told how big he was, John L. said, "The bigger he is the bigger the fall." He knocked him down twice until it was over. He was out cold on the floor for 15 minutes.[23] The Frenchman afterwards told Sullivan, "I break wood and fences with my fist, but you break stone."[24]

One paper reported that the tour was in Portland, Oregon, on February 2 and 4. It said that Sullivan would head next to Seattle and Victoria.[25] They might have been in New Tacoma, Washington, on February 5.[26]

Regarding Sullivan's record to that point, one paper said, "Sullivan claims to have met and vanquished 45 men, but many of these do not appear in his record."

Of the sport, Sullivan said that "it will ere long not be considered a disgrace to be a boxer.... It will not be long before the best people of the country will attend boxing contests."[27] Sullivan and his tour had already been making that a truism.

Five days after the La Gouriff bout, on February 6, 1884, over 2,000 people watched Sullivan spar in Seattle. The local *Seattle Daily Post-Intelligencer* said that

> [Sullivan] is a marvel of strength, skill and agility. If there is another man on earth who is equal, certain it is that that man has never been publicly known. He is a master in the art of boxing. The force with which he delivers a blow is simply appalling to ordinary people.... There is nothing comparable to it, unless it be those guns holding several charges, which are discharged one after another.... He is wonderfully agile, and his motions resemble those of a tiger in the act of springing on its prey. No ordinary man has any chance at all before him, and it is idle, foolish, to talk otherwise.

James Lang, a tall, strong, and apparently well-developed man, attempted to win the $1,000 offered for lasting 4 rounds.

> It took just a little less than seven seconds to make Mr. Lang aware of the fact that he had business elsewhere.... In that time he was knocked from side to side as if he were a child, battered to the floor twice and forced to quit. It was simply impossible to withstand the rain of blows and the force with which they were delivered.

Following this, Steve Taylor sparred Gillespie, and then McCoy boxed with Slade. Sullivan returned to give an exhibition of "stroke and parry" with Taylor. They were essentially working with one another, "but the quickness, force and skill with which Sullivan delivered and parried the blows of his opponent were as conspicuous as in his previous contest with the volunteer whom he 'knocked out.'" McCoy then boxed with Gillespie. The finale was a bout between Sullivan and Slade.

> Here was indeed a contest of giants, and one worthy of seeing.... To either of them, however, an ordinary man is as a toy, to be tossed about at will. The rounds were sharp, fierce and exciting. Blows were given and returned of sufficient force apparently to fell an ox, and the exhibition of skill in striking and warding off blows was interesting to even the most unenthusiastic observer. The audience cheered loudly at the end of each round, and at the close retired in good order, apparently well satisfied.

It was said that the Sullivan combination left for Victoria afterwards, set to give an exhibition there, but would be returning in two days.[28] One report said that Sullivan was in Victoria, British Columbia, on February 8, 1884.[29]

An advertisement stated that Sullivan would be appearing twice in Seattle on February 9, first in an exhibition with Steve Taylor, and then with Herbert Slade, boxing 4 rounds with each. Admission was $1.50. "Especial attention will be given to ladies."[30] The tour management was good at having advance advertisements printed in the newspapers of whatever town they were headed to.

As promised, Sullivan again sparred in Seattle on February 9, 1884, before an immense crowd that jammed the hall. The miscellaneous assemblage included prominent citizens. Members of the tour sparred with each other as usual, and then Sullivan and Taylor "fought an interesting and exciting three round contest." Other sparring contests followed, and the final set to was between Sullivan and Slade. It was called a marvelous exhibition which drew great applause.[31]

The Sullivan itinerary reflected that they would be in Dayton, Washington, and Walla Walla, Washington, on the 12th and 13th. They were set to be in Dallas, Oregon, on the 14th, and Portland on the 15th.[32]

On February 18, 1884, the Sullivan combination gave yet another show in San Francisco. About 1,200 people attended. Sullivan was reported to have previously suffered a muscular strain in his leg, but he sparred once anyway. He and Taylor engaged in 3 lively one-minute rounds.[33] Slade did not spar.[34]

It was reported that Slade had severed his connection with the combination when on February 23 in a saloon in San Francisco; a drunken Sullivan butted Herb in the face. Slade grabbed him, threw him to the floor, and held him there until the police arrived and took John L. back to his hotel.[35] However, given that Slade did not spar on the 18th, prior to that incident, it is unclear whether the severance was already in the works. Perhaps Sullivan's actions were in reaction to Slade's separation from the tour.

On March 6, 1884, in San Francisco, Sullivan took on the local Olympic Club's champion, George Robinson, a trained boxer. That same club would later produce future champion James J. Corbett. In early 1883, Robinson had taken on Herbert Slade in an exhibition (before Slade fought Sullivan) and supposedly had the better of it. George was described as a clever boxer and a powerful man, impressing people with his ability to put up 50-pound dumbbells 75 times in succession.[36]

Robinson was listed a year earlier as standing 6'1" and weighing 189 pounds. It was then said that he could raise a 100-pound dumbbell 20 times, a 50-pound dumbbell 58 times, and once raised a 25-pound dumbbell 427 times.[37]

The local paper described Robinson as being a man of muscle and nerve (ironically, as will later be seen). However, Sullivan was special.

> With Sullivan it is a different thing. He is such a prodigy in the fistic world that there seems to be no rule, whether physical or mental, that can apply to him. He is a phenomenon. He is always in fighting condition, notwithstanding his continual sprees. It is his nature to fight. His prowess has never been doubted or diminished by any one with whom he has come in contact. All have succumbed to his fearful blows and terrific "rushes."[38]

The "continual sprees" being alluded to were Sullivan's famed drinking bouts. Amazingly, despite his alcoholism, he remained in excellent condition, although it would eventually catch up with him.

In this match, according to *The National Police Gazette*, Sullivan's first blow barely struck him, but Robinson went down. The crowd booed and hissed as Robinson took every opportunity to go down. Sullivan was unable to land as many effective blows as usual because Robinson went down so quickly. However, John was occasionally able to land uppercuts as George was going down. Sometimes, Sullivan held him up by the head and hit him.

George later said that his objective was to make sure that he was not knocked out. He claimed to have drawn blood from Sullivan's nose. He also said that Sullivan struck him in the 1st round once when he was down, and criticized John L. as having only swinging blows. However, Robinson was branded a coward.[39]

The New York Clipper quoted a California newspaper as saying that Sullivan was to receive ⅔ of the gate receipts and Robinson ⅓. 15,000 people appeared and paid nearly $20,000 to witness the bout. Sullivan weighed 204 pounds to Robinson's 170. Robinson dropped incessantly in each round until he was disqualified in the 4th round for dropping without being hit. During the bout, Sullivan landed several left uppercuts when George was in the act of falling.[40]

The local accounts agreed that Robinson did not last the distance, but was disqualified.[41] The *San Francisco Chronicle* said they fought in a ring roped off on a platform four feet high and 21 feet in diameter. Robinson wore red tights. The police insisted that the fight be fought with regular 8-ounce boxing gloves, considered large at the time.

This account said Robinson disgracefully dropped 66 times in 4 rounds. The fight began with a Sullivan right that barely grazed Robinson's mustache, but he immediately went down. Every time the champion's glove barely landed, George went down and the audience howled, realizing that this was not going to be a fight.

Robinson went down 9 times in the 1st round and 20 times in the 2nd round. Sometimes John landed a hard uppercut, but it was difficult to land solidly because Robinson was so busy quickly going down. He showed no pluck whatsoever, and went down 22 times in the 3rd round. Once, John held his head and hit him with an uppercut. Sometimes Sullivan rolled over on him. John sometimes asked Robinson to keep in the center of the ring, or pointed with disgust at his fallen man, and even once danced a jig while he was down. Mathematically, for the numbers to add up to 66 knockdowns, Robinson must have gone down 15 times in the 4th round.

George was warned by the referee not to go down without being hit on penalty of losing the fight. However, in the 4th round, he hit the deck voluntarily 3 times without being struck, and the referee decided to stop it and award the fight to Sullivan. Robinson's second apparently also threw up the sponge. This local account indicated that Robinson did not last the 4 rounds, but rather lost the fight "by three wind blows," meaning that he had lost on the foul of going down without being struck.[42]

The San Francisco Daily Examiner said the pavilion was jammed with 12,000 people, and there were 5,000 more outside. There were only about six women present. The fight took place in a 24-foot ring with two ropes. Sullivan wore flesh-colored tights.

Before the bout took place, William Muldoon, Sullivan's trainer and second, took the platform and said,

> This affair tonight was intended to be a knockout contest with gloves. A little difficulty, however, has arisen today in regard to the gloves. I hold in my hand one of the three-ounce gloves that Sullivan used in his fights.... It was intended that, the same should be used here tonight, but the authorities would not allow it.... The gloves to be used are 8-ounce—the only ones they will be allowed to fight with. The men are going to fight on their merits, and Sullivan is going to try to knock Robinson out if he can, although it might be considered a miracle for a man to do so with these gloves.

The crowd then hissed and hooted their displeasure over the fact that the authorities had insisted on larger 8-ounce gloves rather than the usual 3-ounce ones. Fans today would laugh at this, because an 8-ounce glove is about the smallest that is used. Back then, they were seen as large pillows. Not only did smaller gloves mean that the punches had more power, but there was less glove space present to block punches, which left little room for error.

Regardless of glove size, when the fight began it was obvious that it was not going to be a fight at all. Sullivan led with a left that glanced off Robinson's shoulder, and he went down. Robinson rose, dodged a punch, and landed one, but then went down when Sullivan led for him. George rose and landed a right on the nose, but it was to be not only the last blow that he landed, but the last that he threw. It was evident that he was afraid to take a punch. Time and again he dropped down even at the slightest Sullivan feint. He dropped eleven times in the 1st round "without receiving a blow that would have hurt a boy."

In the 2nd round, Robinson dropped six times from blows that were nothing, and the seventh time he was knocked off his feet by a powerful right. He went down three more times. When he tried to drop the tenth time, Sullivan caught him with his left and held him up while he landed an uppercut to the jaw. George only received slight punishment on the twelfth and thirteenth times he went down. Sullivan appealed to the referee, who cautioned Robinson to behave himself. Twice more George went down just to kill time, contrary to the rules. Sullivan did land one good hit on the forehead when Robinson was preparing to drop.

In the 3rd round, the crowd became loud and uncomplimentary towards their local champion. Robinson looked groggy and went down seven times, receiving only one full blow to the face. He was again cautioned, but continued to drop at the slightest provocation, and sometimes with none at all. Once when Sullivan threw, George fell and John stumbled and fell on Robinson, striking him accidentally in the fall. Robinson's claim of foul was not allowed. After he had fallen down sixteen times in the round, Sullivan landed a "staggerer" to Robinson's neck that legitimately dropped him. Robinson rose and played his game to escape punishment.

In the 4th round, Robinson dropped eight times, only being hit on the third and eighth times, while the others were from pushes or feints. After about a minute had elapsed, the referee stepped in and said something which could only be heard by those nearest the platform, and Robinson went to his corner to retire as his second threw up the sponge.

"Muldoon then announced that the fight had been given to Sullivan on the ground that Robinson had violated the rules by dropping to the floor without being struck." It is unclear how many times he went down in the bout, but it was at least 51 if you total the number of knockdowns in this account.

Robinson's response to being called a coward was that he had not contracted to knock Sullivan out, and that he had decided beforehand to act on the defensive.[43] Even a trained boxer like Robinson stood no show with Sullivan. He had fought to last rather than to win, using Tug Wilson tactics.

One paper said that Sullivan earned $10,000 for knocking Robinson down 60 times and that Robinson received $5,000 for doing so.[44]

This bout was witnessed by a young amateur named James J. Corbett, who would many years later challenge Sullivan.

The Sullivan itinerary said that they would be in Los Angeles from March 12 to 17, San Bernardino on the 18th and 19th, and Tucson and Tombstone, Arizona, on the 21st and 22nd.

In Tucson, Arizona, on March 21, 1884, Sullivan sparred 3 rounds with McCoy that were timed at 1:45, 1:30, and 1:05 minutes respectively. McCoy was described as an active, wiry fellow with a vigorous style. Sullivan was constantly the aggressor in the 1st round, pushing his opponent, never standing in defense. The 2nd was uninteresting, as McCoy vainly tried to hit Sullivan, who easily kept him at arm's length. They did some good slapping in the 3rd, and Pete was allowed to land a couple punches. After an intervening exhibition between McCoy and Gillespie, Sullivan sparred Taylor 3 short rounds that only lasted 42, 35, and 30 seconds respectively.[45]

They next headed to Tombstone. There is a secondary source published in 1949 that claims that while there, Sullivan fought and quickly knocked out a negro cowboy named Jim, but this has not been confirmed by a primary source.[46] Unfortunately, the March 1884 editions of *The Tombstone Epitaph*, the most local newspaper, are unavailable to determine the veracity of the claim. Sullivan always stated that he never boxed a black man (although he came close a few times), and no primary source ever questioned his assertion.

The semi-local *Arizona Weekly Citizen* only said that while Sullivan was in Tombstone on March 23, 1884, he visited five bandits in the jail who were awaiting execution. One bandit told John L. that he knew a man who could beat him—the sheriff. Sullivan responded that the sheriff didn't look like a fighter. "Well, he ain't ... but he'll knock five of us out in one round next Friday morning, all the same."[47]

The itinerary said they were next headed to Deming, New Mexico, on the 24th, and venues in Texas including El Paso on the 25th, Fort Worth on the 29th and 30th, Denison on the 31st, Sherman on April 1, Dallas on the 2nd, Corsicana on the 3rd, Waco on the 4th, Austin on the 5th, San Antonio on the 6th and 7th, and Houston on the 8th.[48] *The National Police Gazette* said they would also go through Montana.[49]

A report said that the combination would appear in Dallas, Texas, the first week of April.[50] They appeared in Fort Worth on the last day of March and were reported to be planning to be in New Orleans in early April.[51]

On April 9 and 10, 1884, Sullivan's tour performed in Galveston, Texas. Seats were advertised for $1.00.[52] The "respectable was largely in the majority" of those in attendance.

On the 9th, after a preliminary, Sullivan sparred Pete McCoy, who was called the most scientific middleweight in the world:

[Sullivan's] arms cut through the air with almost inconceivable rapidity in blow upon blow upon McCoy, which, though lightly dealt, resounded throughout the theater. Pete stood up gamely through his three rounds, and exhibited his science at every move.

After another exhibition, Sullivan boxed Taylor, who was listed as taller and about equal in weight with Sullivan.[53]

A fighter named Al Marx said he wanted to box the champion in an attempt to win $250 if not knocked out. Marx was from Kansas (though born in Pennsylvania), but had been living in Galveston for the past year. He was 23 years old and claimed to be 6–0 in his fight career.

Sullivan and Marx boxed in Galveston on April 10, 1884. Marx was described as beefy with a chubby face, and his "generally soft look excited a spasm of sympathy." Sullivan said "that he was sorry for the young man and didn't want to hurt him more than he could help."

Marx came out and landed a lead right to Sullivan's collarbone. John countered with his left, which landed on the eye and staggered Marx. Al recovered quickly and threw two blows that fell short, and was hit by another well directed blow that dropped him. He rose and made a rush, landing a few body shots before being sent back down with a bloody nose. He rose in a groggy state, but rushed again. A few blows of infighting took place, but Sullivan drove him back until a body shot dropped him for the third time.

Sullivan advanced to strike him again when he rose, but "realizing the helplessness of his enemy, said: 'Do you want any more?' 'No,' was the gasping reply and this ended the bout. Time—55 seconds." Marx said that being hit by Sullivan was like being hit with a piledriver encased in a football.

After some other sparring sessions, Sullivan and Taylor wound up the exhibition with their own sparring.[54]

In late April, Marx would fight Jim Trainor, an old time prize fighter, and defeat him in 66 rounds over 1 hour and 8 minutes under London rules with soft gloves. The fight was stopped as a result of Trainor's foul of going down to escape punishment.[55] A man who was a plaything to Sullivan was a good fighter when in with others.

While in New Orleans, John said,

Well, I have been on the road very nearly seven months. I have visited almost every State and Territory in the United States; had a good time; knocked out twelve men, including Robinson, and have cleared over $100,000....

All those announced as the "coming men" have dropped quick enough.... I will be done with fighting in about six months. I don't believe there is anyone too anxious to meet me, but I will meet all comers within that time.... England has ... sent her best men over here and I have defeated them.[56]

Sullivan sparred in New Orleans on April 13 and 14, 1884, the auditorium being crowded on both occasions.[57] On the 13th, he first met Pete McCoy. Sullivan was described as

a man weighing 230 pounds, [who] moved as rapidly and was spryer on his feet than the majority of light weights. Sullivan uses both hands well and hits clean. He dodged and guarded splendidly, leaped into the air to throw all his weight into the blow.... Once Sullivan hit out and caught McCoy square in the face. McCoy was knocked about a dozen feet and narrowly escaped going over the footlights.

A secondary source said that Sullivan sparred McCoy 2 rounds.[58] After another exhibition, Sullivan met Steve Taylor, who was nearer Sullivan's size. "The champion showed what he was capable of and although he was bent more upon showing science than hitting hard, the crowd could judge of his capabilities."[59]

Still in New Orleans, they again exhibited the following evening, on April 14. Sullivan was set to spar Mike Donovan, who was listed as 152 pounds, but a report a couple days earlier said he was 180 pounds. Donovan and Sullivan had sparred on at least two previous occasions.

Donovan first sparred McCoy. Mike was described as quick, clever, game, and a straight hitter having skill, coolness, and in and out two-handed fighting abilities. Two exhibitions followed.

Against Donovan, Sullivan "moved with the easy step of a panther, and was rapid in his movements to a degree wonderful for a man of his size." Donovan showed his skill, but "Sullivan showed he had not forgotten his old trio of rushing, feinting with left and landing with right hand." The crowd applauded when John rushed and showered in three or four blows before Donovan could get away.

Two exhibitions followed, and then Sullivan ended the show with a set-to with Taylor, who had earlier sparred Gillespie. This was more of a give and take affair, and Sullivan gave better than he took. Several blows delivered with more power than contracted for did some damage. Sullivan demonstrated many of his tricks, such as jumping into the air and putting all his weight into the blow, throwing his hand from behind his back, ducking, and showing all the elements of a champion pugilist.

Although it was said by the local paper that no one attempted to win the $1,000 offered to anyone who would stand up to Sullivan for 4 rounds, it meant that no white fighter was willing to do so. "Some colored giant is said to have offered his services, but Sullivan declined to fight a colored man in public."[60] Sullivan's drawing of the color line would later become significant, but at the time, no one squawked about it.

The itinerary listed the tour as scheduled to be in Mobile, Alabama, on April 15, Montgomery on the 16th, in Columbus, Macon and Savannah, Georgia, on the 17th to 20th, Charleston, South Carolina, on the 21st, Augusta and Atlanta, Georgia, on the 22nd and 23rd, Chattanooga, Tennessee, on the 24th, Birmingham, Alabama, on the 25th, and Nashville, Tennessee, on the 26th.[61]

The company was in Chattanooga, Tennessee, on April 27, 1884, performing for an all male audience. Acting on a tip, the chief of police incorrectly thought that Sullivan was an imposter and asked for his identification. Sullivan "raved like a mad bull and swore roundly." He told the chief, "—if you don't believe I'm Sullivan, you just send any man in the house on the stage and if he faces me five minutes I'll give him $1,000. ... there's but one Sullivan,——, and I'm the man." No one took up the offer. The exhibitions were said to be tame and disappointing. Sullivan said that he intended to abandon the ring as soon as he reached home.[62] Again, this was a sign that Sullivan needed a rest.

The following day, on April 28, 1884, Sullivan and his company were in Memphis, Tennessee. The crowd of 1,000 to 1,500 persons featured large numbers of representative citizens, and even a few ladies were present. The 24-foot ring was elevated 3 feet from the floor.

First McCoy sparred Mike Donovan 4 rounds. Then Sullivan sparred Donovan for 3 or 4 rounds (the local paper contradicted itself). Donovan displayed courage and did his best to land a blow. It was obvious that Sullivan made efforts not to punish him. Another exhibition took place, and then Sullivan and Taylor boxed in what was called the most spirited contest of the evening.[63]

Sports were a growing craze in America. One newspaper commented,

Within a few years the popularity of athletic sports has increased to such an extent that its influence has reached all classes of people.... There are many ways in which athletics affect the lives of young men for the better if they are inclined toward dissipation.... There is also a certain mental benefit in all athletics.... For example, when a man stands up to box he must keep a cool, clear head and his wits about him or his opponent will get the better of the game.[64]

In an interview, Sullivan was quoted as saying of his career,

I never had but one fist fight in my life ... and that was with Paddy Ryan.... I sent him to grass in nine rounds, consuming 10 minutes and 23 seconds. I have had about fifty glove fights.... I claim to have worked a revolution in the public sentiment by substituting gloves for the naked fists.... What causes the early decay of so many of the champion fighters? Too much heavy drinking.[65]

The day after the Memphis exhibition, on April 29, 1884, in Hot Springs, Arkansas, Sullivan knocked out Dan Henry in the 1st round. *The National Police Gazette* said that the 6', 190-pound Henry was from Hot Springs, and was trying to win $1,000 for lasting 4 rounds. He "sparred vigorously" but was "deficient as a tactician," and was knocked out in the 1st round. Still, "he evinced no disposition to retire until he saw he would be badly used up. He escaped with only slight bruises."[66]

When in Little Rock, Arkansas, Sullivan was asked about a fight he just had in Hot Springs (the Henry bout). Sullivan said, "Yes, I polished him off in fifteen seconds."[67]

As advertised, Sullivan sparred in Little Rock, Arkansas, on April 30. Admission was $1.00. The local ad said that he had defeated 59 men, and would spar twice at every exhibition, four rounds each with two members of the combination.[68]

However, a 217-pound Sullivan sparred Mike Donovan only 2 brief rounds. The Little Rock based *Daily Arkansas Gazette* said, "Donovan did his best but the sledge hammer blows of the champion were too much for him, and he retired after two rounds." Later, Sullivan sparred 3 rounds with Taylor, who held his own, but "stood no show" against Sullivan, whose "lightning blows punished his arms and head and chest. One blow struck across his arm and strained it badly." The writer opined, "There is not probably in America today a man who can stand up against him, and no foreign importations have yet succeeded in doing so." Sullivan said that he planned to leave the business in six months.[69]

On May 1, 1884, back again in Memphis, just two days after the Henry bout, Sullivan met William Fleming, a bricklayer who was known to have once fallen four stories from a scaffold and escaped uninjured. About 3,000 people, said to be the largest crowd in years, packed the building, paying $.50 each to watch Fleming, "of local boxing fame," try to win $1,000 if he could last 4 rounds. Fleming, appearing to be under the influence of whiskey, was introduced as an ambitious Memphis amateur boxer. Sullivan was introduced as the world champion.

As for their fight, *The Memphis Daily Appeal* said that Sullivan rapidly moved to Fleming, who retreated and threw up his left arm. "Like a flash the champion tore down Fleming's guard with his left hand and struck him with the edge of his right under the left jaw. The brickmason fell like a clod, his back striking the chair in the corner, his side striking the hard pine floor with a dull thud." It was over.

The Daily Memphis Avalanche said of the fight that in an instant, John hit him with a left that was partially blocked, but it still staggered Fleming. A right which followed with lightning rapidity caught Will under the left ear, dropping him as if he had been shot dead. His shoulders struck the edge of his chair. Some thought that his spine was broken.

Sullivan and others rushed to his aid. Fleming was totally unconscious for quite some time. Even after a pitcher of water was emptied one glass at a time into his face, head, and back, and they slapped his hands, back, and chest, and rubbed the back of his neck, Fleming would not come to. There was some fear that he had been killed, but he eventually woke up after several minutes. Fleming required assistance to walk away. His jaw swelled up considerably afterward.

Despite Fleming's condition, the show went on. Donovan and McCoy sparred, followed by Taylor and Gillespie. Sullivan and Donovan then boxed. Sullivan was aggressive, pressing him to the ropes at the close of the first 2 rounds. "In the third he stood while Donovan delivered four or five straight from the shoulder directly at his head, dodging as fast as they came with the greatest ease and without moving an inch out of the spot upon which he stood." Sullivan exhibited his historically underappreciated defense. John then managed to grab Mike's head, but Donovan hit Sullivan with two blows in the stomach. However, he received a smack on the ear from Sully before time was called.

Other exhibitions followed, and the last bout was between Sullivan and Taylor, "who is a splendid specimen of manhood and nearer on an equality with Sullivan than any other member of the company. Their rounds were much shorter than the others, and considerably hotter, too." They engaged in "heavy slugging," and Taylor landed a few square shots.

As usual, it was noted that the affair was an orderly one, with not less than 300 of the best men of the city present.[70] Newspapers almost always made it a point to comment on the fact that the exhibitions were orderly and that the best members of society were present, combating the common argument by anti-fight folks that boxing only attracted ruffians and would be the cause of public disorder.

Sullivan in his autobiography said that it only required one punch to knock Fleming out, that the fight only lasted two seconds, and that Will was out cold for 20 minutes. The first question Fleming asked when he came to was, "When am I to meet Sullivan?" After being told that he had already done so, his next question was, "Did I win?"[71]

A report a couple days after the bout said that Fleming had told a friend that "he did not have any idea of whipping Sullivan, but he merely wanted the glory of having stood before him. He got the glory and is immortal." Yes, but he had to suffer for it. This was likely the motivation of many of Sullivan's opponents. They didn't simply want to win the money if they could last, but wanted to prove their courage and to make themselves part of what they already knew would be a legendary story.

However, the fight was a short story: "Sullivan struck Fleming and Fleming struck the floor." As a result, "nothing but a swelled head remains to tell the tale of how he got kicked by a mule."

Sullivan's tour had demonstrated that "muscle is still worshipped as a king." Sullivan's style and popularity were described as follows:

> He suggests the big Corliss engines when in action, and hardly fails to attract the admiration of even the cultured and refined. There is no doubt that if the law did not prevent prize-fighting now to a large extent ... about three-fourths of the population would turn out to see it.[72]

The day after the Fleming bout, on May 2, 1884, in Nashville, Tennessee, a secondary source reports that Sullivan took it easy on 150-pound Enos Phillips, but when he turned up the heat and started battering him in the 4th round, the police stopped it.[73]

The local *Nashville Daily American* said that 1,400 of the best citizens of Nashville turned up for the exhibition, as there was "an unusually small percentage from the lower strata of society." Sullivan was supposed to box a 174-pound man, but the day of the fight he declined to meet Sullivan. As Sullivan's fame grew, so too did opponents' cold feet.

Instead, Enos Phillips, who only weighed about 150 pounds, desired the opportunity. He had been scheduled to meet Mike Gillespie, but at that point, wanted only to meet Sullivan. Sullivan's manager was concerned about their size disparity, and wanted Phillips to meet McCoy, Gillespie, or Donovan, all of whom were within 12 or 14 pounds of his weight, but Phillips insisted on Sullivan. He was granted his wish.

Sullivan looked a little fleshy, but was quite active nevertheless. Phillips "stood up and took his punishment heroically," and even landed a number of counterblows, to the applause of the local crowd.

> Sullivan drove Phillips into the wings three times, and he, of course, had to take a good deal of punishment. The fourth time Sullivan ran him against the back scene, where he bowed his head, and, with his nose bleeding, was receiving buffet after buffet from the champion, when Capt. Kerrigan, the Chief of Police, came from behind the scenes and led him from the stage.

Phillips exhibited pluck "in coming to the score every time, and was still coming when the police interfered and stopped that part of the programme." The local paper said that although Sullivan was evidently striking hard, notwithstanding the punishment, Phillips had more rounds left in him when the police interfered. It sounded though that Phillips was being pounded on when the police stopped it, and they probably feared serious damage would be done to the much smaller man.

This bout has generally been reported as a 4th-round stoppage win for Sullivan, but from the vague description, it appears that this could also have been a 1st-round police stoppage. It could have been 4 rounds if the rounds were counted in London rules fashion—beginning and ending each time Phillips was downed. The only statement given that could give the impression of rounds was that Sullivan drove Phillips to the "wings" three times.[74]

Sullivan's description of the bout in his autobiography supports the impression that it had a London rules flavor in terms of how each round ended. He said that Phillips "endured my blows for two minutes, and, although thrice driven into the wings of the stage, manfully toed the mark for the fourth round. He had been punished so severely that he was taken off the stage by force."[75] Obviously if it only lasted two minutes, then there could not have been 3-plus rounds under Queensberry rules, but rather less than 1 round.

The Nashville Banner gave the impression that it was actually one round of boxing. It said that Phillips had "bull-dog courage, but in the hands of the great slugger he soon got punishment enough to last him for some time." Enos landed a left to the champion's mouth, riling John L., who began to fight in earnest. Phillips was being punished severely when the police interfered. "The crowd cheered frequently during the round, but evidently had no sympathy for Phillips." The phrase *during the round* gives the impression that it only lasted one round, if calculated based on Queensberry rules.[76]

Several set-tos followed this bout, between Donovan and McCoy, Taylor and Gillespie, McCoy and Gillespie, Sullivan and Donovan, and Sullivan and Taylor, and all displayed "a great deal of science."[77] "They slugged each other unmercifully, giving and receiving blows which would have killed or crippled less experienced men."[78]

Some local writers lamented the moral effect that such exhibitions would have. One said, "The whole proceedings were brutal and disgusting throughout.... They tend to make sluggers and roughs of the boys who witness them. It is hoped no other performance of the kind will ever be tolerated in this city."[79] Another opined,

> Have we sunk so low in morals and respectability that the "best citizens of Nashville" turn out en masses [sic] to witness the brutal and demoralizing scenes of the prize ring—so low that the leading and representative paper of the city must needs commend and praise such things in order to gratify the tastes of its readers?

Yet, Sullivan had an allure, such that in his presence, many of those who had previously denounced such performances turned "denunciation into praise and commendation."[80]

About that time, one writer for *The National Police Gazette* said of Sullivan,

> To claim that John L. Sullivan is a well-formed physical specimen of a man, does not begin to express the idea. Sullivan is perfection itself, and mother nature has done tenfold more for him than he has ever done for himself, although he is perfectly cultured in his profession. He can strike out with either right or left, and knock a man down with as much ease and grace as an accomplished lady can gently and languidly handle an opera fan. No effort, no particular determination or energy does he seem to put forth in his art, but all comes as natural and easy as the balmy breezes of May.[81]

The combination itinerary listed them as scheduled to be in Louisville, Kentucky, on May 3.[82] *The National Police Gazette* said that Sullivan wound up the successful Louisville show with Taylor, "who made a good showing with the champion, although by no means his equal."[83]

Sullivan was supposed to exhibit in Cincinnati, Ohio, on May 4, but the mayor prohibited it. Sullivan instead pitched in a game of baseball. The tour was set to exhibit in Vincennes, Indiana, on the 5th, Evansville on the 6th, and St. Louis on the 7th and 8th.[84] The advertisement for the Vincennes show claimed that Sullivan had vanquished 59 men. However, the tour did not show up there, and likely went to Evansville on the 5th.[85]

Pete McCoy left the combination to prepare for a scheduled May 18 fight with Duncan McDonald (which Pete won with a KO31). On May 7, 1884, in St. Louis, Missouri, Sullivan instead sparred with a new heavyweight named Florie Barnett, who made a favorable impression, but was handicapped by superfluous flesh. After an intervening exhibition, Sullivan sparred with Taylor, who was said to be slightly under the weather. The crowded house went home satisfied.[86]

On May 8, the St. Louis police chief would not allow a local man the chance to fight Sullivan 4 rounds for $1,000. Sullivan said that he would pay the man's expenses to travel to Illinois, where they would be allowed to fight, if he was willing. Sullivan again sparred with Barnett and Taylor.[87]

The tour was in Michigan in places including East Saginaw on May 17 and 18th, Bay City on the 19th, Jackson on the 20th, and Detroit on the 21st and 22nd. The tour closed at Toledo, Ohio, on May 23, 1884.[88]

They arrived back in New York on May 26, 1884, and took a hiatus. Years later, a member of the group said that Sullivan toured the continent for eight months with nine people, and that during that time John knocked out 39 men.[89]

Sullivan's national tour had been quite lucrative. One secondary source said it had achieved profits of around $80–100,000.[90] One member of the Sullivan troupe claimed they made $110,000.[91] Sullivan in his autobiography said the total receipts were a little over $187,000, with expenses of about $42,000, making the profit $145,000.[92] Years later,

Sullivan claimed to have generated $400,000 from his exhibitions during the 1883–1884 winter season.[93]

By comparison, the highest paid baseball player, even by as late as 1887, received about $5,000 per year.[94] A U.S. senator only made $5,000 per year up until 1907. A university professor might make $2,500 per year. Sullivan had often made more than their annual salaries in a single fight or exhibition.[95] As of mid–1884, John L. Sullivan was still only 25 years old.

CHAPTER 10

Unfinished Business and Prelude to a Grudge Match

Upon his return to New York in late May 1884, Sullivan discussed with Charlie Mitchell a potential rematch. Sullivan said that he was willing to make the match as long as the winner took the entire gate admission receipts. Initially, Mitchell was not agreeable and the fight was not made. Sullivan left for Boston.[1] However, on June 6, the two came to an agreement for 65 percent to go to the winner and 35 percent to the loser. The match was set for June 30 in New York. Sullivan supposedly trained in Boston with Goss and McCoy.[2]

Sizing up the match, one writer said that Sullivan had "unquestionably improved to a great degree in boxing skill." Mitchell, already a scientific master, had grown larger and stronger. The admission for the fight was $2, with $20 and $25 for boxes.[3]

June 30, 1884, was the night of the fight, but John L. showed up quite drunk and called the match off. Sullivan was about as well known for his drinking as his fighting prowess.[4] He claimed that his condition was due to lack of sleep for two days and the effect of some medicine.[5] However, throughout his career, it was not atypical for stories to be written about how drunk John L. was and the mischief it had gotten him into.

The New York Clipper reported that nearly 5,000 disappointed people had packed Madison Square Garden. Sullivan entered the ring and gave an incoherent speech excusing himself. "Gents: I am not in fit condition to spar tonight. Some will say I'm drunk, but I'm dead sick." No one believed him.

It had been hoped that Sullivan had learned his lesson about drinking, "but some men cannot learn. The fiasco ... added to the peculiar jollities of his Western trip, proves conclusively that Sullivan has no control over his appetite for drink." It was opined that if Sullivan did not gain control of his drinking, it would "ere long break down his constitution and land him where he was before the set-to with Joe Goss, which may be said to have been the starting point of his unprecedentedly successful career."

Apparently, though, Mitchell was not at his best either, having been suffering from malaria, but he was willing to spar. He graciously excused Sullivan. "I know Mr. Sullivan is very sick, and I don't think it would be fair for me to ask him to spar."[6]

In an interview a month and a half later, Sullivan said, "You know as well as anybody that I was sick and unable to fight Mitchell or anybody else in Madison Square Garden that night. This has been the regret of my life, but I will make amends for it before long."[7]

In his autobiography, Sullivan said that he had not prepared for the contest because he had been led to believe that the police captain would not allow it to take place. He had also heard that Mitchell was not really all that interested in meeting him. So, thinking the match would be off, he ate and drank excessively and was in no condition to fight.[8]

The Mitchell match was not immediately rescheduled. Therefore, some could specu-
late that there was something to Mitchell's earlier claim that John L. was less than anxious
to meet him again.

Almost a month and a half after the fiasco, on August 13, 1884, in Boston, Sullivan
performed in three 3-round sparring exhibitions on the same day, against Dominick
McCaffrey, Steve Taylor, and Tom Denny. This was significant because McCaffrey would go
on to win an October 1884 4-round decision over Mitchell, and Sullivan would in 1885 fight
McCaffrey in an official bout.

The Boston Herald said that the exhibition was a benefit for local councilman Denny
and was not supposed to be of a serious nature. Amongst the spectators was Charlie Mitchell,
whom Sullivan asked to spar, but Mitchell declined.

World champion Sullivan first boxed McCaffrey, who was introduced as the middle
weight champion. They sparred 3 interesting and scientific rounds. McCaffrey seemed afraid,
but boxed well. Sullivan mostly used his left hand. "Every now and then, however, John
would rush in on McCaffrey like an avalanche, and, after delivering a few half length arm
hits, would let the Pittsburg pugilist escape. In truth, it must be said that McCaffrey got in
the most blows and showed most science." McCaffrey landed a number of lefts to Sullivan's
ear and face, and even drew some blood from John's nose. "Of course, John was at a disad-
vantage in not being at liberty to exercise his giant strength."

After some other exhibitions, Sullivan boxed with Taylor, who was closer in size to John
than was McCaffrey. Therefore, "Sullivan let himself out more and did better. Two or three
times he chased Steve around the ring and hammered him well." Additional exhibitions followed, and then Sullivan boxed beneficiary Thomas Denny, who made a good showing.[9]

The Boston Daily Globe said that it was the finest show of physical skill and activity that
the world could afford. The boxers demonstrated highly developed artistry, and it was appreciated. Sullivan seemed to be in good condition, but it was also said that he looked a bit
fleshy.

Against McCaffrey,

[T]he bout was in every way a friendly one, and no hard hitting was indulged in.... John evidently didn't let himself out except at intervals, when with a quick shuffle of his feet, and a few
rapid passes with his left he would send McCaffrey scudding across the stage in a way that would
have laid him open to some pretty severe punishment had the champion the inclination to
administer it. McCaffrey, however, showed himself a most clever sparrer, and kept his adversary
at work all of the time.

Sullivan made no special exertion, but particularly in his bout with Taylor, "showed
by the agility of his movements and the rapidity with which he dealt his blows that he can
still lay good claim to the title of champion." However, the Taylor bout was "entirely friendly."
Councilman Denny gave a creditable showing and evidenced what he used to be when he
was young. 4,000 people attended.[10]

Afterwards, Mike Donovan was interviewed, and said of Sullivan,

"He can settle any man in the world, sure, and the bigger the man against him, the better it is
for him. Let me give you a pointer. I was with him in Hot Springs when they picked a terrible
big fellow for him to knock out. I felt of this fellow at the hotel, and I tell you he was something
immense. He had the broadest shoulders of any man I ever saw, was as hard as iron, and
weighed about 240 pounds. I told John of the kind of a fellow he had to meet. 'Is he a big fellow?' says John. 'You can bet,' says I. 'He's a stunner.' 'Then the bigger he is the harder he'll
fall,' says John.... Well, he knocked that big fellow out in just two punches. He hit him there

once," and Mr. Donovan landed his left under the reporter's chin. "Then he cross-countered him and he went down. When he came to the fellow was silly.... When he was traveling he used gloves with about an ounce of hair in each of 'em.... In Memphis he knocked a big fellow out in 11 seconds. The fellow was out, didn't come to for 20 minutes.... Well, the man laid there and Sullivan rubbed him and slapped his hands, but he couldn't bring him around. You could hear people in the audience saying, 'He's killed him,' and it's my opinion they would have killed Sullivan if the man had died. Finally the fellow came to, and Sullivan lifted him up, but he staggered like a drunken man.... I tell you that Sullivan thinks no more of knocking a man out than I do of eating an apple."[11]

In Boston on August 25, 1884, a 164-pound Dominick McCaffrey fought 148-pound Pete McCoy. Initially it was reported that McCoy was the better fighter. He was stronger at wrestling, and threw Dominick down a number of times. Yet, this was illegal under Queensberry rules. Dispatches initially said that McCoy knocked McCaffrey down twice in the 3rd round. However, later reports said that McCaffrey was not knocked down, but thrown down. This might explain why the audience was in a pandemonium and a number of people jumped on the stage. A general melee ensued. Sullivan, acting either as referee or as McCoy's second (possibly both), knocked down a half-dozen or so McCaffrey supporters. Some said that it was all started by Sullivan, who punched out a local sport who had been "chaffing" him. The police stopped it and the bout was declared a draw.

It was speculated that McCoy had been acting on the advice of Sullivan, who desired to see McCaffrey worsted.

Up to the time of Councilman Denny's benefit in Boston ... Sullivan and McCaffrey had been warm friends; but when the latter on that occasion stopped a couple of rushes by the champion (who had again been partaking too freely of the ardent and was not in good form) and had rather the best of their set-to, Sullivan's sentiments toward the young Pennsylvanian underwent a change, and he seemed to depend on his especial favorite, McCoy, to secure for him the revenge he wanted.

Before his bout with McCoy, McCaffrey had issued a broad challenge to any man in the country, "barring Sullivan." However, after the McCoy incident, McCaffrey said that he wanted to fight Sullivan. He issued a challenge to fight under the rules of the London Prize Ring for $1,000 to $2,500 a side. "As I am the only man who ever bested Mr. Sullivan, he cannot with credit to himself decline to meet me."[12]

On October 13, 1884, in New York, McCaffrey fought Charley Mitchell in a 4-round bout. McCaffrey won, but some questioned whether he deserved the victory. According to *The New York Clipper*, the 1st round was tame, with McCaffrey mostly on the defensive. The 2nd was livelier, each scoring well, but the more aggressive Mitchell doing the better work and once sending Mac to the ropes. The 3rd round was similar, with Mitchell aggressive and Dominick clinching often. However, one right staggered Charley. In the 4th round, Mitchell forced Mac to the ropes, but after a break, it was seen that Mitchell was cut over the eye. They fought hard and fast. Mitchell landed more often and with the most effect, forcing matters. Towards the end, McCaffrey was weak and reeled.

The general belief was that a draw would be proclaimed, and with such a verdict at the termination of so even a contest, all reasonable, fair minded men would have been satisfied ... but great astonishment was expressed when the announcement was made that McCaffrey had won.

Mac had fought well, but the local paper opined that "it is not right that he should have honors thrust upon him to which he is not clearly entitled."[13] Still, his showing against a man such as Mitchell further legitimized McCaffrey's challenge to Sullivan. A week later, Mitchell and Jack Burke fought to a 4-round draw.

During October 1884, a secondary source indicates that Sullivan toured around a bit, giving some exhibitions, possibly in Pennsylvania, West Virginia, Ohio, New Jersey, Kentucky, and Indianapolis, but this is unconfirmed.[14]

It would not be until late August 1885 that Sullivan and McCaffrey were able to meet (the authorities prevented an April 1885 meeting), and not until 1888 that Sullivan would fight Mitchell in a rematch (politicians would not allow an 1886 bout).

CHAPTER 11

Accepted, but Not Quite

On November 10, 1884, in New York, a 196-pound John L. (who later claimed he was 225) took on 205-pound, 6'2", 42-year-old John Laflin. Sullivan and Laflin had previously sparred 3 semi-friendly rounds in March 1883 and Laflin had acquitted himself well.

This time, in a more serious bout, *The New York Times* reported that in the 1st round, Laflin fought in a cowardly manner, constantly attempting to grab on for dear life around Sullivan's neck. When Sullivan finally freed himself, he struck him a blow that knocked Laflin down into a corner and "spattered his gore onto the spectators." A right dropped him for the second time. Laflin remained on the canvas and did not rise. Backers of both men entered the ring, and it seemed that the fight was over. It was a 1st round knockout— or was it?

Laflin was assisted to his feet by his second, and about 30 seconds after he was down, he was allowed to continue, despite the fact that it was a Queensberry rules bout, which required him to rise unassisted within 10 seconds. Again, this demonstrates the time's ongoing transition between the London rules (which allowed for 30 seconds following a knockdown) and the Queensberry rules. It perhaps also demonstrated the desire to give the crowd sufficient entertainment for their money. Often, Sullivan was willing to continue if, after recovering, his opponent desired to do so. There were a number of aspects to this fight that gave the impression of a mixture of London and Queensberry rules.

Sullivan knocked him down three more times in the re-commenced 1st round, for a total of five knockdowns. Laflin continued grabbing Sullivan, and even prevented himself from going down by grabbing the ropes.

Sullivan slowed up a bit in the 2nd round, fatigued by trying to free himself from Laflin's grasp, but dropped Laflin at the end of the round.

The National Police Gazette differed, saying that Sullivan dropped Laflin twice early on in the 2nd round, and then with a single blow sent Laflin from the center of the stage to his corner. Laflin was struck multiple times and initially saved himself from another knockdown by holding onto the ropes. However, a rain of blows knocked Laflin around the ring like a drunken man and down he went again, being struck while down. After rising, further blows dropped him yet again.[1]

The Times went on to say that Laflin was dropped in the 3rd round by a backhanded blow while holding onto Sullivan's neck. He was chased around the ring and battered to the floor by one of Sullivan's famous rushes. The round ended and his backers dragged Laflin to his corner.

In the 4th round, Laflin was staggered by a blow, and another sent him down. He lay there, and was lifted to his feet by his backers (in London rules style), but "his legs refused to sustain him, his arms hung limp, and his head fell back."[2] This gave the impression that he was knocked out.

The Gazette said Laflin was thrown down once in the 4th round, and was assisted to his feet. Sullivan knocked him into a corner "with such force that his body seemed to rebound and his head rung on the timbers as though it were cracked." He went down, was lifted up, and was carried to his corner. The referee then decided the bout in favor of Sullivan.

The New York Herald called it 4 unscientific rounds of hugging and slugging. It said that Laflin's blows made little impression on Sullivan. The fight was for the full receipts of the house, which Sullivan won when the referee decided in his favor (which referees did even in the event of a knockout). It had its own version of the fight:

Round 1: After beating each other wildly about the head and neck Sullivan forced Laflin down. They attacked each other again, grappled, and Laflin was sent down. He rose and was caught around the neck. After a tussle, John L. pitched him against the ropes. Laflin's face was covered with blood. They hugged and hit as best they could with their unencumbered hands. Eventually, Sullivan drove him into a corner and knocked him down.

Round 2: Laflin fought hard, but Sullivan landed a stiff blow to the ear, and as Laflin staggered, John L. threw him down. The police captain came up to stop it, but he was convinced to allow it to continue. They rushed into each others' arms and it was give and take. At one point, Laflin swung John L. around onto the ropes and landed a dozen blows as Sullivan hardly made an effort to stop them, "and stood staring blankly at his opponent without any regard for the punishment until he got his wind."

Round 3: Laflin punched with both hands until a Sullivan blow to the ear dropped him again. They rushed at each other and Laflin did well in the exchanges. Laflin pressed John to the ropes and hit him until Sullivan rallied, landing some hard blows in succession that staggered him. He pressed Laflin to the ropes and held him over them. When they broke and met again, Sullivan "struck the most telling blows of the night." It was in this round that Sullivan knocked Laflin into a corner with such force that his body rebounded and his head rung on the timbers. Laflin went down and had to be picked up and carried to his corner.

Round 4: For a while, they swung wildly and ineffectually in close. However, Sullivan landed a right, and then striking round handed blows, forced Laflin into his corner and knocked him down. "Again Laflin was brought to his corner and his seconds tried to bring him out again. But although he arose and moved forward unsteadily at their solicitation the time had elapsed and the round was declared finished." This gives the impression that the cornermen were allowed to assist him in rising and recuperating even during the round, again indicating the somewhat hybrid Queensberry/London rules quality of the bout. It also contrasts the other accounts by indicating that the round ended.[3]

The New York Clipper said that Laflin was a man of magnificent physique and that Sullivan's recklessness of living had left him in less than his best shape. After Laflin was dropped in the 1st round, he spent his energy on trying to save himself with clinching. Sullivan exerted himself too much by trying to throw Laflin off. "Laflin was down three times in the first round, and once more than thirty seconds elapsed before he rose, instead of the ten allowed by the rules under which they fought." This confirms that it probably should have been a KO1 win for Sullivan.

The 2nd was similar, but when Sullivan grew fatigued, Laflin attacked and forced him against the ropes. However, Sullivan recovered himself and attacked again.

In the 3rd, Laflin was dropped again and he resumed hugging, ignoring the orders of the referee and the jeers of the crowd. Sullivan finally threw him off and knocked him down multiple times, "the last knockdown quite settling him; but he was picked up and carried to his corner before the expiration of time." Again, it seemed that he had been knocked out and illegally (if boxing under Queensberry rules) assisted before the round ended. Police captain Williams wanted to end it, but was convinced to allow it to continue.

Laflin was weak and unsteady in the 4th, and was punished. He was dropped by a right, "which decided him to cut it without further ado. He was assisted to his feet by his seconds ... and upon getting to his corner removed the gloves, whereupon the referee awarded the victory to Sullivan."[4] This gave the impression of a retirement.

Really, this fight should be considered a KO1 or no worse than a KO4. The majority of accounts give the impression that Laflin was either retired or unable to continue. He was occasionally assisted to his feet prior to the conclusion of the rounds and given additional rest following knockdowns, all in London rules fashion. But this seemed to be combined with the three-minute clock continuing to run, in Queensberry rules fashion, even after Laflin was dropped and assisted to his corner, giving the impression that Laflin lasted the distance.

Years later, Mike Donovan said of the fight that "Laughlin" had no nerve, for he simply jumped around and clinched. At one point, he rushed and clinched and pushed Sullivan back into the ropes, but as Sullivan rebounded, Laughlin was decked by a lightning right to the neck and was counted out.[5]

Sullivan's final 1884 defense was against 162- to 165-pound Alf Greenfield, the English veteran of the game who had a reputation for being a very scientific boxer. He stood 5'8¾" and was about 31 years old. A few years earlier, some said that Greenfield was a man who had a chance against Sullivan.

Most of Greenfield's bouts had been fought under the London rules. He fought Pat Perry for 56 minutes before they were stopped by the police. Alf won an 1878 bout with Sam Breeze that lasted 58 minutes. He defeated Jimmy Highland that year in 1 hour and 15 minutes. He punished Denny Harrington over 1 hour and 25 minutes, but lost on a bogus claim that he hit Denny while he was down. In 1880, James Stewart of Glasgow was defeated on a foul in 20 rounds over 1 hour and 20 minutes.[6] Greenfield had an 1881 28-round bareknuckle draw lasting 1 hour and 20 minutes against Tug Wilson, but apparently Wilson had been considered the better man. Greenfield was also said to have had an 1883 3-round decision victory over Jack Burke.[7]

The Sullivan-Greenfield bout was originally scheduled to take place one week after the Laflin fight, on November 17, again in New York City. Unfortunately, New York's mayor, who wanted to end prizefighting, pressured the police to prevent the Sullivan-Greenfield fight. Boxing had become quite popular and well attended by all classes of society, and well followed by the media, but the political climate still resisted its acceptance.

The two boxers were arrested a couple days before the bout on suspicion that they were going to violate the law by having a prizefight. They were brought before a judge. Sullivan said and Greenfield echoed that it was their intention to give an exhibition of the science of self defense over 4 rounds. There was to be no referee, further demonstrating that it was just an exhibition. The money was to be split 65 percent to Sullivan and 35 percent to Greenfield, not based on a winner.

The judge decided that as long as they "intended to engage in a friendly sparring match not calculated to injure either party" the law would not be violated. This required that "the blows are to have no relation to the injury or exhaustion of either party." However, the police could stop the bout and arrest them if "several blows are struck which are likely to cause injury or to inflame passion or the passions of the bystanders."[8]

The legal proceedings had delayed the bout for one day, so it took place on November 18, 1884. *The New York Herald* said that the ring had three ropes and eight posts. Both men wore white tights and stockings. Greenfield was listed as 31 years old, 5'9" and 160 pounds. Sullivan was listed as 26, 5'10¼" and weighing 198½ pounds. *The New York Times* listed Alf as 5'9½" and 165 pounds to John's 196 pounds. It was noted that no referee was chosen, but rather a "master of ceremonies," in light of the police interest in the bout, so as to avoid having it be perceived as a fight.

Greenfield was described by *The Times* as thoroughly game, not acting as if he was

afraid. He dodged John's rushes and used his agility with counters. *The Herald* said that both began the bout holding their lefts well out in front and keeping their rights covering the ribs. The 1st round was competitive, both exchanging, with Sullivan more of the aggressor, Greenfield countering and holding his own. Alf was knocked about and momentarily crowded to the ropes. Greenfield did not have much power and Sullivan was just getting started. The round had nothing of the "fast and furious order." *The Times* said that after Alf was knocked into the corner, he did not care to get close to John again.

The Herald said the 2nd round would "have proved a very spirited round had not there been official interference. Sullivan had woke up, and was anxious to crowd his adversary." Sullivan sent in sledge-hammer blows, but Greenfield returned them and retreated. One of Sullivan's lunges of rights and lefts cut Alf's left eye. The blood dripped over Greenfield's shirt. Sullivan himself had been cut behind the ear. Greenfield

Alf Greenfield. From Billy Edwards, *The Portrait Gallery of Pugilists of England, America, Australia* (Chicago: Athletic Publishing Co., 1894). Clay Moyle, www.prizefightingbooks.com.

landed some clean shots, but they lacked Sullivan's steam. According to *The Times*, Greenfield held a few times and the crowd hissed.

Regarding the conclusion, *The Herald* said,

> While Sullivan was thumping his antagonist on the ropes, right and left, and it looked as if the stranger was getting side winders, crushers and slashers in such quick succession that it would go hard with him, though he was fighting back with courageous recklessness, the law stepped in, and the fight was at an end before the three minutes had expired.

The Times said that Sullivan had "rained a series of tremendous blows upon his opponent and battered down his guard. In another moment Greenfield would have been numbered with the victims of Sullivan who have gone before, when Capt. Williams suddenly pushed between them." *The Herald* said the master of ceremonies announced that both were under arrest and that Sullivan had won.

The 1st round was a scientific exhibition, but the 2nd had been a slugging match in violation of the law. When asked what he thought of the turn of events, Sullivan responded, "What——do you think I think?"[9]

The New York Clipper said that Sullivan had held back in the 1st round, not using his famous rushes or hurricane style. As a result, the quick, well-scienced Greenfield did well. Alf landed more often, though on the retreat, and his blows did not seem to make any impression on John.

Sullivan became more aggressive in the 2nd round. When John grew close, Alf would grab him around the neck, at which the crowd hissed. They exchanged some blows, and then Sullivan made a rush and landed some hard punches. Alf again grabbed him by the neck. When they separated, it was seen that Greenfield's forehead had a gash, from which the blood flowed. It was unclear whether the cut came from a blow or a head butt. John rushed him to the ropes and sent in both hands in quick succession. Greenfield grabbed around the neck again. At that point, the police captain stopped the bout. The round had only lasted 2 minutes and 15 seconds. The master of ceremonies declared that Sullivan was the winner, "presumably because of Greenfield's persistence in hugging, and his tardiness in 'breaking' when ordered. On the score of points, it might have been decided a draw." About 4,000 people were in attendance.[10]

Years later, Mike Donovan said that a Sullivan right sent Greenfield spinning across the ring, and that when he went in to finish, Alf held on for dear life. The police thought there was a danger of a knockout, so they stopped it. "It was a lucky thing for Greenfield that the police interfered."[11]

The two were arrested and tried for engaging in a prizefight, ironic because Sullivan had been allowed to engage in multiple fights in New York that were even more brutal (including the week before), most of which were attended by politicians and police. For whatever reason, they decided to crack down on these exhibitions.

The trial took place a month later, on December 16, 1884. Luckily, although the police testified for the prosecution as its only witnesses, their testimony turned out to be favorable for the boxers. The superintendent testified that he had ordered their arrest when he saw Greenfield hanging onto Sullivan's neck with blood on Alf's forehead, and he had "thought they were about to fight." He admitted that he had never seen a genuine prize fight. He also admitted that he had told the police commissioner that the 1st round was all right and that Sullivan "could have knocked Greenfield if he wanted to." This demonstrated that restraint was exhibited.

Captain Williams said that he had seen numerous sparring matches between police-men where there was blood flowing, and they used smaller gloves than had Sullivan and Greenfield. Williams said of the match, "I didn't see any great severity about the blows." The defense claimed that the blood was actually caused by an accidental head butt.

A member of the force said that when Greenfield grabbed Sullivan, John "remained passive." Another police captain said, "I didn't see any hard blows struck. The men were smiling at each other. There was no knock down." The district attorney was not pleased with the testimony.[12] It was clear that the police were trying to help them out. The boxers were acquitted.[13]

Unfortunately though, the police and political pressure seemed to hover over and influence many Sullivan bouts. The masses accepted boxing long before the law was fully prepared to do so.

Still in New York, on New Year's Eve and twice on January 1, 1885, Sullivan sparred Mike Donovan in the concert scene during performances of *The Lottery of Life*. It was a mild set-to, though scientific.

Sullivan and Greenfield had become friends, given their common interests in opposing the charges against them. They agreed to spar 4 rounds in Boston on January 12, 1885.

Although it had its exciting moments and Sullivan clearly proved his superiority, the rematch was overall fairly tame. However, there was an external reason for this. The police captain said that he had told Sullivan that he and Greenfield could punch as hard as they wanted to as long as all was fair, "and there was no knocking out." He said that Sullivan shook his hand and agreed. Sullivan's performance was limited by his legal concerns. It could not be a knockout fight.

Of John's condition, the police captain said, "Sullivan is all right (in regard to intoxi-cation), but he has shamefully abused himself, and it shows." According to the local press, his reputation as a drinker was causing him to lose some popularity. "There was a time when Sullivan could pack the largest building in the city with men from every walk of life, and reap a pecuniary benefit of thousands of dollars, for a few minutes of not very exhaustive labor. That time has gone by."

Sullivan wore white tights and a pink shirt. Greenfield was bare-chested. Their difference in builds and weight was markedly apparent, John being obviously bigger. Sullivan was called the "champion of the world" by *The Boston Herald*, and Greenfield "was billed as the cham-pion of England."

Sullivan forced the fighting the whole way through. He landed a number of head jar-ring blows in the 1st round and had the best of it. "Sullivan had it all his own way, striking hard and getting few and light returns."

In the 2nd round, Sullivan used his rushes to get Alf either to a corner, stake, or the ropes, and pounded on him. Greenfield began hugging and the crowd began hissing.

In the 3rd round, the "world's champion struck England's champion three terrific blows on the side of the head to start off with, and before he could recover from this attack he brought his right glove full on the neck, and Greenfield went full length upon the floor—a half knockdown." Greenfield then hugged to survive. This was called the most exciting round, "and that is not saying much." Sullivan attacked and made a rush, "holding out his dangerous left arm like a ramrod, smiting him fiercely on the face. In the rapid in-fighting which ensued, Greenfield was knocked down and through the ropes in Sullivan's corner." When Alf rose, he ran away, which brought the crowd's hisses. John caught and hammered him. Alf landed a hard left, his best of the fight, but Sullivan forced him to a corner and staggered him with a neck blow.

In the 4th and final round, Greenfield mostly danced about to survive, but "Sullivan hit him just about as he pleased." Alf landed a right and left, "but he might just as well have hit the side of a house, for Sullivan did not budge." The crowd hissed at Alf's sprinting around as a show of fear. At one point, Alf "came to a sudden stop as the result of a right and a left blow from Sullivan, and many thought he was asking him to hit a little lighter. From this some got an idea that the whole thing was arranged between the men." Sullivan confirmed in his autobiography that Greenfield repeatedly asked him to let up on him, and that he did so. John subsequently fought him to the ropes and landed three moderately hard blows. Alf ran away and time was called. The referee declared Sullivan the winner.

Afterwards, Greenfield said that no one knew as much about fighting as Sullivan, and no one hit as hard. He asked the crowd to excuse his hugging and running, saying that a man had to show generalship to fight Sullivan, but that John had shut him off.

Sullivan said, "I have treated Greenfield with respect, and if I was allowed to go on— but for the order of the captain—I would have done better work." The report called it a tame affair, but apparently this was because of Greenfield's tactics and the restraint Sullivan showed owing to the police captain's directive that there was to be no knocking out.[14]

The Boston Daily Globe also called Sullivan the champion of the world and Greenfield the English champion. It said that Sullivan had been the more scientific and skillful of the two, despite the fact that his condition did not appear to be the best. He was extremely fleshy with an inflated stomach. A reference was made to the common belief that he was usually under the influence of intoxicants.

Of the fight, it said that Sullivan did almost all of the leading. Greenfield threw back occasionally, but often resorted to clinching. In the 2nd round, Greenfield ducked a right, but not far enough, for it caught him on the ear and dropped him. He rose and leaned against the ropes, but Sullivan stood in the center of the ring and paid no heed to those who called upon him to finish Alf. It was clear that John was carrying him. Eventually, they resumed, and Greenfield clinched, often to the crowd's hisses. In the 3rd round, Alf clinched and backed away. It was more of the same in the 4th. "No one in the hall held any other opinion but that Sullivan could easily have settled Greenfield."[15]

Just a week after his rematch with Greenfield, on January 19, 1885, Sullivan fought a rematch with Paddy Ryan, this time wearing four-ounce gloves under Queensberry rules. Unfortunately and surprisingly, it was held in New York. Given that Sullivan had just been tried in New York for violating the anti–prize fight law, it did not make sense to hold the bout there. Perhaps Sullivan was emboldened by his acquittal.

The police said that any slugging would force them to interfere. Yet, that seemed almost impossible given how hard Sullivan hit. Ryan said of him, "It's a mistake to suppose he can't hit hard. His stroke is like a kick from a mule. When he hit me on the neck under the left ear, at Mississippi City, I never knew what struck me."[16]

Captain Williams said, "If the men get to fighting I shall arrest them. I will not permit any knocking out business." Upset with the police as witnesses in the Greenfield trial, the district attorney sent two subordinates to attend the exhibition to gather evidence. The mayor said, "Prize fighting cannot be conducted with impunity in this city so long as I am Mayor."

A judge proclaimed before the fight that it should be prevented by the authorities and that he would grant a warrant if requested, "on the grounds that a breach of the peace has been arranged for; on the grounds that for the time being Madison Square Garden will be transformed into a disorderly house, in which will be gathered thieves and other disreputable characters."[17]

No wonder so many newsmen often made a point to mention the fact that many of the most reputable members of society attended Sullivan bouts, or that the affair was an orderly one. This was necessary to demonstrate that boxing had penetrated all social classes and did not cause a breach of the peace. However, the political climate in New York and many other places at that time was still against boxing.

Sullivan was said to be fat, weighing over 220 pounds. Ryan on the other hand had trained down from 225 to 195 pounds.[18] The 1st round barely got underway when the police stopped it. The New York Times reported that Sullivan began with "a little gentle sparring," as he "had taken a lesson from his last experience in Madison-Square Garden, and evidently intended to do no heavy hitting." If the fight was not brutal and just a mere exhibition of skill, the combatants would not offend the law.

However, Ryan attacked and got in two heavy blows. Sullivan then "threw discretion to the wind," attacked, and in "a second he had broken down Ryan's guard, and in another second it would have been all up with the Trojan. But Inspector Thorne had carefully watched the fight, and he crawled under the ropes when the first heavy blow was struck." The crowd hissed when the fight was stopped, as it had only lasted one minute and eight seconds.[19]

The New York Herald said that a huge crowd of 10,000 was present. "The weights given out were 197 for Ryan, who looked much bigger despite the vast amount of work he had done, and 212 pounds for Sullivan, who did not look that weight."

From its description, Ryan landed a number of good blows. In a clinch, Ryan held Sullivan's head and hit him twice to the ribs. From the outside, Ryan countered some Sullivan blows, and also got the best of some inside exchanges. After a clinch, Inspector Thorne jumped on the stage and stopped the fight.

Both men went to their corners thinking that the fight would be resumed, but the inspector would not yield. The crowd howled its disappointment. "The referee said he considered it no fight, but the popular verdict was that Ryan had the call. No arrests were made. The total time of fighting was 90¼ seconds." Really, the result was inconclusive, owing to the bout's short duration. The police had warned them not to slug, and they had, so technically they were within their rights to stop it.[20]

The New York Clipper said that 6,000 people attended the match, with the seats sold for $1 and $2. Sullivan looked fat. It said that barely 30 seconds elapsed before the police stopped it. They made a few exchanges and there was a clinch. Each put in some heavy shots at close range, in the midst of which Inspector Thorne and Captain Williams, "seeing that the blood of the boxers was up," stepped in and ended it. The crowd had been excited by the boxers' energy, and so when it was stopped, expressed their disappointment with hisses and groans. The police refused to allow it to go on. "The encounter was too brief to be regarded as having the slightest bearing on the question as to the present relative merits of the men. So far as it progressed neither had a whit the better of the other."[21]

This fight is often listed as a KO1 win for Sullivan, but that is probably less than fair to Ryan under the circumstances. Sullivan's own hometown paper said that Ryan had been doing well at the time it was stopped.[22] It should be considered a no contest, as that was the decision of the referee, and properly so. There had not been sufficient fighting to determine the better man.

Two and a half months later, on April 2, Sullivan was supposed to fight Dominick McCaffrey in Philadelphia, but a judge put out a warrant for their arrest charging them with conspiring to create a breach of the peace.[23] Despite its popularity, once again boxing came up against the legal barrier. The bout would have to wait.

Jack Burke. From Billy Edwards, *The Portrait Gallery of Pugilists of England, America, Australia* (Chicago: Athletic Publishing Co., 1894). Clay Moyle, www.prizefightingbooks.com.

Almost five months after the Ryan no contest, on June 13, 1885, in Chicago, 26-year-old Sullivan took on 23-year-old Jack Burke in a scheduled 5-round bout. The 170-pound, 5'8½" Burke was born in Ireland, but raised in England. Mike Donovan said that Burke was Jewish. He had some good credentials, having had his first fight at age 15, and he had even won an amateur middleweight tournament. In 1881, he fought Charley Mitchell to a bareknuckle 25-round draw in a fight that lasted 1 hour and 47 minutes until darkness put an end to it. Burke lost an 1883 3-round decision to Alf Greenfield, but disputed it, saying that many spectators disagreed with the decision. About that time, he only weighed in the 150- to 165-pound range.[24]

On October 6, 1884, Burke sparred Steve Taylor and had the better of it, knocking Taylor down in the 1st round.[25] In late October 1884, Burke and Mitchell fought again, in a competitive, gloved, 4-round battle that resulted in another draw.[26] A November bout between them resulted in an 8-round draw.[27]

A secondary source indicates that Burke fought

a December 1884 5-round draw with Jake Kilrain, and in February and March 1885 had respective 5-round decision wins over former Sullivan opponents Captain James Dalton and Alf Greenfield.[28] A primary source confirms that Burke defeated Greenfield in a 5-round decision in Chicago on March 2, 1885.[29] Other sources say that Burke also defeated Greenfield in 7 or 8 rounds in 1885, likely in late March.[30] Thus, Burke was a very experienced, capable and worthy opponent. He was no worse than Mitchell and better than Greenfield.

According to a non-local source, at around 237 pounds as a result of his excessive drinking, Sullivan was fat and less than his best for the bout.[31] Two local papers said that Sullivan was not in good condition, having a big paunch, though John denied a story of his having been drunk while in Philadelphia. *The Chicago Herald* said that Sullivan weighed fully 210 or 215 pounds with a fat belly, and had two large boils on the back of his neck. Burke looked hard and firm at 170 pounds.[32]

Sullivan was dressed in white, with a sleeveless flesh-colored silk shirt. Burke was stripped to the waist, with white tights and green socks and belt. 10,000 to 12,000 people were in attendance. They fought the scheduled 5 rounder wearing 4-ounce gloves.

1st Round

Chicago Tribune (CT): Burke went down "by the overpowering force of the big fellow's onslaught." Burke attacked Sullivan's ribs, and after they clinched, he attacked again, but Sullivan rushed and sent him down with a right to the left shoulder.

Chicago Herald (CH): Burke began by dodging blows. They mixed it up until there was a clinch, where they fought on the inside, with Sullivan continually swinging his right, "knocking Jack down, not however, so much by the hit as because Jack was off his balance when it came." Burke landed some counters, but took some blows to the back, which showed marks.

2nd and 3rd Rounds

CT: Burke was more defensive in the 2nd and 3rd rounds, except when he attempted to counter Sullivan's rushes with a left to the face or ribs. Burke was pushed to the ropes and hurled to the stage about six times in each of the 2nd and 3rd rounds, but remained clear headed and fresh relative to the hard working John L.

CH: Burke was smiling in the 2nd round, but a jolt to the back of the neck jarred him. Burke continued countering and using his defense. The round ended with some cautious sparring, with no one hurt.

In the 3rd, Jack landed a left to John's chin. An angered Sullivan made one of his famous rushes. They exchanged blows and Burke clinched after successfully eluding John's right.

4th Round

CT: Following a clinch, Sullivan threw Jack across the ring. The perturbed Burke attacked and twice struck John with his left to the face. Another Sullivan rush "swept the lighter man to the staging with a crash. No sooner was he on his feet than down he went again, both times being simply carried off his pins by the weight of his big opponent."

CH: Sullivan rushed him to the corner, but was clinched. Shortly thereafter, a body blow floored Burke. After another Sullivan rush, John sent in rights to the back that again sent him to the floor.

Sullivan in 1885. A line art version of this photograph appeared in *The National Police Gazette*, July 11, 1885. Billy Edwards, *The Portrait of Pugilists of England, America, Australia* (Chicago: Athletic Publishing Co., 1894). Clay Moyle, www.prizefighting-books.com.

Sullivan bore him down simply by superior weight and heavier hitting, but he had not punished Burke very severely. By mistake time was called and the men took their seats nearly a minute before the round was over, but they went together again in heavy short arm work, in which Jack got the worst of it, although he took his punishment gamely. Sullivan forced the fighting over into Burke's corner, fighting him onto the ropes, and Jack dropped once or twice to avoid punishment.

5th Round

CT: Burke was sent to the floor five times in the round by the swarming Sullivan's arms and shoulders, but this account indicated that he never went down simply to avoid punishment. At the conclusion of the round the referee declared Sullivan the winner.[33]

CH: Sullivan went at him with a fierce rush that sent Jack down. John attacked ferociously, leading with his right and pressing Burke to the ropes, sending in right and left "for all he was worth." Burke fought back, but "had to drop to avoid the punishment." This clearly differed from *The Tribune's* account, which said that Burke did not go down to avoid punishment. The referee told Sullivan to get back to his corner, but he did not obey. Burke rose with a quick spring to avoid Sullivan's rush. The round and battle ended with the men clinched. Neither of them was used up, but "Sullivan had done the better fighting and the referee awarded him the match."[34]

Sullivan was critiqued by *The Tribune* as not being as good as he had been two years before, but that "despite the abuses to which he has subjected himself, he is still head and shoulders above any pugilist in the ring today." Despite the effects of excessive drinking, John L. could still overpower his opponents. Apparently, though, Burke had acquitted himself well, being "worthy of his past record. ... he made a creditable showing ... [in] a fight which in point of skill and courage showed him the champion's equal at every point."[35]

Some non-local sources said that the police had influenced Sullivan's performance. *The National Police Gazette* said that in the 3rd round, Sullivan became a bit too ferocious and a policeman warned him. *The Brooklyn Daily Eagle* confirmed that when Sullivan scowled and his eyes flashed, the police lieutenant "shook his cane over the ropes and said warningly, 'John!' Sullivan retreated and the round ended." This demonstrated the fine line that fighters had to walk in order to avoid violating the law. Perhaps when time was called early in the 4th round, it was actually intentional, the master of ceremonies seeking to give Burke a break and prevent a knockout. *The New York Clipper* said, "It is manifest that Sullivan made no serious attempt to knock Burke out, being content to demonstrate his superiority as a fighter." Most non-local sources confirmed that Burke was dropped multiple times in the last two rounds, and also went down to avoid punishment. The decision for Sullivan received cheers.[36]

Sullivan in his autobiography said that he never trained a day for the fight, but that "Burke was but a mere boy in my hands."[37] Mike Donovan years later said that "Burke did the sprinting act—the same as McCaffrey had. He was a clever fellow on his legs, and his skillful sprinting and ducking saved him. He certainly could not have lasted another round.... [Sullivan] would have put Burke out in a round had he been in shape."[38]

A couple weeks after fighting Sullivan, Burke fought Charlie Mitchell to a 6-round draw.

CHAPTER 12

Mystery of the Seven-Round Decision

After the June 1885 Sullivan-Burke fight, Dominick McCaffrey's manager Billy O'Brien, who was present, issued a challenge to Sullivan. "McCaffrey's the only man Sullivan's afraid of.... He saw McCaffrey knock Jack Stewart out in thirty seconds."[1] Stewart had in 1881 boxed Sullivan 3 rounds. Sullivan and McCaffrey arranged for a bout which took place on August 29, 1885, in Cincinnati, Ohio, two and a half months after the Burke fight. It was to be 26-year-old Sullivan's fourth and final defense of the year.

McCaffrey was just under 22 years of age, stood 5'9¼", and weighed in the 165–178 pound range. This Pittsburgh native was known as a scientific boxer. He had fought Mike Cleary to a 5-round draw. In 1884, he won a 5-round decision over Jack Walsh, but many felt that Walsh was his equal. McCaffrey had knocked out Canadian champion and former Sullivan opponent Jack Stewart in 30 seconds. A 162-pound McCaffrey gave an exhibition with 223-pound John Flood and appeared to have the better of it. Sullivan had stopped Flood in 8 rounds under London Prize Ring Rules with gloves.

Sullivan and McCaffrey had sparred 3 rounds one year earlier, in early August 1884, and Mac demonstrated good science. Later that month, John witnessed his friend and sparring partner, 148-pound Pete McCoy, fight the 164-pound McCaffrey, but it was declared a draw when Sullivan and members of the crowd engaged in a fistfight. McCoy apparently threw the larger Dominick down a number of times. Sullivan made it clear that he did not think all that much of McCaffrey.[2] Since then, the perturbed McCaffrey had been openly challenging Sullivan.

In October 1884, McCaffrey defeated the only man to have decked Sullivan, Charlie Mitchell, "champion of England," in a 4-round decision. Some felt it should have been a draw. However, this made him a legitimate contender.[3] A scheduled April 1885 bout between Sullivan and McCaffrey had been prevented by the authorities.

The Sullivan-McCaffrey fight was filled with controversy that historians discuss today. There is some debate regarding for what length the fight was scheduled, what the terms for the decision were, how many rounds were actually fought, when the decision was rendered, and who actually had the better of it. All of these issues will be analyzed.

Some accounts indicate that the bout was scheduled for 6 rounds or to a finish. Some believe that meant that if the two continued to fight after 6 rounds, the bout would not terminate until someone was knocked out. Others felt it meant that the fight would be 6 rounds, or less if someone was knocked out. Some believed it was a fight to the finish. Still others believed it was merely scheduled for 6 rounds. Apparently, the fight was only supposed to be 6 rounds, but the stipulated length of the bout may have changed a number of times, confusing the participants and the media.

Some secondary accounts indicate that the combatants fought for 7 rounds and that

Sullivan refused to continue after the 7th round. If it was supposed to be a fight to the finish, then although Sullivan appeared to be the better fighter, his refusal to continue the bout would be a bad mark on his "win" and has been used as a criticism of Sullivan. These accounts also report that the decision was announced for Sullivan several days later as being a 6-round win. This has caused some controversy because decisions were supposed to be rendered at a bout's conclusion.[4] Some of the eventual controversy may have been generated either by Sullivan haters or McCaffrey supporters.

Some primary source accounts indicate that the fight ended after 6 rounds and the decision was given to Sullivan at that time. This appears to have been the version put forth by many non-local newspapers which published *next day* fight reports as it being a 6-round decision for Sullivan. They were right about the decision, but wrong about the number of rounds fought.

The local primary source accounts indicate that 7 rounds were fought. That said, even those accounts support that there may have been some confusion regarding just how many rounds were fought or intended to be fought, so it is not a cut-and-dried issue. As will be discussed, the extra round might have been the result of the referee's mistake, not because the participants agreed to it. Even the accounts that said 7 rounds were fought agreed that the referee awarded the bout to Sullivan after its conclusion.

Confusion regarding the propriety of the decision actually resulted from the belief that the fight was not to be decided on the merits, based on points, but that Sullivan was required to knock McCaffrey out in order to win. However, the police likely affected the ultimate terms under which they were allowed to fight, and may have affected the way in which Sullivan fought.

The truth regarding these issues is somewhat muddled, but is more favorable for Sullivan than some historians believe. *The National Police Gazette* two weeks after the bout provided a somewhat ambiguous account that appears to be an amalgamation of multiple sources, and reveals the general confusion about the bout that has prevailed to this day.

The article indicated that Sullivan weighed 210 pounds and was not in his best physical condition. It said that Sullivan's condition was markedly different than it had been when he fought for "the championship of the world" in 1882, when he took on Paddy Ryan.

McCaffrey was described as mostly defensive in the 1st round, utilizing Tug Wilson tactics, dodging and eluding, clinching, slipping and falling. In the 2nd, Dominick continued fighting defensively, ducking and running about. He landed a hard punch, but a powerful Sullivan counter left uppercut landed solidly, and McCaffrey thereafter fought "more warily." He clinched, but was pushed and knocked into the ropes, taking punches to the body and head. Dominick did land a few light blows.

In the 3rd round, in a clinch, the two hit each other about the ears, and McCaffrey went to his knees. After a punch under the right ear, body blows followed and McCaffrey went down again, retiring to his corner "very groggy." In the 4th, Dominick fought to survive as he was driven to the ropes, landing a counter to the neck. Sullivan rushed and Dominick partly went down, grabbing John's hips.

McCaffrey landed a shot in the 5th, but seemed to voluntarily go down to avoid Sullivan's onslaught. The round ended with Dominick on the ropes. In the 6th, they clinched, and "both went down heavily, with Sullivan on top." Some secondary accounts have indicated that this is the point when the bout was stopped, blaming Sullivan for a foul, but this article stated that the bout continued, with McCaffrey punching at Sullivan until he was countered and they clinched again and the round ended.[5]

After the bout concluded,

> McCaffrey then went over to Sullivan, both shook hands and the referee gave his decision, which was that Sullivan was the winner, but no one heard it.... The referee said, but in a tone to be heard only by those nearest the platform: "I decide that all through the contest Mr. Sullivan has had the best of it. Besides that on one or two occasions when McCaffrey went down he struck Sullivan on the leg."

It mentioned nothing about there being a 7th round. The way McCaffrey acted after the 6th round in shaking hands gave the impression that he understood the bout was over. From its description of the fight, it certainly seemed that Sullivan was the better man. The exhibition was called poor. McCaffrey had landed as much as Sullivan, but his lighter weight and force made him appear weak.

Later, it said that "McCaffrey claimed he injured his right hand during the contest. He claimed the referee should have decided the affair a draw.... Sullivan will not accept McCaffrey's challenge to fight with bare knuckles to a finish within three months because he is under engagement with a minstrel troupe." There, the dispute is not the conclusion of the bout but that McCaffrey was upset at the decision and wanted another chance in another fight, to the finish.

McCaffrey was also reported to have said, "We fought 7 rounds, and at the end of the seventh round I says to Sullivan and his seconds: 'Here, now we're here let's fight to a finish.' 'No,' says Sullivan, 'this match was for 6 rounds, and we've fought 'em.' Now what could be fairer than my proposition?" Yet, nothing was said in the article about there having been a 7th round. Even if there was an extra round fought, clearly Sullivan believed that it was supposed to be a fixed duration, 6-round bout.

However, oddly enough, earlier the article stated that "it was mutually agreed and ratified in the protocol that the men should battle to a finish." Obviously, a finish fight had no rounds limitation. Why then would McCaffrey have shaken hands and the referee rendered a decision? Ultimately it is left unclear exactly how it all went down, but the general impression from the article was that both understood that the fight was over and that McCaffrey, albeit not entirely satisfied by the decision, understood that he had lost, and wanted another chance.[6]

The New York Times' day after the fight report had a slightly different view of matters, but also revealed the confusion. It called the fight "tame and bloodless" and "little more than a clever sparring match of six rounds with three-ounce gloves." The crowd was disappointed by the lack of slugging.

McCaffrey was described as being in better condition than Sullivan at the end of the 6th. However, the fight description appears favorable for Sullivan, who was likely more fatigued because he had done most of the work. Sullivan was listed as being 205 pounds to McCaffrey's 160 pounds. This version said that McCaffrey went down to his knees twice in the 1st round. He tried to keep away in the 2nd. In the 3rd, Dominick was pushed to the ropes and a blow to the neck caused him to slip and fall to his knees. The fight slowed in the 4th round, but McCaffrey was again sent to the ropes. Sullivan chased him in the final two rounds, but Dominick ducked and retreated until it ended.

It too noted that the referee's decision was inarticulately announced in a manner which only few could hear. However, it was in Sullivan's favor because he had forced the fighting and scored the most points. Thus, a decision was rendered immediately after the bout.

The article was somewhat critical of the decision, indicating that the crowd felt it should have gone the other way, but not for the reasons one might think. "If the agreement was that they were to fight six rounds on exactly equal terms, the decision cannot be found fault with, but it has been the understanding all along that if McCaffrey was not knocked out in six rounds he was to be considered the winner." The criticism of the decision was lodged under the belief that it was one of those deals where Sullivan had agreed that if he failed to knock out his foe within the stipulated number of rounds, then McCaffrey would be deemed the unofficial winner and entitled to a monetary bonus. However, as will be discussed, legal circumstances may have prevented the bout from being fought under those terms.

Interestingly, also in *The New York Times* was a more local August 30 report out of Toledo, Ohio, indicating that when the referee was questioned regarding his decision, he stated that he had made no decision.

> He thinks Sullivan had the best of the fight so far as fighting points were concerned, but if the Boston boy was to knock out McCaffrey in six rounds he failed, as the Pittsburg lad came up smilingly every round. He has not seen the agreement as yet under which they fought, and cannot, in consequence, render a decision.

If there was any uncertainty, it was only regarding whether Sullivan was supposed to knock him out. Thus, it seems clear that if it was to be decided based on points, Sullivan won, but the referee may have been concerned that the agreement was for Sullivan to knock him out, which had not occurred. The contest had been decided on points for Sullivan, but if someone had produced a contract with terms requiring Sullivan to knock McCaffrey out or lose, then the referee might have changed his decision. He likely only wavered and hedged

Dominick McCaffrey. From Billy Edwards, *The Portrait Gallery of Pugilists of England, America, Australia* (Chicago: Athletic Publishing Co., 1894). Clay Moyle, www.prizefightingbooks.com.

afterwards because of the criticism by those who believed that Sullivan was required to knock him out.

The other issue was whether the fight should have been continued to a finish. After McCaffrey had "heard the referee's decision he fired up, and demanded that the fight go on to a finish, but Sullivan's friends paid no attention to him." Thus, it appears that Mac asked for the fight to continue only after the decision was already rendered.

It was reported a couple days after the bout that McCaffrey's proposition to fight to the finish was for the fight to take place within the next three months. Sullivan countered with different monetary terms, and for the fight to take place within three weeks. "This proposition has been sent to McCaffrey and has not yet been heard from."

There was apparently some ambiguity in the original terms of the contest regarding the agreed upon duration.

> The written agreement provided that the fight should be six rounds or to a finish. Sullivan claims that the clause "or to a finish" was to cover a fight of less than six rounds. McCaffrey's understanding was that the clause was to be taken literally without any reference to the six rounds.[7]

The impression here is that if the fight was to be one to the finish, it would have simply said that, rather than alluding to the 6 rounds. Certainly, it was an odd phrasing, because a fight to the finish should have been stated as being just that, and a fixed duration bout should have simply been listed as such as well. Combining the two phrases was somewhat of a contradiction and a unique oddity.

As will be seen in other fight descriptions, it was likely not anticipated that more rounds would be fought. The "or to a finish" phrasing was not mentioned in pre-fight accounts regarding how long the bout was scheduled, nor did it exist in some post-fight accounts of the terms. "6 rounds, or to a finish" might have been the offer sent by Sullivan when they were negotiating terms, meaning that John was willing to accept a fight of either 6 rounds, or one to the finish. The general discussion of the bout, though, was that it was to be a 6 rounder.

A couple of weeks before the bout, *The Brooklyn Daily Eagle* reported that "six rounds, Marquis of Queensberry rules are to be fought." In fact, the title of the article was "To Fight Six Rounds."[8] *The New York Clipper* a week before the fight also reported that they were to fight 6 rounds, Queensberry rules.[9] Thus, it appears understood that it was going to be a 6-round bout.

Bolstering the likelihood that it was a fixed duration bout was the fact that the legal authorities made an attempt to prevent it. On August 29, the day of the fight, John L. "signed a bond in the sum of $1,000 by which Sullivan is bound not to engage in any fight or contention, commonly called a prize fight.... This, it is maintained, does not include a glove contest or a sparring exhibition."[10] This circumstance would have negated any previous contract terms to the contrary, and it may have also affected Sullivan's performance. With the law looking over his shoulder so as to prevent brutality, not only could it not have been a fight to the finish, but there may have been an expectation for John L. to limit his slugging.

The Police Gazette later reported that the referee had reaffirmed his decision for Sullivan, stating that the authorities had forbidden a knockout or slugging, and so as it was understood that it was merely a boxing exhibition, he decided on points.[11] Of course, if the authorities had forbidden a knockout, then the fight could not under those circumstances be continued and fought to a finish, nor could Sullivan be expected to knock him out without being subject to arrest and bond forfeiture. Thus, it had to only be a 6- round points bout.

Other national post-fight reports suggested that Sullivan was more cautious in the bout because he had signed the bond as a result of the anti-fight pressure, and because the sheriff had been present and had instructed them to behave. This bolsters the referee's argument that scientific points were to count, as well as the argument that it could not have been a finish fight.[12]

However, some of Sullivan's comments indicated that he was trying to knock McCaffrey out, and he even claimed to have done so. In one interview, Sullivan alleged that McCaffrey was knocked out in the 2nd and 3rd rounds, and was down over a minute. He also claimed that Dominick was illegally assisted to his feet by his cornermen in the 3rd round. However, the referee did not award John the fight at those times because he was afraid of the howling pro-McCaffrey mob, most of which had revolvers. Sullivan apparently had in his possession six photographs of the fight, three of which showed Mac lying down in a heap looking as if he was knocked out.

However, *The New York Times* quoted Sullivan as providing an excuse for why he failed to knock him out, saying, "How could I knock a man out ... who kept running away from me?" It said that there was "little doubt that Sullivan wanted to administer a good punishment to his adversary." Either way, Sullivan did not claim to be holding back.

Some reports indicated that Sullivan was declared the winner (in part) on account of a foul, McCaffrey possibly having kicked, punched, or grabbed Sullivan's legs. The referee may simply have mentioned McCaffrey's fouls to further justify his decision. Sullivan claimed that McCaffrey illegally tried to throw him several times by grabbing him around the legs.

Sullivan also alleged that McCaffrey's brother pulled a gun and told him that if he hit his brother Dominick, that he would blow Sullivan's brains out. Thus, John L. believed that the referee was frightened and reluctant to disqualify Dominick, despite the rule violations.[13] In his autobiography, Sullivan said Mac's brother pulled the revolver in the 3rd round.[14] This might explain why the referee made a points decision, but referenced the rule violation by Dominick as part of his justification, although McCaffrey had not been disqualified. Of course, this claim also has its holes, because if the sheriff was there, it is unlikely that such events could have happened when Sullivan claimed they did without his brother being disarmed and arrested. However, there may have been so many armed fans that the sheriff did not attempt to do anything, or he may have failed to notice. There is support for the allegation that a gun was pulled after the fight.

As usual, the local papers, *The Cincinnati Commercial Gazette*, *The Cincinnati Evening Post*, and *The Cincinnati Enquirer*, further assist in settling the confusion.

As of August 16, *The Brooklyn Daily Eagle* reported that McCaffrey said he would weigh about 178 pounds when he entered the ring against Sullivan.[15] A couple weeks before the bout, *The Cincinnati Commercial Gazette* reported that Sullivan was not in fighting trim, weighing 230 pounds, or 40 more than his best weight. It said that he was not going to make much of an effort to lose the weight because he felt that he would do up McCaffrey without trouble. A week before the fight, McCaffrey was listed as standing 5'8½" and weighing 165 pounds to Sullivan's 235 pounds.[16]

Yet, *The Cincinnati Evening Post* as of August 25 said that Sullivan had been training and had worked off most of his superfluous flesh. Obviously, he wasn't that overconfident, as had been previously reported. As of the 27th, Sullivan said he was weighing 208 pounds.[17]

The Commercial Gazette on August 28 also reported that Sullivan had managed to get rid of considerable flesh, but said that his weight was still several pounds over his usual. He felt confident, though, saying that he could whip McCaffrey as he pleased.[18] The day before the bout, McCaffrey boxed Dennis Kelleher in preparation.[19] At that point, Dom said that he would enter the ring at about 167 pounds.[20] *The Enquirer's* next-day fight report listed Sullivan as being 210 pounds to McCaffrey's 165 pounds. Dom was listed as standing 5'9".[21]

Regarding the scheduled length of the bout, on August 23, *The Evening Post* reported that a telegram from the champion confirmed that the fight would be with four-ounce gloves, "six rounds, Marquis of Queensberry rules, 'or to a finish.'" Apparently, negotiations as to the terms of the bout were ongoing, and what Sullivan likely meant was that he was agreeable to a fight of either 6 rounds, or one to the finish. A report out of Pittsburg the day before from McCaffrey stated that they would fight to the finish. However, subsequent discussion of the fight gave the impression that it was to be a 6 rounder.

A gentleman named John F. Kennedy laughed at the idea that Sullivan would knock out McCaffrey in the 1st round with one punch, and was willing to wager that Dominick would last *the full 6 rounds.*[22]

On August 26 (three days before the fight), *The Cincinnati Commercial Gazette* advertised in a big headline, "SULLIVAN AND MCCAFFREY WILL FIGHT SIX ROUNDS." This paper said that Queensberry rules would govern, that once a man had his knees off the ground "he is up, and, being up, may be struck by the contending pugilist, who may stand over him till he rises or attempts to do so." Commands to break were to be instantly obeyed. They were to fight in a 24-foot ring, with three-ounce or lighter gloves.[23]

When discussing the fight, most reporters and experts referred to it as a 6 rounder. William Muldoon gave his pre-fight analysis:

> I believe moreover that he will fight Sullivan cleverly, adopting the keeping away from him as his tactics, and thus possibly staying with him throughout the six rounds. But I think that Sullivan, without a day's training, can lick any pugilist living, if Sullivan is in good health and not drinking.... I have never yet seen his face flushed by a blow from the best of them, and he has never received a black eye or bloody nose.... Sullivan's advantages are many: His activity—that of a light weight, his strength—greater than that of any pugilist who ever lived, and his wonderful reach.[24]

However, a passenger on a train upon which Sullivan was traveling claimed that Sullivan had been drinking all night and was thoroughly intoxicated. It was also reported that the local Law and Order League was attempting to discover whether there were any legal means to prevent the bout.[25]

Sullivan was arrested on August 27 and taken before a judge. A $1,000 bond was required and Sullivan pledged that there would not be a prizefight, but only a three-ounce gloved boxing match.[26]

The signing of the bond, in conjunction with Sullivan's prior legal troubles, may have affected his performance. With $1,000 on the line, as well as the threat of arrest, John was much less likely to attempt to score a knockout. That said, after the bout, the excuse John made for not knocking him out was not the law, but Mac's survival tactics. Certainly though, the climate was of the restrictive kind, making it impossible for the bout to be one to the finish. It had to be a limited rounds bout.

The question posed by one reporter was "Will they fight, spar, hippodrome or have a glove contest, or will the authorities interfere?" The sheriff said that he would only allow a sparring match, and that he and his officers would be on hand to prevent any brutalizing contest.[27]

Admission for the bout was originally advertised for $3, $2, and $1.[28] However, on the day of the fight, after half an hour of sales in the morning, the tickets jumped to $6, and eventually, brokers were asking for $20 for a first class front seat.

At 3:05 p.m. on the day of the fight, it was announced that a change was made to the terms of the fight and that it was "to be fought to a finish if not settled in six rounds." This supports those who later said that the fight was supposed to go on to a finish. However, at 3:15 p.m. the sheriff said that he would maintain order and only allow a contest in strict accordance with the law. This was his way of saying that there could not be a fight to the finish. Could the announcement of a finish fight have been a way to further stimulate ticket sales?

Both pugilists wore sleeveless shirts, flesh-colored tights and hose, and rubber-soled shoes. William Tate of Toledo was the referee. One *Commercial Gazette* writer asserted that Sullivan's only correct title was champion of America, though noting that he was practically and frequently called champion of the world.[29]

The Enquirer said the bout was witnessed by 15,000 people "of every element of society," including women. It lasted 7 rounds, after which Sullivan was declared the winner and "still the champion of the world." *The Evening Post* said that the fighting began at 5:45 p.m., and 7 plucky rounds were fought.

The Cincinnati Evening Post (EP) was actually able to publish a same day, evening fight report on August 29, 1885. It and *The Cincinnati Commercial Gazette* (CG) were much more pro-Sullivan than *The Cincinnati Enquirer* (E). *The Enquirer* provided a following morning report, while *The Commercial Gazette* report came out two days later.

The fight by rounds:

1st Round

EP: During the round, Sullivan landed a terrific body blow which sent McCaffrey to the ropes and onto his knees, though Mac landed one on the way down. After a clinch, Sullivan struck Mac, who fell against the ropes again and clinched.

E: This article somewhat minimizes Sullivan's good points and maximizes McCaffrey's. Regarding the fight, Sullivan began aggressively, but Dominick ducked and clinched and hit John in the face. Sullivan rushed at him, but "while McCaffrey avoided being hit by anything but half-arm blows, he was borne down in the north-east corner." Sullivan continued his rushing tactics but could not land cleanly. McCaffrey was taken to the ropes, but landed a punch on John's head. Dominick fell to his knees along the ropes, but rose and clinched. After escaping, he led and landed a punch on Sullivan, "the first clean blow of the round."

2nd Round

EP: They exchanged blows and clinches to the enthusiastic cheers of the crowd. "Honors so far are easy."

E: Dominick began the round eluding and crowding Sullivan. John pushed McCaffrey to the ropes, but Dominick escaped by using a left to the face. Clinching followed to neutralize the subsequent Sullivan rush, and McCaffrey "got off with very little punishment."

Dominick then landed "two stingers with his left full in Sullivan's face," which apparently hit the nose.

3rd Round

EP: Sullivan "led and caught McCaffrey, who fell to his knees." Overall, Dominick's defense held up. However, Sullivan ducked a blow and landed a straight counter right to the face that floored McCaffrey. He then fought McCaffrey to the ropes.

E: Sullivan seemed confused by McCaffrey's tactics and was more cautious, asking McCaffrey why he never forced the fighting. Dom responded that Sullivan was the one who was supposed to knock him out in two punches (apparently what Sullivan had boasted), and asked Sullivan, "Why don't you knock me out?" Dominick continued to elude, until on the inside, "Sullivan's dexter mauler played on the neck and face of his antagonist." McCaffrey hit him in the ribs. A right on the back of John's neck injured Dominick's hand and rendered it useless. In close, Sullivan landed "several half-arm blows on his face and neck" and "McCaffrey was again forced down on the ropes. He arose and resumed the battle."

4th Round

EP: Sullivan led and clinched, forcing Dom through the ropes. After another clinch, Mac led and struck John with a stinger on the jaw. He clinched to avoid Sullivan's blows. Regardless, "It was apparent that Sullivan would win. Sullivan hit McCaffrey two terrible blows on the jaw and forehead, knocking him to his knees."

E: The first two minutes of the round were taken up by Dominick's ducking and hugging Sullivan around the neck, with only inside short arm blows landing. In the breakaway, Sullivan "landed a good blow on the forehead and scored a clean knock-down." Sullivan's rush sent him to the ropes, and a right under McCaffrey's eye drew blood.

5th Round

EP: McCaffrey continued clinching immediately after punching so as to avoid blows, and this angered Sullivan. A Sully straight right to the face brought first blood from McCaffrey. Sullivan "reached him with his left, and McCaffrey went to his knees, but reached Sullivan as he went down. McCaffrey is a little groggy." There was a fight in the crowd at the end of the round.

E: "Sullivan rushed and swung his right and drove the Pittsburger before him, and the latter went down on a push." This is likely the point where all the controversy regarding the length of the fight was caused, owing to the referee's mistake, not the intent of the parties.

> This was a short round, one minute and forty-five seconds being occupied, owing to a mistake of the referee in permitting the men to go to their corners after a fall. McCaffrey was on the floor seven seconds. Dan Murphy, in his anxiety to have Sullivan win, called out time. Mr. Donohue denied time was up, and cried for the men to resume fighting, but Referee Tait, in the confusion that prevailed, ordered the men to their corners.

Having them go to their corners after a fall was very London rules style and should not have happened, causing only half of the round to be fought, and giving Dominick extra recovery time.

The round was not supposed to end and should have continued, so it is possible that perception was that the subsequent fighting which occurred after they went to their corners was considered to be a continuation and completion of the 5th round, rather than as an additional round. Probably because of this mistake, extra fighting resulted, either to make up for the short round or because in the confusion the timekeeper lost track. It clearly was not what was originally intended.

6th Round

EP: To begin the round, Mac, "though badly punished, came pluckily to the front," landing a left to Sullivan's face. Sullivan seemed tired but Mac waited for him to lead. Both were wary and playing for wind, meaning that they took a break in this round.

E: Both were more cautious, but Sullivan remained the aggressor and McCaffrey the matador. Sullivan attempted to no avail to draw him in with feints.

7th Round

EP: Sullivan forced the fighting and managed to get Mac into a corner. They exchanged blows and clinches for the rest of the round, Sullivan being the aggressor. "The decision of the referee could not be heard, some claiming a draw, others a decision in favor of Sullivan. The referee declared Sullivan the winner."[30]

E: The round began like the previous one, and each time Sullivan attacked, McCaffrey was able to avoid the blows. In a clinch, both went to the floor, Sullivan on top. They resumed, each attempting to regain their wind, but time was called.

The local papers gave their post-fight analysis. *The Evening Post* said that Sullivan won the hardest battle of his life. However, its description gave the impression that Sullivan was clearly the better man. *The Commercial Gazette* agreed.

The Enquirer was the dissenter, being critical of Sullivan's performance and very high on McCaffrey, feeling that he had won or at least earned a draw. "McCaffrey can claim the honor of giving Sullivan the hardest tussle of his life. ... at the end of seven good rounds, he was on hand smiling and serene, anxious for more of the medicine, while Sullivan was only too glad to quit."

After the last round, McCaffrey offered to fight to a finish, but Sullivan gave no reply. Then, McCaffrey's brother got into a fight with one of Sullivan's representatives. A revolver was drawn by McCaffrey's brother, but Sullivan and Dominick broke up the melee. Clearly, these were not the type of circumstances where a boxing match was going to continue.

Although the referee gave the decision to Sullivan,

> [T]here are very few persons who do not condemn the decision as outrageous. At best the fight should have been declared a draw, as McCaffrey made equally as good a showing as his opponent. In fact, most people are of the opinion that he had the best of it. In the whole seven rounds of fighting Sullivan never landed a clean blow at long range, while McCaffrey planted his hands right in the champion's face no less than five times.

This article also said of the decision and length of the bout, "The referee declared at the end of the seventh round, for, by some mistake, there was an extra round, 'Sullivan has the best of it,' yet the vast audience that saw the rounds from first to last considered it a draw."

Although there were 7 rounds fought, clearly this extra round was the result of a mistake rather than the original intention and agreement of the boxers. There was obviously confusion by Sullivan and some national reporters regarding just how many rounds were fought because it was advertised as being a 6 rounder, and because one round was truncated.

McCaffrey was complimented for his clever dodging and generalship, being described as a "wiry, active, agile fellow, who jumped round and round like a cat." The referee was criticized as biased for failing to declare a foul when Sullivan hit McCaffrey several times while he was down after a fall.

It is clear that the underdog, smaller McCaffrey "had the sympathy of the crowd." They appreciated his defense and the fact that he was able to last. Yet the same article's description of the fight does not necessarily seem all that favorable towards McCaffrey. It sounded as if he mostly fought to survive, and was down on his knees a number of times.

Of the fight, Sullivan said, "It is a matter of impossibility to fight a man who is continually either running away from you or hugging you like a child would its mother. I am not a sprint-runner."

McCaffrey's interview followed. "'He did have me down; that's so,' he responded while viewing the cut. 'But he didn't knock me down. It was his brute strength, not his science.' ... 'He is the stronger man, of course, but if I didn't show more science in the contest I will never spar again.'"

It was noted that many did not realize that the referee had decided the fight on the merits, points taken into consideration.

> There as elsewhere the mistaken idea prevailed that Sullivan was compelled to knock McCaffrey out, and as that was not done, there was considerable comment. Most of the spectators of the contest did not know that it was decided on its merits, the best points made being taken into consideration.

Apparently, they incorrectly believed that Sullivan was required to knock him out. This may have accounted for the crowd's sympathy and impression that McCaffrey had won or at least earned a draw.

It also said that the referee later hedged regarding whether he had made a decision. He stated that he had not awarded a decision to Sullivan, but had merely said that Sullivan had the best of the fight. "This is curious speech to come from a referee who decided a fight."[31]

A couple days later, *The Evening Post* reported McCaffrey's displeasure at the decision, quoting him from an interview he gave the evening of the fight:

> Who did the cleverest work? Why, I tell you, young man, there was never such clever dodging done in a ring as I did today.... I stopped him every time. He stopped me, too, I'll admit, and did it very cleverly. Often, I couldn't get at him when I wanted to, but he never got at me once.

Note that he did not complain that the fight was supposed to continue. He also spoke of the post-fight melee:

> McCaffrey emphatically denied the report that his brother had pulled a revolver on Arthur Chambers, claiming it was a stranger who raised the rumpus, and that he (McCaffrey) took the revolver away from him. The Pittsburg boy showed no marks of the encounter, save a slight scratch on the right cheek, where the skin was broken by one of Sullivan's vicious upper cuts.

McCaffrey claimed that he deserved to win the match and believed that he could knock out Sullivan with bare knuckles. His trainer said, "The conditions were that if Sullivan did not whip McCaffrey in six rounds the fight was to go on to a finish. Mac was ready and anxious to go on, and if he is not entitled to the entire gate receipts, he is at least entitled to one-half." Gate receipts were split in the event of a draw. Declaring Sullivan the winner meant that the greater share of the gate receipts went to John, which explains why McCaffrey and his trainer were so upset at the decision. Sullivan in his autobiography claimed that he made about $5,200, but it was likely more.

One of Sullivan's backers rhetorically asked, "Who won the fight? Sullivan, of course. Why, in the third round, McCaffrey's brother had to pick him up off the ropes. The fight should have been given to us then and there, but the referee ordered the men to their corners. A minute and forty seconds had been lost." Under Queensberry rules, a fighter had to rise from a knockdown unassisted and continue within 10 seconds. This too confirms that there was a short round.

The referee gave a statement from his hometown of Toledo, Ohio. "He says that the match was a regular farce, and that as Sullivan displayed the most science, and that as McCaffrey did nothing but dodge to escape punishment, he based his decision on each man's individual merits." Another report out of Toledo said,

[The referee] says that Sullivan had the best of the fight from the beginning; that Sullivan had the opportunity to knock out McCaffrey, but for some reason did not take advantage of it; does not know whether Sullivan agreed to knock McCaffrey out in six rounds or not; if that was the agreement he did not do it; his decision is in favor of Sullivan; a clever big man can do a clever little man every time; the decision was on the merits of the fighting.

It is interesting that the referee noted that Sullivan could have knocked him out but did not. Again, the question arises whether Sullivan was simply unable to do so because of his poor condition, Mac's tactics, or because he was holding back, fearful of the law.

It was also said that Sullivan had been drunk ever since the fight was over.[32]

The Cincinnati Commercial Gazette said that the average citizen was unable to decide whether the match was a genuine scientific contest or a farce. "He is sure it wasn't one of those 'slugging matches' he has read about." This supports the version that the bout was tame, that either McCaffrey purely fought to survive, or that Sullivan did not or could not make much of an effort to stop him, or both. Perhaps Mac's science kept it tame.

Another writer criticized that McCaffrey had used clinching as a way to avoid blows, in addition to other defensive tactics used to neutralize and survive rather than to win:

A clinch stops the fisticuffs, and the referee orders them to part. Thus a clinch may be practiced as a dodge to escape blows. This was McCaffrey's great tactics....
McCaffrey's play was to keep out of the way of blows, and by dodging to keep through six rounds with out getting knocked out.... McCaffrey's tactics were to evade, dodge back, duck his head, dodge forward into Sullivan's arms, and dodge down to his knees. He played this game with expertness and activity; but this was not fighting....
On the other hand, the beholder could not tell for certain whether Sullivan was doing his best to knock out McCaffrey. As it looked, there were many times when if he had followed up quickly he could have finished the other one. And his antagonist's blows seemed unable to get in with any force on Sullivan.

McCaffrey had engaged in what The Commercial Gazette had previously called "the eternal dodging and monkeying of the old ring." This author said that the fight had not been brutal, but "gentle enough for an entertainment for a peace society convention." In fact, the writer complimented this new limited form of fighting where fists were muffled with mittens, where there was no wrestling, throwing and falling upon, or holding the head with one arm and punching it with the other, and where a clinch was followed by a break. This form of fighting was said to have brought about a revival of the ring, where police protected rather than prevented bouts. "Convenient places and police regulations have enabled men of wealth and high social and political station to attend these displays."[33]

There was some post-fight discussion regarding what the terms of the fight were. It was said that a New York correspondent reported that the original proposed agreement was for 6 rounds, or to a finish, scientific points to be considered, with the winner to take the gate receipts. Sullivan objected to the clause which stated that scientific points were to count, and so it was removed. However, the referee was not shown the agreement, and when he took his place on the day of the bout, he "merely stated that it was for a six-round glove contest for the championship of the world." Of course, no one corrected him or disagreed, so the fighters and managers were on notice.

When asked for his decision, the referee said that all through the contest Sullivan had the best of it, and besides that, on one or two occasions, when McCaffrey went down, he struck Sullivan on the leg. The paper was critical of the statement by the referee that Mac had struck him on the leg because no claim of foul had been made and the referee did not at the time call attention to it. Thus, it had to be decided on scientific points, the very thing to which Sullivan had apparently not agreed.

> The generally understood conditions were that Sullivan was to knock McCaffrey out in six rounds, if not sooner, the latter clause being expressed by the words "or to a finish." The whole matter of conditions is in a muddle, no two persons understanding them in the same way.

That summed it up. Apparently that paper understood the phrase "6 rounds, or to a finish" to mean that Sullivan had to knock him out in 6 rounds or less, consistent with what many in the crowd had believed.

Less than a week after the bout, *The Cincinnati Enquirer* published the articles of agreement, which were signed on July 31, 1885. They simply stated that it was to be a "six round glove contest, Marquis of Queensberry rules to govern." This article also mentioned that Sullivan had objected to a clause stating that scientific points were to count. McCaffrey's manager said that the referee would have decided it a draw had he reviewed the terms before the bout. However, nothing was mentioned about Sullivan being required to score a knockout, nor did those terms mention anything about a fight to a finish. They also said that three-ounce gloves were to be used, though this paper said that one-ounce gloves were actually used. The winner was to receive 60 percent of the gross receipts.[34] Clearly, there had been some confusion as to the terms, which may of necessity have been subsequently modified to satisfy the legal concerns which arose after they were originally agreed upon.

Sullivan issued a challenge to McCaffrey to fight to a finish within three weeks. "A private meeting is suggested, as it would be almost impossible to carry a public fight through in any State without official interference." This bolsters the argument that a finish fight would not have been allowed by the police when they had fought.[35]

Regardless of the confusion, in reviewing multiple descriptions of the bout, it seems that Sullivan had the best of it. McCaffrey fought mostly to survive, and his blows had little to no effect. Given the legal circumstances, the bout was not going to be allowed to go farther than it did. Most reporters and members of the public generally considered Sullivan to have been the world champion, unconcerned by or unaware of the version where Sullivan stopped fighting or was unwilling to continue. Some felt that Sullivan was required to knock McCaffrey out to win, but this was unclear. Public admiration of Sullivan certainly

did not wane after the bout. However, this fight did provide some fuel for those who won-
dered how well John could do in a fight to the finish with someone who could last a long
time, especially if John continued drinking and failed to maintain his physical condition.

The two never fought again. A year and a half later, in 1887, McCaffrey was knocked
out in the 2nd round by 175-pound Patsy Farrell.[36]

CHAPTER 13

The Plateau and the Break

Sullivan had fought four times in 1885, but after the August McCaffrey bout, John L. subsequently became less active, not fighting in an official bout again for just over a year. Sullivan stated that he was tired of chasing men around the ring and was considering retiring. He had actually been discussing the idea of retirement for the past year or so. He was wealthy and perhaps a bit weary of fighting, having been boxing's dominant figure for the past five years. He eventually tried to make arrangements for some bouts, but continued to run up against legal obstacles.

During the interim, Sullivan engaged himself with the Lester and Allen's minstrel show for 21 weeks doing statuary acting at a salary of $500 per week. All he had to do was pose as statues of ancient and modern gladiators. He started traveling with them on September 20, 1885, and continued this business until May 1886.[1] Sullivan began realizing that he could make money without having to get into the ring. People would pay merely to see him. He would further capitalize on this reality of fame a few years later.

In May 1886, Sullivan arranged a rematch with Charlie Mitchell in Chicago, but the fight fell through because citizens appealed to the mayor to prevent it. It was rescheduled for July 1886 in New York, but the mayor there also prevented it from taking place. John then became a partner in a New York saloon business.[2]

Sullivan still managed to fight a couple times in late 1886, and also gave a number of exhibitions. On September 18, 1886, in Alleghany City, Pennsylvania, a 205–210 pound Sullivan took on 5'10½", 185- to 187-pound Frank Herald. The powerful Herald had a number of wins, including KO22 "Sparrow" Golden, KO1 Jim Cannon, and KO1 Mike Conley.[3] One paper called him the "new wonder."[4]

A semi-local source, The Philadelphia Press, presented its own special reports out of Pittsburg. At first, consistent with the legal impediments that Sullivan had been running up against lately, the local authorities did not want to allow the bout. However, the mayor allowed it to be licensed with the agreement that there was to be no slugging or knocking out. In order to exclude "the tough element," the admission price was set at $2 minimum. Actually, it was $2 for the promenade, $3 for a seat, and about ¼ of the 1,000 in attendance paid for the $5 location. The Pittsburg Dispatch said 3,000 attended.

Although the police were told that it was merely going to be a scientific sparring exhibition for points, they were suspicious. "Private talk among the people directly interested showed conclusively that the contest was to be nothing short of a real fight."[5] The New York Clipper reported that it was a scheduled 6 rounder for a stipulated percentage of the admission receipts. The boxers represented that they were to simply spar scientifically, for points, "the old gag, which the officials of New York, Jersey City and Brooklyn declined to swallow—being, in all probability, the nearest correct."

The day before the fight, *The Pittsburg Dispatch* reported that Herald was weighing 186 pounds. Sullivan said that he felt well and had not touched a drop of liquor in eleven weeks. The *Dispatch*'s day-after-the-fight report said that Sullivan tipped the beam at 210 pounds, with Herald at 187.[6] Both the *Philadelphia Press* and *Philadelphia Inquirer* agreed that Sullivan weighed 205 pounds but looked larger, while Herald weighed 186 and looked small compared to Sullivan.

Sullivan entered the ring before Herald, attired in white trunks and light blue stockings, with the national colors for his belt. Herald wore drab tights and a blue belt. Reports of the glove size varied, with claims of 2, 3, and 4 ounces.

The National Police Gazette, Philadelphia Inquirer (using a Pittsburg report), *Philadelphia Press*, Associated Press (AP), and *New York Clipper*, as well as *The Pittsburg Dispatch* and *Pittsburgh Daily Post*, mostly agreed upon the facts, but with some variations:

In the 1st round, initially both were cautious. Sullivan feinted, smiling nonchalantly. He kept his right across his breast and his left well out. John was the aggressor, but Herald kept at a distance, dancing around with agility, "lithe and active as a cat." Herald moved about until an aggravated Sullivan eventually made a rush at him and landed a right to the stomach. Herald countered to the chest, but received a right on the nose that "sent him flying half across the ring." Herald then fought hard, exchanging blows with John for a while, but his punches had little effect. A succession of clinches followed. Eventually, during a clinch, Herald was pushed over the ropes. The referee ordered them to break, but the maddened fighters did not listen. They had to be pried apart by their attendants and forced into their chairs, the round ending just a bit early as a result. The AP said the round lasted 2¾ minutes.

The New York Clipper said of the

Frank Herald. From Billy Edwards, *The Portrait Gallery of Pugilists of England, America, Australia* (Chicago: Athletic Publishing Co., 1894). Clay Moyle, www.prizefightingbooks.com.

1st round that Herald generally clinched when Sullivan rushed. By the end of the round, Herald was slightly bleeding at the nose. "The round might be called a succession of clinches and breaks, and neither man could do much execution."

The 2nd round began cautiously, but was to be a much more exciting round, as Herald fought more. At first, Sullivan followed him and feinted, looking for an opening. Eventually Frank attacked, but once embraced by Sullivan on the inside, was hit by multiple rights to the head. Herald slipped away and landed a good right under the eye, which was the only clear blow that he landed. A stunned Sullivan "seemed staggered for an instant, and was apparently too surprised to do more than protect himself from the blows that Herald was showering on his guard." However, Sullivan gathered himself and dropped Herald with a huge uppercut under the chin. Frank quickly rose and clinched. "The fight had become a mere rough-and-tumble. Herald slipped and fell again, when the Chief of Police and his officers rushed in and with difficulty separated the men." Both fighters were anxious to continue but were not allowed to do so.

Sullivan then made a dash at a reporter who was also acting as Herald's timekeeper. The reporter reached for his revolver, but the police disarmed him and Sullivan was forced to his chair.

Sullivan later asked the police chief, "What did you stop us for? ... I just wanted to get another good square crack at that fellow Herald, and I would have paralyzed him." The chief responded, "I know that ... and that is just why I stepped in between you at that juncture."

The Philadelphia Press and *New York Clipper* said of the 2nd round that Herald continued moving, but Sullivan followed and tracked him down until he finally got into range and they mixed it up. After Herald landed a left to the jaw,

> Sullivan smashed him straight on the mouth with such force that he fell to the floor like a log. His head struck the boards with such force that the sound echoed through the building. The police at once rushed into the ring and declared that the fight must end. Both fighters desired a resumption, but the Chief said he was satisfied that Herald would be either seriously injured or killed if the fight continued.

It was also said that Herald was dropped "by one of the most terrific blows that ever came from a man's shoulder. The blow seemed almost fatal. So much so that the police, numbering about eight, rushed on the platform and stopped the fight." When compared to McCaffrey, Herald was credited as being a better man and putting up a better showing.

The Pittsburg Dispatch said of the 2nd round that Herald missed his right and was countered with a right and left that dropped him. He quickly rose and was struck by a right to the jugular, lifting him off his feet onto his back. The police began mounting the stage. Herald rose and Sullivan hit him with a left to the ribs before he was clinched. The police chief then stepped between them and announced that it must stop.

One non-local source said that

> Herald's blows did not affect Sullivan in the least, except to make him angry, while it was only a question of time when Herald would be stopped, and might be badly injured in addition. This was so evident to the police that the contest was ended when Herald was knocked down in the second round by an upper-cut.

It credited Herald, though, for doing some good infighting and showing no fear.[7]

The crowd was upset at the stoppage, howling and yelling. The referee announced that Sullivan was the winner. "I give the fight to Sullivan ... as he manifestly had the best of it up to the time of the interruption by the police." This was much to the chagrin of Herald's management, which correctly claimed that he was ready and willing to continue. Some writers implied criticism that there was a decision, because Herald was still able to fight on. However, *The Clipper* revealed that the referee had based "his decision on the clause in the agreement providing that, in case of police interference, the man who had the better of the encounter should be declared the victor." Thus, there appeared to be an agreed upon justification for the referee rendering a decision, despite the fact that the bout had been prematurely terminated and both men willing to continue.[8]

Despite Sullivan's year of inactivity, he still had what it took, and he afterwards demonstrated his conceit. He gave a speech saying, "I have had clearly the best of the fight as you have seen and as the referee has decided. I will say that it is no shame to Herald to be defeated by a pugilist of my ability.... I remain your kind and sincere friend, John L. Sullivan." Later when asked what he thought of Herald, he said, "Why, he is like all of the rest of them, no good.... I had figured on going easy in the first round in order that he might think he was a fighter.... He said I tried to throw him over the ropes. Why, he is a chump."

Sullivan also provided some insight into some of his strategies. When asked why he didn't knock Herald out when he had him in a corner, Sullivan responded,

> Why, there's no use in hitting a man when you first chase him into a corner. He is always dead wary to get out, and the chances are you won't find him, while if you let him out he will think you are getting tired or afraid and the next time he gets there why he will be off his guard, and you can punch him. People may say what they please about fighting, but I tell you that a good fighter is a man who uses his brains. He has to know what he is doing and how to do it.
>
> My objective point in hitting is the corner of a man's shoulder, and if he ducks his head he is bound to get it in the neck. A man will break his dukes if he goes hitting at his antagonist's skull.[9]

Some said that Sullivan in part won his fights through fear. "Sullivan frightens his man every time. They lose their nerve the moment they face him." Another said, "They all know that if John gets in a blow they are virtually done for. This makes them nervous and they lose their heads."[10]

Almost three weeks later, on October 7, 1886, Herald was knocked out in the 6th round by Joe Lannon.[11] Lannon would later become a Sullivan sparring partner. In November 1886, Herald was knocked out in the 1st round by Jake Kilrain.

Sullivan in his autobiography said that after the Herald match, another touring combination was formed, which included Joe Lannon, Steve Taylor, George La Blanche (other sources spell his name Le Blanche; for consistency, my text uses the La spelling), Jimmy Carroll and Patsy Kerrigan. They opened in Racine, Wisconsin, and then went to Minneapolis and St. Paul, as well as other cities, on the way to San Francisco.[12]

The weekly *New York Clipper* reported in early November that the Sullivan combination had been engaging in a Western tour, but had not been creating the expected furor, owing to the absence of locals willing to take Sullivan on.[13] Local reports confirmed that men willing to face Sullivan had been growing scarce, so combination members sparred with each other.

An October 25 report said that Sullivan had been in Chicago and was headed to Minnesota. Traveling with him were George La Blanche, known as the "Marine," Steve Taylor, Jimmy Carroll, Dan Murphy, Jim McKeon, Pete McCoy, and George Weir, the "Spider." Kerrigan and Lannon were not mentioned (they likely toured with him at a later time). $1,000 was being offered to anyone who could stand up before Sullivan for 4 rounds.[14]

On October 28, 1886, in New York, the dedication of the Statue of Liberty, a gift from

France, took place. It had taken ten years to design, construct, transport, and reassemble. The next day, on October 29, the Sullivan combination performed in Stillwater, Minnesota, to a good house.

Each set-to between combination members lasted 3 rounds. First, George La Blanche, who earlier that year had been knocked out in the 13th round (reported as La Blanche's first loss)[15] by world middleweight champion Jack Dempsey in a very good fight, sparred heavyweight Tom Hinch. Next, Jimmy Carroll and Steve Taylor boxed, then Sullivan and Hinch, Carroll and La Blanche, and finally Sullivan and Taylor.[16] One report said that Sullivan was in excellent condition at 231½ pounds, and no one was willing to stand before him for 4 rounds.[17]

George La Blanche (Library of Congress, Prints & Photographs Division).

On October 30, they performed in St. Paul. One local newspaper said that judging by the reception given, Sullivan was the most popular man in Minnesota. "Never in the history of Northwestern sport has a larger crowd gathered to see any pugilistic contest." One said that the audience numbered over 4,000 people, filling every chair in the rink. Another local source said the audience numbered 3,000.

First, 165-pound Hinch, called the Illinois champion, and the 200-pound Taylor sparred. Next, the 5'7", 165-pound La Blanche knocked out a 140-pound local man in the 1st round. La Blanche then sparred 3 rattling rounds with the much smaller Carroll.

Sullivan, "the champion of all champions," then sparred with Hinch. Sullivan contented himself with just demonstrating his defense.

> [Sullivan's] cleverness was the feature of this contest ... the only work Hinch could do was to attempt to hit the champion. In this he was entirely unsuccessful and the man who has never had a blackened eye or scratched body from fighting easily managed to keep Hinch at a distance.

Following this, Taylor sparred Carroll 4 slow rounds, and Hinch sparred 3 even rounds with Jack Keefe. Sullivan and Taylor then closed the show in a 3 rounder. Sullivan was more aggressive this time, and his "celebrated rushes were gently illustrated, as were those wicked lefts which have been known to crack a two-inch plank."

A fighter had been scheduled to box Sullivan in an attempt to stand up for 4 rounds, but he did not appear. Such cowardice (or intelligence) was expected when it came to standing before Sullivan. One paper called the exhibitions tame and disappointing.[18]

They exhibited in Minneapolis on November 2. Jack Keefe was advertised as being willing to attempt to last 4 rounds, but the local newspaper accurately predicted that Keefe would be a no show, for he wouldn't have lasted ten seconds. The resulting exhibitions were called tame hippodromes.[19]

Almost two months after fighting Herald, on November 13, 1886, in San Francisco, a 28-year-old Sullivan fought a rubber match with 33-year-old Paddy Ryan, perhaps owing to the disappointing premature manner in which their second bout was terminated as the result of police interference. They wore four-ounce gloves, and Ryan probably weighed about 220 pounds.[20]

A primary source accounting of the fight alleged to have been released out of San Francisco, repeated verbatim in at least four sources, including The National Police Gazette, indicated that Ryan began the fight aggressively, hitting Sullivan with two rights on the cheek. The two fought savagely, with Ryan mostly doing the leading early in the 1st round. The fighting was so severe that Paddy began to show signs of fatigue towards the end of the round, and upon seeing this Sullivan made a rush, but was clinched, ending the round.

In the 2nd round, Ryan was again the aggressor and landed to both the body and head, but had less effective power owing to his fatigue. Sullivan noticed this and began forcing the fight more. Ryan was dropped three times, the impression being that each knockdown was the result of body blows, although it is somewhat unclear. Paddy clinched to avoid punishment.

They slugged in the 3rd round,

Paddy Ryan. From Billy Edwards, *The Portrait Gallery of Pugilists of England, America, Australia* (Chicago: Athletic Publishing Co., 1894). Clay Moyle, www.prizefightingbooks.com.

but Sullivan forced matters, being fresher. John L. dropped Paddy with a right to the jaw. The hurt Ryan rose and threw a left that was blocked, and Sullivan again landed a right, sending Ryan "down as if shot out of a cannon. It was a knock-out of the cleanest kind. Ryan laid on the floor utterly unable to move." The police entered the ring, but it did not matter because Paddy was out cold. Sullivan picked him up and carried him to his corner.[21]

The local *San Francisco Examiner* said that Ryan was aggressive in the 1st round, and towards the end of the round threw "some heavy sledge-hammer blows that reached his opponent's face," while Sullivan mostly used his left and only delivered a few hard blows.

Sullivan "commenced work" in the 2nd round and delivered a "terrific short-arm blow on the chin" that dropped Ryan, but Paddy quickly rose and attacked again. However, the tiring Ryan's blows had lost their force. Blows to the head and body dropped Ryan twice more.

In the 3rd round, a blow under the left ear knocked Ryan through the ropes. He rose, and Sullivan "struck out like a battering ram, showering blows upon the defenseless face of his opponent and the latter again fell through the ropes with a crash, bleeding from the mouth." Sullivan knelt down, lifted the unconscious Paddy up, and carried him to his chair.[22]

The San Francisco Chronicle said 9,000 persons, which only included about 6–8 women, paid for tickets priced at $2.00, $1.50, and $1.00. They witnessed Sullivan easily knock out Ryan, as John seemed to be a "giant toying with a child."

A number of exhibitions constituted the warm up, including one between Con Riordan and Steve Taylor. Riordan would years later be killed in a sparring session by future champion Bob Fitzsimmons.

Sullivan appeared "a trifle too fleshy," but it didn't matter. Very little slugging was done in the 1st round, and although Paddy tried to force matters and landed the most blows, they had little effect. Sullivan appeared to be feeling him out.

In the 2nd round, Ryan continued forcing and landed a right. Sullivan responded with a left and right to the jaw, which rattled Ryan. John avoided an attempted body blow and dropped Ryan with a straight punch to the forehead. Ryan was dropped twice more. The only thing that saved him was the fact that his glove came off when he rose, giving him extra recovery time while the glove was readjusted. Sullivan had it his own way until the end of the round, when he sent Paddy down once more with a blow to the forehead.

In the 3rd round, Paddy's glove again came off amidst the combat. After it was replaced, Sullivan fought him all over the platform and into a corner, where a right landed to the jaw and dropped Ryan. As soon as Paddy rose, he was again knocked down, this time for good. When Paddy's seconds rushed over, John waved them off, picked Paddy up, and carried him to his corner.[23]

Following this win, the new Sullivan combination traveled east, again giving exhibitions. Said to be traveling with Sullivan were Steve Taylor, George La Blanche, Duncan McDonald, called the champion of the Northwest, champion lightweight James Carroll, and Daniel Murphy and James McKeon of Boston. "This combination has more genuine representatives of the fistic art than any ever organized." On December 24 and 25, 1886, the combination appeared in Leadville, Colorado, before a packed theater.[24]

At that time, Sullivan's skill was being more appreciated. *The Denver Daily News* reported that an expert writer from *The Chicago Herald* wrote the following:

You have heard of hundreds of men, when speaking of Sullivan, say, "He wins by brute strength," and I have seldom seen a man who advanced the truth, which is that Sullivan is as clever as any man. His unquestioned ability as to being the hardest hitter ever seen has caused the overlooking of the fact that his blow is always planted where it will do the most good, either upon the jaw or jugular—again, it is certain that could an adversary so land his blow, Sullivan would fall as quickly as another, and yet having knocked out about sixty men, he has never been harmed.

The truth is that Sullivan is a careful, scientific fighter....

Do I think his equal as a pugilist ever trod the earth? Certainly not....

Even in imagination the ancients never conceived such a hitter as Sullivan.[25]

The tour exhibited to a crowded house in Colorado Springs on December 27, 1886. Sullivan gave a sparring exhibition against tour member Duncan McDonald. The 6', 174-pound McDonald had fought Pete McCoy in May 1884. Against McCoy, McDonald broke his right hand in the 3rd round, but fought on for 2 hours and 15 minutes before suffering defeat in the 31st round.[26]

In July 1886, McDonald had fought a 6-round draw against a young, promising amateur boxer named James J. Corbett, who would later become world champion. McDonald was clearly a skilled veteran who knew how to work with someone. There were rumors, not unfounded, that although he and Corbett put on a good show, it was really a friendly arrangement (a hippodrome). McDonald and Corbett might have actually been sparring partners who traveled around giving exhibitions.

McDonald also fought former Sullivan challenger and sparring partner Herbert "the Maori" Slade in August 1886, dropping Slade in the 3rd round before winning an 8-round decision. On September 18, 1886, the same day that Sullivan defeated Frank Herald, McDonald fought a rematch with Slade, this time knocking him out in the 9th round.[27]

A Sullivan-McDonald bout has been listed by most secondary sources as a 4-round draw, but this is incorrect, as the two boxed as touring sparring partners, not in a serious contest.[28] Most secondary sources have failed to realize that McDonald was a tour member who gave a number of exhibitions with Sullivan.

Bolstering that this was just the typical round-robin sparring style of Sullivan's exhibitions and not an actual competition is the fact that on the 27th, McDonald first sparred John Davis for 4 rounds, took a break, and then worked with Sullivan. He would not have first sparred with someone else if he was intending to compete against Sullivan. Set-tos between Walker and Carroll, and Taylor and La Blanche followed. "The event of the evening then took place, being a purely scientific match between John L. Sullivan and Duncan A. McDonald." Calling their exhibition a "purely scientific match" was the paper's way of saying that it was not a serious bout, but merely a friendly sparring exhibition.[29]

It was said to be a highly satisfactory exhibition. "The champion was in fine form, and he delighted the large audience with his exhibition of scientific sparring." One paper said that Sullivan's sparring was part of a joint engagement with a Presbyterian pastor. "The one lectured on physical science, the other illustrated it, and both won applause."[30]

They were set to give exhibitions in Denver on December 28 and 29 before heading to Georgetown, Central, and Cheyenne.[31] *The Denver Daily News* said of their December 28, 1886, Denver exhibition that the crowd filled the 1,000 chairs and intruded upon the standing room and beyond. As was the case on the previous evening, the first exhibition was between John Davis and Duncan McDonald. They slapped at one another for 4 rounds. A number of other exhibitions followed.

[T]he champion of the champions came on, and sparred four of his peculiar rounds with McDonald, who does excellent work both in stopping and leading considering the fact that Sullivan is in front of him, liable at any time to expend a portion of his surplus strength. Sullivan's method of sparring is beyond criticism. It is the basis of the modern school, and to its system of throwing the weight with the leads and follows is due the terrible execution with soft gloves that has become more or less common in Sullivan's time. Sullivan looks a great deal better than he did three years ago when he appeared at the Exposition building with McCoy, Taylor and Slade.[32]

The Denver Tribune-Republican gave its own account of this exhibition show. It said that 1,300 men witnessed the sparring between the most noted and scientific pugilists of the day.

The first bout was between McDonald and Jack Davis. They sparred 4 indifferent rounds, and McDonald was the better man. This was followed by Jimmy Carroll, the champion lightweight of New England, and Dave Walker, then La Blanche and Nathan Brambley, as well as Davis and Walker over 4 tame rounds. Carroll and La Blanche then "gave the only exhibition of the evening which contained any science. La Blanche is without doubt the best sparer, barring Sullivan, that has visited Denver."

Finally, Sullivan sparred with McDonald, who had already worked with Davis. It was said that usually John L. worked with Steve Taylor, but Steve had suffered a sprained elbow. McDonald and Sully sparred 4 rounds.

The two men went at each other as if their lives were at stake. It was give and take, McDonald standing up to his work bravely. Sullivan showed one point of his science by quick movements of his head, completely eluding, on such occasions, the heavy blows which were aimed by McDonald. Sullivan showed his quickness and alertness.... The bout was roundly applauded. Sullivan's weight is 226 pounds, and he is the pink of condition. His physical appearance is that of "The Champion of Champions."

It was said that although most spectators were satisfied, those who knew something of the game realized that the sparrers had generally engaged in "make believe slugging matches" and "sham rough encounters." They were just working with each other and putting on a good show.[33]

The combination exhibited there again the following evening, on the 29th. La Blanche knocked out Professor Smith, the champion Greco-Roman wrestler of the Pacific slope, in the 1st round. McDonald then sparred with La Blanche, "and it was the prettiest exhibition of sparring ever witnessed in Denver. The men proved to be very evenly matched."

Sullivan sparred twice, once with McDonald, and once with Steve Taylor. The wind up with Taylor was "brief but interesting," during which "Sullivan gave a number of his famous 'rushes.'"[34]

A local Georgetown, Colorado, paper reported that the exhibition there on December 30 began with a bout between Duncan McDonald and George La Blanche. McDonald appeared to be the better man. Taylor sparred Carroll. Sullivan then faced McDonald, and "those who have any knowledge of the art could readily see the superiority of the 'big one,' yet the Butte City man is quite an adept." La Blanche and Carroll met in the most even match. The final bout was between Sullivan and Taylor. "Many good points were observed but the cleverness with which the champion ducks his head, thus escaping many a well directed blow, was admired by all. His antagonist stood but a poor show with him."[35]

On January 1, 1887, the combination again performed in Denver before a house that was even more crowded than on the two previous occasions there. The "loud applause which greeted the 'champion of champions' shows to what extent admiration can be carried even for a prize fighter." Sullivan again sparred with McDonald and Taylor, but the prettiest bout of the evening was said to be the one between La Blanche and McDonald. The boxers were said to be heading east, stopping at Topeka and the river towns.[36]

It was reported that at least 615 gloved boxing contests had occurred during 1886.[37] Some old school folks still did not appreciate gloved boxing. A writer for *The National Police Gazette* said:

> Thirteen years ago pugilists fought with bare knuckles and London prize ring rules for the championship, and there was no limit to the number of rounds. Nowadays they fight a stipulated number of rounds with pillows and rules made for convenience, which do not prove who possesses courage and stamina, and yet they style themselves as champions.[38]

Another writer noted the shift in the style of boxing:

> The modern prize fight is a knock-out. It used to be that men would fight one hundred rounds with bare knuckles, while now it is the rule to knock a man out with gloves in a few rounds. It is not that men have less endurance than formerly, for it is not now a question of endurance. The secret is a blow from the shoulder on the side of the neck. Such a blow, fairly planted, knocks a man out. In the modern prize-fight it is a question of skill in getting in this blow. Occasionally two men are so equally matched as to skill that neither can get in this blow until either is too weak to make it effective. In such a fight we have the old contest of endurance.[39]

A reflective Sullivan provided some of his thoughts on boxing:

> The essentials of a thoroughly good fighter are pluck, skill, endurance and a good head on his shoulders. A man fights with his head almost as much as he does with his fist. He must know where to send his blows so they may do the most good. He must economize his strength and not score a hit just for the sake of scoring it.
> I endeavor ... to hit my man above the heart or under the chin, or behind the ear. A man wears out pretty soon if one can keep hammering away in the region of the heart; a blow under the chin or behind the ear will knock out a man quicker than a hundred blows on the cheek or any other portion of the face....
> I can tell pretty well when my man is giving in.... I watch his eyes, and I know at once when the punishment is beginning to tell on him. And when I talk to a man before I stand up before him at all, I can make up my mind whether he is a fighter or not. There is more intelligence required in this business than outsiders give us credit for....
> I do not train ... I know better than to waste my vitality in training.... Now when I meet a man that I think is going to give me some trouble, I will train, but I have not met that man yet.

Sullivan also told of a time when a young man undertook to stand 4 rounds before him. Sully wanted to give the public a good show, so he let the man hammer away at him for a while. After the 2nd round, John asked his second to call out to him about 30 seconds before the next round was over. During the 3rd round, John let him punch away again, and the audience cheered, thinking that the challenger was doing well,

> but at that close range his blows hurt me about as much as you could by fibbing me on the top of the head with a soft glove. There I lay, as snug as you please, taking a great deal of amusement out of the enthusiasm of the audience. Presently my second, who had kept his eyes upon his watch, called out "John," and then I stepped back and landed my young man one under the ear, and that was the last of him.[40]

The Sullivan combination performed before an immense crowd in Kansas City, Missouri, on January 7, 1887.[41]

On January 18, 1887, in Minneapolis, the 211- to 215-pound (sometimes listed as 230), 28-year-old Sullivan took on the approximately 185-pound Patsy Cardiff (sometimes listed

as 200).[42] Cardiff was a worthy contender who had many good wins,
including having an 1885 KO9 over
Billy Wilson (a black fighter who
had an 1885 KO1 over the highly
touted 210- to 220-pound Mervine
Thompson), and victories over former Sullivan foes Professor Donaldson, Captain James Dalton, and
George Rooke. One paper reported
that a 178-pound Cardiff also
scored a June 14, 1885, KO4 over
175-pound Wilson.

In June 1886, Cardiff fought
Charley Mitchell to a 5-round
draw, wherein Patsy dropped
Mitchell and appeared to have the
better of it (though later reports
claimed that Mitchell dropped
Patsy). A few weeks later, in a
rematch with Billy Wilson, Cardiff
knocked him out in the 8th
round.[43]

Cardiff was a Minneapolis
native, and Sullivan in late October
1886 signed to fight him 6 rounds
there. Cardiff said, "Though I may
not whip Sullivan I'll give him a
hard fight and it will be the best
match ever seen in this city."[44]

The local *Minneapolis Tribune*
confirmed the day before the fight
that it was to be a 6-round contest.
It listed the 28-year-old Sullivan as

Patsy Cardiff. From Billy Edwards, *The Portrait Gallery of Pugilists of England, America, Australia* (Chicago: Athletic Publishing Co., 1894). Clay Moyle, www.prizefightingbooks.com.

being 211 pounds. The 24-year-old Cardiff was listed as 5'10" and 185 pounds. The crowd
was the "largest audience ever seen under a roof in Minneapolis."[45] *The National Police Gazette*
said that Sullivan was 229 pounds, while Cardiff had worked down from 200 pounds to
185.[46]

Sources generally report that against the quick, defensive Cardiff, Sullivan broke his
left arm in the 1st round when striking Patsy. A handicapped Sullivan primarily used his
right thereafter, but Cardiff mostly remained cautious until the final round, when he attacked
a bit. The fairly dull bout was called a draw after the 6 rounds were concluded. It was not
revealed until after the fight that Sullivan's arm was broken.

One non-local primary source reported that there was a great deal of clinching in the
bout and that neither man was particularly aggressive or effective. The somewhat contradic-
tory report was unclear regarding whether Sullivan broke his arm or wrist, striking a stake
or Cardiff's neck. Sullivan concealed his injury, but thereafter the action was tame. Cardiff

was unaware of the injury and did not seize his opportunity, as he later "said he expected to be knocked out, and he acted with great caution, knowing Sullivan was only awaiting one good effective blow." Despite this, the report said that the general impression was that Cardiff had the best of the fight, avoiding Sullivan's punches, and getting in three solid blows of his own.[47]

The local *Minneapolis Tribune* called it a "very tame" 6-round gloved contest. At first, Cardiff seemed pale, nervous, and panicky. Sullivan began the fight leading with his left, but Cardiff dodged and rushed back at him. A Sullivan rush pushed Cardiff to the ropes. After breaking, Sullivan reached his neck with a punch, but Cardiff struck back and they clinched.

Cardiff made a rush at Sullivan in the 2nd round, pushed him against the ropes, and landed a good blow on the side of the face. Following some ineffective short arm work, very little was done, but the advantage seemed to be with Cardiff.

In the 3rd round, after Cardiff dodged and clinched, he hit Sullivan on the jaw. Patsy made a second rush and landed a right. However, there was little fighting after the 3rd round.

Both were cautious in the 4th round and not much happened. Sullivan led in the 5th and Cardiff dodged and blocked a blow on his shoulder, but nothing significant occurred, as Patsy seemed anxious about the possibility of a Sullivan rush.

Cardiff pushed Sullivan against the ropes in the 6th. Although Sullivan caught Patsy with a blow on the back of the neck, little to no effective work was done by either, and it seemed that Cardiff was eager to have the bout end, although the article also mentioned that Patsy did most of the work.

The referee called it a draw. The local writer opined that "The fact that Sullivan broke his arm ... made the fight, the little there was, entirely Cardiff's, and it ought to have been given him."

It was announced afterwards that Sullivan broke his left wrist in the 1st round and that it had prevented him from fighting effectively. A doctor examined the arm and confirmed that there was in fact a fracture of one of the forearm bones near the elbow (not the wrist).

Sullivan said that in the 1st round he caught Cardiff on top of the head when Patsy ducked a punch, and that it was the first time that he had broken his arm.[48] In another report, John said that as he threw a left uppercut at Patsy, Cardiff ducked and his forehead struck Sullivan's forearm.[49]

Cardiff had done "surprising work," momentarily getting Sullivan to the ropes a few times (in the 1st, 2nd, and 6th rounds), but the fight was dull, with Patsy generally keeping away, concerned about taking too many chances, and Sullivan not doing much owing to his being crippled. This is probably why the referee declared it a draw.[50]

Another local paper, *The Saint Paul and Minneapolis Pioneer Press*, gave an interesting and different take on matters. The day before the bout, it said,

Everyone looks upon the affair as savoring of a hippodrome. As a prominent sporting man said yesterday:
I'll wager a nice little pile that Cardiff is not knocked out. A man who would not meet Mitchell on the square certainly will not go before Sullivan unless there is some sort of an arrangement made before hand. You will find that either Sullivan has put up a forfeit that he will not knock Cardiff out, or else the latter has an understanding with the police whereby they will insist upon the largest kind of gloves being worn, and also interfere and stop the fight the moment Cardiff is getting the worst of it.[51]

Thus, there was some suspicion that the 6 rounder would be tame even before it took place. However, the terms were for 75 percent of the receipts to go to the winner and 25 percent to the loser, which would seem to provide an incentive for the men to try their best to obtain the winner's share.

The following day's report said that "The Whole Affair Has the Appearance of Being an Out-and-Out Hippodrome." 5,000 people had paid to attend the dull bout. This writer believed that its tameness was proof that it was a fixed fight where both men had essentially agreed to do little.

The referee's draw decision was criticized.

His decision should have been in favor of the Northwest champion, for Cardiff did more of the fighting, thrice rushing the champion to the ropes, and getting in three clean blows to Sullivan's one. In the fourth round not a single lead was made, and in the fifth there was but one exchange of blows, neither landing squarely. After the close of the sixth round Sullivan's manager announced that the champion had broken his left hand early in the fight, and as a consequence, was compelled to let up. The crowd did not believe this, and every one cried hippodrome.

However, the local doctors did confirm that Sullivan had broken the radius bone of the left hand. Still, the local writer nevertheless felt that there was an arrangement.

Even with his left hand helpless Sullivan could have taken all the fight out of Cardiff had he felt so inclined. The fact that Cardiff made such a good fight is evidence that there was some sort of an arrangement made before he went on the stage. No one for a moment supposed that he would go at the champion the way he did, unless he knew he would not be hurt.

The next day, the paper said that there were many who questioned the genuineness of Sullivan's break, and also questioned the decision. "The opinion was quite common that the referee should have given Cardiff the fight." Cardiff wanted to meet Sullivan again in a fight to the finish.[52]

Sullivan as of 1887 (Library of Congress, Prints & Photographs Division).

The local *Irish Standard*, a weekly paper, reported that Sullivan's arm was claimed to have been broken in the 2nd round. "The fight was decided a draw, although the general opinion is that Patsey had the best of it."[53]

The National Police Gazette reported that many disgusted spectators, unaware of the injury, called the bout a hippodrome (a fake), due to its dullness. Two doctors said that the radius was broken midway between the wrist and elbow, and would require at least 60 days to heal.[54] Other reports confirmed that Sullivan had broken one of the smaller bones in his forearm.[55] John traveled to New York, where the left arm had to be re-broken by a doctor because it had been set improperly.[56]

Sullivan was not impressed by Cardiff, although he generally was not one to compliment his opponents. A week after the fight he said of Patsy, "He ran about the ring like a sucker and a coward, and failed to notice that something wrong had happened to me."[57] In his autobiography, Sullivan incorrectly claimed to have been declared the winner.[58]

Cardiff was later quoted as saying "Had I known ... that Sullivan had broken his arm, I think that today I would be the recognized champion of the world; for I would have gone at him and forced the fighting until I should have put him to sleep."[59]

Years later, of the fight, Cardiff stated, "I knew that the left was gone, but I thought a good deal of my jaw when he began poking that right at me, and am well satisfied that I got off so easy."[60]

Mike Donovan said of Cardiff that he "was very clever, but lacked nerve. He did nothing but clinch, clinch.... He was a good runner and sprinted all through the bout."[61]

There was some talk of a rematch being arranged, but they did not fight again.[62] Cardiff in August 1887 fought another good fighter named Pat Killen to a 10-round draw, but in June 1888 was knocked out by the 190-pound Killen in the 4th round.[63]

In March 1887, Sullivan's arm was removed from plaster of Paris.[64] On March 28, 1887, in Hoboken, New Jersey, he gave two 4-round exhibitions on the same day, one with Joe Lannon, and the other with Steve Taylor. Lannon was the man who had scored an October 1886 KO6 over Frank Herald. However, Lannon was just coming off a March 8, 1887, 11th-round knockout loss to Jake Kilrain, who also had a victory over Herald.

Before the sparring, Sullivan

Joe Lannon. From Richard K. Fox, *Life and Battles of John L. Sullivan Ex Champion Pugilist of the World* (New York: Richard K. Fox, 1891). Clay Moyle, www.prizefightingbooks.com.

gave a speech asking the crowd to excuse his imperfections because he was still nursing his arm. The men proceeded to spar in a friendly, tame manner, and John used his left very little.[65]

An Australian source said that John mostly threw only rights, but told sparring partner Lannon, "Let her go, Joe, don't be afraid." Sullivan let himself out a little in the 4th, landing some stinging rib shots. After a couple other exhibitions, Sullivan sparred Taylor, again using his left very little. Sullivan "was badly winded, and showed that he was greatly out of training." That said, his rights were still quite powerful, and one of them crashed across Taylor's face and made him reel and stagger off the stage. Sullivan said, "That was a little harder than I intended."[66]

On April 1st in Baltimore, Maryland, Sullivan again sparred with Steve Taylor.[67]

On May 7, 1887, almost four months after Sullivan had broken his arm, Jake Kilrain (whose original name was John Joseph Killion or Killian), backed by Richard K. Fox's *National Police Gazette*, challenged Sullivan to fight for the championship, depositing a forfeit of $1,000 with *The New York Clipper*. The challenge was not accepted because Sullivan was apparently still recuperating from his arm injury. At that point, Kilrain claimed the world championship by default, which was naturally recognized by Fox's *Gazette*. Title disputes are not a modern invention. The public still considered Sullivan champion.

The 5'10½", 180-pound Kilrain and Sullivan had apparently sparred 3 rounds back in 1880, wherein Jake received "some hard punishment," and again in 1882, when Sullivan agreed to take it easy. An 1889 source reported that Sullivan's friends and the referee said that the two had boxed in a 4-round contest and that Sullivan had defeated Kilrain.[68] An 1884 *National Police Gazette* confirmed that Kilrain "has had several friendly set-tos, with John L. Sullivan." An 1888 source said that they had met at a benefit in South Boston at Revere Hall in 1882. Sullivan said that he gave Jake a good punishing. Four persons who witnessed their contest said that they boxed 3 rounds and Kilrain was bested. Sullivan said that they met again about two years later at a benefit in Monument Hall, Charlestown. "Godfrey was to have sparred with me, but he wanted too much money, so Kilrain was selected to take his place. Before Kilrain would put on the gloves he made me promise that I would not punish him hard."[69]

Jake in 1883 bested Pete McCoy

Jake Kilrain. From Richard K. Fox, *Life and Battles of John L. Sullivan Ex Champion Pugilist of the World* (New York: Richard K. Fox, 1891). Clay Moyle, www.prizefightingbooks.com.

at a Sullivan benefit. That year, Kilrain stopped in the 3rd round George Godfrey, who was considered the top American black fighter.[70]

On March 26, 1884, Kilrain fought Charley Mitchell to a competitive 4-round draw. According to *The National Police Gazette*, Kilrain was dropped in the 4th round. Overall, Jake had acquitted himself well and some felt that with further development, he could be a champion, but "at present he is no match for either Sullivan or Mitchell." *The New York Clipper* said that Kilrain performed well against Mitchell, was the aggressor, and did most of the fighting and landed more blows, but that Mitchell's punches were the more effective. No knockdown was mentioned.[71] A late March 1884 *Gazette* issue said that Kilrain was "willing to fight any man in the world, barring Sullivan."[72]

In May 1884, Kilrain scored a KO3 over William Sheriff in a bout stopped by the police.[73] Kilrain next fought Mike Cleary to a 4-round draw, but the spectators felt that Jake was the better man. In December 1884, Kilrain fought a 5-round draw against Jack Burke, but Kilrain was considered to be the better fighter. In late 1884, Kilrain's financial backer said that he would put Jake in with any man in the world except for Sullivan.

In 1886, Kilrain won an 8-round decision over Jack Ashton (though many felt it should have been a draw), and scored a November KO1 over recent Sullivan challenger Frank Herald and a KO2 against Joe Godfrey (different from George).

On March 8, 1887, Jake knocked out Joe Lannon in 11 or 13 rounds (reports differ). Lannon had the 1886 KO6 over Herald, but had earlier in 1886 lost a 6-round decision to George Godfrey. Lannon would later rematch Godfrey in 1889, fighting to a 15-round draw.[74]

Kilrain had good results, but not necessarily compelling enough at that point to force a Sullivan match. Still, although Sullivan's arm injury was initially a valid excuse for not fighting Kilrain, it would be another two years before Sullivan fought him. 1887 was the first year that Sullivan began markedly reducing the number of serious bouts he fought per calendar year. The January Cardiff fight was his only 1887 title defense. John L. only fought one title bout per year from 1887 to 1889.

Sullivan drew some criticism for not fighting Kilrain. Some believed that because he failed to accept the challenge, he forfeited his title. In June 1887, *The New York Clipper* (which held the forfeit money posted by Kilrain) wrote, "John L. Sullivan having, for some reasons which cannot have any weight in sporting law and usage, declined to accept the challenge regularly issued by Jake Kilrain, the title of champion-pugilist of America ... is forfeited to the challenger."[75]

The rest of the world did not necessarily recognize Kilrain's claim. In Australia, *The Referee* said,

> As soon as the unprecedented bruiser John L. Sullivan broke his arm a new aspirant for the boxing championship instantly arose.... In America, Fox seems to be the despot of sport. ... the despot decided that in spite of everything, Kilrain was to be champion.... This was harmless ambition, and no doubt Sullivan smilingly calculated at the time what a deal of cheap advertising the new aspirant was getting, and what a big house there would be when they met.

Fox matched Kilrain to meet Jim or Jem Smith of England for the world championship, but the Australian paper was critical.

> Neither men are competent to fight for the Championship of the World, and there are several pugilists today that are classed before either of them. Smith has done nothing yet to merit the public prominence bestowed upon him, while everybody expects to see Sullivan mow down Kilrain when they face one another.[76]

Sullivan continued giving sparring exhibitions. On July 4, 1887, in Hartford, Connecticut, after umpiring a baseball game there, he sparred with Lannon.[77]

On August 8, 1887, in Boston, 3,000 people watched Sullivan receive the most costly championship belt ever made. It was later said that the belt was worth $10,000.[78] John was no doubt the people's champion. He sparred with Mike Donovan and Steve Taylor.[79]

CHAPTER 14

The European Tour

In late 1887, Jake Kilrain, recognized as champion by *The Gazette* and *The Clipper*, traveled to England to meet then–English champion Jem Smith. Of the Smith-Kilrain championship fight, Sullivan said, "It is a big advertising scheme by a certain very foxy newspaper manager. Pugilists in general take no stock in it, and I hear it seldom discussed among those with whom I associate. Championships won by wind are frail honors."[1]

On October 27, 1887, Sullivan set sail for Liverpool, England, beginning his long contemplated European tour. He was set to appear in England, Scotland, Wales, Ireland, and Paris, France. Jack Ashton, who had lost a close 1886 8-round decision to Kilrain, went with Sullivan as his sparring partner. Sullivan said that he wanted to challenge Charley Mitchell while there, "and shut him up," as well as Jake Kilrain.[2] Jake was already there.

Sullivan in his autobiography said that he exhibited in London, Birmingham, Liverpool, Manchester, Newcastle-on-Tyne, Leicester, Nottingham, Derby, Sheffield, Preston, Oldham, and other cities. In Ireland, he appeared in Dublin, Waterford, Cork, Limerick, and Belfast. In Scotland, he visited Glasgow, Dundee, Aberdeen, and Edinburgh. The only place that he visited in Wales was Cardiff, arriving there after his Nottingham exhibition. He claimed to have boxed in 51 exhibitions.[3]

Sullivan arrived in London, England, on or about November 5, 1887.[4] Many noblemen were amongst the 1,800 in attendance at his first exhibition, which took place on November 9. England's current champion, Jem Smith, was present, and Sullivan said that he would like to eventually face him. However, Smith was already scheduled for his match with Kilrain.

Bare above the waist with pink fleshings and an American flag around his waist, a 222-pound Sullivan sparred Jack Ashton. They went at it hammer and tongs in the 1st round, and John used his rushes to the delight of the audience. "That Ashton stood up under such hurricane blows proves that he is a tough one." The 2nd and 3rd rounds were just as spirited. "Several times Sullivan said to Ashton, 'Don't be afraid, give it to me,' and Ashton complied to the best of his ability, but he was scarcely more than a child in the bean-eater's hands." After the 3rd, Ashton's second told them to shake hands, for it was over. However, the audience wanted one more round, because it had been announced as a 4 rounder. Eventually, they boxed a 4th round, which was quite hot.

"Exclamations of amazement at Sullivan's agility, considering his weight and condition and hard work of the previous rounds, were heard on every side." Jem Smith said, "Well, he's a hot 'un." A member of the club said, "Sullivan, why he's a cat and a locomotive combined."[5]

Sullivan quoted the next day's newspaper notice as saying that Ashton was lighter than Sullivan, but about the same stature.

While both men were remarkably quick and agile, the rapidity and springiness of Sullivan's movements created the deepest impression, and evoked universal admiration.... Once an opportunity occurs he delivers a perfect bombardment of blows with a speed which the eye can scarcely follow. In attack he seems literally to throw himself upon an opponent with puzzling and disconcerting suddenness and impetuosity.[6]

Sully was scheduled to appear in Birmingham on November 12 and 14, Sheffield on the 17th, Wolverhampton on the 18th, Leicester on the 19th and 21st, Bolton on the 22nd, Manchester on the 23rd, and Leeds on the 24th, and in a twelve-night engagement in London, each time facing Ashton.[7]

8–9,000 people turned up in Birmingham, England, to watch the second night of boxing by the Sullivan combination (on the 12th). He first sparred Ashton, who was described as a clever boxer. "Ashton was let off lightly." The wind-up was between Sullivan and former opponent Alf Greenfield. They sparred 3 rounds, during which John "used his left with good effect, and made one or two of his hurricane rushes. The set-to was generally of a light, but scientific character, Greenfield making a very creditable display."[8] John L. said that the two-night show had brought together 19,000 people.[9]

Sullivan was the talk of the town.

Kilrain and Mitchell have been completely snuffed out by the arrival in Birmingham of John L. Sullivan. The name of Sullivan has been a household word in the mouths of pugilists on both sides of the Atlantic for years. It is small wonder, then, that his admirers—and they are many— should give him a welcome scarcely accorded to a royal prince. Sullivan is certainly a superior class of pugilist.

Sullivan was warmly received in Manchester and other large towns. In Wolverhampton, against Ashton, Sullivan's "brilliant display of science and his finely built form" was "greatly admired." "His quickness in attack and marvelous defense was the subject of admiration, and the way in which he delivered his blows was watched with the greatest interest." Their science brought forth great applause.[10] Sullivan was a hit.

On November 29, Sullivan and Mitchell signed an agreement to fight with bare knuckles for $2,500 a side. Sullivan wanted the ring limited to 16 feet, but Mitchell successfully resisted, insisting on the typical large 24-foot ring. "Mitchell taunted Sullivan repeatedly, one remark so incensing the American that he proposed that they settle the matter by a fight on the spot, but wiser counsels prevailed."[11] Mitchell liked engaging in head games.

On December 5, 1887, Sullivan began the second week of his engagement in London. The prices of admission were doubled, but the house was still full. "His performances during the preceding week yielded a profit of over $500 per night."

Future engagements included Ireland, Scotland, and England again, with Sullivan set to be giving almost daily exhibitions. John's intention was to continue exhibiting until late January, when he would go into training for the Mitchell fight.[12]

On December 8, 1887, Sullivan and Ashton provided entertainment at the London Aquarium, and then gave a separate, private exhibition at the Pelican Club.

They sparred for the Prince of Wales on December 9, 1887. First, Jem Smith sparred Greenfield. Then Sullivan sparred Ashton. The prince was "duly impressed by the massiveness of the Bostonian, his skillful and powerful boxing and the wonderful agility displayed by him."[13]

Sullivan said that the local paper quoted the prince as saying, "He is the quickest big man I ever saw." When asked what would happen if John L. met Smith, the prince said,

"Sullivan has the weight, the height, the reach, and undoubted pluck.... That put together generally wins the fight."[14]

During the next week, Sullivan exhibited in Ireland. Sullivan said that 15,000 people gathered at the steamboat landing for his December 11 reception in Dublin. He also met enthusiastic receptions in Waterford, Limerick, Belfast, and Cork. John said that he made more money in one week in Ireland than he did in six weeks in England.[15]

On December 19, 1887, Jake Kilrain fought English champion Jem Smith. The 24-year-old Smith was 5'8½" and weighed around 170–182 pounds. It was said that he was undefeated since beginning his career in 1881. Amongst his many victories, in 1883, he defeated Bill Davis in 1 hour. In 1884, Harry Arnold was defeated in a hard glove fight in 14 rounds over 55 minutes. Woolf Bendoff was defeated in the 12th round in 48 minutes. In 1885, Jack Davis was quickly knocked out and didn't wake up for two hours. Smith's most significant fight took place in February 1886, when he fought Alf Greenfield for 1 hour and 8 minutes. It was declared a draw, but Greenfield was "carried senseless from the ring."[16] Following that bout, there was some discussion regarding a potential Smith v. Sullivan match. Sullivan said that if Smith wanted to win the world's championship, he would need to come to America to fight him.[17] Smith did not come.

Kilrain proved his staying power by fighting Smith in a marathon 2-hour, 30-minute, 106-round bareknuckle fight that ended in a draw due to darkness. The description of the fight gives the impression that it was mostly a wrestling match, the two usually ending the rounds by throwing each other down. However, there were also many knockdowns as the result of punches, and Kilrain was the one scoring those, generally having the best of the fight. Still, by the 104th round, Kilrain appeared to be more fatigued than Smith, and the lighting was becoming poor. They considered stopping it then, but continued for another couple of rounds before agreeing to end it.[18] Most considered Kilrain to have been the better man. *The National Police Gazette* continued hyping a potential Kilrain-Sullivan match, calling Kilrain the world champion. It believed that Jake had the endurance and skill required to outlast Sullivan.

While in Edinburgh, Scotland, Sullivan said, "My desire is to fight Kilrain. I whipped him once and can do it again, and well they know it."[19] Sullivan successfully exhibited in Edinburgh, Glasgow, Dundee, and Aberdeen.[20]

The Sullivan combination appeared in Cardiff, Wales, on January 5, 1888. Sullivan sparred Ashton and also had a set-to with a local boxer named William Samuells. Sullivan "toyed with him during the first two rounds." The crowd cheered their man, thinking that he had been doing well, on the merits.

However, in the 3rd round,

> [Sullivan] let himself out just once, but the blow he planted on Mr. Samuells' caput proved sufficient to lay him flat and knock all the fight out of him. When he rose from the floor ... the local boxer stepped to the front of the stage and acknowledged that he was no sort of a match for Sullivan, whom he was convinced had simply been playing with him before putting the right mauley where it would do the most good.[21]

Sullivan said that his tour of Great Britain closed in January 1888 with an exhibition in Portsmouth.[22] He then went into training for his Mitchell match.

Apparently, Sullivan tried to arrange a bout with Smith, including a bareknuckle fight, but his offers were refused. Sullivan proposed to box Smith 6 rounds with gloves, saying that if he failed to knock out Smith within 6 rounds he would forfeit 200 pounds to him.

If Smith were to be beaten, he would lose nothing. "Any of the offers I have advanced to Smith are open to Kilrain. Can any man living make more sacrifices or concessions than I have? Surely Smith must come to the front or wilt like a wet rag."[23] There were no takers.

Sullivan continued training for the Mitchell fight. "It is pretty generally known that when Sullivan arrived here last November he scaled, stripped, 238 pounds, and was very 'beefy.'" However, John had been training diligently. He went on 3-hour walks and ran 3 or 4 miles, in addition to his other work. In February, Sullivan was reported to weigh 206 pounds and was expecting to enter the ring weighing 190 pounds.[24]

After losing to Sullivan in 3 gloved rounds in 1883, Charlie Mitchell in 1884 had fought Jake Kilrain to a 4-round draw, possibly knocking him down in the process. An 1884 rematch with Sullivan was scheduled, but John L. showed up drunk and called the match off. Mitchell was subsequently defeated by Dominick McCaffrey in a disputed 1884 4-round decision. He ended the year by meeting Jack Burke in a 4-round draw and a light 3 rounder.

In 1885, Mitchell was defeating Mike Cleary again when the police stopped it in the 4th round and it was declared a draw. 6- and 10-round draws with Burke followed. A May 1886 match with Sullivan in Chicago was prevented by the authorities. Mitchell then fought a 5-round draw with Patsy Cardiff. One report said that he dropped Patsy once, although another said Patsy dropped Mitchell. A July match with Sullivan in New York was also prevented by the authorities. Mitchell had fought some other bouts in the intervening years, including some exhibitions with Jem Smith and Jake Kilrain.[25]

On March 10, 1888, in Chantilly, France, over one year after his last defense against Cardiff, Sullivan again took on England's Charley Mitchell, this time under bareknuckle London Prize Ring Rules. It was Sullivan's first bareknuckle fight since his 1882 bout with Paddy Ryan. Sullivan said that he fought the "bombastic sprinter boxer" for a purse of 500 pounds.[26]

Reported weights for the fighters vary, including 162, 166–168, or 170–185 pounds for Mitchell, and 200, 204 or 215 pounds for Sullivan. Mitchell was 26 to Sullivan's 29 years of age. For the first time in a championship fight, Sullivan was

Charlie Mitchell. From Richard K. Fox, *Life and Battles of John L. Sullivan Ex Champion Pugilist of the World* (New York: Richard K. Fox, 1891). Clay Moyle, www.prizefightingbooks.com.

forced to prove that he could endure a lengthy battle. They fought for 39 rounds lasting over 3 hours, outdoors in the cold rain, under muddy conditions.

Mitchell took a beating from John L. and went down multiple times, sometimes from hard rights, and other times from light blows. It was technically against the London Prize Ring Rules to go down voluntarily in order to get a rest or avoid punishment, and could be grounds for disqualification. However, the actual rule left some leeway for interpretation, stating,

> It shall be a fair "stand up fight," and if either man shall willfully throw himself down without receiving a blow, whether blows shall have previously been exchanged or not, he shall be deemed to have lost the battle; but this rule shall not apply to a man who in a close slips down from the grasp of his opponent to avoid punishment, or from obvious accident or weakness.[27]

The spirit of this rule was often violated, as it was by Mitchell, and this helps explain why so many bareknuckle bouts lasted so long. Referees generally overlooked this foul, as was the case in this fight.

Overall, Mitchell used guerrilla tactics, fighting mostly to survive, scoring only occasionally, hoping that John would eventually wear himself out or that he could close Sullivan's eyes. Mitchell's survival tactics included jabbing, moving, and occasionally going down and getting his 30–38 second rests. Mitchell drew some blood from Sullivan in about the 8th round. Charley's spiked shoes sometimes managed to cut Sullivan's lower legs or feet (they were allowed to wear shoes with three spikes in them), and he also landed some low blows. Still, Mitchell's face was lumped and bruised from Sullivan's blows.

Eventually, after 3 hours had elapsed, it was agreed to declare the bout a draw because little was happening at that point owing to the fighters' fatigue, hurt hands, and the muddy conditions. Sullivan had not knocked his man out, but then again, Mitchell's survival tactics in the hope that John L. would fatigue himself to the point of vulnerability had not worked either. Sullivan was too tired to stop him, but Mitchell was too fatigued and hurt to turn the tide of the fight.

The New York Times reported that the whole fight favored Sullivan. Sullivan dropped Mitchell with rights to the head to end the 1st through 3rd rounds. Mitchell moved about the large 24-foot ring to survive. In the 6th, Charley dropped to avoid a right hand and was cautioned against breaking the rules. Sullivan eventually grew fatigued from chasing him around the 24-foot ring, and the rain and muddy turf did not help matters, slowing John up.

The 32nd round lasted 27 minutes, as the rain was "falling in torrents." The 39th round lasted 30 minutes. Both were weak and fatigued and their blows had lost their steam. As it was clear that "no definite result was likely to be reached" it was suggested and agreed that the bout be declared a draw, after 3 hours and 11 minutes. Mitchell had a lump on his jaw, his left eye was banged up, and his body was bruised.[28]

The National Police Gazette reported that Mitchell weighed 170–185 pounds. It agreed that Mitchell tried to move for the first 3 rounds and was knocked down to end each, coming up for the 4th with a lump on his left temple. A right to Mitchell's eye ended the 4th. He dropped from a right in the 5th and a blow to the cheek in the 6th. Sullivan fell in the 7th, with Mitchell on top of him. Charley was usually carried to his corner, but Sullivan walked.

A Mitchell left in the 8th drew first blood from Sullivan's nose. After landing a right to John's eye, Mitchell went down to avoid retaliation. A right to the arm dropped Charley in the 9th. Sullivan's eye was looking bad by the 10th. Mitchell went down that round amidst a Sullivan rush, and did the same in the 11th. He clearly fell without a blow in the 12th, the claim of foul being disallowed. Charley had some excuse because the muddy ground was slippery. A right to the neck dropped Mitchell in the 13th. Mitchell was laughing in the 14th, but a right to his mouth drew blood, and a right to the ear dropped him. Charley again went down to avoid punishment in the 15th.

The article then noted that from the 16th round to the end, they would talk to each other and then punch, and then Mitchell would run away or go down. Sullivan's right eye was bad; his lips were swelling and nose bleeding, while Mitchell's temple had a big lump.[29]

The San Francisco Chronicle reported that Mitchell's agility had saved him from defeat. He fought with skill and cunning, going to the ground whenever the slightest push would justify it. The champion's right arm began to puff up in about the 12th round, when the sleet began to fall, and it was not used very often. The rain continued until the 32nd round. It was very cold and the grounds were in terrible condition, resembling a pigsty.[30]

Sullivan in his autobiography said that Mitchell engaged in his sprinting tactics, running around the large ring. Mitchell would sometimes drop without a blow, and a number of times from a mere tap. "Mitchell adopted a saving game throughout." Sullivan was fouled repeatedly by being spiked. John was very cold, and had badly bruised the muscles of his right arm in the 5th round when striking Mitchell's head. He felt that Mitchell did not go in to win the 500 pounds, but to save his own, "which, thanks to the big ring, the weather and my accident, he succeeded in doing." He also said that Mitchell's "whole game was to avoid me, not to fight me."

One observer said that the fight had been "a walking tournament the greater part of the time." Mitchell danced about continually, and Sullivan had rendered his right hand useless from a blow to the head in the 5th round. Mitchell's blows were not strong enough to tire out Sullivan.[31]

The Boston Herald had the most detailed comprehensive accounting of the fight, followed by *The Boston Daily Globe*. *The Sydney Referee* also printed reports. *The Herald* said that Mitchell was knocked down 15 times, but not out. It reported that Mitchell weighed 162 pounds to Sullivan's 204. *The Referee* said that Mitchell "played a splendid 'get away' game," working the London rules system very well.

Here is an abbreviated round-by-round accounting, mostly describing how the round finished unless something significant occurred. *The Herald* version is provided first, followed by *The Globe* where there is a significant difference, and *The Referee*:

Round 1: *The Herald* said that Mitchell began cautiously, with Sullivan on the attack. Less than a minute into the fight, a left to the neck staggered Mitchell, and then a right to the jaw sent him down. *The Globe's* version said that both punched and blocked, and Mitchell dropped to avoid punishment. *The Referee* said Mitchell was knocked down with a left 7 minutes and 7 seconds into the bout.

Round 2: They exchanged blows, but a right and possibly a second blow sent Mitchell down. *The Herald* later mentioned a blow to the eye dropping him. *The Referee* said a right to the eye dropped Mitchell 50 seconds into the round.

Round 3: Sullivan landed a strong left to the stomach. In pursuit, John sent in a left that dropped Charley. *The Globe* said that Sullivan asked Mitchell not to run around, and dropped him with a right. *The Referee* said a scrambling hit dropped Mitchell in 3 minutes and 20 seconds.

Round 4: According to *The Herald*, Mitchell dropped down to avoid punishment, while *The Globe* said a right to the eye sent him down. It noted that Mitchell had a lump on his head.

Round 5: A left and right sent Charley down.

Round 6: *The Herald* was unclear as to how this round ended, but *The Globe* said that Charley went down from a blow to the cheek. However, Mitchell had landed some good body shots during the round.

Round 7: They exchanged and Mitchell rushed in to clinch and forced John down, falling on him. *The Herald* later mentioned a scratch by Mitchell's nails bringing blood from Sullivan's face. *The Referee* said Mitchell threw Sullivan.

Round 8: After only one minute had elapsed, Mitchell fell without a blow, but the claim of foul was not allowed. *The Globe* noted that Mitchell drew first blood and landed to the belly, but agreed that he went down to avoid a return. *The Referee* said that Charlie's rights had made Sullivan's mouth and left ear bleed and swell. Sullivan's right eye was partly damaged as well.

Round 9: Mitchell fell from an open handed hit on the back from the right. *The Globe* said the blow was a right to the ribs. It later noted that from rounds 9 to 15 there was a "fearful storm," during which Sullivan was visibly shivering and his teeth chattering. Mitchell was mostly on the retreat throughout.

Round 10: One version said that Sullivan again slapped Charley's back and he fell, while the other said that Mitchell got down in the face of a Sullivan rush. Sullivan's left eye was in bad shape. *The Referee* said that other than his swollen left eye, Mitchell seemed unharmed to that point. Mitchell's spikes cut Sullivan's boot.

Round 11: Mitchell either went down from a blow to the eye, or went down on the slippery ground to avoid punishment. *The Referee* said that Mitchell landed his left, but Sullivan bore him down without landing a blow after 50 seconds. As Mitchell was carried to his corner, he said, "Well, I think I shall begin to fight now."

Round 12: Mitchell landed a left to the stomach, but was dropped from a blow to the jaw. *The Globe* said Mitchell fell without a blow, but then rose upon the claim of foul and continued. He went down again, though, shortly thereafter, to avoid punishment. According to *The Referee*, Sullivan rushed furiously, boring Charlie down without a punch. However, Mitchell was laughing, cool, and confident.

Round 13: Charley retreated and went down from a light exchange. *The Globe* said he went down from a right to the neck.

Round 14: The rain was heavy and the men killed time for a minute under the circumstances. Charley led with his left but a counter right to the chest dropped him. *The Globe* said a blow on the mouth drew blood from the laughing Mitchell, who then hit John in the temple. Charley was dropped from a right to the ear.

Round 15: Not much happened, but apparently Mitchell went down to avoid punishment.

Round 16: *The Herald* said that a left to the stomach sent Charley down only 7 seconds into the round, the shortest round to that point. Most rounds had thus far lasted 1–3 minutes. *The Globe* differed, saying that Mitchell moved away, there were slight exchanges, and then Charley went down from a right. *The Referee* said that Mitchell landed a heavy left to the nose. Sullivan then rushed and landed a left and right, knocking Mitchell down. Time: 2 minutes, 50 seconds.

Round 17: John landed a left and a light right, but Charley went down to prolong matters. *The Globe* noted that Mitchell was shaky. *The Referee* said that Sullivan floored Mitchell with a left to the chest only 10 seconds into the round.

Round 18: A counter to the jaw sent Mitchell down only 33 seconds in. *The Referee* said that Sullivan's eyes were both bad, but he knocked Mitchell down with a blow to the top of the head.

Round 19: Sullivan's shin was spiked. Charley went down after an exchange, possibly from a right to the temple. It is also possible that he rose and continued, but went down to avoid Sullivan.

Round 20: After some exchanges, Charley was sent down from a blow to the stomach.

Round 21: There was more heavy rainfall, and Mitchell went down from a left to the body. *The Referee* said that Sullivan was swinging his arms like windmill sails, while Mitchell was sparring beautifully. Sullivan's left ear was cut in two or three places. A Sullivan rush sent Mitchell down after 3 minutes and 15 seconds.

Round 22: According to *The Herald*, Sullivan's teeth began chattering and his bare skin turned blue with cold. Charley went down from a right on the neck or the eye, depending on the version.

Round 23: Mitchell either went down from a left to the neck or was fought down. *The Referee* said that the rain came down in torrents, and Sullivan did not like it. Mitchell pounded his face, which was very swollen about the eyes and mouth. The fighting was pretty much the same through the 28th, with Mitchell "fibbing and getting away, Sullivan rushing and getting well stopped."

Round 24: Charley landed a left to the stomach, and then threw himself down. *The Globe* said he landed twice on the mouth but went down from a right to the neck.

Round 25: A Mitchell left to the mouth caused Sullivan's lip to swell and blood to flow. A Sullivan right to the cheek sent Charley down. *The Globe* account differed, saying that Charley had the best of it and landed to the body, and then went down to avoid a Sullivan right.

Round 26: The sun came out and Mitchell went down from a light exchange, possibly to avoid punishment.

Round 27: Sullivan drove Mitchell about the ring and used his left well in exchanges, either forcing him down, or Mitchell going down to avoid blows.

Round 28: Sullivan's bare hands were in bad condition, and Mitchell had slightly the better of some early exchanges, but ended the round by falling, the round being a bit longer than usual, clocked at just over 4 minutes. *The Globe* said there were some fierce exchanges, and Charley was sent down. *The Referee* said Mitchell stopped a right, but slipped down after 1 minute and 25 seconds.

Round 29: Both landed well, but Mitchell fell, this round lasting almost 6 minutes. *The Referee* said a left to Sullivan's mouth drew blood, and the betting shifted to even at this point. Time: 4 minutes and 15 seconds. *The Herald* continued discussing each round, but *The Globe* simply provided a less than informative synopsis of the rest of the fight.

Round 30: The rain again fell heavily. The two exchanged some blows, and Mitchell threw himself down, in a more normal 2½ minutes. *The Referee* said that word spread that Sullivan's right hand was gone. The round was all in Mitchell's favor. "Mitchell ended the round when it suited him by stopping a well-meant lead and getting down. Time, 6 min. 50 sec." Although the rain had stopped for a while, it resumed, coming down in sheets.

Round 31: This was a very long round, lasting 21 minutes. They again had many exchanges, and finally Mitchell in a clinch bore Sullivan to the ropes and pushed him down.

Round 32: John drove him around the ring until clinched. Two lefts to the face sent Charley down, the round lasting 7 minutes. *The Referee* said Sullivan's teeth were chattering and he seemed to be in a critical state. It said the round lasted 23 minutes and 30 seconds.

Round 33: After a series of exchanges, Mitchell was driven around the ring and fell after almost 5 minutes had elapsed.

Round 34: It was apparent that Sullivan's hands were in really bad shape and that he was weak from chasing Charley around the ring. Much time was spent walking around between light exchanges. The 14-minute round ended with Mitchell slipping down in a clinch.

Round 35: Mitchell went down in an exchange, this round only lasting about 3½ minutes. *The Referee* said that during the 33rd and 35th rounds Sullivan seemed unsteady, but the ground was so bad and slippery that Mitchell couldn't do much.

Round 36: Mitchell attacked, landed to the body and "settled the Yankee down," but it is unclear how the short round ended. The suggestion is that Mitchell threw or wrestled John down. No historian has ever indicated that Sullivan ever went down from a blow in this fight.

Round 37: Mitchell landed some punches and walked about. Eventually, John drove Charley to the ropes and down, the round lasting almost 3 minutes. *The Referee* said that Mitchell had the best of it in the 36th and 37th rounds. Sullivan seemed dazed and could not land.

Round 38: *The Referee* said that Sullivan was vicious in the 38th, but could not land a significant blow, as Mitchell fell comfortably.

Round 39: One account said that this round lasted 38½ minutes. Both fell from weakness and on three occasions by mutual consent retired to their corners to receive attendance and have clay removed from their shoes. Finally it was suggested that a draw be declared, and both agreed.

The Referee said that there was a great deal of walking around and conversing amidst the fighting and feinting, the round lasting 31 minutes and 49 seconds. When Mitchell retreated, Sullivan said, "Now then, let's have a round." Eventually, they both went to their corners by mutual consent. They resumed, sparring ineffectively for several minutes. A bystander remarked that the fight had lasted 3 hours. After some more fighting, they again went to their corners for attention by their seconds. During subsequent sparring,

> Mitchell was understood to express some impatience, and Ashton, who was standing near him, at once chimed in with, "If you don't like it why don't you agree to a draw." Mitchell still sparring, "I'll draw if John likes.... What did you say, John? Shall it be a draw?" Sullivan replied, "I don't mind," whereupon Baldock said, "Then shake hands; it's a draw."

The Referee said the fight had lasted 3 hours, 10 minutes and 55 seconds. Mitchell's left eye was almost closed and the parts above very swollen. His body had several marks. Despite having scored all the knockdowns and almost all of the throw downs, Sullivan looked worse. His right eye was almost closed, and the left wasn't far behind. The left ear was cut and the lobe was swollen, with the blood oozing from the inside. Blood trickled from his nose and lips.[32]

Excepting the external damage, Sullivan had the better of it overall, yet was criticized by some for being unable to stop Mitchell. The fight was used as a sign that Sullivan was slipping. After all, he had easily defeated Mitchell in 3 rounds with gloves years earlier.

One paper said, "Mitchell's blows were quick, but puny as a baby's, while Sullivan stalked around, a mere shadow of what he was.... The secret is now in every one's mouth that Sullivan's fighting days are finished."[33]

Richard K. Fox, when asked if Sullivan was as good a man as he was five or six years ago, responded, "Not by any means. Sullivan has been drinking hard for several years and has undermined his constitution to an alarming extent. No man can expect to drink almost continuously and not injure his health. I tell you John L. Sullivan is not the man he once was." Sullivan was said to have been weighing 240 pounds when not in condition.[34] Fox's *Police Gazette* later said that Mitchell had lowered Sullivan's colors and made him take a back seat in pugilism.[35] Another newspaper wrote,

> Sullivan has taught us afresh that physical vigor cannot be preserved by burning the candle at both ends. After years of dissipation, Sullivan pretended to reform, and then we were told that he was as good a man as he ever was. The student of physiology knew better. A man cannot trifle with his body.... He abused his system in every way.... The moral is that men who would retain their physical or mental powers must lead regular lives. If they indulge to excess the shadow of decay will early fall upon them.[36]

The criticism of Sullivan, although not without foundation, was a bit unfair. The critics failed to consider the fighting conditions and how Mitchell used the London rules to his advantage. Under the London rules, Charley had plenty of recovery time between knockdowns, making it difficult for Sullivan to finish him. This was made even more difficult because Mitchell occasionally violated the rules by going down without being struck or went down from light blows. Also, Charley prolonged matters by moving about and forcing Sullivan to chase after him in the very large, muddy, outdoor ring under less than ideal cold and rainy conditions.

It was noted that Sullivan might have been able to finish him at times had he pressed matters more. However, it should be considered that in a fight to the finish, John had to pace himself because if he did not finish Charley off, he could have been left so spent that it would be he who was knocked out. Thus, to a certain extent, he had to allow Mitchell to move and walk about. Consider this in conjunction with the fact that even when Sullivan did track him down, Charley could quickly drop to avoid trouble, and so all of John's efforts could be for naught. Also, without gloves and in the cold, it was more difficult to consistently punch hard over time because of damage to the hands, rendering them less useful. No wonder so many of these bareknuckle fights lasted so many hours. Mitchell's tactics in this bout partially demonstrate why the London rules had outlived their usefulness and were not favored by Sullivan.

Sullivan a month later said,

> I never claimed to run as fast as Charley Mitchell, and the Chantilly fight was a sprinting match throughout.
> I would have won anyhow had not my arm been hurt in the fourth round, but among the circumstances which militated against me are the unfairness of the referee, Mitchell's foul play in spiking me at every opportunity ... the partiality of the timekeeper, an Englishman, who timed the intervals between the rounds from Mitchell's reaching his corner, and not from where he fell; I also charge him with having lengthened each rest interval from twenty-five all the way up

to seventy and eighty seconds, and, lastly, the rainstorm, which blew straight into my corner ... with such violence, in fact, as to knock out even several men who were not fighting.[37]

After giving so much of themselves, the day after the illegal fight, the two men were captured by the police, spent a night in jail, paid $600 bail, and then left the country.[38]

This was Sullivan's only 1888 title defense, although that is somewhat understandable after having had such a lengthy and grueling fight.

CHAPTER 15

The Color Line

Two months after the Mitchell fight, on May 15, 1888, in Boston, 3,000 people attended a Sullivan benefit. John L. sparred with Jack Ashton "in a scientific, but by no means exciting, manner."

More interesting is the fact that on this occasion, Sullivan was willing to spar the top American black fighter: colored heavyweight champion George Godfrey. Godfrey was born in 1853 and began boxing in about 1879. By 1888 he was 35 years old. He weighed about 170 pounds and stood 5'10¼".

Sullivan had possibly been matched to box Godfrey back in 1881, but the police prevented the bout just before they were about to begin.[1] Sullivan indicated that in about 1883 or 1884 at a benefit in Charleston, "Godfrey was to have sparred with me, but he wanted too much money, so Kilrain was selected to take his place."[2] John L. refereed a match for the colored heavyweight championship between Godfrey and Professor Hadley in February 1883, which Godfrey won by a 6th-round knockout.[3]

Jake Kilrain fought Godfrey in 1883, stopping him in the 3rd round, although Godfrey years later claimed this was spin on Kilrain's part and that it was just a 3-round exhibition.[4] Kilrain said it was scheduled for 6 rounds and that he "hit the darky so hard that he quit in the third round." *The National Police Gazette* consistently reported the fight as being a 3rd-round stoppage win for Kilrain, even as early as 1884.[5]

An Australian source said that Godfrey had the better of an 1886 6-round bout with Joe Lannon, but the white referee called it a draw owing to racial favoritism.[6] Jake Kilrain subsequently scored a KO11 or 13 over Lannon.

On this evening, Godfrey appeared in the hall and was announced by the master of ceremonies as being there to spar Sullivan for a sum of money. However, it appeared that neither Godfrey nor Sullivan were aware that they were to spar. *The New York Clipper* said,

> Immediately afterwards Sullivan appeared on the stage, attired in full dress, and stated that, while the announcement that Godfrey was to spar with him at the benefit had not been made with his knowledge or consent, he was prepared to box George, if the latter desired it, as he had often stated, and would give him a fair sum. To this Godfrey responded that he had not come to the hall prepared to box anyone, but that he would spar Sullivan at any other time for any amount of money named by the latter or for the gate receipts.[7]

This was interesting because Sullivan had generally said that he would not box a black man in public. This was one of the times, however, that he expressed a willingness to do so. In the future, Sullivan would continue to oscillate about whether he was willing to box a black man.

The Boston Herald's local report said that the master of ceremonies asked if Godfrey, colored pugilist, was in the hall. Godfrey announced that he was. The master of ceremonies then said that he was announcing on behalf of Sullivan that he would give Godfrey money to stand before him in a 3- or 4-round gloved contest. Godfrey said that it was unexpected and that he had not come prepared for it. "They advertised that I had been offered a sum of money to appear here tonight and spar Mr. Sullivan. They did not come near me.... If Mr. Sullivan had come to me personally and asked me to spar with him, I would have been happy to do so for nothing."

Sullivan then said that he had not authorized the statement, that it must have been his former manager. That said, he was willing to do it. "I am here to spar Mr. Godfrey, if he is ready to spar me, as he has often stated, and I will spar him as the master of ceremonies has just told you." Godfrey replied that he would have to do so at another time, as he had not come prepared to spar with anyone.

Then Sullivan troupe members George La Blanche and Jack Ashton took turns challenging Godfrey to spar anywhere and anytime. Godfrey responded that he had offered $1,000 to fight Ashton the previous year.[8] The crowd then responded and drowned out his voice. George insisted, "I am black, but I have a right to my say." Ashton replied, but it could not be heard. Eventually the master of ceremonies broke up the argument and they left the stage.

Instead, Sullivan and Ashton sparred and went right to work in fast give and take fashion, although no powerful blows were exchanged. The spectators enjoyed the 4 rounds.

> On all sides people might be heard commenting on Sullivan's remarkable dexterity and cleverness. His movements betokened a light-weight boxer, rather than a man of his actual division.... John L. took matters with a coolness that seemed positively marvelous, and the admiration of his old time admirers was increased a hundredfold.[9]

Sullivan and Godfrey never did box.

On June 4, 1888, in New York, Sullivan sparred in tame and short set-tos with Mike Donovan and Jack Ashton. The exhibitions were called "devoid of excitement."[10] Sullivan subsequently took a vacation from the ring.

A definite mar on Sullivan's otherwise magnificent reign is the fact that he at times openly refused to fight blacks, citing the color line. The color line was a social line drawn by those who believed that whites and blacks should not mix in any area of life on the same level, including sporting competition. Generally, Sullivan's position was not much of an issue during most of his reign, as no black contender particularly stood out, and John L. was considered invincible anyway. The press did not really care that he drew the color line until he drew it against the world's recognized best contender in the late 1880s, Australia's Peter Jackson.

That said, at that time, the color line was considered acceptable by most Americans and was a reflection of the general social trend. Blacks could serve or work for whites, but they couldn't compete with them. The colored heavyweight championship had existed long before Peter Jackson. Professor Charles Hadley had been its champion in early 1883, until he was stopped by Godfrey.[11]

To provide a context for race relations, on October 15, 1883, the U.S. Supreme Court declared the Civil Rights Act of 1875 unconstitutional. That act had provided for equal accommodations and privileges for colored persons at inns or hotels, and in railroad cars and theaters. The court declared that the act was not consistent with the U.S. Congress' powers under the 13th or 14th amendments because it was no infringement of those amendments to refuse to any person the equal accommodations and privileges of an inn or a place of public entertainment, and to do so was not a badge of slavery or involuntary servitude implying subjugation. Justice Harlan was the lone dissenter. Black leader Frederick Douglass felt that the decision was "a step backward and places the United States in the rear of the civilized nations of Europe and America. Its moral effect will, he thinks, be mischievous." It was said that the colored people in the South would not be affected by the decision anyhow.[12]

This decision was reflective of the view at the time that Congress could not legislate social equality. Whites and blacks had different positions in the social order and the law could not change that fact. In fact, the ruling led to states passing laws actually mandating separation of the races, and these laws were upheld. This philosophy generally was reflected even in sport. Sullivan's position was the norm rather than the exception.

However, boxing seemed to have more progressives and dissenters from this policy than any other sport. Even the media often criticized the color line. This was in part because it was believed that the sport was so low on the moral totem pole that exponents of the art were not in a position to draw such distinctions. Thus, ironically, boxing, the sport considered to be the most depraved, was one of the few areas of life where strong arguments for fair play and equal competition were often lodged. Some boxers drew the color line, and others didn't. Some were consistent in drawing the line, while others used it selectively.

Peter Jackson stood 6'1¼" and in his prime usually fought between 190 and 210 pounds. He was born in 1861 in St. Croix, British West Indies, but eventually moved to Australia, where he began his boxing career in 1882. Training at Larry Foley's famous gymnasium, Jackson had his first bout in 1883. Peter Jackson was famous for his quick left-right combinations to the body and head, good uppercut, defensive skills, and endurance. He was not considered a big puncher, but usually cautiously and methodically broke his opponents down.

Jackson was no novice, having fought quite often in Australia, where boxing was legal. His only loss came early in his career, in 1884 when he was knocked out in the 3rd round by fellow Australian Bill Farnan (also called Farnam) in a Queensberry rules bout. Farnan was listed in America as 5'9", 32 years old, and 165 pounds.[13] According to an Australian report, in their fight, Jackson dropped Farnan in the 1st round with a punch to the jaw, followed by one to the ribs. He again dropped him with a punch to the neck. However, in the 2nd round, the durable Farnan attacked, staggering Jackson with a body shot. Farnan grabbed Jackson, and hit him "hard between wind and water, the effects being instantaneously shown by the darky seeming to double up." Thereafter, Farnan had the better of it. In the 3rd round, Jackson was punished with body shots and was fought down and out along the ropes.[14] Farnan was called the "antipodean Sullivan."[15] Jackson was only a growing and developing fighter at the time, and initially was not thought that highly of.

Later in 1884, a Jackson and Farnan rematch was stopped by the police in the 6th round when Jackson supporters broke into the ring determined not to allow their man to be roughed up by the stronger Farnan, causing it to be declared a draw. Jackson was seen as more scientific, but as less able to take a punch. "That Jackson ought to win there can be no two opinions, as Farnan has no science ... and is evidently a bit of a glutton in the way of taking his gruel—a quality which the darkey evidently does not possess, being liable to get out of order about the stomach."[16]

Farnan was thought of as a tough guy with little skill, and was laughed off when he was considered as a match for Sullivan in 1885. An Australian paper said,

Farnan may be a good rough-and-tumble fighter among his own set, but it makes us shudder when we picture him before Sullivan—or even facing our own Larry Foley.... As a matter of fact, *Farnan has no science*, and when he fought Jackson in Sydney—we did not see the Melbourne affair—the darky was all over him in the first round; but Jackson was very wild, and struck half his blows with open hands, and appeared afraid of his man. Should Farnan and Foley meet, we shall not be surprised if Farnan does not show for a second round.[17]

Peter Jackson. From Billy Edwards, *The Portrait Gallery of Pugilists of England, America, Australia* (Chicago: Athletic Publishing Co., 1894). Clay Moyle, www.prizefightingbooks.com.

In March 1886, Jackson knocked out Mick Dooley in the 3rd round, two months before Dooley stopped future champion Bob Fitzsimmons, when Bob retired after the 3rd round.

Jackson continued improving and in September 1886, the more mature Jackson won the Australian heavyweight championship with a KO30 over Tom Lees. Lees had twice knocked out Jackson's conqueror, Bill Farnan, in 12 and 4 rounds respectively in 1885 and 1886.[18] Jackson had proven that he possessed the strength and stamina required for fights to the finish.

Some of the world's best fighters at that time were coming out of Australia. Jackson, Bob Fitzsimmons, Jim Hall, and Frank Slavin, amongst others, would all be highly regarded fighters in years to come, and all were groomed in Australia. Most had been taught at the Larry Foley boxing school, where weekly gloved boxing bouts took place before spectators. Jackson was considered to be the best man in Australia. In late April 1888, having already gained world notoriety for his ability, just over a month after Sullivan fought Mitchell in their 39-round draw, Jackson set sail for America.

The first view Americans had of Jackson was in June 1888 in San Francisco against Con Riordan, a boxing teacher at the Golden Gate Club. Riordan was 165 pounds to Jackson's 200. They boxed 4 rounds and Jackson was impressive. He was quick on his feet, clever at ducking, accurate with his punches, throwing them straight from the shoulder, without swinging, and was good at getting in and out. Jackson's counterpunches swelled Riordan's lip.

Impressed spectators were quoted by the local *San Francisco Daily Examiner* as saying, "Fear alone ... will prevent Sullivan from meeting him.... The white fighters will draw the color line tighter than ever, now."[19] Generally, *The Examiner* was very high on Jackson and would be the most anti–color line American newspaper.

American black George Godfrey was also clamoring for a title shot at that time. *The National Police Gazette* said that Sullivan had refused to fight Godfrey on the ground that he would not fight a colored man. It called this a mistake, noting that its champion, Jake Kilrain, "did not run behind the door and peep through a crack when Godfrey wanted to meet him and arrange a match."[20] Back in 1883, Jake had stopped him in the 3rd round.

Of Godfrey, *The San Francisco Examiner* noted that "those who are recognized as the champions do not care particularly to face him, not because he has not backing enough, but because he is a man of color."[21] It was later in 1888 said that Godfrey had "repeatedly challenged John L. Sullivan and other claimants to the championship, but never got a battle."[22] This seemed to be including Kilrain as a champion who refused to meet Godfrey during the time that Jake was calling himself champion. Kilrain said, "It is not customary in this country for white men to fight colored men for the championship, but I will fight any man."[23] Yet, no match between Kilrain and a black fighter was made while he called himself "champion."

The color line was viewed by some as a legitimate and acceptable social barrier preventing whites from mixing with blacks. It was seen by others as a mere excuse for cowardice. *The San Francisco Daily Examiner* addressed the issue of the color line in sport when it was attempting to arrange a match between Peter Jackson and California champion and hot prospect Joe McAuliffe, stating that in America, "competition is free to all." Some felt that McAuliffe's position in drawing the color line was un-American, while others felt that he would "degrade himself by fighting the dusky Australian." A judge was interviewed and quoted as saying, "I consider if any pugilist objects to meeting him it will be merely a subterfuge and a virtual acknowledgment that the Australian is a better man, whom the other is afraid to fight." A policeman noted, "The only case I know of ... in which the color line was utilized is in connection with the colored pugilist Jackson.... I suppose the excuse is as good as another to avoid a dangerous man." Some believed that the color line was "a remnant of the feeling that once existed between master and slave."[24]

In late June 1888, Jackson and a top local Jewish pro named Joe Choynski boxed 4 rounds. The approximately 160- to 165-pound Choynski had apparently boxed state heavyweight champion Joe McAuliffe and made a "clever stand" against him, but no other details were provided.

Against Choynski, Jackson again demonstrated his ability, although it was noted that no local pugilist was as clever as Choynski, and that his quick work forced Jackson to make some effort.[25] Choynski would eventually become a top world contender who was willing to take on anyone, white or black.

The San Francisco Daily Examiner wrote:

At no time in the history of pugilism have affairs looked so bright as they do now. The presence of Peter Jackson, the Australian champion, who asks for nothing better than to meet America's best man, has done a great deal to bring about this state of affairs. The only drawback to the situation is the perceptible reluctance of the State's heavy-weight champion [Joe McAuliffe] to meet Jackson, putting his refusal under the ridiculous head of drawing the color line.[26]

The Australians back home took note of the fact that the San Francisco papers were unanimous in declaring Peter the cleverest sparrer that had been seen on the coast. "[H]is quickness in ducking away and coming up at beautiful hitting distance instantly behind or beside his opponent is noted ... one of Jackson's best points." An Englishman told an Australian reporter, "Well, I consider he's the cleverest man I ever saw. I did not always say so to you, because you and all Australians are so mad about your nigger: but now he's gone I tell you. If he's as game as he's clever there is none can beat him."

The Australians criticized the American color line:

The painful part of all this is that the Americans make his colour a bar to fighting him, a thing that should never have obtained in any country, least of all in the land whose sons actually went to war with their own brothers for the emancipation of these very negroes, whose descendants they now refuse to box with, eat with, or sit beside. Then there is another feature, and that is that in manner, deportment, and decency of living Peter Jackson is to Sullivan and a lot more like him as a schoolgirl is to a slum virago.... It is only these windbags, these men who don't want to meet men who mean real fight, that raise this black shield between them and the chance of defeat at the hands of a coloured antagonist.[27]

In the meantime, in San Francisco, on August 24, 1888, Jackson took on the fighter considered to be the best American black, Boston's George Godfrey. As they were both being avoided, they fought each other. Economics had nothing to do with the avoidance of Jackson and Godfrey, as they were both big draws. "[T]here was not a single absentee" from their fight.[28]

Godfrey was listed as weighing 164 to Jackson's 172 pounds, but the report of their fight indicated that they both looked ten pounds larger. They rarely had official weigh-ins, so reports of weights often varied.

In this Queensberry rules bout, although from the beginning it appeared that Jackson was the better man, Godfrey "fought hard, gamely and took the severest ring punishment. How he managed to stand up under Jackson's left and right handers over the heart is almost beyond comprehension." In the 2nd round, Jackson blocked a Godfrey right and then countered with a left to the chin that dropped George. It was the only knockdown. Godfrey continued fighting hard, but Jackson was much better at hitting and not being hit.

A Jackson right to the body in the 4th round caused a thud that "sounded like that of a baseball bat fetching a side of beef." However, Godfrey had the ability to take it, and fought right back, staggering Jackson with a right. Jackson retreated but hit him with a left, "drawing a copious rivulet of the crimson from Godfrey's left eye." Jackson had him hurt in the 5th, but Godfrey continued to absorb the punishment and fight back, occasionally putting Jackson on the defensive and landing some solid blows of his own.

In the 9th, Jackson asked Godfrey if he wanted him to kill him, essentially suggesting that George should retire. However, the game Godfrey could withstand punishment and kept coming back, so Jackson paced himself and gradually broke him down over many rounds with blows to the head and body. George was essentially whipped by the 16th round, and started clinching more. Jackson was fatigued, so it took a bit longer to end matters.

Pete went at him in the 19th round with both hands. After being hit with multiple lefts to the stomach, Godfrey, still standing, said "I give in," and retired. "It was a wonder he held out as long as he did."[29]

Godfrey afterwards said, "I don't know if anybody else can lick Jackson, but I know that I can't. He is a very hard man for anyone to reach, and the person that can beat him has not many equals."[30] Analyzing Jackson's performance, *The Examiner* stated,

> Jackson's fighting qualities astonished many of those present, while a few were disappointed with his hitting powers.... Jackson struck at and hit one of the hardest men in the world, one whose powers of endurance are acknowledged by all as superior to those of almost any other fighter. If Jackson's well-directed blows did fail to knock out Godfrey, it was not that they were so weak, but that Godfrey's endurance was so great.[31]

Sometime in August 1888, John L. Sullivan became seriously ill.[32] Speaking of his afflictions, Sullivan said,

> I had typhoid fever, gastric fever, inflammation of the bowels, heart trouble, and liver complaint all combined. During this sickness I was obliged to keep my bed for a period of nine weeks, leaving it on Monday the fifteenth day of October, 1888, the day I was thirty years of age.... During this illness I had been given up on two occasions by doctors.... From this sickness I contracted what the doctor termed incipient paralysis, having no use of my legs except with the assistance of crutches, which I had to use for six weeks.[33]

Mike Donovan also said that for a long time Sullivan was not expected to live. "When he recovered he was only a shadow of his former self."[34] This illness took a lot out of John L. and it was amazing that he was eventually able to recover as well as he did. Medical knowledge at that time was quite limited. Even by as late as 1900, the average life expectancy for a male was only about 48 years.

In late October, just after he ended his bed rest, Sullivan announced that he was willing to fight Jake Kilrain. On December 7, 1888, Sullivan made the official challenge to Kilrain to fight under London rules for $10,000 per side. The articles of agreement were signed on January 7, 1889. However, because of Sullivan's necessary recovery from his serious gastric and typhoid fever, as well as the training required for a finish fight, the contest was not set to occur until July 1889.[35]

Sullivan and Kilrain were scheduled to fight in what would wind up being the last heavyweight championship prize fight, the last fought under London Prize Ring Rules with bareknuckles, to determine who the real champion was. It was odd that Sullivan had again agreed to fight under the old system, but it still had its prestige, and John felt that he had something to prove. Clearly, after having failed to stop Mitchell, Sullivan wanted to defeat Kilrain under the London rules.

Those who had seen Kilrain fight Jem Smith in England thought that Kilrain would defeat Sullivan. A London report said,

> There is not one impartial man in this city who believes that Sullivan has a three to one chance in a prize ring encounter with Kilrain.... Nearly all the sporting men at the clubs were of the opinion that Kilrain will win, and they think Sullivan is aware he has no chance.[36]

Certainly, this was perceived as quite a legitimate title match.

In the meantime, in late December 1888, Peter Jackson had his second official fight in America. Although California champion Joe McAuliffe had initially drawn the color line, *The San Francisco Examiner* "pointed out to him the nonsensical position," and realizing that if he did not face Peter Jackson "it would be considered a palpable sign of weakness," McAuliffe agreed to face Jackson. This change of position "was hailed with delight by every lover of sport."[37]

Fighting McAuliffe was important for Jackson, because in 1887 Joe had knocked out Paddy Ryan in 3 rounds, giving him a national reputation. Prior to meeting Ryan, McAuliffe had defeated Mike Brennan in 44 rounds over 3 hours. Subsequent to the Ryan victory, in 1888 Joe had wins over Frank Glover in 49 rounds, and Mike Conley, the Ithaca Giant, stopping Conley in the 2nd round.[38] McAuliffe was a top contender.

Jackson fought McAuliffe on December 28, 1888, also in San Francisco. The 27-year-old Jackson weighed 204 pounds to 24-year-old McAuliffe's 219 pounds. Joe stood 6'3¼". McAuliffe's abilities were so well respected that he was the betting favorite.[39]

Fighting under Queensberry rules, Jackson knocked out McAuliffe in the 24th round. The next day's *San Francisco Examiner* report was titled, "The Color Line ... Peter Jackson Knocks Champion Joe McAuliffe Under It." Jackson was hailed as both a better boxer and fighter, being "too skillful, too quick, too scienced, too much of a general, and 'our big Joe' bit the dust." Jackson had the best of it during the entire fight, and "chopped him to pieces in as masterly a manner as was ever witnessed in the history of the squared circle.... Jackson is a short-odds horse in the race for the world's laurels of modern fistiana. He has earned the chance, and earned it well."

Jackson generally inflicted punishment and was able to avoid McAuliffe's hard blows. *The Examiner* said that Joe did have a bright moment in the 10th round, landing a powerful right to the back of the head which brought Jackson to the floor. *The San Francisco Chronicle* saw this a bit differently, saying that Jackson's foot slipped, and as he clinched, Joe threw a punch and Peter rolled to the floor. It said that it was not a knockdown, but the crowd roared anyway. *The Examiner* said Jackson recovered and landed a body shot and uppercut, but was again hit by a right, making him a bit more cautious.

Jackson had a very good 15th round, hitting Joe often with every type of blow. In the 16th, "Jackson still did the rushing, but he was always careful not to take chances against Joe's right."

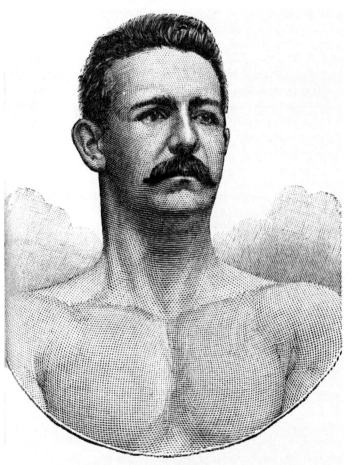

JOE McAULIFFE

Joe McAuliffe. From Richard K. Fox, *Life and Battles of John L. Sullivan Ex Champion Pugilist of the World* (New York: Richard K. Fox, 1891). Clay Moyle, www.prizefightingbooks.com.

In the 18th round, after an exchange, Joe went to his knees by the ropes. *The Chronicle* said that his feet had crossed and he was tripped up, but did note that Joe suffered a beating in this round. *The Examiner* said Peter hit him to the body, weakening him, and at that point Joe seemed almost defeated.

Joe was dropped in the 19th round by a body shot, and continued to absorb blows to the body and head. *The Chronicle* did not mention this knockdown.

After continuing to break him down with his consistent pounding, Jackson stopped McAuliffe in the 24th round, dropping him with a straight right to the nose. When he went down, it looked as if the blows "had almost knocked the life out of him. His eyes seemed almost closed, his nose was fearfully swollen, and his body was covered with great red blotches which marked where every blow had landed."[40]

Of the knockout, McAuliffe said, "I had no idea of going down, but my legs sunk under me, and that's all there was to it. I didn't know I had been knocked out until my seconds had helped me to my corner." Joe complimented his foe, stating, "Peter Jackson is the best boxer I ever knew, and those who say that he can't hit hard ought to let him try it on them. They'd soon learn their mistake. He is quick and smart as a man can be, and in addition to his skill he is a nice, gentlemanly fellow."

Jackson was complimented for his "extraordinary skill in keeping away from McAuliffe's crushing right and never planting a blow when he would risk getting one in return." It was noted that Jackson could duck faster than McAuliffe could strike.

San Francisco's black population rejoiced at Jackson's victory:

> The colored population of San Francisco have not had such a jubilee since Mr. Lincoln signed the Emancipation proclamation.... Every one of them had money on Jackson, but deeper even than the pleasure of winning was their joy at the victory of race.... Every one that had bet jingled coin in his pocket, and for once was disposed to dispute the superiority of any other race than his own.

Such statements were a sign that boxing had symbolic social implications which extended beyond a mere single sporting event, and may in part explain why the color line was so important to many whites.

Jackson said that he was willing and anxious to meet Sullivan or any other top contender, such as Jake Kilrain, believing that he could defeat anyone, and that "No man can hurt me." "If they draw the color line on me I will claim the championship anyhow. That is a 'chestnut.' They cannot avoid meeting me by such a plea."

However, it was clear that Sullivan would not fight him. Sullivan's backers indicated that he "had long ago declined to meet any colored man in the ring, or any man who stands up with a colored fighter."

Some felt that Jackson's victory was not good for boxing. "Many regret that Jackson won, on the ground that no first-class Eastern pugilist will care to fight a colored man, and they think it will have a tendency to lessen the regard of outsiders for boxing if a black man demands the championship."[41]

Others supported Jackson's right to fight Sullivan and questioned John's commitment to the color line. The president of the California Athletic Club, which financially backed Jackson, expressed his opposition to the color line being drawn:

> It sounds strange to me that John L. Sullivan has drawn the line. It is a well-known fact that at his benefit in Boston he challenged George Godfrey, the colored man, to go him four rounds there and then. Godfrey did not see where the money would come in as Sullivan proposed to do

the business "for fun," so he refused. I have heard it stated, too, that when Sullivan was here some years ago he accepted quite a large sum of money and promised to spar Bill Williams, a colored man, six rounds at the Pavilion. The only reason he did not do it was that his manager could not get a license.

Another boxing club delegate said of Jackson,

He has fought his way to the front honestly and fairly, and his color must be lost sight of by those who would lay claim to championship honors. Kilrain, Sullivan, and others cannot afford to draw the color line under the circumstances. It would lay them directly open to the charge of cowardice. I do not think the color line, which the war effaced, will stand between Jackson and the championship.[42]

It was unclear just how strong or consistent Sullivan's views were regarding the separation of the races. Apparently, Billy Wilson, a black pugilist, was a nine-year member of a sculling crew in which Sullivan was a double stroke.[43]

Years later, it was said that Sullivan was "on record that he was once stripped to meet George Godfrey in Boston, when at the last moment the police interfered." Some sources indicate that this may possibly have occurred back in 1881.[44] One foreign source alluded to this earlier match with Sullivan having been arranged. "Godfrey was once matched to fight John L. Sullivan, but the friends of the latter gave the affair away.... The tickets were all sold, the spectators present, and the men stripped and in the ring, when the police broke in."[45] Perhaps Sullivan's willingness to fight Godfrey had only been for show. That said, Sullivan was quoted as saying that he and Godfrey were once set to spar, but that George wanted too much money.[46]

Sullivan had apparently been willing to meet a black fighter named Johnson in 1882, but Johnson pulled out at the last minute.[47] Race was not an issue in 1883 when Sullivan took on Herbert "the Maori" Slade, who was called "the half breed Maori." Slade had even been a member of Sullivan's tour. Slade would be the only fighter that Sullivan ever boxed with who was not entirely white. He was half-Maori, but that was not "colored," at least in Sullivan's perception. Slade was a Pacific islander, not of African descent.

Before meeting Slade in 1883, Sullivan refused to box American black C.A.C. Smith on account of Smith's color. In early 1884, Sullivan said that he would never spar a colored man in public, but would box Bill Williams in a private room.[48] Sullivan confirmed in April 1884 while in New Orleans that he would not meet a colored man in public.[49]

Yet, Sullivan was willing to meet Godfrey in public in May 1888, when neither Sullivan nor Godfrey was aware of a match but the announcer said that they were going to spar. Sullivan did not object, but the unprepared Godfrey declined the meeting, offering to fight at a later date.[50] Perhaps Sullivan only expressed a willingness to box him because he knew that Godfrey was not prepared and would not accept at that time. Godfrey said that he wanted to meet John at a later date, but the fight was never arranged. In early 1889, Sullivan refereed a bout between Joe Lannon and Godfrey, a mixed race bout, declaring it a draw after 15 rounds.[51] Certainly, Sullivan's stance was not consistently held.

It was reported by the New York correspondent of *The London Sporting Life* that as of January 7, 1889, Sullivan had been on another wild spree, i.e. drinking excessively. It too criticized Sullivan's drawing of the color line:

His flat refusal to meet Peter Jackson, on the thin excuse of his objection to fight a coloured man, was already sapping his new found popularity.... Sullivan has already put himself on record as refusing to meet a negro, and he now says that under no consideration will he meet Jackson. Many sporting men construe this as an acknowledgement of Jackson's great fighting powers.... Would it not be a curious thing if Sullivan was whipped by a nigger, and a British subject at that?[52]

Regardless, by that time, Sullivan and Kilrain were scheduled to fight each other, which was a very big fight. Thus, John L. initially had a legitimate excuse for not facing Peter.

On April 24, 1889, in Brooklyn, New York, Sullivan sparred with Jack Ashton. John L. looked fat and soft. Although the crowd was charged $1 and $1.50 to witness the exhibition, the rounds only lasted half a minute and the boxing was described as light and not particularly interesting.

John L. seems to be quick with his hands and to get home on the neck with considerable precision and force. He is not himself at all, though, and those who knew him when he was downing everybody with the greatest ease remarked the difference. However, allowance must be made for his recent sickness.[53]

Another report said that Sullivan made a clever display, and though he was not as agile as before his illness, he was able to more than hold his own with the conqueror of Joe Lannon, and the exhibition of skill and quickness evoked applause.[54]

On April 26, 1889, in San Francisco, Peter Jackson took on Patsy Cardiff, who had fought Charley Mitchell to an 1885 5-round draw, and had fought Sullivan to an 1887 6-round draw. Cardiff also had an 1885 and 1886 KO9 and KO7 over Bill Wilson, a black fighter. However, in 1888, Cardiff was stopped in the 4th round by Pat Killen. Killen also had an 1886 KO4 over Mervine Thompson, a very strong 210–220 pounder, and an 1887 KO2 over Duncan McDonald. In September 1889, Killen would be stopped in the 7th round by Joe McAuliffe, whom Jackson had already defeated.

For this one, Jackson weighed in at 200 pounds, while Cardiff may have been slightly larger than 185 pounds.[55] According to the local *San Francisco Chronicle* (SFC), Jackson was superior in every respect from the very beginning, hitting the body and head with both hands, although Patsy did occasionally land a good counterpunch. Jackson smiled throughout, and the only mark he had at the end was a small lump on his forehead where he was head butted in the 1st round.

The San Francisco Examiner (SFE) was more critical of Jackson, saying that although he was a clever boxer, he lacked finishing power, depending on defeating his opponent "by jabbing him into insensibility and not by a clean knock-out." Altering its previous opinion, it called Jackson overrated, but this criticism seemed to be a bit picky. What Jackson lacked in power he made up for in ring intelligence, defense, and endurance. Regardless of its criticism, its version still said that in the "hard and vicious" fight, "Jackson displayed his wonderful quickness and ability to dodge at short range. He had decidedly the best of the slugging."

1st Round

SFC: Cardiff utilized some foul tactics, such as grabbing Jackson by the legs, in addition to a head butt.

SFE: Cardiff tried to push Jackson over the ropes, which received cries of foul. A Cardiff counter to Jackson's nose brought first blood.

Nothing was particularly interesting about the 2nd round.

3rd Round

SFC: Cardiff grabbed and tried to throw Jackson. They both did some good infighting.
SFE: Cardiff clinched around the waist and tried to break Peter's back.

4th Round

SFE: It was competitive early in the fight, but in this round, Jackson began hitting him easily with his left on the face and avoiding most counters.

5th Round

SFC: Cardiff again grabbed Peter's legs. Patsy's left cheek was bleeding and his eye puffed.
SFE: Cardiff landed a good counter that staggered Peter a bit. Patsy again tried to push him over the ropes. They exchanged often in the round, but Jackson landed more and got the better of it.

6th Round

SFE: Patsy attempted to knee Peter in the stomach while grabbing his waist, to calls of foul. Cardiff also hit with an open hand, and was admonished for that. A Jackson right under the ear dropped Cardiff, who rose weakly. Peter again hurt him with a hard left on the nose. At this point, it appeared that Cardiff was a beaten man. *The National Police Gazette* also indicated that Cardiff was dropped in the 6th round, but *The Chronicle* did not mention this.

7th Round

SFE: Jackson hit Cardiff's nose often.

8th Round

SFC: "Jackson sent in one telling smash on Patsy's gory lips, and Patsy tottered. Jackson immediately swung his right and brought Cardiff to the floor with a blow on the chin." Cardiff hugged and tried to grab Peter's leg.
SFE: Patsy was punished in the round, and a right under the ear sent Cardiff down for the second time in the bout. Additional blows sent him back to the ropes. Jackson pounded on him, and then asked, "Do you give up?" However, Patsy refused and continued to take his beating.

9th Round

SFC: Between the 8th and 9th rounds, Cardiff's cornerman rubbed some resin on Patsy's glove, which was illegal, but it was discovered prior to the beginning of the round and was removed. In the 9th, Cardiff seemed just about out of it, and turned to his second as if asking him to stop it.

SFE: Between rounds his cornerman rubbed rosin on Patsy's gloves, but he was caught and the referee alerted. Pete jabbed away, but was caught by one right that backed him off for a while. However, Jackson eventually forced Cardiff to the ropes. Patsy was just about knocked out at the bell, and Jackson seemed to pity him a bit.

10th Round

SFC: Jackson landed hard lefts and rights to Cardiff's jaw, and Patsy held onto the ropes. Jackson stopped momentarily and asked Patsy if he wished to give in, but apparently he gave the wrong answer because Peter then continued pounding on him and Patsy turned his back and bent over the ropes. At first, Cardiff's cornerman attempted to get him to continue, but seeing that he was essentially knocked out hanging on the ropes, retired his man by throwing up the sponge.

SFE: Rights and lefts sent Patsy back into his corner against the ropes, dropping his hands. His cornerman urged him to fight, but he said, "I can't fight." He continued to be hit. Jackson paused a moment, waiting for him to raise his hands in the ready position, but he did not. Cardiff was unable to continue. The referee stepped in and raised Jackson's hand, saying, "Out."[56]

Peter Jackson was clearly the best heavyweight around, other than Kilrain and Sullivan. His manager felt that Peter could defeat both, saying that the only man who could whip Jackson was the Sullivan of old.[57] Throughout 1889, Jackson continued boxing regularly in exhibitions and fights.

CHAPTER 16

End of an Era

In May 1889, John L. Sullivan moved to wrestler William Muldoon's farm to train for his early July bout with Jake Kilrain. It was thought to be important to get Sullivan away from the metropolis, a climate which was "not healthy enough for a man so easily led from the paths of sobriety." Muldoon was a strict disciplinarian who insisted on Sullivan's getting into the best shape of his life for this fight to the finish. He was also a champion wrestler who could help Sullivan with his wrestling skills in preparation for a London rules bout.[1]

One writer analyzed the upcoming fight:

There never was a fighter like John L. Sullivan.... In the plenitude of his powers no man could successfully resist him.... He is now backed against Jake Kilrain ... to fight under London ring rules, and he can't wrestle a little bit. Purely a Queensberry fighter, he has never thought it worth his while to acquire an intimate knowledge of cross-buttocks, grapevine twists or inside checks, and now Billy Muldoon is to try and teach him in a few weeks what men who have a natural aptitude for wrestling find it difficult to acquire in years....

If he is able to land with anything like his old-time severity on Jake's jaw, neck or stomach, the contest will be as short and sweet as a donkey's trot. Kilrain ... may attempt to imitate Mitchell's tactics and make a waiting fight of it, but no man that ever lived can evade Sullivan if he is well and strong on his legs. He is the quickest big man that ever fought in the ring, and when he once gets an opponent in the ring that is the end of that man's chances. Mind that is when he is well and strong.[2]

Sullivan and Muldoon in preparation gave wrestling exhibitions in Detroit, Cincinnati, New Jersey, and New York, each time attracting full houses. Mike Cleary was also brought in to spar with John. Kilrain had Charley Mitchell as his trainer.[3] Sullivan's training generally included things like wrestling and sparring, hitting the punching bags, shadow boxing with weights, jumping rope, swimming, running, and taking 1- to 3-hour-long walks.

A month before the fight, one newspaper said the general belief was that Sullivan would lose. Billy Edwards said, "I had a look at Sullivan last Friday, and assuredly he is not the man he was.... He and Kilrain are of the same age, but one has taken good care of himself and the other hasn't. If they had met five years ago Kilrain would have stood no show." Describing Kilrain, he said, "He never does anything for show. He's all business in the ring.... He is a two hander and a jabber from way back. Besides that he's got a right that is able to put Sullivan or anybody else to sleep. He's as good a general, too, as ever put up his hands.... If there is a meeting it will surprise me if Sullivan wins."[4]

Still, there were many who were just as sure that Sullivan would win. Middleweight George La Blanche picked Sullivan. Jimmy Carroll said, "With Sullivan's wonderful hitting powers and his great cleverness he ought certainly to win." Jack Dempsey said that Kilrain would give John little more than a pleasant sparring bout before being knocked out. William

Muldoon said that Sullivan was working hard and was weighing 218 pounds, and expected to be 195 by fight time.[5]

One of the more important sub-stories of the fight was the fact that the governors of Mississippi, Louisiana, and Alabama, not knowing exactly where the fight would take place but suspecting that their states were the likely locations, all issued edicts that the fight would not be allowed to occur in their states. The fight's exact location had to be kept secret for fear that the fight would be prevented.

Mississippi governor Robert Lowry had been governor back in February 1882, and was then unsuccessful in his attempts to stop the Sullivan-Ryan prize fight. The month after that fight, on March 7, 1882, an act was passed by the state legislature making prize fighting a misdemeanor punishable by up to a year in jail and/or a $500–$1,000 fine. Lowry called upon all state officers to prevent the Kilrain-Sullivan fight, and said that he was willing to use the state militia if necessary. Alabama and Louisiana granted Lowry permission to allow troops from his state militia to pass through their states if needed in order to stop the fight or arrest the combatants. Lowry also offered a $500 reward for the arrest of Sullivan and Kilrain, or half that amount for either man.

About five days before the fight, Kilrain was listed as weighing 185–188 pounds. He walked 20 miles and hit the punching bag for two hours, in addition to other exercises. Sullivan was said to have removed all of his superfluous flesh. A few days before the bout, John L. did two hours of work in the morning, and two more in the evening. He tossed the medicine ball, skipped rope for twenty or more minutes, did calisthenics with light dumbbells, and punched the bag.

A couple days before the fight, Muldoon said that Sullivan was weighing 203 pounds and would weigh 205 upon entering the ring. Muldoon said that both Sullivan and Kilrain would wear a protective plaster reaching above the waist and around the body. Apparently, the rules did not prevent such thing.[6]

The fight had been building for a couple years, with *The National Police Gazette* billing Kilrain as champion, and therefore it was a fight that the general public was excited about. Most considered Sullivan to be the champion, but the fight was to settle any cloud over the championship, which Kilrain had claimed since 1887. Jake was coming off his 106-round draw with Jem Smith, and was seen as a legitimate threat to Sullivan. Tickets were being sold for $10 and $15.

Analyzing the mass popularity of these men and the sport, one writer commented,

> There must be something esthetic in a contest that involves human muscle directed by fistic science. It cannot be that ten millions of people in the United States are today devouring with avidity the least details of the coming mill, if there be not in such a struggle something that appeals to other than our brutish instincts. Candor compels us to say that many of our educated and refined people are excited over the event.... The brutality in man's nature gives no adequate explanation, for men who are not brutal are eager to witness the fray.... There is in us all an unconscious worship of physical perfection in the human form.... To this admiration ... is added the peculiar pleasure felt at any exhibition of scientific skill.... The well-directed blow, the parry, the swift counter blow—this is not brutality; it is skill. We instinctively admire it in every other sphere—why not in the realm of prize fighting?[7]

Opinions were mixed as to who would win the fight. Some were impressed with Kilrain's performance against Smith, and felt that Sullivan would not be sufficiently recovered from the effects of typhoid fever. Ex–American bareknuckle champion Tom Allen picked Kilrain to win. Paddy Ryan picked Sullivan, saying that when fit, no living man could defeat him.

"You might as well try to make an impression on a lamppost with your fist as on Sullivan's face or body." Another said, "Science will not avail much against such blows as Sullivan will deal out."[8]

At 2 a.m. the morning of July 8, 1889, it was learned that the fight would take place on that date in Richburg, Mississippi, about 7 miles from Hattiesburg, and 103 miles from New Orleans. Richburg was essentially the estate of Charles Rich. On the afternoon of the 7th, a special train took the Sullivan party from New Orleans to the fight site. The ring was pitched outside the day before the fight.[9]

Jake Kilrain. From Billy Edwards, *The Portrait Gallery of Pugilists of England, America, Australia* (Chicago: Athletic Publishing Co., 1894). Clay Moyle, www.prizefightingbooks.com.

It was Sullivan's first defense in one year and four months. It was a scheduled fight to the finish, and only Sullivan's third bareknuckle fight. His first such fight had also taken place in Mississippi, over seven years earlier in 1882 against Paddy Ryan. It was to be the last bareknuckle heavyweight championship fight fought under London Prize Ring Rules.

The Daily Picayune said that over 2,000 people witnessed the fight, but *The Times-Democrat* said that over 3,000 attended. It had earlier been reported that the bout was for an unprecedented stake of $10,000 a side. One paper said that the winner would be paid more money than any pugilist had ever received for any pugilistic event. It estimated that after expenses, the winner would clear about $22,000 for the fight.[10] Another paper said the amount of the stakes and gate money combined was $50,000.[11]

As usual, there are some factual variations based on which primary source is reviewed, but the overall gist is the same. *The Daily Picayune* and *Times-Democrat* versions will be provided first because they were the papers located closest geographically to the fight site. They will occasionally be followed

Building the ring and stands for the Sullivan-Kilrain fight (Library of Congress, Prints & Photographs Division).

by what other reports said, such as *The Boston Herald*, *The Boston Daily Globe*, *The National Police Gazette*, *The New York Daily Tribune*, and *The New York Times*. With some subtle variations, the sources mostly agreed on what happened, but not necessarily when it happened, having varying accountings of each round. When viewed as a whole, though, the stories are essentially the same. Because the fight was so long, generally, how the round concluded is what will be provided unless something particularly significant occurred during the round.

Sullivan wore green tights with white socks and black shoes. Kilrain wore black tights. Sullivan's plaster reached several inches above his waist. Kilrain's plaster was not as large and mostly covered his back.

The Times-Democrat reported that Jake's friends said he weighed 195 pounds. Sullivan had been weighing about 205 pounds, but was reported to have gained some weight in the days leading up to the fight.

> Sullivan was by far the heavier man and so pronounced is this impression that it is difficult to believe that the big fellow's weight was accurately stated in the figures given out concerning it.... Had it been stated that Sullivan weighed 217 pounds and Kilrain 197 the statement would have gained ready credence.

The Picayune reported that Sullivan claimed to weigh 207 pounds. Mitchell said that Kilrain weighed 195 pounds, although at another time he said he weighed 190. After the fight was over, that evening, Kilrain was weighed at 183 pounds. It would not be surprising for a fighter to lose 12 pounds during a grueling fight in the broiling sun.[12] Both men stood 5'10½" and were 30 years old.

The thermometer showed 108 degrees Fahrenheit. Some reporters suffered from heat prostration, and they weren't fighting.[13] *The Daily Picayune* said that it was so hot that many observers almost fainted. Kilrain and Sullivan were afterwards red from sunburn.[14]

After some debate, John Fitzpatrick of New Orleans was agreed upon by both sides to be the referee. Fitzpatrick was originally a spectator, and was asked to do the honors when neither side could agree on a referee. He admitted that he was not very conversant with the rules, but said that he would do as best as he could. He said that the 30 seconds time between rounds would commence from the time a man went down.

Initially, the local sheriff said that there could be no fight. However, the managers engaged in coaxing and convincing.

[A friend of the sluggers] politely met the sheriff and posse at the ring side, showed them all possible attention and courteously escorted them inside the ring. The sheriff entered his protest against the fight, and, with his deputies retired to a choice spot, specially set aside for them, witnessed the brutal exhibition.

In an interview given four days after the fight to *The Times-Democrat*, William Muldoon admitted that he had bribed the sheriff.

I walked up to him and put $250 in his hand. "Here, says I, is $250 and Duffy will give you as much more." He hadn't more than felt the money till he sang out: "Well, gentlemen, I am powerless to stop you, because I've only got six men and you 3000," and on he sneaked.

The fight began at 10:15 a.m.:

Round 1

The *Daily Picayune* (DP) said there was no chance for any fighting as Kilrain immediately clinched, got Sullivan across his hip, and threw him to the ground, landing on top of him after only 5 seconds had elapsed.

The *Times-Democrat* (TD) reported that both men carried the left low and only moderately extended. Jake held his right loosely across his chest with the forearm extended upward. John held the forearm tightly against his chest in an almost horizontal position, looking anxious to counter. After a few passes, Sullivan led short, and Kilrain grabbed him by the neck and used a hip-lock to throw John to the ground, falling on top of him. The round lasted no more than half a minute at the most.

Other sources said that Kilrain was a good wrestler, ending the 1st round only 12 seconds in by throwing John to the ground.

Round 2

DP: Kilrain rushed in and wrestled, with both eventually falling side by side in a dog fall. Time: 2 minutes.

TD: Sullivan had a slight bruise on his back from the fall ending the 1st round, but he was smiling. Sullivan grabbed Kilrain by the waist and hit him in the ribs. Jake jumped cleverly out of the way of the next punch. They came together again and both went down, with Sullivan on top. Time: About 1½ minutes.

Others said that after Sullivan landed a right to the body, they wrestled down, *The Police Gazette* and *Boston Daily Globe* indicating that it was Sullivan who initiated the throw down.

Round 3

DP: Sullivan slightly staggered Kilrain with a right to the neck. Jake hit below the belt twice, and the second time it appeared deliberate. Sullivan landed his big right twice in succession to the ribs. Kilrain clinched and swung his right on the neck. Sullivan tried to wrestle, but Kilrain threw Sullivan instead, both going down. Time: 5 minutes, 30 seconds.

TD: They clinched and engaged in tremendous infighting, both landing to the ribs with such force that the sound of the blows could be heard around the ring. Sullivan's fists seemed to bury themselves inside of Jake's side, a sight that was "absolutely sickening." John also landed strong blows to the heart. Jake got away and danced about. When they came together again, Sullivan was wrestled down. It was one of the most terrific rounds of the fight. Despite the fact that Kilrain landed a number of heavy blows and had the best of the fall, Sullivan's rights to the ribs and heart did more damage. The punishment that Kilrain received in this round seemed to weaken him. Time: 3 minutes.

The Police Gazette said that a Sullivan blow to the stomach in this round made Jake turn pale, and that after this point, he seemed whipped. Most sources indicated that after the 3rd round, Kilrain was not the same.

The New York Daily Tribune mentioned that Kilrain twice struck Sullivan below the belt. *The New York Times* echoed that there were cries of foul to Kilrain's low blows, with *The Boston Daily Globe* saying that there were half a dozen thrown. *The Boston Herald* said that Sullivan hit the body and kidneys, and they fell down together in a clinch to end the round, *The Globe* saying that it was Sullivan who was thrown down.

Round 4

DP: The men conversed during the round, and Sullivan wore a smile of self-confidence. Charley Mitchell coached Kilrain and said, "Go in Jack: you know he can't hurt you." Sullivan replied to Mitchell, "I wish I had you in the center, you sucker." John landed a light left to the nose that drew just a slight speck of blood. Sullivan rushed in with his head down and Kilrain caught him under his arm and threw him on his back. Time: 2½ minutes.

TD: Kilrain would jump away after Sullivan feinted. After wrestling for a moment, both men landed a number of head shots in fierce and rapid exchanges. Kilrain landed a blow to the neck hard enough to knock an ordinary man out, but Sullivan laughed contemptuously and danced backwards to avoid the follow up. They sparred, evaded and clinched for a bit, until Sullivan lowered his head and rushed in. Jake jumped to the side and grabbed his neck, twisting it as they both went down from the force of the rush. Time: 3 minutes.

Round 5

DP: Kilrain seemed distressed as Sullivan came forward looking fierce. Sullivan stalked Jake, who walked around in a circle as the crowed jeered. After a number of exchanges, Sullivan landed a left to the jaw, Kilrain clinched, and both fell with Sullivan underneath. Time: 2 minutes.

TD: After rapid exchanges, Sullivan landed a vicious uppercut to the eye, which momentarily staggered Jake. After some more fighting, Kilrain landed an effective right to the ribs around the heart, which hurt Sullivan. A clinch followed and both went down, Sullivan underneath.

Round 6

DP: Kilrain was offensive and landed a punch to Sullivan's right ear that started the blood flowing. Kilrain was allowed the claim of first blood. The aroused Sullivan landed a right to the head that dropped Kilrain, scoring the first knockdown. Time: 1 minute.

TD: When Sullivan led for the ribs, Jake cross-countered on the ear with such force that the blood streamed down John's neck. He had scored first blood, one of the betting points. Sullivan grinned savagely. Jake led for the stomach and landed, but Sullivan paid it no mind and immediately cross-countered to the neck, dropping Kilrain to the grass limp and half-senseless, the first knockdown of the fight. The crowd cheered the result of another betting point.

Round 7

DP: When Sullivan released Kilrain from a hold and was about to strike him, Jake went down to avoid punishment, and was carried to his corner. Time: 2½ minutes.

TD: Sullivan rushed in but Kilrain stepped aside and grabbed and twisted John's neck. Jake's hold slipped from the perspiration and he went down. Time: 20 seconds.

Round 8

DP: It was evident that Kilrain had abandoned his aggressive plan and was trying to save himself, adopting Mitchell's tactics of delay and walking around the ring. Several times John said, "Come here and fight."

The Boston Herald said Sullivan taunted Kilrain, saying, "Stand up and fight ... you're the champion, you know. Come, prove your title." *The Police Gazette* and *The Boston Globe* said that Kilrain seemed frightened and playing a waiting game, moving and walking about the ring. Sullivan asked him why he didn't come on and fight.

The DP said that eventually, Kilrain punched Sullivan's right eye, cutting him and drawing blood. Kilrain closed in, back heeled and threw Sullivan. Time: 1½ minutes.

TD: Kilrain's right eye was badly discolored. He danced away from Sullivan, laughing. Some spectators called Jake a cur. They exchanged some, and Jake eventually landed a left under the right eye that opened a gaping cut, the blood flowing freely. Sullivan was now cut on the ear and under the eye. In a clinch which followed, Sullivan threw Jake down. During the round, a section of seats came down, but the fighters paid it no mind.

Round 9

DP: Kilrain was aggressive again and rushed in. A Sullivan right made Jake look weak. Another right to the neck dazed him. Sullivan followed up and Kilrain moved about. A right to the pit of Kilrain's stomach dropped him, doubled up on the turf. Kilrain was in distress and his body showed signs of the punishment, revealing a deep hue. Time: 15 seconds.

TD: A Sullivan counter to Jake's ear caused blood to flow. Kilrain clinched, but was pushed off. In proper range, Sullivan landed a right to the left ear and then fought him down with a follow-up rally. It looked as if Jake would be done for pretty soon.

The *Globe* and *The Gazette* said that from this round through the 14th round, the rounds did not last beyond 30 seconds, and sometimes they did not even last 10 seconds before Kilrain went down.

Round 10

DP: Sullivan quickly scored a knockdown with a punch to Kilrain's right cheek. Time: 10 seconds.

TD: Sullivan feinted with the left, and when the weak Kilrain tried to stagger out of the way, Sullivan sprang forward and landed a crushing right to the side of the head that dropped Jake "as though stricken with a pole-ax."

The Tribune indicated that a heavy right dropped Kilrain.

Round 11

DP: Kilrain was slow to come to the scratch and was warned by the referee. A right to the jaw sent Jake down. "Kilrain was carried to his corner as if he weighed a ton. His flesh was quivering and he showed signs of distress. Time: 1½ minutes."

TD: Kilrain staggered to the scratch and was too weak to avoid Sullivan's rush. Jake was knocked down with a crushing left hand blow to the neck.

Round 12

DP: Sullivan landed several uppercuts. Jake landed a good one to the eye, but Sullivan got Jake in a neck hold and threw and fell heavily upon him. Time: 1½ minutes.

TD: A right to the heart caused Jake to fall forward in an attempt to clinch, grabbing John's neck. Sullivan fought him down with repeated rights and lefts to the neck and ear. Some said that Kilrain was gone.

Another source said the crowd hissed at Kilrain when he was chased down and fell just as a blow was coming at him.

Round 13

DP: As Kilrain clinched to avoid punishment, Sullivan pushed him and Jake fell. Time: 1 minute.

TD: Kilrain showed some pluck, but his blows were so weak that Sullivan did not even bother to parry them, preferring to counter. Kilrain was damaged to the ribs, ear and neck. He was quickly fought down, and his seconds carried him to his corner.

Others said that Kilrain landed and tried to grab, but John hit him hard in the face and dropped him. *The Gazette* mentioned Kilrain spiking Sullivan in this round and said that Jake slipped down to avoid punishment.

Round 14

DP: Both came up smiling, but Kilrain's seemed forced. Sullivan looked at Jake with scorn as Kilrain walked around the ring. After some feints, Sullivan made a rush and landed to the head with both hands, knocking Kilrain out. Time: 1 minute.

TD: Kilrain cleverly avoided punishment. In a clinch, Sullivan slipped down, his back striking against one of the ring posts.

Another source said they exchanged some blows, but this time it was Sullivan who slipped and fell in a clinch.

Round 15

DP: This was the longest round of the fight. Sullivan carried his left low and his wrist looked swollen. Sullivan's left foot was gashed by Kilrain's spikes. Kilrain walked or ran away whenever Sullivan came within rushing distance. The crowd shouted that it was not a foot race. Eventually, Sullivan landed a right to the neck and Kilrain fell, John going down with him and falling on Jake with his knees. Time: 7 minutes.

TD: Sullivan wore a grim smile, but Jake seemed somewhat recovered. During some rapid exchanges, an uppercut to Kilrain's nose brought blood, but Jake countered with a heavy punch to the stomach. Kilrain began moving around more and kept well away from Sullivan, a perceptible change in tactics. The crowd responded, "You cur!" At one point, Kilrain spiked and gashed Sullivan's left foot. Kilrain said that it was accidental. Sullivan asked him to be more careful. They engaged in some infighting in which Sullivan got the best of it. While breaking away, Sullivan landed a right to the ear and followed up with a left to the ribs, which dropped Kilrain.

The Boston Globe said that Kilrain made the round a foot race, causing the crowd to yell, "Make him fight!" Sullivan taunted him, saying, "You are a champion ... a champion of what?" John hit him with a right to the jaw, and then Jake fell in a delayed reaction.

The Herald said that Jake spiked John, but then went down from light blows.

Round 16

DP: Kilrain pursued dirty tactics, twice clearly fouling John by hitting him low. The crowd jeered at Kilrain for generally keeping away. Occasionally Jake would land a good punch to the head or body, but would then go on a long walk, pursuing guerrilla tactics. Eventually, Sullivan punished the body, and following him to a corner, landed a blow to the right ear that knocked him out. Time: 4 minutes.

TD: Sullivan forced matters. Kilrain countered, but Sullivan fought him down near a corner.

The Globe said Kilrain was trying to position John where Sullivan might miss a lead and strike a ring post. Sullivan hit him in the jaw and was about to repeat the punch when Kilrain went to the grass without being hit. Sullivan and his seconds put up a mild protest.

Round 17

DP: Cleary asked for a show of hands, and Kilrain's open palm displayed traces of rosin. However, there were traces of rosin in Sullivan's hands as well, and both their hands were washed.

During the round, in a clinch, Kilrain tried to throw John, but Sullivan threw him instead, falling on Jake. Time: 4 minutes.

TD: As Jake was coming to the scratch, the referee accused him of having rosin on his hands. Jake washed his, but accused John of having rosin as well, saying that if he had something on his hands resembling rosin, it was likely due to coming in contact with the plaster Sullivan wore over his stomach. Sullivan also washed his hands.

Although Jake landed a stinging right to the eye, in the follow-up exchanges, he was fought down by Sullivan. In the corner, Cleary sucked the blood out of Sullivan's eye.

Others agreed that illegal rosin was discovered in Jake's hands and it was removed. *The Herald* said that Sullivan landed body shots to the ribs, "the sound of the blows being like a smith's anvil under the hammer. Kilrain got in a stiff one under John's left eye in the closing moments, cutting a deep gash and starting the blood. In a wrestle Kilrain back-heeled John, and fell on him." *The Globe* said it was Sullivan who threw Jake and fell on top of him.

The Times-Democrat said that from the 18th to the 21st rounds, Sullivan had the best of it, fighting Kilrain down in each round.

According to *The Boston Herald*, over the next number of rounds, very little action took place. Kilrain would go down from light blows or sometimes without being struck at all, in addition to the occasional wrestle down.

Round 18

DP: The cut under Sullivan's left eye was bleeding. John followed Jake around and landed a right to the chest, from which Kilrain dropped in order to avoid further punishment. Time: 1 minute.

TD: Kilrain missed a punch and received a slight tap to the breast in return that sent him down.

The Globe felt that Kilrain fell without being struck.

Round 19

DP: Sullivan landed a right to the ribs and held Kilrain up to keep him from falling. Later, when John was about to strike out with his right, Kilrain dropped down to avoid punishment. Sullivan complained to the referee, but Kilrain rose, Sullivan landed two body shots, and Kilrain went down again. Time: 3 minutes.

TD: Kilrain ducked a right, but in doing so went down to one knee. He quickly sprang up again only to receive a knockdown blow to the neck.

The Globe said John asked Kilrain, "Do you want to wrestle, fight or race?" A punch to the ribs dropped Kilrain, who rose, and then fell again without being struck. *The Gazette* said that he went down from a punch to the head.

Round 20

DP: Sullivan landed a light right to the body and Kilrain fell. Sullivan called the referee's attention to Kilrain's survival tactics, and asked him to make Kilrain fight. Time: 30 seconds.

TD: Sullivan staggered Kilrain with a stomach blow. Jake punched back and fell from the force of his own blow.

The Globe said Kilrain went down without being struck at all. The Tribune and The Gazette said that Kilrain went down from a "roaster" to the ribs, but also mentioned that Kilrain often went down without being hit. This was technically illegal, but the referee did not disqualify Kilrain.

Round 21

DP: Kilrain seemed groggy, especially after Sullivan landed a right to the nose. After a mere push, Jake fell down. Time: 15 seconds.

TD: Jake's left side was horribly discolored. On the inside, Sullivan landed his left and right on the neck and ribs and Kilrain fell to the ground with a groan.

The Globe said Kilrain went down without being struck. The Gazette said Kilrain fell from a blow to the jaw.

Round 22

DP: Sullivan hit him in the ribs and Kilrain dropped to escape further punishment. Sullivan's rib shots were especially effective. That particular spot was very inflamed and bothered Jake. Time: 15 seconds.

TD: Sullivan knocked him down with a right to the ribs.

The Globe said Sullivan made a protest when Kilrain went down, saying that he never touched him. The Gazette said that Jake went down from a blow to the ribs, a punch that Sullivan said missed.

Round 23

DP: Sullivan hit his ribs with both hands. "As usual, at the slightest push Kilrain went to grass, and, in exasperation, Sullivan jumped on him with both knees, striking him in the head. It was a foul, but was not allowed. Time: 1 minute and 45 seconds."

TD: After being punched to the heart, Kilrain tried to clinch, but John grabbed his waist, threw Jake down, and dropped down upon him with his whole weight, both knees landing on Kilrain's neck and head. Some excitement followed, as Kilrain's seconds claimed that the fight should be awarded to them on a foul, but the referee disallowed the claim. One accused the referee of having money on the fight. The referee called him a liar.

The Globe and The Gazette agreed that Kilrain hit Sullivan's damaged eye, trying to get it to close shut. When Jake fell, John fell on top of him, and Jake claimed that John punched him in the stomach with his elbow.

Round 24

DP: Kilrain continued to walk away and the crowd jeered. However, in avoiding one of Kilrain's blows, Sullivan slipped to one knee, and Kilrain taunted him, saying that John was pursuing his tactics. Time: 2 minutes.

The Sullivan-Kilrain fight. John L. is on the left (Library of Congress, Prints & Photographs Division).

TD: Sullivan landed a blow to the ear that staggered Jake. As John followed up, Kilrain threw up his right hand to stop a Sullivan punch and fell down, partly from the force of stopping the blow, and partly from weakness.

Another source said that Kilrain went down from a blow to his elbow, which hurt John's hand.

The TD said that the 24th, 25th, and 26th rounds were decidedly in Sullivan's favor, although in the 26th he was thrown by Kilrain.

Round 25

DP: A neck blow glanced off, but Kilrain fell down nevertheless. Sullivan sat down in his corner for the first time in the fight. Time: 30 seconds.

TD: Sullivan landed a sharp punch to the ribs and followed with a rally which sent Jake down.

Others said that Sullivan continued hitting the sore spot under the heart, and landed a good one to Jake's nose, causing it to swell up. *The Herald* said Kilrain received three terrific blows to the body that sapped his strength. His left side below the heart was "red as scarlet from the repeated visitations."

Round 26

DP: Blood streamed from Kilrain's ear. They wrestled and Kilrain gained the fall over Sullivan by using a cross buttock to down him. Time: 1½ minutes.

TD: Kilrain back-heeled and threw Sullivan.

The Globe and *The Gazette* said Kilrain did better and threw Sullivan to the ground.

Round 27

DP: John landed a right to the jaw and pushed Jake, who fell heavily. Time: 3 minutes.

TD: A blow to the neck, right to the breast, and another on the left ear knocked Kilrain down.

The Globe and *The Gazette* said the 27th was more action packed, at one point both men giving and taking powerful blows for about 20 seconds until Kilrain fell. Sullivan's left eye was well puffed up and swelling. *The Herald* noted that in this round, Kilrain's left started a little mouse under Sullivan's right eye.

In subsequent rounds, Jake continued going down from slight taps or from fear of being hit. According to *The Tribune*, after the 27th round, the "next twelve rounds were but a repetition of the former ones, Sullivan getting the best of them all, landed several heavy blows on Kilrain's side, the latter falling regularly to avoid punishment."

The Times-Democrat said that from the 27th to the 43rd rounds, "Kilrain was playing a waiting game, much to the disgust of the crowd." Jake would walk and move about the ring, generally avoiding John and killing time. "The referee also objected to Kilrain's tactics. During all this dodging and dancing around, however, Kilrain had managed to land again and again on Sullivan's stomach."

Round 28

DP: Sullivan landed a right to the body and Jake dropped to avoid punishment. Time: 2 minutes.

TD: Sullivan landed a punch to the damaged ribs which doubled Jake up, and John followed with a savage uppercut to the eye which dropped Jake.

Another source said that it was a good round. A punch to Sullivan's eye seemed to hurt him. Kilrain ran away when John rushed him, but when he went to the ropes, Jake was struck on the jaw and went down to one knee.

Round 29

DP: Sullivan landed a right to the breast, and as Jake attempted to clinch, sent Kilrain down with a left on the jaw. Time: 1 minute.

TD: Kilrain tried to close in, but John stepped aside and hit him on the shoulder, and then, pushing him off at arm's length, dropped Jake with a right to the neck.

The Gazette said Kilrain hit the injured eye, and then in a clinch slipped out to the ground.

Round 30

DP: After Jake walked around stalling for time, Sullivan rushed at him, but Kilrain dropped to escape punishment. Time: 1 minute.

TD: The round was very short. Kilrain tried to close in, but Sullivan pushed him and Jake fell.

According to *The Herald*, the referee finally warned Jake not to fall without a blow, on penalty of losing. Kilrain nevertheless continued to fall in the next two rounds from light or nonexistent blows.

Round 31

DP: Sullivan hit Kilrain's damaged eye. After John landed a left to the mouth and a light punch to the body, Jake went down. Time: 1½ minutes.

TD: Kilrain landed a nice counter right to the left eye, but Sullivan landed twice to the damaged ribs, the second blow knocking Jake down.

Round 32

DP: Sullivan landed a right to the ribs and followed with a rush, under which Jake dropped to avoid punishment. Time: 1 minute.

TD: In a clinch, Kilrain pushed Sullivan's head back with his open hand. Sullivan said, "Don't put your fingers in my eyes, you bloody coward." Sully landed a left and right to the ribs, knocking him down.

Round 33

DP: A light left to the nose sent Jake down. Time: 1 minute.

TD: An uppercut to the nose dropped Kilrain.

Another account said that Kilrain looked quite tired and his nose bled after being struck.

Round 34

DP: This was a slugging round, as Kilrain took the initiative. However, Sullivan's body blows were terrific, and an uppercut knocked Jake down. Time: 45 seconds.

TD: Sullivan rushed in and landed a right and left to the nose and ribs, from which Kilrain went down.

Others said Kilrain was dropped either by a blow to the neck or the nose.

Round 35

DP: Kilrain clinched and wrestled, but Sullivan threw Jake down and rolled over on top of him. Time: 2 minutes.

TD: Sullivan threw Jake and fell on him.

Another source said that John wrestled him down and fell with his whole weight on Kilrain's abdomen.

Round 36

DP: Sullivan hit him with both hands and Kilrain went down. Jake kicked John while he was down and Sullivan turned to the referee and said, "What do you think of that?" Time: 3½ minutes.

TD: Kilrain walked around for a while until a blow to the chest dropped him.

Round 37

DP: A number of blows were exchanged, and when Sullivan tried to counter Kilrain, Jake fell before the blow landed and the crowd jeered at him. Time: 4½ minutes.

TD: Kilrain mostly avoided Sullivan. John landed to the stomach and Jake countered to the right eye, but went down in the rally that followed.

Another source said Jake moved around the ring and then went down from a light blow.

Round 38

DP: Kilrain walked around and the crowd called upon him to fight. After an exchange of blows, Kilrain went down from a punch to the face. Time: 4½ minutes.

TD: Kilrain walked around, but Sullivan refused to follow, standing in the center of the ring. Sullivan complained to the referee, who told Jake that he must fight. The crowd yelled, "Fight, fight." He eventually engaged in some exchanges. When they came together, Sullivan knocked him down with an open-handed blow. To this point, the fight had lasted about 1 hour and 22 minutes.

Another said the referee directed Jake to fight, which he did for a bit, until he was forced to the ropes and dropped by a hit on the side of the face.

Round 39

DP: Jake continued moving about. He blocked a blow with his hand and fell. Sullivan's second claimed a foul for going down without punishment, but it was not allowed. Time: 3 minutes.

TD: Kilrain in stopping a left to the ribs went down. The crowd cried "Foul."

Others said that the spectators howled "Foul" when Kilrain went down without being struck in the 39th through 41st rounds, although *The Gazette* said that he went down in the 41st from a punch to the ribs.

Round 40

DP: Kilrain again engaged in his usual tactics and dropped to escape punishment. Time: 2½ minutes.

TD: A left to the ear dropped Jake.

Round 41

DP: Sullivan landed a right to the body and to the chest, as well as an uppercut. When they tried to clinch, Kilrain fell. Time: 1 minute.

TD: After receiving a right to the ribs, Kilrain staggered and fell just in time to escape another blow.

Round 42

DP: Kilrain rallied and landed some good straight blows to the head and body, as well as some uppercuts. Sullivan wrestled with him, getting him in a neck hold and nearly twisted Jake's head off, throwing him down and falling on top of him. Time: 2½ minutes.

TD: Kilrain went down and Sullivan dropped on him with his knee to Jake's neck. Mitchell claimed foul, but the referee said they must fight on.

Others said they engaged in some furious fighting for about 20 seconds, until Kilrain was thrown and Sullivan sat down on his head, to cries of foul, which were not allowed.

Sullivan would occasionally fall on top of Kilrain when he was down, which was a foul, and Kilrain occasionally went down without being hit, which was also a foul, but these fouls were disallowed and generally overlooked by the referee. Although the referee was criticized for not being well versed in the London rules, he was fair in that he overlooked both Kilrain's deliberate drops to the floor without being struck, and Sullivan's dropping down on Jake.

Round 43

DP: Sullivan continued landing telling rights, and easily stopped Kilrain's blows or pushed him away. In a clinch, they hit each other with uppercuts. Sullivan laughed. A right to the neck dropped Jake. Time: 1½ minutes.

TD: Jake went down from a tap on the back of the neck which he had ducked to avoid.

Round 44

DP: Sullivan began vomiting. Kilrain's seconds urged him to go in and take advantage, but he refused to do so. When John recovered, he got in two hard rights to the body, and Jake went down. Time: 1½ minutes.

Mike Donovan, who was in Kilrain's corner, after the fight said that he told Jake to go at Sullivan when he was vomiting, but that Jake said, "No, I won't, Mike; no I won't ... John, I won't hit you while you are vomiting."

TD: Sullivan came to the scratch vomiting, and despite Donovan's calling upon Kilrain to attack, he did not, and waited for John to finish. As soon as he was done, Sullivan appeared fresher and stronger. From this point to the end, Kilrain gradually grew weaker. Sullivan sent him down with a left and right to the ribs.

Other sources agreed that when Sullivan came to the scratch vomiting, Jake refrained from approaching. According to *The Herald*, Kilrain said, "I don't want to hit you while you're in that condition ... will you give up?" Sullivan responded, "Give it up! ... you're crazy. I've got you whipped." The *Tribune*, *Times*, *Globe* and *Gazette* all said that Kilrain asked him to call it a draw. Sullivan replied, "No, you loafer." He then attacked and dropped Kilrain, possibly by punches to the ribs. *The Herald* indicated that the vomiting had deterred Jake's attack, and when it was over, John quickly recovered and fought even harder. The referee later said that Kilrain offered to make it a draw, but Sullivan responded, "No, we'll fight it out."

Round 45

DP: "Sullivan got out of the way of Kilrain's blows as cleverly as if the fight had just commenced." John hit him with a right to the ribs and to the jaw. Kilrain fell without punishment. Sullivan then jumped into the air and came down with both knees upon Kilrain's head. A foul was claimed but it was not allowed. Time: 1½ minutes.

TD: Sullivan again dropped on Kilrain's neck with his knees, but the referee insisted that they should fight on.

Others said that Kilrain was again cautious, moving and walking around, fighting only occasionally, and going down easily. Either Kilrain was dropped by a body blow to end the round or they fell in a clinch. The Tribune said the round ended with Sullivan landing to the body and the jaw, then stamping on Jake, the cry of foul being disallowed. The Times agreed that he was stamped upon. The Globe and The Gazette said Sullivan jumped on his head with his knees.

Summarizing the rest of the fight, The Times-Democrat said that Kilrain was knocked down several times, and often a push would provide him with the excuse to fall down. On two occasions, Jake fell suspiciously. The punishment to the ribs and heart combined with the heat of the day took the strength out of him.

Round 46

DP: Sullivan had the best of a rapid exchange of blows until Jake fell. Time: 1 minute.

TD: John landed a right to the nose, and Jake slipped down in an attempt to avoid a follow-up blow.

Another source said that after Kilrain landed a good one on John, an enraged Sullivan pounded on his ribs "until they cracked."

Round 47

DP: After Sullivan landed both hands to the jaw and Jake clinched, John threw and fell upon Kilrain. Time: 1 minute.

TD: Sullivan had the best of a rally, then threw Kilrain and fell upon his neck.

Non-local: When Jake dropped to the ground, Sullivan rolled over him.

Round 48

DP: Kilrain rushed in and fell from a shove. Time: 30 seconds.

TD: After a short rally, Kilrain went down.

Non-local: Jake again went down just from the mere attempt at a punch by Sullivan, with Sullivan possibly falling on top of him again.

Round 49

DP: An easy right to the chest caused Jake to drop. Time: 30 seconds.

TD: Kilrain led to the stomach but was knocked down with a cross counter to the jaw.

Round 50

DP: When Sullivan cornered Kilrain, Jake dropped without being hit. Again a claim of foul was made but apparently not recognized. Time: 2 minutes.

TD: After Sullivan staggered him, Jake in trying to escape stumbled and fell rather suspiciously. The claim of foul was not allowed.

Non-local: Kilrain hit the body and head, and then backed away and dropped.

Round 51

DP: John landed a right to the ribs and Jake fell just as Sullivan was about to repeat the blow. Time: 2 minutes.

TD: Sullivan struck Jake open-handed on the jaw and Kilrain went down.

Non-local: Kilrain clinched, both tried to throw each other in close, and then Jake slid down.

Round 52

DP: Sullivan landed on the ear and Kilrain went through the ropes to escape punishment. Time: 30 seconds.

TD: Kilrain was driven to the ropes and fought down.

Non-local: Sullivan dropped him with a blow to the neck.

Round 53

DP: Kilrain kept away, with Sullivan following and laughing. Blood flowed from Jake's mouth. When John went to hit him, Kilrain fell and Sullivan went down on top of him. Time: 3 minutes.

TD: Both walked about until Sullivan closed in. Kilrain went down and John fell on him.

According to *The Herald*, Sullivan landed hard shots to the ribs and nose to send Jake down.

Round 54

DP: Sullivan grabbed Jake by the neck and threw him down. Time: 1 minute.

TD: Sullivan twisted Jake's neck and fell upon it as both went down.

The Herald said that after Sullivan threw him to the ground, he fell on Kilrain. *The Gazette* said John fell on Jake's head.

The Tribune indicated that Kilrain was gradually growing weaker, and the crowd becoming discontented with his tactics of retreating and falling from slight blows, which continued in subsequent rounds, with Sullivan occasionally falling on top of him.

Round 55

DP: Kilrain ran away, ignoring the jeers of the crowd, though he was eventually warned

The Sullivan-Kilrain fight (Library of Congress, Prints & Photographs Division).

by the referee. Kilrain landed two rights to the neck, causing a cut which bled. Sullivan landed a light blow in return, and Jake dropped, grabbing John's legs. A foul was claimed but not allowed. Time: 2½ minutes.

TD: Jake walked away and leaned on the ropes for support. The referee told him he must fight. Advancing, he received a blow to the nose and was fought down in a clinch. As he went down, his hands touched John's legs and a claim of foul was made but not allowed.

Round 56

DP: Kilrain fell to escape punishment. Time: 1½ minutes.

TD: In dodging a right, Jake dropped down.

Round 57

DP: Sullivan gave him a light tap on the face and Jake went down without punishment. Time: 2 minutes.

TD: Kilrain missed a right to the body and fell from the force of his own lunge.

Round 58

DP: In a clinch, Sullivan threw and fell on top of Kilrain. Time: 30 seconds.

TD: Kilrain grabbed Sullivan's neck, but his arm slipped over his head and he went to the ground.

Round 59

DP: When John grabbed him with his right, Jake fell before John could do anything. Time: 1 minute.

TD: Kilrain went down rather suspiciously in a rally.

Round 60

DP: Sullivan feinted and Kilrain fell. Time: 2 minutes.

TD: Kilrain was knocked down from a right to the ribs.

Round 61

DP: Kilrain rushed in and Sullivan fell to his knees in dodging to avoid a clinch. Kilrain's people jeered at John, who then apologized. Time: 10 seconds.

TD: Kilrain went down in a rally.

Round 62

DP: Sullivan hit the ribs and chased him around until Kilrain fell to escape being hit. Time: 1½ minutes.

TD: Kilrain went down from a slight tap to the ear. They had been fighting for 2 hours.

According to *The Herald*, John grabbed Jake's head and hit it with his right to the face repeatedly, something perfectly legal under the rules.

Round 63

DP: Kilrain walked around. Sullivan feinted and Kilrain dropped without a blow. The crowd jeered. Time: 3 minutes and 15 seconds.

TD: A right to the ribs dropped Kilrain.

The Globe and *The Gazette* said Kilrain went down from a "rib-roaster."

Round 64

DP: A tap sent Jake down. Time: 2¾ minutes.

TD: Kilrain went down in a scramble.

The Globe and *The Gazette* said Jake again went down without being stuck, to disallowed cries of foul.

Round 65

DP: Kilrain killed time, and John accused him of cowardice. Sullivan landed both hands to the face and Jake went down. Time: 30 seconds.

At this point, no one would bet against Sullivan.

TD: Sullivan pushed him down. Fearing that Sullivan would jump upon him, Jake put up his leg and spiked Sullivan's thigh. Sullivan turned to the referee and asked, "How is that?"

Round 66

DP: Kilrain fell from a light punch. Time: 30 seconds.

TD: Jake looked dazed and helpless. He tried to hit the stomach, but was knocked down by a swinging right.

Non-local: Jake went down by a slight blow.

Round 67

DP: Kilrain did not toe the line on time and had to be called several times to rise. During the round, Sullivan finally cornered him, landed two body shots and a right to the face in rapid succession, and Kilrain fell under the ropes. Time: 1½ minutes.

TD: Sullivan dropped Kilrain with a blow to the breast which sent him under the ropes.

Another source said a left to the ribs dropped him.

Round 68

DP: Sullivan hit the ribs and face and knocked him out. Time: 1½ minutes.

TD: An uppercut dropped Kilrain.

The Gazette said a vicious uppercut dropped Jake in the 68th, although *The Herald* said this occurred in the 69th. *The Gazette* said Jake was dropped by a right in the 69th.

Round 69

DP: John landed a right to the body and Jake dropped to avoid further punishment. Time: 30 seconds.

TD: A right and left to the ear and jaw sent Kilrain down.

Round 70

DP: Kilrain slipped to one knee to escape. Time: 30 seconds.

TD: A blow to the ribs dropped Kilrain.

Non-local: Sullivan landed many times, and when Jake tried to wrestle John down, it was Kilrain who slipped and fell.

Round 71

DP: Sullivan at one point held Jake up to keep him from falling. After cornering Kilrain, Sullivan landed a right to the neck and Jake dropped to one knee. Sullivan saw that the end was near. Time: 1 minute and 30 seconds.

TD: The very short round ended by a right to Jake's left ear.

Non-local: Jake feinted and backed away, but was dropped by a rib shot.

Round 72

DP: Kilrain went down from a shove, and while on the ground tried to spike Sullivan. Sullivan asked the referee what he thought of that. Time: 30 seconds.

TD: Kilrain fell from an open-handed blow or push on the chin. Jake was very groggy.

Non-local: Sullivan landed multiple times and Jake went down to avoid punishment.

Round 73

DP: "The fight was virtually over. What with the heat of the sun, in which he had been for two hours, the punishment he received and the evident superiority of his opponent it was simply a matter of a few more rounds when nature would get the better of Kilrain's stubborn courage." A right to the ribs dropped Jake. Time: 1 minute.

TD: A right to the ribs dropped Kilrain.

The Herald said two body shots under the heart sent Kilrain to the grass, although *The Tribune* and *The Gazette* said he went down to avoid punishment.

Round 74

DP: More walking around and Jake fell. Time: 1 minute.

TD: A right to the neck dropped Kilrain.

Non-local: A mere slap or slight blow caused Jake to fall down.

Round 75

DP: Sullivan led with his right and Kilrain fell in stopping it. "The referee warned him against going down without punishment. It was not Kilrain's fault. He could not stand up anymore." Mitchell ran over to John's corner and asked if he would give Jake $1,000 if he gave up. Sullivan said yes but his backers said no. Kilrain stood to make no money if he lost. Mitchell was about to negotiate further but Mike Donovan threw up the sponge, retiring Kilrain. Jake objected, but Donovan "said that he did not wish to be a party to a murder." Sullivan was declared the winner.

Donovan afterwards said,

> I threw up the sponge because I saw that there was no chance of continuing the fight without endangering our man's life.... Kilrain was game to the last, but I believed him to be in danger of sunstroke and, besides, the blow over his heart, which Sullivan landed, bid fair to the serious in its effects.... I do not consider that Sullivan was ever in his life the man he is now.

Years later, Mike Donovan said that he wanted to give up the fight for Jake in the 50th round because he knew that Kilrain had no chance and might be killed, but that Mitchell would not allow it. He said that Jake was so weak that he was falling from exhaustion.

Unlike those who felt that alcohol during the fight was of no help, Donovan said,

"Kilrain could never have gone through this fight without whisky, of which he drank over a quart between the rounds." Apparently, the whiskey helped to dull the pain.

He said that Kilrain was dropped by a right to the body to end the 75th round. Jake was carried to the corner, clearly all gone. Donovan decided to stop it then. "I will not be a party to manslaughter." As he threw up the sponge, he saw Mitchell in Sullivan's corner. He later learned about Charley's attempted negotiations.[15]

TD: Kilrain staggered out of his corner and wandered about in a dazed condition along the ropes. Sullivan went after him and with a moderate blow to the chest knocked him down. Mitchell asked Sullivan if he'd give Jake a present if he gave in. Sullivan said that would be all right, but his backer refused. Sullivan replied, "That settles it then; we'll fight." However, Donovan then threw up the sponge. Mitchell initially disputed the propriety of this action as Kilrain was willing to continue, but after some discussion, the sponge was again thrown up, this time with Mitchell consenting.

The Herald said a heavy body shot to the ribs sent Jake down to end the 75th round, but The Tribune said Jake went down from a slight blow to the jaw and was warned by the referee. The Times agreed that he was going down to avoid being knocked down and that he was cautioned.

Just before the 76th round was to begin, The Herald said that Charlie Mitchell went over to Sullivan and asked him what he would give Jake if he gave in, but the response was that he would give him nothing. The Tribune and The Times differed, indicating that Mitchell asked Sullivan if he would give Jake a "present" if Kilrain gave in, and Sullivan agreed. Another one of Jake's seconds threw up the sponge and the $20,000 prize money was Sullivan's. The Times said that the sponge was thrown up before Sullivan had answered Mitchell's inquiry.[16]

The Brooklyn Daily Eagle praised Sullivan for refusing to buy the battle from Charley Mitchell, despite a broken finger and painful foot from the spiking. When offered the fight if he'd make a $1,000 present, Sullivan responded, "I came here to whip Kilrain, and I'm going to do it or die in the ring. I want no draws or compromises." Mitchell then threw up the sponge. It was said, though, that Sullivan decided afterwards to give Kilrain that amount for his suffering and efforts.[17]

A special dispatch to The Boston Herald said the fight lasted 2 hours and 35 minutes. The New York Daily Tribune reported that the fight lasted 2 hours and 18 minutes. The New York Times clocked it at 2 hours, 16 minutes and 25 seconds. The most local Daily Picayune at one point said it lasted 2 hours and 13 minutes, but at another said it lasted 2 hours, 16 minutes and 23 seconds. The Picayune was based in New Orleans, a mere 105 miles away from Richburg, and claimed to have had bulletins before any other paper. The Times-Democrat said it lasted 2 hours and 15 minutes, "counting the close of the seventy-fifth round as the end of the fight, though as a matter of fact the decision of the Kilrain party to abandon it was not satisfactorily demonstrated until about three minutes later."

The Daily Picayune said that Kilrain wept at his defeat. He was psychologically and physically crushed. His body was badly bruised and his head showed the traces of punishment. His mouth was badly swollen, a bleeding cut disfigured the upper and lower lips, the left eye was puffed and swollen, and the left ear was cut and swollen. Although the crowd had often jeered his tactics during the fight, it felt sympathetic towards him afterwards and collected $500 for his relief. It reported that Sullivan had won $22,000 plus his share of the gate receipts. Of course he would have to split it with his financial backers, which included *The New York Illustrated News*, Jim Wakely, and Charles Johnston.[18]

Muldoon said that the only injuries to Sullivan were a black eye, cut ear, slightly swollen face, and hurt wrists and hands. The local paper reported that Sullivan's foot was gashed from Kilrain's spikes. One eye was a little bruised, and the other one had a small cut over the eye and another one on the cheek below. His side was a little bruised. The following day's report said that both of John's hands were badly puffed and his left wrist badly swollen.

Another paper said that Kilrain was suffering severe bodily pain and mental agony from the bout. Sullivan was not unmarked. His ear and cheek were cut and his eyes swollen and discolored.[19]

To summarize the fight, Sullivan was the aggressor from the beginning, mostly attacking the body, initially finding it difficult to land as effectively to the head as he was used to, perhaps because of Jake's defense, perhaps in an attempt to save his hands. Kilrain was aggressive at first. However, he soon learned that he could not defeat Sullivan in this manner. Sullivan's body shots sounded like "a smith's anvil under the hammer," and wore him down. Kilrain tried to extend the fight as long as he could, hitting, moving, wrestling and dropping, killing time, hoping that Sullivan would tire. According to *The New York Times*, at one point, Sullivan said to Kilrain, "Stand up and fight like a man; I'm no sprinter!" His tactics were similar to Charley Mitchell's in that he at times fell down when hit lightly, and at other times fell when not even struck at all. Trainer Mitchell must have instructed him on the use of these tactics. Jake occasionally landed some good punches, perhaps hoping to close John's eye, but was too afraid to do much more, moving about so much that the referee had to tell him to fight. The rounds typically did not last over a minute and were often much shorter. Sullivan had the best of it throughout, although it was a hard fought battle.

The Tribune concluded, "At no time, excepting when Sullivan's stomach gave evidence of weakness, was there a doubt as to the final result of the fight." *The Times* reported that the body punishment in the 3rd round "was said to have done more than anything else to decide the battle." This sentiment was echoed a day later by *The Herald* and *The Globe*, stating that Kilrain was beaten after the 3rd round. Even *The Picayune* agreed that "Sullivan hit Kilrain a blow in the short ribs in the third round which settled the contest."[20]

There were actually some day of the fight afternoon reports because it concluded around 1:00 p.m., but their accuracy was questioned. Some were wildly wrong, saying that Sullivan won in 8 or 9 rounds, that Kilrain had won, or that Sullivan had broken Kilrain's jaw in the 3rd round, etc. The final report was that Sullivan had won in the 72nd round, only slightly wrong.[21]

The Times-Democrat noted that

The Northern evening papers ... are models of inaccuracy.... It seemed to be fashionable last Monday to send off bogus news, and such was the anxiety of the papers to give something that they gladly accepted anything they came across, whether they believed it or not. They waited impatiently for some information from New Orleans, and when they could get nothing, apparently invented it. We mention this fact, because journalism of this kind seems to be coming into favor in America. It is the duty of the press to expose and crush it at the very start....

The press has not the same time as the historian to examine facts, and is therefore liable to err sometimes, but to invent news or publish news which it knows to be false, is a degradation which cannot be tolerated.... Let it be understood that the public can credit the newspapers. If it ever gets to doubting them, journalism has a dark future ahead.[22]

Initially, Sullivan kept away from reporters, saying that many of them had little regard for the truth. He acknowledged that he had fouled Kilrain, but not until after Jake had fouled him. He could have been given the fight many times on fouls, but was glad to prove that he was a finish fighter. He said that he had whipped Kilrain 11 years ago and knew how to fight him. He also said that the blows to the stomach did in Jake.

Regarding his 44th round vomiting, John L. said that his seconds gave him a drink of whiskey and that it did not mix well with the tea he was given. He felt stronger after vomiting.

Of Kilrain, Sullivan said, "Jake is a good fighter, and he gave me a better fight than I ever got before."[23] He also said that Kilrain had given him more punishment than any other man before him. "Of course, he hardly fought fairly, going down, as you know he did, numbers of times without a blow. Still, he took by far more punishment than I believed he would."[24]

Sullivan later said, "I knew after two or three rounds I was the sole master of the situation.... If Kilrain had stood up and fought like a man, I think I could have whipped him in about eight rounds."[25] Trainer Muldoon agreed that Kilrain was not in the fight after the 6th round, and although game, was outclassed.[26]

In his typical defiance, Sullivan refused to accept Richard Fox's *Gazette* championship belt, "feeling that it is not necessary in establishing the fact that he is the champion pugilist."[27] He had previously referred to it as a dog collar. Sullivan was not the first nor was he the last champion to feel that way about belts. Sullivan said that he was going to retire and would never enter the ring again, and that others could fight for that belt. He noted that no one that Fox had backed had been able to defeat him.[28] Another report said that Sullivan would never again fight bare knuckle, but only with gloves.[29]

Nothing but praise was heaped upon Sullivan. *The Picayune* concluded that Sullivan "was as cautious as any prize ring tactician who ever lived. He made no wild rushes, did not lay himself open to injury, and made every blow count." It believed that "Sullivan, when in condition, is an enormous ox who cannot be hurt." One man commented that if John had used his rushing tactics he would have been licked, but he fought a cool scientific fight and not a slugging match. The paper summarized that

> Kilrain was crafty and cool ... wrestled nicely for two rounds and kept warily out of the way after Sullivan's body blows had reduced his wrestling chances, got in some good hits until he found Sullivan imperious and himself growing weaker constantly, and then devoted himself to getting hurt as little as possible, getting all the rest he could, and staying in the ring as long as possible. In short, Kilrain is a general and a clever fighter, but was only a chopping block for Sullivan.... Pony Moore poured brandy down his [Kilrain's] throat after each round, and it is doubtful if this did him good.[30]

The Times-Democrat said, "From first to last Sullivan never lost control of his temper more than momentarily, and cool, calculating judgment never for one instant forsook him." Kilrain was called a powerful man, a hard hitter, and a clever general, but despite his shiftiness, "Sullivan proved equally cunning, and until he had found his opponent so completely worn out as to be unable to administer a dangerous blow he never afforded him an opportunity of landing one.... John L. Sullivan has proved himself a marvelously scientific boxer." It also said, "After the thirtieth round those who counted on the Bostonian's lack of endurance began to look blank and blue. After the middle of the fight the victory of the champion was foreordained." One writer noted that Sullivan was careful to hit the neck and body so as not to injure his hands to a great extent.

Muldoon was complimented for allowing Sullivan to put on seven pounds of weight before the fight in order to combat the fact that he would lose weight during the heat, which helped his strength and vitality.[31]

Joe Coburn said that Sullivan was "a perfect wonder" and the greatest fighter in the world, even though he "did not think Sullivan was as good a man today as he had seen him in other years, but was satisfied that he would never be asked into the arena again." John L. had proven himself. Coburn calculated that Sullivan's share of the proceeds would come to $20,000. "Were I called on to fight Sullivan ... I would say, 'Sullivan, take the money; I don't want it: it belongs to you.'"[32]

Former fighter Tom Allen said that Sullivan looked to weigh 220 pounds.

> He must have the constitution of ten mules, for in spite of the heat, which was simply terrific, his flesh suffered but little, his wind the best I ever saw, and he did not blow much at any time. He did not seem to care any more for Kilrain than an ordinary man would for a child. He did not sit down ten times during the entire fight and laughed at Kilrain's efforts to hit him.... I don't think Kilrain could have whipped him with a ball bat.[33]

The referee observed that Kilrain was game but overmatched on this extremely hot day. Kilrain spiked Sullivan many times, but he could not determine if it was intentional. Of Sullivan, he said that he "is simply a wonder.... I do not think we'll ever see his like again."[34]

Sullivan's trainer, William Muldoon, said,

> I don't think a man was ever born who could have whipped Sullivan yesterday.... I have always been anxious to prove to the public that he is a natural born fighter and could fight a long and scientific battle if necessary.... I consider Kilrain the greatest heavyweight fighter outside of Sullivan.[35]

One reporter said, "Even his most sanguine advocates could not believe before the battle that his staying qualities were such as he showed them to be."[36] Sullivan had proven his science and endurance.

Even Richard K. Fox had to give Sullivan his justly due compliments. He was out over $25,000 as a result of the stakes, wagers and expenses he had put up for the fight. He said that he had never had any doubt that Kilrain would win, because he was intelligent, knew about Sullivan's tactics, believed Sullivan would wear himself out, and also because Kilrain had endurance. "By this fight Sullivan has proved that he is a first-class pugilist in every respect. He is a stayer as well as a slugger." He admitted that Kilrain had the worst of it from start to finish.[37]

Lem Fulda, president of the California Athletic Club, said,

> The best way to be a fighter is to be born a fighter, and Sullivan was born that way.... Kilrain was whipped because Sullivan hurt him and he could not hurt Sullivan.... He can strike harder blows and more of them, he can stand more fatigue and more punishment, his blows are too powerful to be stopped, and his strength too great to be weakened, and he is so much the physical superior of any other man in the ring that a few touches of science more or less make no difference.[38]

The fight was huge. It was reported that "not since the days of the war were the people of New York city so absorbed in any one event as in the great fight. The interest was intense and universal. It was extraordinary and unprecedented. Nothing else was talked about."[39]

The fight made Sullivan legendary. Because most of his bouts were short, either because John L. knocked his opponents out quickly, or because the fights were scheduled for a limited duration, Sullivan had not often had to prove that his style and skill could work in a lengthy bout, and some still doubted this as a result of his performance against Mitchell, even though he had had the better of it against him.

Against Kilrain, Americans had witnessed Sullivan demonstrate his determination and stamina in a lengthy, over two-hour fight to the finish, in a winning effort against another large, strong, well-conditioned and well-respected fighter. As an editorial to the New Orleans *Times-Democrat* said, "It is not likely that anybody will want to meet the big Boston Slugger very soon. Just now he is the most famous person in the country, and now more highly valued than ever will be the privilege of 'shaking the hand that Sullivan shook.'"[40]

Yet, it wasn't quite over. Another fight after the fight would have to be fought. Mississippi governor Lowry was hell bent on having the men tried for engaging in an illegal prize fight and secured a warrant for their arrest. Not everyone was happy about the fight, and many supported the governor's actions. An editorial writer for Jackson, Mississippi's *Clarion-Ledger* wrote,

> [I]n defiance of civilization and decency, these "sluggers" ... by the aid of railroad officials, the Western Union Telegraph Company, civil officials and sympathizers of the ring, defied the law of the State.... [T]he sheriff could have stopped the fight if he had made the slightest attempt.... The law approved in 1882, passed just after the Sullivan-Ryan fight, should also be amended as to make prize-fighting a felony, with increased penalty, as it is in a majority of the States.... [E]very effort will be made to return them that they may answer for the great outrage and crime committed on the soil of Mississippi.[41]

On July 11 in Nashville, Tennessee, police arrested and removed Sullivan from a train. True to form, he did not go without a struggle, and resisted arrest. In a scuffle, he drew back to strike a policeman, but the police chief stuck a pistol in his face and told him that if he struck, he would kill him. He was cuffed and dragged off the train. Sullivan's backer Johnson was also arrested. Muldoon narrowly escaped arrest:

> They were about to place me under arrest when I said to them: "What do you mean? I am no prize fighter. Do I look like one? I am a gentleman, and it is your duty to protect me and not to offer me an insult." They at once abandoned me and devoted their efforts to securing the Big Fellow and Johnson.

Their attorneys applied for a writ of habeas corpus, requesting their release based upon the fact that prizefighting was a misdemeanor in Mississippi, not a felony, and therefore not an extraditable offense. A judge agreed and let them go.[42] Muldoon, not shy about admitting to a bribe, said that both the Nashville lawyer and the judge had been paid $500 each.[43]

Still, the Mississippi governor persisted in chasing down the pugilists wherever they might go, and many reporters and politicians agreed with his vigilance. Some analysis revealed a twinge of existing regional tensions. *The Clarion-Ledger* wrote, "What mattered it that the encounter was forbidden by special act of the Legislature? What cared the first citizen of classic Boston that the Governor of a Southern commonwealth had issued a proclamation forbidding the proposed outrage upon society, decency, law and order?" Although it was said that "generally speaking, the newspapers of the country, both North and South, have spoken fairly of Gov. Lowry in his efforts," it also quoted *The Chicago Tribune* as saying,

> They taught the arrogant Mississippian that the North is still in the saddle, and that Northern men, when it pleases them, will invade his State and set all its laws at defiance. They are not to be bulldozed. They are not to be scared away like colored citizens. It is a pity, that the black voters of Mississippi have not the nerve and manhood of the men who took possession of the State this week.... It might be a fine scheme for the colored men to hire Sullivan and a few of his companions to look after their interests at the next election.

The southern paper took umbrage at this opinion. "If he thinks the sluggers can do so much bulldozing, why not get up a car-load of fellow-toughs around Chicago and come down here and just wipe us off the face of the earth?" However, this was not the unanimous Chicago opinion. *The Chicago Inter-Ocean* said, "It is only unfortunate that the law would not hold him and return him to the tender mercies of Mississippi, whose law he violated."[44]

With the law still after them, Charley Mitchell and Mike Donovan skipped over to Canada to avoid arrest.[45]

Sullivan was arrested in New York on July 31, 1889, on a requisition warrant signed by that state's governor, and he was transported back to Mississippi. Upon reaching that state, Sullivan "was treated more like a conquering hero than a common criminal. The President of the United States would have attracted less attention than this man Sullivan." At first he was allowed to stay at a hotel, but the governor ordered him placed in jail, which was done. Sullivan then gave a $2,000 bond for his appearance at trial and was released.[46]

Within a month, Sullivan was tried and found guilty of violating Mississippi's anti–prize fight law. Despite multiple petitions requesting only a fine, he was sentenced to twelve months' imprisonment. The judge called the fight a "gross affront to the laws of the State," and "a studied disregard and contempt for law." Sullivan apparently smiled when the sentence was pronounced. He was allowed out on bond pending appeal. Referee John Fitzpatrick was also convicted, but only given a $200 fine.[47]

It was said that Richburg's Charles Rich, host of the fight, was the county contractor for county prisoners. He would have charge of Sullivan, "and, you may be assured, will treat him kindly."[48] Even if Sullivan had to do time, it was not going to be difficult, given whom his jailer would be. Still, no one would want their liberty constrained for a year.

Kilrain was captured at the end of August.[49] Oddly enough, Jake was acquitted of the prize fight charge, but found guilty of an assault charge and sentenced to two months in jail and a $200 fine. However, Kilrain served the time as a "laborer" for Rich, the fight benefactor who was determined to keep him out of jail. He purchased Kilrain's services under the prison contract system. "Rich is one of the wealthiest, most popular and influential young men in Marion county, and when he undertakes to do a thing, he usually succeeds." Naturally, Kilrain was treated as an honored guest and did not actually spend the time in jail.[50]

Sullivan said that while he was awaiting the result of his appeal, he was idle for a year, with the exception of five or six weeks when he traveled with a show called the *Paymaster*, wherein he would give sparring exhibitions with Joe Lannon, being paid $1,000 per week.[51]

Eventually, in March 1890, Sullivan's conviction was overturned by the Mississippi Supreme Court on a technicality—the indictment was defective.[52] In June 1890, a grand jury found a fresh indictment against Sullivan, who (most likely pursuant to a plea agreement) pleaded guilty and was sentenced to a $500 fine, which he immediately paid.[53]

Sullivan's legal and other expenses related to the case totaled $18,675.[54] Prize-fighting simply wasn't worth it. As Sullivan said,

> [B]reaking these particular laws has been very expensive to me, for in all the fights that I have been in under the London Prize-Ring rules, I have not only lost money, but have also had the care and worriment incidental to arrests, trials, and penalties. It has always cost me more money to get out of my fights under those rules than I have ever gained from them.

The strong legal impediments further explain the death of the London rules system. Sullivan contrasted this with the Queensberry rules, where "the contest usually takes place in a hall of some description under police supervision, and the price of admission is put purposely high so as to exclude the rowdy element." Of course, Sullivan had occasional legal troubles with the Queensberry system as well, but certainly not to the same extent as with the London rules.

Sullivan was also happy to see the death of the London rules system because he felt that the rules themselves did not allow for a legitimate, quick or entertaining determination of who really was the better fighter.

> Under the Marquis of Queensbury rules no clinching is allowed, no wrestling, and the superiority of the contestants is judged by the actions of their hands.... Under the London Prize-Ring rules ... [c]ontests last too long to demonstrate which is the superior man, and the length of time occupied does not depend on the superiority of the man as a fighter or boxer, but the contemptible trickery possessed.... Gentlemen and business men of all vocations cannot afford to give up the time to witness fighting under the London Prize-Ring rules, for the reason that it takes too long.... The London Prize-Ring rules allow too much lee-way for the rowdy element to indulge in their practices. Such mean tricks as spiking, biting, gouging, concealing snuff in one's mouth to blind an opponent; strangling, butting with the head, falling down without being struck; scratching with nails; kicking; falling on an antagonist with the knees; the using of stones or resin, and the hundred other tricks that are impossible under the Marquis of Queensberry rules...[55]

Bareknuckle boxing had existed in modern times for over 170 years, at least since Figg in 1719. It had extended from Broughton and his rules in 1743 to the London Prize Ring Rules in 1838, all the way to July 8, 1889. It was over.

CHAPTER 17

Retired?

After defeating Jake Kilrain, John L. Sullivan did not defend his title for the next three years. At 30 years old he had been dominant for a decade, and was growing tired of the fight game. Sullivan had proven all that he wanted or needed to prove. He essentially retired after the Kilrain fight, and said so. It was reported just after the fight that

> Sullivan says that he will never enter the ring again under any consideration. He has done his share of slugging during his rather brief career in the fistic arena, and wanted no more of it. He certainly did not intend to fight the California negro, for the simple reason that he considered it entirely too degrading for a white man to place himself on an equality with a negro.[1]

Another newspaper echoed this report, quoting Sullivan as having said, "But I'll never fight again."[2] Still another quoted him as saying, "Anybody who wants the championship now can come to me and I'll give it to 'em."[3]

Sullivan preferred a stage career at that point, performing in plays such as *The Paymaster* and eventually, *Honest Hearts and Willing Hands*. However, during that time, he hedged and wavered on whether he was retired. Certainly, his title was not considered vacant and no new champion was recognized. He was still considered the champion by the public, which understood that Sullivan needed some time off after such a battle as he had just had. He had earned it. Sullivan would occasionally spar in some short 3-round friendly exhibitions each year, but nothing serious.

Like some of the champions who followed him, Sullivan realized that he could capitalize upon his championship status without having to risk it in the ring. Fame enabled him to make money simply by allowing people to see him. He became more of a businessman, as often fighters do. His invincible status allowed him to do this without defending his title.

Two months after the Kilrain fight, on September 9, 1889, in New York, Sullivan boxed in a friendly sparring exhibition with Mike Cleary, and looked good. "Sullivan never appeared to better advantage in a scientific set-to. He looked well physically, and he was quite as quick upon his feet and with his head and hands as upon any previous occasion."[4]

The prospect of a Sullivan-Jackson bout still lingered. An Australian paper criticized the color line:

> There can be nothing more false than the idea that sneaking behind the colour-line will protect a white man from the charge of cowardice in refusing to meet a black, or enable him to hold fictitious honours. No man can call himself or be called champion while he refuses to meet and fight a black challenger.... There is no doubt but that this colour line has to go. It is against all manliness and courtesy—a fungus growth of an effete generation of self-styled champions; and the false security of these colour-line drawers has got to have the bottom knocked out of it, and that very shortly.[5]

Sullivan's racial prejudice had shades and contours. In late September 1889 he discussed a potential candidacy for Congress. When asked what his policy would be regarding the present race troubles in the South, he said,

> When it comes to flogging men at night, whether they're black or white, I'm against it. See? I'd like to go down there on a committee. I'd stop all such foul work. I will not go into a ring with a negro, but by Jupiter, I wouldn't stand by and see another white man lick him without reason.[6]

Peter Jackson continued fighting. On November 10, 1889, in England, in a gloved match, Jackson defeated English champ Jem Smith via disqualification in the 2nd round. In the 1st round, there were many heavy exchanges. In the 2nd, Smith appeared to be winded. "Jackson forced the fighting and knocked the English champion all over the ring." Jem was dazed and his "supporters were appalled to find him hugging the rope as if quite exhausted." However, Smith then got inside, wrestled and threw Jackson to the ground in London rules style. Smith had lost his cool because Jackson had essentially outfought him and beaten him up. Jem then tried to resume the fight with bare knuckles. The police stopped him and the referee awarded the fight to Jackson. "Smith was beaten at all points," and "his claims to being in champion 'form' are exploded."[7] In defeating Godfrey, McAuliffe, Cardiff, and Smith, Jackson had clearly earned the right to a title shot.

The Australian press continued attacking Sullivan for refusing to meet Jackson.

> [S]o long as he raises that false, unmanly, disgraceful side issue as to color, and refuses to meet the only man on earth whom good judges consider likely to defeat him, Peter Jackson to wit, the world will not accord him champion honors. No man can be champion of the world while he allows the challenge of any other man in that world, whatever his creed or color, to pass unheeded.[8]

However, in America, Sullivan's separatist views were consistent with the majority. The "negro race" was seen as an inferior race to be viewed with suspicion and not to be allowed to mix with whites on the same level. The Times-Democrat said, "When the negro race is left to itself it relapses into that state of barbarism in which it originally existed." The Houston Free South said, "[T]he young negroes—who are termed 'coons' and never knew what slavery was, are a nuisance—a curse to the South." The Williamsburg Journal said, "It is the fixed policy of the Republican Administration to 'draw the line,' to establish a white-man's Republican Party in the South, and thus leave the colored man out in the 'cold.'"[9]

Racism did not just exist in the South. The Times-Democrat alleged that color prejudice was actually stronger in the North, but hypocrisy tried to conceal it. It noted that northerners were extremely upset that some blacks had recently been recruited in the South as postmasters. It called attention to the fact that northern merchants would not hire blacks as clerks and salespersons, no matter how deserving. White northern mechanics refused to work with negroes. Northerners would not work under a negro foreman, though such was not uncommon in the South. In New Jersey, blacks were not allowed to bathe in the ocean at the same time as whites. It asked of the North,

> Does not a colored servant cook your meal, another wait on your table, another shave your face...? Well, then, I am unable to see why it is that if you can take your breakfast from black hands, you can't also take your letters and newspapers from the hands of negro postmasters....
> There is nothing extraordinary about this particular manifestation of the color prejudice. There are other exhibitions of the same feeling, in the North as well as in the South, which are even more remarkable....
> While such things are true at the North, it is arrant hypocrisy for Northerners to prate about

the "insane prejudice" of Southerners against the negro. The truth is that this color prejudice is entertained by most white people—by a great many who concede that it seems unreasonable, and yet who confess that they cannot get over it....

We must remember that it is only about thirty years since Abraham Lincoln, in his famous joint debate with Douglas, in answering on the 18th of September, 1858, the question whether he was "really in favor of producing a perfect equality between the negroes and white people," replied:

I am not, nor ever have been, in favor of bringing about in any way the social and political equality of the white and black races. I am not, nor ever have been, in favor of making voters or jurors of negroes, nor of qualifying them to hold office, nor to intermarry with white people; and I will say in addition to this that there is a physical difference between the white and black races which I believe will forever forbid the two races living together on terms of social and political equality.[10]

In early December 1889, it was reported that a rich white widow wanted to marry Peter Jackson. Providing insight into how race-mixing was viewed in America, the report said, "Of course a marriage between a white woman and a negro, even though it be a champion pugilist, would be unlawful, but they could get around this either by going three miles out at sea ... or going to some foreign country," but "even these evasions and delays will not be necessary, for it is stated that the would-be bride herself has a strain of negro blood in her veins."[11]

Still, discussion of the potential Sullivan-Jackson match was ongoing. *The Sydney Referee* quoted an American expert who sized up the two.

The Sullivan that Peter Jackson is to meet is only the remnants of a great man. In his day he was the greatest glove-fighter the world ever saw. He is the man that popularized glove-fighting in the United States.... For a big man he is a marvel for activity and precision in delivering a blow. He swings the right across about as quick as most men can shove out the left hand. For four rounds he will pound a man about, regardless of size, same as he would handle a sand-bag or punching ball. The left does but little execution, and for that reason he depends solely upon the deadly right. Some pugilists say that cleverness would pull a man through, and avoid the rushes that Sullivan makes, but that is a great mistake. No man can stand up under his hurricane work with the big gloves on, and the bigger the man the poorer his chances are of giving him a stand-off. The only man to defeat Sullivan is one after the Mitchell order, and even then it is odds on John L. It won't be much to Jackson's credit to defeat Sullivan as he is now, because the great slugger is past his prime ... I must say, however, that people who have seen the Australian darkey admit that for four or six rounds his chances of defeating John L. are slim, but if he can by good fortune survive for that length of time he would be afforded an excellent opening of gaining the day.[12]

On December 25, 1889, in Ireland, Jackson scored a KO2 over Irishman Peter Maher, who quit before the 2nd round was over.[13] In subsequent years, Maher would make a name for himself as a hard punching contender.

Regardless of the current American social norms, Sullivan's color stance came at the cost of some criticism by those in the press who believed in equal opportunity when it came to the sport of boxing. Perhaps some of the negative press was getting to him, because Sullivan was inconsistent in his color line stance. Despite his previous representations, as of late 1889 and early 1890, Sullivan was not definitively ruling out the possibility of a Jackson match, nor was he definitively retired. In December 1889, Sullivan was quoted as saying,

I admit having said, however, that I was willing to meet Jackson for a suitable purse and stake.... Everybody knows perfectly well that I will meet Jackson, Kilrain or any other man living who can get sufficient backing.... Next year I shall be ready to talk business with Kilrain, Jackson, or Slavin.[14]

Another rising contender who had challenged Sullivan in 1889 was Frank "Paddy" Slavin, another Australian. He stood just over 6 feet tall and weighed about 188 pounds. His record included an 1887 KO10 Mick Dooley, KO9 Martin "Buffalo" Costello, and KO2 Bill Farnan (the only man to hold a win over Jackson), an 1888 KO1 Dooley, and 1889 KO3 over Jack Burke (who in 1885 went the 5-round distance with Sullivan and in 1887 had an 8-round no decision "draw" with Jim Corbett).

In late 1889, Slavin fought Jem Smith to a 14-round bareknuckle London rules draw, but it was clear that Slavin was the better man. It was only a draw because the police stopped it owning to fan interference with the fight.[15] Slavin's fight with Smith occurred shortly after Jackson had easily defeated Smith on a 2nd-round disqualification in a Queensberry rules bout. Slavin was more than a legitimate contender, but John L. Sullivan was not considering any match at that time.

In February 1890, Jackson and Sullivan gave separate sparring exhibitions during the same week at the same place in Hoboken, but on different nights.[16] In one of those exhibitions on February 7, 1890, Sullivan boxed Joe Lannon 3 rounds before a packed house. Although they did not engage in rough work, the spectators applauded and were satisfied.[17] Sullivan sparred Lannon in Hoboken on February 12, boxing 3 rounds that had enough life to evoke applause.[18] Again on the 13th, a crowd of nearly 1,000 paid $.75 or $1.00 to see them spar 3 rounds. Peter Jackson was in the audience.[19] Sullivan was scheduled to give an exhibition in Troy, and was set to proceed to Mississippi.[20]

Frank Slavin. From Billy Edwards, *The Portrait Gallery of Pugilists of England, America, Australia* (Chicago: Athletic Publishing Co., 1894). Clay Moyle, www.prizefightingbooks.com.

Jackson that same week in Hoboken worked with Billy Elluger and Jack Ashton. Sullivan saw Jackson spar with Ashton and said that Peter was a very clever boxer.[21] Apparently he was attempting to get a look-in at Jackson for pointers as to how to defeat him, or to see whether he was really willing to fight him.

There were some negotiations for a Sullivan-Jackson match. A report a month later said that the proposed meeting between them was in status quo.[22] Certainly at that point, Sullivan did not definitively say that he was drawing the color line, demonstrating the inconsistency of his apparent social or moral stance. These negotiations clearly were not in good faith, as Sullivan had before and after made it clear that he was not going to fight Jackson. This began the history of many champions negotiating championship bouts with top black contenders, but not really ever intending to fight them.

In Australia, *The Referee* continued calling Sullivan a coward, and provided an explanation for why he was giving the illusion of moving from his color line stance:

> From all appearances John L. Sullivan is bluffing most pronouncedly in his pretended negotiations for a fight with Peter Jackson. He was on bed rock, when in desperation, and seeing plainly that unless he came down off his cowardly color line pedestal, Jackson would be hailed Champion of the World, he suddenly coiled up the line and announced his willingness to meet the Australian Champion for a purse, if any club would give one. The California Club at once sprang into the breach and offered 15,000 dol. or 3000 pounds, for the two to fight for. Seeing that there was an absolute danger that he would actually be matched with and have to fight the Australian champion-extinguisher, Sullivan then changed front, and with his usual braggadocio and insulting manner and language announced that he would fight any white man the club chose to match against him for 10,000 dol., or 2000 pounds, but he wanted double for niggers....
>
> Now we are told that Sullivan has again raised his demand, and wants 25,000 dol.... All this means one little word—bluff! Sullivan is frightened to death at the idea of meeting our long-armed, lithe-limbed champion, and will resort to any means, however despicable, to avoid a meeting with the man he dreads. Having withdrawn his old safeguard, the color line, he falls back on quibbling for a stake that is simply ridiculous as a means of getting out of a fight altogether. ... he knows perfectly well that by imposing such prohibitory stakes he evades all possibility of a meeting.... Hence Sullivan is safe, and can still boast himself champion while resorting to a mean subterfuge to avoid risking his hide and his title. The whole Press of America is against Sullivan and his cowardly and unmanly objection to fighting colored men.[23]

Peter Jackson was clearly the most worthy contender at the time, but he was black, and consistent with the racial separatism of the day, Sullivan would not fight blacks. Throughout his reign, John L. was willing to fight any white boxer, but he never did take on any black fighter. It was ironic that the most revered American sports figure, the symbol of power, dominance and courage, refused to fight blacks.

Amongst his many bouts and exhibitions, in March 1890, Jackson scored a KO2 over Jack Fallon (stopped by police). In May, Jackson had another significant fight when he took on Ed Smith (a white boxer) in a 5-round bout in Chicago. In the early 1880s, Smith had fought Charley Mitchell to a 1 hour and 40 minute draw battle.[24]

Of the May 19, 1890, Peter Jackson–Ed Smith fight, *The Chicago Tribune*, a local paper, reported that Jackson was 20 pounds bigger and they fought with four-ounce gloves. *The San Francisco Examiner* said the 5'10½" Smith weighed 175 pounds. It said that Jackson forced the fight throughout, while Smith alternated between defensive and aggressive tactics. *The New York Clipper* said that Smith had "decidedly the worst of the five round engagement.... Smith is said to have been knocked down five times in the opening round and twice in the fifth."[25] Local and non-local sources reported the rounds as follows:

1st Round

Chicago Tribune (CT): Smith drew first blood with a right to the mouth. Jackson then attacked and landed a right to the eye, scoring a knockdown. Smith clinched and went down several times to avoid the knockout.

San Francisco Examiner (SFE): Jackson floored him three times, but Smith continued to fight hard, even landing a good right of his own, making Peter smile.

2nd Round

CT: Smith landed several times, but so did Jackson. A right sent Smith down again, and as soon as he rose, he was dropped yet again. However, Smith continued fighting hard.

SFE: Jackson "began a fierce onslaught on the white man, who made little resistance beyond clinching and going down." However, Smith did land a left that sent Peter back a bit, and followed up with a number of good blows. Jackson came back and punished the body. Smith clinched and slipped down.

3rd Round

CT: Smith would clinch and go down.

SFE: They clinched often, but Smith then rushed Jackson to the ropes. Peter retaliated and punished him until the bell rang.

4th Round

CT: Ed landed often in this round.

SFE: Smith fought hard for a bit, then clinched for a while and used survival tactics. He then smashed Peter with a right and "laughed at him and used ugly language." A furious Jackson attacked and hit the left eye with his left, raising a lump and drawing blood.

5th Round

CT: Jackson tried to finish him, but could not land a telling blow.

SFE: Smith landed a good left and right, and some body punches. Jackson attacked fiercely and was clinched. They exchanged some blows, and at the end of the round, Smith attacked and forced Peter to the ropes when the bell rang. Jackson was declared the winner. Smith had a lump on each cheek bone, his nose was bruised, and the left side of his head was swollen. Jackson had a swollen mouth and lump under his left eye.[26]

The local *Chicago Tribune* was critical of Peter, stating that while the decision in his favor was just,

> the fight has proven that Sullivan is a better man than the Australian black. Jackson lacks two requisites necessary for a first-class man—the quality to finish and to follow up an advantage. Smith seemed able to hit him when and where he pleased, and showed that a good man can always find Jackson's face. Smith's blows lacked force. Jackson showed no ability that would stop the famous rushes of Sullivan.[27]

This critique seems a bit harsh, given that Jackson had proven a pretty good defense over the course of his career, having taken and avoided big shots by Godfrey, McAuliffe and Cardiff, and although he was not a killer puncher, had shown enough strength and stamina to drop and stop all of them. Also, he dropped Smith often in the short bout, and Sullivan himself had his fair share of fights where his opponents went down and survived.

Furthermore, Ed Smith was simply very tough and not easily taken out. In late 1890, it took George Godfrey 23 rounds to stop Smith. Godfrey had in early 1890 scored a KO16 over Patsy Cardiff.[28] Smith would eventually win some important battles and become a top contender.

Jackson's results did not matter. Sullivan was not fighting anyone at that time, let alone a black man. That same week in May, in New York, Sullivan and Joe Lannon appeared giving 3-round exhibitions as part of the play called *The Paymaster.* "The fistic gladiators appear attired in regulation evening dress, instead of ring costume." Despite the non-serious nature of their exhibitions, they received nightly ovations.[29] Generally, but for these type of friendly exhibitions, that year (1890) Sullivan was inactive, not engaging in any real contests.

Members of San Francisco's California Club witnessed a July 1890 Sullivan exhibition and were "not highly pleased with the champion's appearance. They found Sullivan giving boxing exhibitions in a swallow-tail coat with Joe Lannon, and they appear to think that this style of contest is about all that the eminent Boston slugger will be ever again good for."[30]

In late August 1890, Sullivan began performing in the play *Honest Hearts and Willing Hands,* touring the country.[31] Acting had become his profession.

In September 1890, Frank Slavin stopped Joe McAuliffe in the 2nd round.[32] Although this win was after Jackson's 1888 KO24 over Joe, McAuliffe had subsequently come back with a May 1889 KO8 Tom Lees (against whom Jackson had scored an 1886 KO30) and a September 1889 KO7 over Pat Killen (who had an 1887 KO2 Duncan McDonald and June 1888 KO5 Patsy Cardiff). Thus, this quick and easy victory over a tough and well respected contender further highlighted Slavin's merit.

Seeing that no bout with Sullivan was going to take place, in August, Jackson returned to Australia and gave regular exhibitions there. On October 21, 1890, in Australia, Jackson, "colored champion pugilist of the world," took on fellow Australian Joe Goddard in a very tough, grueling battle. Goddard had such victories as 1889 KO11 Owen Sullivan, KO4 Jim Fogarty, and 1890 KO21 Mick Dooley. He generally weighed around 186 pounds.

The local Australian paper, *The Referee,* said that Goddard was a vicious, aggressive, strong rusher who kept the pace fast. He was said to have little skill, but more than compensated for it with "boundless energy, pluck, dash, and devil." He was also called "a modern Hercules, and planks his faith upon his grit and staying powers ... he is the most perfectly trained man in the world."

Jackson and Goddard fought viciously in the 1st and 2nd rounds, each landing well. In the 1st, Peter landed his straight punches, but that only set loose the slumbering demon, and Goddard was on top of him, smashing in lefts and rights to the body and head, causing Jackson to reel away, staggered and shaken. He collected himself, dodged and landed lefts, but Goddard beat down his guard and with his whirlwind of blows again had Jackson in trouble. Peter smashed him in the mouth with his left, but could not beat him back. It "was quite evident that the white man held his own, and many people were inclined to think he had a bit the best of the three minutes."

In the 2nd round, Goddard "bounded across the stage like a lion." Peter stood up well to him and landed a good right. After a clinch, they exchanged blow for blow to the body and head and it looked as if one or the other would be knocked out. They slowed momentarily before Goddard was at him again, "and in spite of Peter's great swiftness of foot he bore down on him ... and another frantic, desperate, savage rally followed, in which Joe more than held his own until the cry of corners sent them apart."

Goddard again dashed at Jackson in the 3rd round. Peter landed a hard right and countered strongly. After a rally, "Jackson came away like an electric eel, and drove a superb left on the front of the chin, bringing Joe to the boards as if he had been kicked by an elephant." Despite this knockdown, Goddard sprang at Jackson and beat him back. "Joe held his own, fighting grimly, desperately, fiercely, as if the very pride of race and color had entered into his heart." However, "suddenly Peter saw an opening, and shooting his right clean across he dropped his determined foe once more to the boards." Still, Goddard "rose and sprang at his man and drove him over the ring by sheer vim and pluck. Peter smashed him over the eye with the left and made it get on the bulge, but Joe smiled sardonically and went for more." Despite the two knockdowns, the strong and aggressive Goddard was undeterred and continued fighting hard.

The 4th was again fierce. A flush left on the chin again dropped Goddard, but Joe continued setting the pace. Peter dodged cleverly and landed his jab as Joe pressed. "Over and over again he flung himself full upon Pete and took his gruel like a white man, never flinching, never quailing, game, grim and almost reckless he fought as no man had ever been seen to fight in the Southern Hemisphere before." The crowd cheered. Despite the apparent pounding, the local newspaper said, "Goddard went to his corner with a decided lead."

Goddard went at him again in the 5th, but Pete drove him back with long heavy lefts to the face. Still, Joe gave him no rest. "All through the three minutes he was rushing and pounding, and it took Pete all he knew to keep his end up under the cyclonic pressure." An American source said they both went down at the same time in this round, but the local primary source did not mention this.

Both were a bit weary in the 6th, but Goddard kept plugging away, and had Jackson mostly defensive. "Jackson did mighty little besides dodge out of danger, for now it was a case of the huntsman hunted, for the knocker-out was in danger of being sent down."

Jackson began aggressively in the 7th and landed a strong left. However, Joe then "punched him from one end of the ring to the other, Pete seeming fairly paralyzed by the tornado." It appeared that Pete was weakening, and "for a spell it looked as if Joe was going to win. Pete fell, but got up again quickly, and then the tongues of the throng were let loose." They fought "like dervishes, until the struggling, seething mass of humanity formed a sight such as one might hope to see in hell when it's nigh boiling point, but Peter was equal to the occasion."

They were cautious for a bit in the 8th and final round, but then they went at each other for a finish for about sixty seconds. "Peter weakened, and Joe drove him all over the place. Hurling himself bodily on the great African boxer he sent him reeling from him like a child, and at the call of time it looked as if Pete had met his Waterloo."

One judge had it for Goddard, one for Jackson, and the referee decided to call it a draw. The local report said, "The fight was a grim one, but nearly all present agreed that Goddard had the best of it." That said, the bout description gives the impression that a draw was appropriate. Some might say that Jackson deserved the win given that he was the one who had scored the clean knockdowns.

After the fight, it was said of Goddard that "he has now established a claim to be considered a phenomenon in his own style, and it looks as if that wicked natural style of his will carry him right into the front ranks of the very best fighters the world possesses." Goddard became a top contender known for his punch, toughness and durability.[33]

This bout raised the question of whether Jackson really could compete with Sullivan. Goddard had nowhere near the talent or skill of John L. If Joe could give Jackson a rough time of it, then how would Pete do against a man like Sullivan? Frank Slavin had demonstrated more firepower than Jackson. This made many experts view Slavin as Sullivan's next legitimate challenger. That said, the flip side of this argument was that Jackson had shown that he could endure a rough fight with a strong, tough, well-conditioned rushing fighter. Also, Slavin ducked Jackson while they were both living in Australia.

In late 1890, *The Referee* criticized Sullivan for continuing to claim the status of champion even though he was not accepting legitimate challenges from fighters such as Slavin.

> Sullivan still clings to the title of Champion of the World, and that sign is attached to his name on the advertising bills of the theatrical Company that he is traveling with....
>
> Slavin probably would not be so eager to meet John L. Sullivan if the latter would drop the title of Champion of the World, which everyone who is conversant with prize-ring ethics, rules ... is well aware that Sullivan has no right to the claim....
>
> According to the rules governing the Championship a Champion holds that title as long as he accepts all *bona-fide* challenges and defends it against all-comers. When a champion fails to carry out this programme he ceases to be looked upon as a champion....
>
> Sullivan has no excuse to offer for his failure to pick up the gauntlet Slavin throws at his feet, except that he claims that he is an actor.

Despite this, the author did not feel that Sullivan's inaction was a result of fear, still favoring John L. in a potential match with Slavin.

> Sullivan has the youth, height, weight, courage and the battering abilities, and by combining agility and muscle with common sense and good judgment, he should be able to prove that he is still a champion, no matter how great a pugilist Slavin may be.[34]

The National Police Gazette chose to give Slavin its championship belt and call him the champion of the world. Sullivan did not care, going back into semi-retirement mode:

> I have retired from the prize-ring for the present.... Whatever fighting I may do hereafter will be as a sort of recreation. My business is acting....
>
> Whether I meet Slavin or not, no man will ever dare to accuse me of cowardice. If our business continues to be as good as it has thus far, my bit this season will amount to 25,000 dollars, and it's a whole lot better to make money this way than to get it as I did in Mississippi. I had to spend all the money I made out of the Kilrain fight in getting myself free.[35]

Sullivan could turn an easy buck merely by allowing the public to see him act, and did not have to pay lawyers to defend him against criminal charges for fighting. He also didn't have to train, and could eat and drink all he wanted. He was reaping the rewards of his well-earned fame.

> Wherever the champion goes he is the centre of attraction.... The secret of his prominence is the fact that even in this age, when brains are superior to muscle, there is still enough of the old animal instinct left in humanity to admire the physically perfect, and Sullivan is popularly supposed to be the physical superior of any man in the world. This is the reason people flock in crowds to see him "act." They don't care a picayune for his "acting." They want to see a curiosity, the man able to "lick" any other man in the world.[36]

Of course, maintaining that fame and prestige would eventually require Sullivan to fight. But for the time being, boxing was far from his mind.

On April 27, 1891, Australian heavyweight Frank Slavin arrived in America and asked Sullivan whether he would consider a match. Sullivan said that he had a contract for a year to appear on the stage, and "besides that, he was out of the ring for good and would never under any circumstances enter it again."[37] Another report said that Sullivan was making good money in the theatrical profession and had bid goodbye to the ring forever.[38]

Still another contender emerged at that time. In 1889, scientific boxer James J. Corbett stopped Joe Choynski in the 27th round, and in 1890 easily won decisions over two former Sullivan title challengers, defeating Jake Kilrain in 6 rounds and Dominick McCaffrey in 4 rounds.

On May 21, 1891, in San Francisco, in a gloved Marquis of Queensberry rules bout to the finish, 200-pound Peter Jackson took on 185-pound James J. Corbett. The scientific bout lasted 61 rounds over 4 hours, until it was declared a no contest when it appeared that neither was going to score a knockout any time soon and the bout had become exceedingly slow. Both fighters well distinguished themselves as skillful boxers, many saying Corbett the more so. This made Corbett a well-respected top contender.[39]

However, an Australian report said that it was a "painfully slow affair" and that "the general opinion was expressed that Sullivan in his best day could have made mighty small work of the pair of them in the one night."[40] Jackson's bouts with Goddard and Corbett probably made Australians view Slavin as their hope for the championship more than Jackson.

It was reported in mid-1891 that Sullivan "has at last retired from the ring" and that "the next battle will decide the championship.... It lies between Slavin, Jackson, and Corbett."[41]

On June 16, 1891, Frank Slavin knocked out Jake Kilrain in the 9th round. This was somewhat significant because in March 1891, Kilrain had stopped top American black George Godfrey in the 44th round. Corbett had come nowhere near to stopping Kilrain in their 6 rounder.

CHAPTER 18

Changing His Tune

One month after the Corbett-Jackson bout, on June 26, 1891, in San Francisco, John L. Sullivan sparred James J. Corbett in a 4-round exhibition, both wearing formal dinner attire at Sullivan's insistence. John did not want anything serious, and it wasn't. Still, this exhibition showed that Corbett was on Sullivan's radar, and John likely wanted to size him up.

The next day report quoted Sullivan as saying to Peter Jackson, "I can lick any man in the world, Jackson ... you and Slavin and all the niggers and Australiana, and I'm going to do it." Jackson replied, "I am willing to have you try, Mr. Sullivan."[1] Sullivan again appeared to be changing his tune about being retired, as well as his position regarding the color line.

Still, Sullivan did not arrange a fight. Instead, in July 1891, he took a trip to Australia with Jack Ashton. On the way, they visited Honolulu and gave an exhibition there. They arrived in Australia on July 21, 1891.[2] While there, John said, "I may fight again, and I may not." It all depended upon whether he was "offered sufficient inducement to again put on the gloves when I return to America." That inducement would have to offset the easy money that he was already making. "But, as I said before; I'm doing splendidly at the business I'm in now, and as men fight for money it'll have to be made well worth my while to throw over an easy and lucrative living to go in for such a tough job as fighting."[3]

Sullivan in his Australian shows would spar 3 rounds with Ashton. He said that he exhibited in Sydney for a while, then Melbourne for three weeks, as well as Ballarat for three nights, Bendigo for two, Adelaide for three, Cathlenain for one night, Maryborough for one, and Stahl for one evening. They were there for about six and a half weeks.[4]

These exhibitions gave Australians a chance to see Sullivan and compare him with their champions. For the first time, their tune about Sullivan changed. Seeing him made them realize just how good he was.

> [A]nd though not in any sort of condition ... he has enough of his old vitality left in him to show what a marvelous man he has been, and still would be if he would deny himself some of the luxuries of life and get into something like shape. He is remarkably quick upon his feet for so big a man, and shoots out his left hand as cleverly and as neatly as a youngster, whilst his heavy right arm, of which we have heard so much, comes across like a mule kick. Considering the pace the man has lived for the last seven years, he is a marvel, and must have been blessed with a constitution like a horse.[5]

Another Australian writer said, "He gave us a taste of his capabilities as a pugilist whilst here with Jack Ashton, and I for one consider him a fistic phenomenon and I do not think the man breathes who can make a certainty of downing him." That included even Australia's own Frank Slavin.

209

[O]ur great athlete, with his big, game heart, powerful frame, unbounded confidence, quickness, strength and wonderful hitting power, will need to have every muscle braced, every nerve strained, for in this American giant he will meet such a man as the world only breeds once or twice in a century.[6]

A later report said, "I always held the opinion that Slavin was a world-whipper for certain until I saw John L. Sullivan spar."[7] Sullivan told the Australians that he and Slavin would meet one day.[8]

John might have been considering fighting again, but it wasn't going to be against Jackson. *The Referee* reported,

John L. Sullivan, although he once stripped to fight George Godfrey in Boston, and once signed an agreement to fight Peter Jackson at the California Athletic club if the club would offer a 20,000 dol. purse, made the following statement: "I vowed before the public years ago that I would never fight a colored man, because I thought, and still think, that a white man is lowering himself too much when he faces a nigger. Why, God had a view in making them black, and I earnestly believe it was because they were always doomed to be our inferiors. Leaving this aside, if I ever lower myself so much as to step into the ring with this man Jackson, his aspirations will be cut short."[9]

While in Australia, Joe Choynski told the press there that Sullivan was the king of the ring and could defeat Goddard, Jackson, Slavin, or anyone else. "I don't think the man ever put on a glove who could have a look in it with him when he's well, and you can take what I'm telling you for Gospel, and good Gospel at that."

When asked by Smiler, a well known Australian writer, whether Sullivan could land his right swing on a big shifty fellow with a good jab like Jackson, Choynski responded,

You have never seen Sully fight, Smiler. His right arm don't do any swinging; it comes across like a flash of lightning with a jerk, and if he misses he's so quick you can't get your head out of range before it's back ready for another shot at your jaw, and how it does fly, ping, ping. I think he'll land on Jackson right enough if he meets him....

People in this country don't understand the color line, and therefore they can't grip Sullivan's prejudice against Jackson properly, but you may rest easy that John is afraid of no man breathing. Personally, I wish he would fight Jackson, for I know how long the fight would last, and who would win it.

Choynski had seen Jackson fight and had even sparred him, so he had a basis for his opinion. Although Choynski himself did not draw the color line, he understood Sullivan's position and did not believe it was due to fear.

As for Joe Goddard, Choynski complimented him as a good fighter because the Australian had twice defeated Choynski via KO4 in 1891, although he had managed to deck Goddard. However, Choynski also said,

I don't think he'd have a ghost of a show with Sullivan. You see, it's this way. Sullivan is quicker than I am, and he hits with terrible power. If I'd a tenth of Sullivan's force I'd have beaten Goddard both times I fought him, but I hadn't it. Now, it's easy to figure it out. I think, honestly, that John would smash him down with very little trouble.[10]

On October 2, 1891, Joe Goddard won an 8-round decision over Jack Ashton.[11] Sullivan, Ashton, and Joe Choynski left Australia on October 5, 1891.[12]

Once back home, Sullivan said that although he had made up his mind after the Kilrain bout to never enter the ring again, he was now willing to fight one last time, against Slavin. Clearly, though, Sullivan wasn't that eager to fight again because as soon as he arrived back in America, he signed up for another theatrical engagement. It seemed that he was putting it off for as long as possible, enjoying the easy money. He said that his new theatrical engagement would end in June 1892, and he would then have time to get ready for a match with Frank in September or October 1892. However, there were also reports that Slavin and Jackson had already agreed to fight each other in London.[13]

On November 25, 1891, in San Francisco, 2,500 people watched Sullivan spar Paddy Ryan 3 short but lively rounds. Sullivan was fat, but looked thin when compared to the portly Ryan. Despite their weight, they demonstrated great spirit. "Considering his lack of condition Sullivan showed wonderful quickness and hustled around his opponent like a middleweight."

Sullivan gave his interesting view on his training methods. "The fact is I never had a trainer in my life dictate to me. If a man can't train himself no one in the world can do it for him."[14] He also gave some other thoughts on training and learning the art of boxing:

No "professor" or master of sparring can ever claim me as a pupil of theirs. What I know about boxing I picked up from time to time by hard experiences and intelligent observation. I belong to no school of boxers, and have copied no special master's style, and I always fight according to my own judgment. I have always considered it very necessary that a young man, in order to become an accomplished boxer, should have brains as well as muscle. I never knew a thick-headed fellow yet to become skilful in the manly art. A good boxer must be clear and cool-headed, quick to decide, with a keen perception, always able to size up his man at all stages of the game, and know exactly what he's doing, even if he's punched into a dazed condition....

The first thing a "professor" will teach a pupil is to stand in position. He will show him how to turn his toes out, spread his feet so many inches apart, and will try and convince the young man that his style and position is really the only correct one in the world. Now I consider this is all simple rot. My advice is to stand in whatever way is best suited to your purpose—whichever way you can hit your opponent the straightest and hardest blow and avoid a return by getting away quickly.... So with boxing, the position that suits you best is certainly the proper one for you to assume....

Learn to strike straight and clean; swinging blows nearly always leave an opening for your opponent. It is always well to do your leading with the left, reserving your right for a good opening. Wherever you hit your man with one hand let the other fist land in the same spot if possible....

Always watch your opponent.... Just as soon as you see him about to lead, shoot your left into his face, and the force of his coming towards you will increase your blows considerably.[15]

On December 20, 1891, in San Francisco, Sullivan boxed a 3-round exhibition with Joe Choynski, the man whom Corbett had stopped in 1889 in the 27th round. Choynski was quite "willing" and made "earnest attacks." John L. showed some of his defensive skills and landed counters. They hit each other freely, and John exhibited his speed. The 3rd round was "business-like" with each mixing it up, Sullivan seeming "inclined to be gracious." The local report did note though that the pace seemed to be telling on John.[16]

One of Sullivan's backers said,

I like John very much, and I believe that he could whip any man living if he would take care of himself. From what I have heard about him for the past few months, however, I am convinced that he has set his mind on going to the dogs as fast as he can.... He appears to think that he can thrash anybody, and he continues to try and drink all the liquor there is in every town he visits.[17]

Color prejudice prevented Peter Jackson from being allowed the opportunity to prove in the ring with Sullivan that he was the best of the late 1880s and early 1890s. In John L.

Sullivan's eventually famous March 1892 public challenge to "all" contenders he stated, "But in this challenge I include all fighters, first come first served, who are white. I will not fight a negro. I never have, I never shall."[18] Sullivan's refusal was ironic, given that he was famous for uttering, "I can lick any son of a bitch in the world." It was practically his epitaph. He

meant only whites, just as the United States Constitution meant only whites when it asserted that "all men are created equal." In fact, it was a fundamental belief that all men were not created equal. As *The Clarion-Ledger* wrote, "The declaration in the Declaration of Independence of the United States, that all men are created equal is false, utterly false in every particular."[19]

Sullivan was an American icon, and to a large extent represented the era's brand of racial separatism. Blacks were not meant to have opportunities in positions reserved for whites. There was a racial caste line that could not be broken, and merely providing a black the opportunity, regardless of whether or not he could win, would be offensive to that hierarchy. The heavyweight championship was a whites-only position, and only whites could apply. Jackson's excellent career results did not matter, because his race automatically disqualified him from consideration as a Sullivan challenger.

Although there were critics of Sullivan's avoidance of Jackson, many actually praised him for it. One wrote, "I think that the fact that he has faithfully kept his word by not fighting a colored man makes him deserving of much admiration."[20] Just to highlight the time's intense racism, in 1892, there were a U.S. national record 161 black lynchings (since record keeping began in 1882).[21] One Southern paper, responding to U.S. president Benjamin Harrison's attacks on the South's treatment of blacks, defended southerners:

A less than prime Sullivan (Library of Congress, Prints & Photographs Division).

There were no Southern men engaged in the slave trade and no Southern men having slave ships.... I can point out to him and his Northern allies crimes that they have committed against the negro very lately much greater than selling him into slavery—if conspiring against his life is worse.[22]

Sullivan's three-year period of championship fight inactivity is a poor mark on his reign. He seemed to have lost his fighting spirit. His career essentially ended after the Kilrain fight. He made good money in plays and friendly exhibitions, and that was enough for him at that point. He was still considered the champion, but the question is, "For how long can a champion be inactive and still remain the champion?" Sullivan had been so dominant and impressive for so long that apparently he could get away with his inactivity. To maintain his lofty status, though, he eventually had to fight.

To John L. Sullivan's credit, he did take on James J. Corbett in late 1892 in the first heavyweight championship fight to the finish under Queensberry rules. From that point on, heavyweight championships would be fought under Queensberry rules. Although Sullivan was unwilling to fight Jackson, he was willing to take on the man who had equaled Jackson over 61 rounds. Really, Sullivan did not pick Corbett so much as Corbett just happened to be the man who came up with the big money. Although Sullivan's challenge stated that he preferred to fight Slavin, Mitchell, or Corbett, in that order, he was willing to fight anyone but a black man, first come first served, who would agree to a $25,000 purse and $10,000 side bet, winner take all. Corbett was the man who was able to come up with the financial backers, and the match was made soon after Sullivan's March 1892 challenge.

Corbett's quick moving and punching defensive boxing style may have actually been more of a challenge for Sullivan because it presented the perfect foil to Sullivan's aggression. The larger Jackson

James J. Corbett (Library of Congress, Prints & Photographs Division).

James J. Corbett. From Billy Edwards, *The Portrait Gallery of Pugilists of England, America, Australia* (Chicago: Athletic Publishing Co., 1894). Clay Moyle, www.prizefightingbooks.com.

would have stood in his range more. This lends credence to the argument that Sullivan was not afraid of Jackson. If he was, then he would have also avoided the men who were considered to be Jackson's equals or superiors: Corbett or Slavin. Still, Sullivan's attitude of racial separatism, which led to his refusal to fight Peter Jackson, leaves the only hole at the end of his reign.

In the meantime, Sullivan arranged a sparring company and showed in the West, British Columbia, and Manitoba. They also appeared in Philadelphia for a week, Brooklyn for a week, and closed in Boston on June 4, 1892.[23]

In late May 1892 in London, Peter Jackson knocked out Frank Slavin in the 10th round. Defeating a contender as highly regarded as Slavin further highlighted that Jackson deserved championship consideration.[24] Regardless, Sullivan and Corbett were already set to fight on September 7, 1892, and Sullivan was not going to fight Jackson anyway.

The Corbett fight would be Sullivan's last bout as champion, as he would be knocked out in the 21st round by the consummate slick and speedy stick and move fighter.[25] They say that a fighter can never take three years off from serious competition and ever hope to be the same again. That held true for Sullivan, especially given his penchant for drinking, weight gain, and loss of interest in the sport. He was a diminished shell of himself when he lost to Corbett. His career as a great fighter had essentially ended in July 1889.

CHAPTER 19

The Legacy

John L. Sullivan was an exciting, dominant fighting machine for a decade. Because of his superiority, he made gloved boxing a popular money making profession and began its path towards legitimacy.

Few discuss just how many times Sullivan defended his title. If he is considered to have been champion since 1882, when he defeated Paddy Ryan, he made at least 33 defenses, more than any other champion to date. If his world championship began when he defeated Charley Mitchell in 1883, he successfully defended a minimum of 25 times after that, but likely more, through 1889. In truth, he was the world's best gloved fighter as early as 1880, when he easily stopped Joe Goss. The confusion as to when his reign began is owing to the fact that gloved boxing was a new thing and there were no gloved champions prior to Sullivan for him to dethrone. He said that he was the best and he consistently proved it. Sullivan claimed to have knocked out not less than 100 men, 59 of which were during his eight-month tour of America.[1] Very few heavyweight champions throughout history even come close to matching his record.

Today, Sullivan's skills are generally little discussed, and sometimes criticized, but if you carefully review what was said about Sullivan's skills over the years of his reign, it is clear that he knew plenty about the subtleties of boxing, and you will find that John knew well how to slip a punch. He had good enough defense to fight and spar multiple times night after night in his prime years. He only got decked once during that time, by Mitchell, which was a flash knockdown, even though most of his fights were with only 3-ounce gloves. His offense was good enough to hurt and drop fighters of a wide variety of sizes and styles. He was so fast and strong and had such a good chin and defense that almost no one could deal with him at all, no matter what their skill level. And he wasn't just a short rounds slugger. He proved his conditioning in his bouts with Curley early on, and later with Mitchell and Kilrain, so he has to be given a lofty status in history.

Sullivan was a phenomenon—similar to the prime Mike Tyson of his day, but with greater endurance and career longevity. Super fast and strong, he had Floyd Patterson type leap-ins as well as quick Jack Dempsey rushes forward. He was extremely accurate and knew how to find and create openings. He could feint, use set up punches, leap and rush in to surprise his opponents, and throw a variety of punches in rapid combination. Amazingly, he maintained a fast pace in doing all of this. As Sullivan said, "I go in to win from the very first second, and I never stop until I have won. Win I must, and win I will, at every stage of the game."[2]

The Times-Democrat said,

> Sullivan was one of the quickest big men that ever lived; that with all his aggressive ability, which had in reality not been overrated, he was quick as lightning at parrying, ducking, dodging and getting out of the way generally. While his tactics were never to unnecessarily delay a contest, he well

215

knew when it was desirable to rush and when it was prudent to bide his time. In brief, Sullivan, in addition to being probably the hardest hitter that ever stood in a prize ring, was also one of the quickest of big men, a thoroughly scientific boxer by instinct as well as training, and without a superior as a ring general. In this way many boxers of skill and comparatively good sense were ignominiously defeated.[3]

Even Richard Fox, his most ardent critic, had to admit that he was a great fighter after he defeated Kilrain. Even when he was no longer at his best, and had been fat and drunk and not serious about boxing for 3 years, it still took a prime Corbett 21 rounds to take him out. Even a Sullivan recently recovered from malaria and other ailments hurt and dropped Jake Kilrain continually, while Corbett never hurt Jake and was not close to doing so in their decision bout. A younger Sullivan dropped and hurt Jack Burke multiple times, and was said to have had the best of his sparring with Duncan McDonald. Corbett boxed on even terms with Burke and McDonald, some feeling that the latter men actually had the best of their encounters. Most who had seen Corbett and Jackson box thought that a prime Sullivan could defeat both on the same night. Corbett defeated Sullivan when he was many, many years past his prime.

Some analysts today say that Sullivan's opponents were not very good, but many of those fighters were considered the best men of the day and had a fair amount of bareknuckle and gloved experience in lengthy bouts to the finish. Their science was usually commended. During Sullivan's era, rather than being critical of his opponents' abilities, observers throughout the world were unanimous in their acclaim of Sullivan as a rare prodigy, and even compared him favorably with history's greatest fighters. Sullivan's foes could fight, but John L. was so good that he usually made them look like nothing.

Another criticism often lodged is that Sullivan fought a lot of smaller guys, but size does not matter if you know how to use it. History has proven this. Many of the larger fighters at that time were defeated by smaller boxers. In fact, the biggest opponents Sullivan fought were usually taken out the fastest. Few of the bigger men had the courage to step into the ring with him, often pulling out of matches at the last minute. After enough stories of boxers being out cold for 20 minutes and being feared dead circulated around, it is understandable how Sullivan's results could have a chilling effect on many fighters. Experts back then felt that it would take a smaller, quicker man with crafty footwork and skill as well as great condition to even remotely deal with Sullivan. No one was stronger. Great size was often seen as a detriment in a lengthy fight to the finish and most top fighters intentionally trained down in weight for endurance purposes. How many 200-plus-pound fighters exist today or throughout history that could last for two or three hours of bareknuckle fighting in intense cold or heat? Even the 15-round fight only lasted an hour. Sullivan fought Mitchell with bare hands in the cold rain for over 3 hours. He fought Kilrain in over 100-degree heat for over two hours. This was a special man.

Sullivan's only bad marks were the color line and his inactivity at the end of his reign. Could Peter Jackson have defeated him? Jackson wasn't the most powerful fighter. However, his relaxation and lack of power might have actually helped him in a long fight with Sullivan because Jackson had great endurance and could methodically break down strong and tough fighters. He did it with hard punchers like McAuliffe and later Slavin, so he might have done it with Sullivan. Of course, no one thought those fighters had anywhere near Sullivan's talent and ability. Peter struggled with vicious rushers like Farnan and Goddard. The question is whether Jackson could have gotten to the later rounds with Sullivan, or have been unhurt enough to have done anything once he got there. Obviously, it is Sullivan's fault that we will never know the answer to that question. Certainly though, Jackson was sufficiently admired and had strong enough results against top fighters such that he would have had a competitive chance to defeat Sullivan, especially when past his prime in 1892. If Corbett could stop an over the hill Sullivan, then Jackson might very well have done so also. Sullivan's bigotry prevented this great match from taking place.

Perhaps Sullivan knew that he was slipping, that his day to lose would eventually come, and decided that should he be defeated (however unlikely this was in his own mind), he wanted it to be only by a white man. However, Sullivan also reflected the common belief that merely allowing a black man to challenge for the title, regardless of whether or not he could win it, offended hierarchical notions of racial separation and white supremacy. That said, he wasn't always consistent, at times during his career having expressed a willingness to meet a black fighter. This leaves his position open to attack as mere subterfuge.

Sullivan, the legendary champion. From Billy Edwards, *The Portrait Gallery of Pugilists of England, America, Australia* (Chicago: Athletic Publishing Co., 1894). Clay Moyle, www.prizefightingbooks.com.

Sullivan's theatrical manager believed that Sullivan was concerned that he would lose to Jackson.

> Speaking of Jackson, I might say that I know that he can whip Sullivan. Sullivan has tacitly admitted it. He agreed with the California Club to fight him and contracted to do so for a $15,000 purse. Two nights afterward he saw Jackson box in the Music Hall in Boston [January 29, 1890], and the next day he demanded $20,000 for the purse, using his now famous expression, "$10,000 for a white man, $20,000 for a nigger." His demand was acceded to. He did not think it would be, and then he drew the color line.[4]

In Sullivan's partial defense, he defeated Kilrain, who was better than Godfrey. Jackson was only a true challenger when John L. was just about retired and not fighting at all anyway, white or black; and Sullivan did fight Corbett, who had equaled Jackson. Corbett might have actually been more of a challenge than Jackson. Quite frankly, if I had been managing John L., I would have taken Slavin or Jackson before I took Corbett because Jim had the absolute perfect style to defeat Sullivan, sort of like Tunney to Dempsey or Ali to Liston. Jackson would not have moved around quite as much as Corbett did. Jackson was slick and intelligent, but if a boxer didn't have that fast moving, running around footwork like Corbett, he just couldn't withstand the early punishment that John would apply. Also, Corbett had never been decked, while Jackson had once been stopped. There was some question as to Jackson's ability to take it. Even James Corbett agreed:

> I tell you that no one can whip Sullivan who is not as fast as I am. I am not so sure that he wouldn't whip Peter Jackson, for Peter's style would suit him a good deal better than mine. Peter would go and shy with him, and no man can do that with any hope of success.[5]

Perhaps Sullivan's drawing of the color line really was based upon principle, however misguided, and not fear.

During the late stage of his career (1889–1892), John L. was just going for the easy buck with his mostly short friendly exhibitions and plays, and eventually just took whatever was going to be the biggest payday. He would have taken on any white challenger that could match the immense cash challenge of a $25,000 purse plus a $10,000 side bet, regardless of how good they were. He didn't care about how his style matched up with Corbett or Jackson or anyone else. John L. Sullivan had such a huge ego that he could not even conceive of someone being able to defeat him, which is why he made the Corbett bout winner-take-all. Fear was not in his vocabulary. "I never had stage fright in my life; do not know what it is, and do not suppose I could understand it if somebody would try to explain it to me."[6] Ultimately though, the failure to fight or be willing to fight Jackson is a blemish on his otherwise fantastic reign. However, without Sullivan's great reign, we would not even be discussing or caring about whether or not they fought.

Most felt that a prime Sullivan would have defeated both Jackson and Corbett. Neither punchers nor movers and slick boxers could defeat Sullivan at his best. Analysts were unanimous in saying that superior science was not enough to defeat him. Mitchell lasted, but he ran around in a large, 24-foot ring in muddy conditions under London rules, where he could drop or wrestle down to avoid big shots and get 30–38 seconds of recovery every time, which often made fights last forever. Under the Queensberry system against a prime Sullivan, Mitchell only lasted 3 rounds. Kilrain used the same tactics as Mitchell, but took severe punishment and went down often. Basically, those that tried to win and not simply survive were taken out quickly or knocked down multiple times. Even those who were movers and survivors could do little more than that. They could not beat Sullivan. As Sullivan said,

> Whenever I have boxed with men who have resorted to all the trickery and sharp practices which they or their friends could invent, the match has lasted longer than where the men have come up manfully and fought me.
>
> The length of the match has always depended upon the amount of trickery my opponent could resort to and his sprinting abilities.... Now, in the face of such matches the general public give the man who makes the longest fight the credit of being the best boxer or fighter; whereas such should not be the case by any means, for where one man stands up manfully and fights, and does his best to win and is consequently knocked out in short order, the other man does not attempt to win but attempts to make the fight last as long as possible, depending upon police interference and hoping to make a draw, and knowing that the public will give him credit for having made a long fight.[7]

Very few boxers who fought Sullivan to win survived.

William Burns, a fighter and brother of Sullivan opponent Jack Burns, said the following of Sullivan:

> At his best, from 1878 to 1883, in my opinion, he could easily have trimmed Peter Jackson, Jim Corbett, Frank Slavin, Bob Fitzsimmons, Jim Jeffries, or Jack Johnson....
>
> He was as lithe as a cat and his cleverness at dodging was vouched for by the unmarred condition of his face and head after his hectic career.... In the ring, when time was called, he always left his chair like a shot out of a gun, ready and eager for the fray. The impression he gave was one of boundless vitality. Any ordinary man was forced to run to keep pace with his walk.... His whole body seemed to be set on springs.... His hands and head cooperated beautifully at all times. Besides this, he was a natural born fighter, and absolutely fearless.... His left hand was just as deadly as his right and his blows always came straight from the shoulder with the full weight of his body behind them. He was never known to lose his head in a tight place and he always fought a clean fight....
>
> Sullivan was a strong advocate of glove fighting as he considered bare-knuckle fighting too brutal for true sport. His ambition was to see the ring uplifted and its standards raised to a good deal higher plane than those then prevailing.[8]

Sullivan really put boxing on the map as more than just a fringe sport. He was a star who sold gloved boxing as a legitimate sport and successfully brought it to new heights. Without being an immensely talented, dominant and active fighter, he could not have accomplished this. Even James J. Corbett said, "I think he was the most popular pugilist that ever lived."[9]

One newspaper summarized Sullivan's importance to the sport, saying,

> [H]e was the virtual inventor of the modern glove contest. He did better with the gloves than all his predecessors with naked fists and did as much execution with padded hands in four rounds as the old time fighter with ungloved battering rams in hours. He Americanized the manly art, deprived it of much of the brutality and made it possible to decide championships before athletic clubs under the best auspices, before classes of people who formerly took little interest in the sport. Nature intended him for a gladiator, and although he abused nature to a considerable extent not even the best trained rivals could defeat him.... He stood out a central figure in the history of pugilism; attracted to him a following from every corner of the country.[10]

John L. Sullivan revolutionized boxing.

Appendix:
John L. Sullivan's Record

1877–1878

?	Jack Scannell	Boston, MA	KO 1

1879

Mar 14	Jack Curley	Boston, MA	Win in 1hr. 14 min.
Mar 14	John "Cocky" Woods	Boston, MA	KO? 5?—possibly just an exhibition
?	Dan Dwyer	Boston, MA	KO 3?
?	Tommy Chandler	Boston, MA	W 4?

1880

Late '79 or Jan 1880?	John/Jack "Patsy" Hogan	Boston, MA	W 4?
Possibly Feb 1880?	Mike Donovan	Boston, MA	EX 3 or 4
Mar 6	Jerry Murphy	New York	EX
Apr 6	Joe Goss	Boston, MA	EX 3

Actually a KO2, but Goss continued after recovering.

Jun 28	George Rooke	Boston, MA	KO 3

Sullivan said that he subsequently gave several exhibitions with Dan Dwyer.

Sometime that year, Sullivan may have defeated Jake Kilrain in a 4 round exhibition.

In November 1880, Sullivan might have sparred with John Kenny in New York.

Dec 11	John Donaldson	Cincinnati, OH	EX 4
Dec 24	John Donaldson	Cincinnati, OH	KO 10

London Prize Ring Rules with hard gloves, lasting almost 22 minutes.

1881

Jan 3	Jack Stewart	Boston, MA	EX 3
Jan 3	Joe Goss	Boston, MA	EX 3
Mar 21	Mike Donovan	Boston, MA	EX 3

It has been reported that sometime in 1881 while in Boston, Sullivan was set to fight George Godfrey, who was black, but the police prevented the match.

Mar 31	Steve Taylor	New York, NY	KO 2
May 16	John Flood	Yonkers, NY	KO 8

London Prize Ring Rules with gloves, lasting 16 minutes

Jun 13	John Flood	New York, NY	EX 3

Jul 11	Fred Crossley	Philadelphia, PA	KO 1
Jul 11	Billy Madden	Philadelphia, PA	EX

Sullivan and Madden sparred nightly during the following week.

Jul 21	John Buckley/Dan McCarty	Philadelphia, PA	KO 1

Sullivan and Madden possibly gave more exhibitions the following week.

Aug 13	"Captain" James Dalton	Chicago, IL	KO 4
Sep 3	Jack Burns	Chicago, IL	KO 1
Sep 3	"Captain" James Dalton	Chicago, IL	EX 4

In October in New York, Sullivan sparred Steve Taylor in a tame set-to. It was said that his next exhibition would be in Philadelphia.

Nov 5	Billy Madden	New York, NY	EX

It was said that Sullivan was headed to Boston, but would be back to spar in Buffalo, New York, on November 16.

Nov 16?	Pete McCoy	Buffalo, NY	EX
Nov 28	Pete McCoy	Cincinnati, OH	EX
Nov 28	Billy Madden	Cincinnati, OH	EX

Sullivan said that he gave exhibitions with Madden, McCoy, and Bob Farrell (a lightweight) on the way to New Orleans, in preparation for the upcoming match with Ryan.

1882

Feb 2	Joe Goss	New Orleans, LA	EX 3
Feb 7	Paddy Ryan	Mississippi City, MS	KO 9

London Prize Ring Rules, lasting 10½ or 11 minutes.

Sullivan said that after the Ryan fight, he, Madden, Goss, McCoy, and Bob Farrell exhibited in Chicago, Detroit, Cleveland, Pittsburgh, Philadelphia, and New York.

Mar 27	Joseph Douglas	New York, NY	EX 3
Mar 27	Billy Madden	New York, NY	EX 3
Mar 28	Steve Taylor	Jersey City, NJ	EX 3
Apr 15	Pete McCoy	?	EX

Sullivan had been set to meet a black fighter named Johnson, who failed to appear.

Sullivan sometime that year bested Jake Kilrain in an exhibition.

Apr 20	John McDermott	Rochester, NY	KO 3
Jul 4	Jimmy Elliott	Brooklyn, NY	KO 3

Bout fought with gloves, but hybrid rules—only 30-second rests—the bout lasting 7 minutes and 20 seconds.

Jul 17	Joe "Tug" Wilson	New York, NY	W 4/L 4

Wilson knocked or dropped down incessantly to last the distance and claim the cash bonus for merely lasting.

Aug 19	Joe Goss	North Adams, MA	EX 5 (or EX2, EX3)

First exhibition interrupted, but resumed hours later.

Sullivan said that his company signed an agreement to spar six nights a week for twenty weeks at $500 per night, beginning September 4.

Sep 4	Billy Madden	Newark, NJ	EX

The combination exhibited on September 9 in Philadelphia, on the 11th at Pittston, the 12th at Scranton, and the 13th at Wilkes-Barre.

Sullivan and Madden again gave a "decidedly tame" and short exhibition at Wilkes-Barre, Pennsylvania.

Sep 22	Billy Madden	Buffalo, NY	EX
Sep 23	Henry Higgins	Buffalo, NY	KO 3
Oct 16	S.P. Stockton	Fort Wayne, IN	KO 2
Oct 30	Charley O'Donnell	Chicago, IL	KO 1
Oct 30	Pete McCoy	Chicago, IL	EX 3

Oct 31	Pete McCoy	Chicago, IL	EX 3
Nov 17	P.J. Rentzler/Rensler	Washington, DC	KO 1
Nov 17	Pete McCoy	Washington, DC	EX

It was said that the Sullivan combination of sparrers would be in Cincinnati during Thanksgiving week.
Sullivan said they appeared in Chicago on December 10, 1882.

| Dec 28 | Joe Coburn | New York, NY | EX 3 |

1883

Jan 20	Joe Coburn	Buffalo, NY	EX
Jan 23	Joe Coburn	Toronto, ON, Canada	EX
Jan 25?	Harry Gilman?	Toronto, ON, Canada?	KO 3?
Jan 29	Joe Coburn	Troy, NY	EX 3
Feb	Joe Coburn	Rochester, NY	EX
Feb 22	Pete McCoy	Boston, MA	EX 3
Mar 19	Steve Taylor	Boston, MA	EX 3
Mar 19	Joe Coburn	Boston, MA	EX 3
Mar 19	Mike Cleary	Boston, MA	EX 3
May 14	Charley Mitchell	New York, NY	KO 3
May 16	John Flood	NewYork, NY	EX
Aug 6	Herbert Slade	New York, NY	KO 3

Sullivan's tour across America began in late September. One paper reported that the tour was to begin in
Washington, D.C., and Baltimore, then continue to Pennsylvania, West Virginia, Ohio, Indiana, Kentucky, Missouri, Illinois, Wisconsin, Minnesota, Kansas, Nebraska, Nevada, Montana, Utah and California. On the return trip Michigan, New York, and Boston would be visited.

| Sep 28 | Herbert Slade | Baltimore, MD | EX |
| Sep 29 | Herbert Slade | Baltimore, MD | EX |

They appeared in Richmond, Virginia, on October 1. The itinerary showed them to be in Petersburg on
the 2nd, Norfolk on the 4th, Washington, D.C., on the 6th (twice), Harrisburg, Pennsylvania, on the
8th, Reading on the 9th, and Lancaster on the 10th. On October 11, they appeared in Pottsville, Pennsylvania. The itinerary said they would be in Wilkes-Barre on the 12th, Scranton on the 13th, York on
the 15th, and Altoona on the 16th.

| Oct 17 or 18 | James McCoy | McKeesport, PA | KO 1 |

The itinerary said they were to be in Youngstown, Ohio, on the 18th.

| Oct 19 | Steve Taylor | Allegheny City, PA | EX |
| Oct 19 | Herbert Slade | Allegheny City, PA | EX |

On the 20th, they exhibited in Allegheny before 1,000 folks in the afternoon, and 3,000 more in the evening.
They were set to be headed to West Virginia, New Jersey, Ohio, Kentucky, and Indiana, all before the month
was out.
Their itinerary listed them as being in Wheeling, West Virginia, on the 22nd, Steubenville, Ohio, on the
23rd, Newark, Ohio, on the 24th, Columbus on the 25th, and Dayton on the 26th and 27th.
The combination was in Cincinnati, Ohio, on October 28, 1883, filling the house in both afternoon and
evening exhibitions.

| Oct 29 | Steve Taylor | Louisville, KY | EX 4 |
| Oct 29 | Herbert Slade | Louisville, KY | EX 4 |

The itinerary said that they were in Indianapolis on the 30th, Terre Haute on the 31st, Lafayette, Indiana,
on November 1, and Danville, Illinois, on the 2nd.

Nov 3	Jim Miles	St. Louis, MO	KO 1
Nov 3	Steve Taylor	St. Louis, MO	EX
Nov 3	Herbert Slade	St. Louis, MO	EX

Nov 5	Steve Taylor	St. Louis, MO	EX 4
Nov 5	Herbert Slade	St. Louis, MO	EX 2
Nov 6	Steve Taylor	St. Louis, MO	EX
Nov 6	Herbert Slade	St. Louis, MO	EX

One report said that the tour was headed to Quincy, Illinois, on the 7th. However, Sullivan and Taylor were arrested on the 7th for having violated the state's antiboxing laws. Their itinerary said they would be in Keokuk, Iowa, on the 8th, and Burlington, Iowa, on the 9th, and in the following Illinois towns: Peoria on the 10th, Galesburg the 12th, Mendota the 13th, and Streator on the 14th.

| Nov 16 | Steve Taylor | Chicago, IL | EX 4 |

Sullivan possibly also boxed a Hoosier and scored a KO3.

| Nov 16 | Herbert Slade | Chicago, IL | EX 4 |

The combination gave another Chicago exhibition the following day.

Their itinerary listed them as being in Wisconsin over the next week: Racine on the 19th, Milwaukee on the 20th, Fond-du-Lac on the 21st, Oshkosh on the 22nd, and Eau Claire on the 23rd. They then toured throughout Minnesota, exhibiting in Stillwater on the 24th.

Nov 26	Morris Hefey or Hafey	St. Paul, MN	KO 1
Nov 26	Steve Taylor	St. Paul, MN	EX 4
Nov 26	Herbert Slade	St. Paul, MN	EX 4

It was said that Sullivan would be continuing on to other places in the Northwest, including Minneapolis, then to Kansas City and Omaha, and taking a trip on the Union Pacific to Ogden, Utah, then to Montana, and then along the coast.

| Nov 27 | Herbert Slade | Minneapolis, MN | EX |

Sullivan's itinerary reflected that they were to be in Winona, Minnesota, on the 28th, La Crosse, Wisconsin, on the 29th, and then on a tour of Iowa, including McGregor on the 30th, Dubuque on the 1st and 2nd of December, and Clinton on the 3rd.

Dec 4	Mike Sheehan/Shean/Shehan	Davenport, IA	KO 1
Dec 4	Steve Taylor	Davenport, IA	EX
Dec 4	Herbert Slade	Davenport, IA	EX
Dec 5	Herbert Slade	Davenport, IA	EX

They were said to be exhibiting in Muscatine, Iowa, on the 6th. The itinerary, which may not be accurate, said they were to be in Marshalltown on December 7, Oskaloosa on the 8th, Ottumwa on the 9th and 10th, and Des Moines on the 11th. From Iowa, they were to go to Lincoln, Nebraska, on the 12th, and Omaha on the 13th, before coming back to Iowa on the 14th to exhibit in Council Bluffs. They then were set to be in St. Joseph, Missouri, on the 15th and 16th. Kansas was next, in Atchison on the 17th, Leavenworth on the 18th, Lawrence on the 19th, Topeka on the 20th, and Wyandotte on the 21st. Kansas City, Missouri, was to be visited on December 22. The itinerary said they were to be in Pueblo, Colorado, on the 26th. They in fact wound up in Denver on that date. Another report slightly conflicted, saying that the combination was scheduled to appear in Kansas on December 18, Missouri on the 19th and 20th, Kansas again on the 22nd, and then to head to Denver, Colorado.

| Dec 26 | Steve Taylor | Denver, CO | EX |

They were in Leadville, Colorado, from December 27 to the 30th, and Sullivan said that they were given a grand reception.

1884

The Sullivan itinerary reflected that they would be in Denver on the 1st, in Cheyenne, Laramie City, and Rawlins, Wyoming, on the 2nd through 4th, Salt Lake City on the 5th and 6th, and Ogden, Utah, on the 7th.

| Jan 9 | ? | Butte, MT | EX |

The combination exhibited there, but there was no next day report.

Jan 10	Steve Taylor	Helena, MT	EX 3
Jan 10	Herbert Slade	Helena, MT	EX
Jan 11	Steve Taylor	Helena, MT	EX
Jan 11	Herbert Slade	Helena, MT	EX
Jan 12	Fred Robinson	Butte, MT	KO 2
Jan 12	Herbert Slade	Butte, MT	EX

Exhibitions took place on the 13th as well.

The itinerary reflected that they would be in Salt Lake City on the 15th, and then in Nevada towns including Reno on the 17th, Carson City on the 18th and 19th, and Virginia City on the 20th.

The combination was in Nevada City on Monday, January 21, Sacramento on Tuesday, January 22, Stockton on the 23rd, and San Jose, California, on Thursday, January 24.

The combination sparred in San Francisco on January 25 and 26. On the 25th, Sullivan sparred Taylor 3 rounds and Slade in 3 short rounds. On the 26th, Sullivan sparred Taylor in 3 short rounds, and then Slade.

Sullivan said that he would appear in Oakland on Monday and Tuesday, January 28 and 29, and then go to Oregon, and then return to San Francisco. It was said that the tour would then head to Texas and New Orleans.

Feb 1	Sylvester La Gouriff	Astoria, OR	KO 1
Feb 1	Steve Taylor	Astoria, OR	EX 3
Feb 1	Herbert Slade	Astoria, OR	EX

One paper reported that the tour was in Portland, Oregon, on February 2 and 4th. It said Sullivan would head next to Seattle and Victoria. They might have been in New Tacoma, Washington, on February 5.

Feb 6	James Lang	Seattle, WA	KO 1
Feb 6	Steve Taylor	Seattle, WA	EX
Feb 6	Herbert Slade	Seattle, WA	EX

It was said that the Sullivan combination left for Victoria afterwards, set to give an exhibition there, but would be returning in two days. One report said Sullivan was in Victoria, British Columbia, on February 8, 1884.

| Feb 9 | Steve Taylor | Seattle, WA | EX 3 |
| Feb 9 | Herbert Slade | Seattle, WA | EX |

The Sullivan itinerary reflected that they would be in Dayton, Washington, and Walla Walla, Washington, on the 12th and 13th. They were set to be in Dallas, Oregon, on the 14th, and Portland on the 15th.

| Feb 18 | Steve Taylor | San Francisco, CA | EX 3 |

Slade severed his connection with the tour.

| Mar 6 | George M. Robinson | San Francisco, CA | WDQ 4 |

Robinson went down 28–66 times to avoid being knocked out, until disqualified for falling without a blow.

The Sullivan itinerary said that they would be in Los Angeles from March 12 to 17, San Bernardino on the 18th and 19th, and Tucson and Tombstone, Arizona, on the 21st and 22nd. On the 21st in Tucson, Sullivan exhibited 3 short rounds with McCoy and 3 short rounds with Taylor. They next headed to Tombstone. The Sullivan itinerary went on to say that they would exhibit in Deming, New Mexico, on the 24th, and venues in Texas including El Paso on the 25th, Fort Worth on the 29th and 30th, Denison on the 31st, Sherman on April 1, Dallas on the 2nd, Corsicana on the 3rd, Waco on the 4th, Austin on the 5th, San Antonio on the 6th and 7th, and Houston on the 8th.

A report said that the combination would appear in Dallas, Texas, the first week of April. They appeared in Fort Worth on the last day of March and were reported to be planning to be in New Orleans in early April.

Apr 9	Pete McCoy	Galveston, TX	EX 3
Apr 9	Steve Taylor	Galveston, TX	EX
Apr 10	Al Marx	Galveston, TX	KO 1
Apr 10	Steve Taylor	Galveston, TX	EX
Apr 13	Pete McCoy	New Orleans, LA	EX
Apr 13	Steve Taylor	New Orleans, LA	EX

| Apr 14 | Mike Donovan | New Orleans, LA | EX |
| Apr 14 | Steve Taylor | New Orleans, LA | EX |

The itinerary listed the tour as scheduled to be in Mobile, Alabama, on April 15, Montgomery on the 16th, in Columbus, Macon and Savannah, Georgia, on the 17th to 20th, Charleston, South Carolina, on the 21st, Augusta and Atlanta, Georgia, on the 22nd and 23rd, Chattanooga, Tennessee, on the 24th, Birmingham, Alabama, on the 25th, and Nashville, Tennessee, on the 26th.

On April 27, the company exhibited in Chattanooga, Tennessee.

Apr 28	Mike Donovan	Memphis, TN	EX 3 or 4
Apr 28	Steve Taylor	Memphis, TN	EX
Apr 29	Dan Henry	Hot Springs, AR	KO 1
Apr 30	Mike Donovan	Little Rock, AR	EX 2
Apr 30	Steve Taylor	Little Rock, AR	EX 3
May 1	William Fleming	Memphis, TN	KO 1
May 1	Mike Donovan	Memphis, TN	EX 3
May 1	Steve Taylor	Memphis, TN	EX
May 2	Enos Phillips	Nashville, TN	KO 1/KO 4

Possibly a KO 1 if Queensberry rules, but a KO 4 if counted in London rules fashion.

| May 2 | Mike Donovan | Nashville, TN | EX |
| May 2 | Steve Taylor | Nashville, TN | EX |

The combination itinerary listed them as scheduled to be in Louisville, Kentucky, on May 3. Sullivan sparred Taylor.

The tour was set to exhibit in Vincennes, Indiana, on the 5th (but did not show up), Evansville on the 6th, and St. Louis on the 7th and 8th. On May 7 and May 8, 1884, in St. Louis, Sullivan sparred with a new heavyweight named Florie Barnett, and also Taylor.

The tour was in Michigan in East Saginaw on the 17th and 18th, Bay City on the 19th, Jackson on the 20th, and Detroit on the 21st and 22nd. The tour closed at Toledo, Ohio, on May 23, 1884.

On May 26, they arrive back in New York.

| June 30 | Charley Mitchell | New York, NY | |

The night of the fight, Sullivan calls it off due to "illness," but most believed he was drunk.

Aug 13	Dominick McCaffrey	Boston, MA	EX 3
Aug 13	Steve Taylor	Boston, MA	EX 3
Aug 13	Tom Denny	Boston, MA	EX 3

Exhibitions were to benefit Councilman Tom Denny.

They possibly toured in Pennsylvania, West Virginia, Ohio, New Jersey, Kentucky, and Indianapolis.

| Nov 10 | John M. Laflin | New York, NY | KO 1/KO 4 |

Laflin was actually knocked out in the 1st round but allowed to continue, in London rules fashion.

| Nov 18 | Alf Greenfield | New York, NY | W 2 |

Police stopped the bout when they began slugging.

In New York, on New Year's Eve and twice on January 1, 1885, Sullivan sparred Mike Donovan in the concert scene during performances of *The Lottery of Life*.

1885

| Jan 12 | Alf Greenfield | Boston, MA | W 4 |
| Jan 19 | Paddy Ryan | New York, NY | NC 1 |

Police intervened and the referee declared it no contest.

| Apr 2 | Dominick McCaffrey | Philadelphia, PA | |

Police prevented the bout.

| Jun 13 | Jack Burke | Chicago, IL | W 5 |
| Aug 29 | Dominick McCaffrey | Cincinnati, OH | W 7 |

Sullivan engaged himself with the Lester and Allen's minstrel show for 21 weeks doing statuary acting at a salary of $500 per week. All he had to do was pose as statues of ancient and modern gladiators. He started traveling with them on September 20, 1885, and continued this business until May 1886.

1886

In May, negotiations for a Mitchell rematch fell through when the mayor of Chicago would not allow it to take place there. It was rescheduled for early July in New York, but the mayor of that city also prevented it.

Sep 18	Frank Herald	Alleghany City, PA	W 2

Police stopped the bout, but pre-fight terms allowed for a decision in the event of interference.

Sullivan in his autobiography said that after the Herald match, another touring combination was formed which included Joe Lannon, Steve Taylor, George La Blanche, Jimmy Carroll and Patsy Kerrigan. One report said that traveling with Sullivan were George La Blanche, "the Marine," Steve Taylor, Jim Carroll, Dan Murphy, Jim McKeown, Pete McCoy, and George Weir, "the Spider." They opened in Racine, Wisconsin, and then went to Minneapolis and St. Paul, as well as other cities on the way to San Francisco.

It was reported in early November that the Sullivan combination had been engaging in a Western tour. They performed in Stillwater, Minnesota, on October 29, 1886. Sullivan sparred Tom Hinch and Taylor 3 rounds each. On the 30th, they performed in St. Paul. Sullivan again sparred Hinch and Taylor 3 rounds each. They also appeared in Minneapolis on November 2.

Nov 2	?	Minneapolis, MN	EX
Nov 13	Paddy Ryan	San Francisco, CA	KO 3

On December 24 and 25, 1886, the Sullivan combination appeared in Leadville, Colorado. Traveling with Sullivan were Steve Taylor, George La Blanche ("the Marine")(called La Blanche), Duncan McDonald, champion of the Northwest, James Carroll, champion lightweight, and Daniel Murphy and James McKeon of Boston.

Dec 27	Duncan McDonald	Colorado Springs, CO	EX

Sullivan sparred McDonald in a purely scientific match.

They were set to give exhibitions in Denver on December 28 and 29 before heading to Georgetown, Central, and Cheyenne.

Dec 28	Duncan McDonald	Denver, CO	EX 4
Dec 29	Duncan McDonald	Denver, CO	EX
Dec 29	Steve Taylor	Denver, CO	EX
Dec 30	Duncan McDonald	Georgetown, CO	EX
Dec 30	Steve Taylor	Georgetown, CO	EX

1887

Jan 1	Duncan McDonald	Denver, CO	EX
Jan 1	Steve Taylor	Denver, CO	EX

They were said to be headed east to Topeka and river towns.

The Sullivan combination performed in Kansas City, Missouri, on January 7, 1887.

Jan 18	Patsy Cardiff	Minneapolis, MN	D 6

Sullivan broke a bone in his left arm.

Mar 28	Joe Lannon	Hoboken, NJ	EX 4
Mar 28	Steve Taylor	Hoboken, NJ	EX 4
Apr 1	Steve Taylor	Baltimore, MD	EX

On July 4, 1887, in Hartford, Connecticut, after umpiring a baseball game there, Sullivan exhibited with Joe Lannon.

Aug 8	Mike Donovan	Boston, MA	EX
Aug 8	Steve Taylor	Boston, MA	EX

In November, Sullivan embarked on a European tour. Sullivan said that he exhibited in London, Birmingham, Liverpool, Manchester, Newcastle-on-Tyne, Leicester, Nottingham, Derby, Sheffield, Preston, Oldham, and other cities. In Ireland, he appeared in Dublin, Waterford, Cork, Limerick, and Belfast. In Scotland, he visited Glasgow, Dundee, Aberdeen, and Edinburgh. The only place that he visited in Wales was Cardiff, arriving there after his Nottingham exhibition. He claimed to have boxed in 51 exhibitions.

He first exhibited in London, England, with Jack Ashton on November 9, 1887. He was scheduled to appear in Birmingham on Nov. 12 and 14th, Sheffield on the 17th, Wolverhampton on the 18th, Leicester on the 19th and 21st, Bolton on the 22nd, Manchester on the 23rd, Leeds on the 24th, and in a 12-night engagement in London, each time facing Ashton. In Birmingham, Sullivan first sparred Ashton, and then took on Alf Greenfield for 3 rounds.

Nov 28	Jack Ashton	London, England	EX 3

On December 5, 1887, Sullivan began the second week of his engagement in London. On December 8, 1887, Sullivan and Ashton provided entertainment at the Aquarium, and then gave a private exhibition at the Pelican Club.

Dec 9	Jack Ashton	London, England	EX 3
Dec 12	Jack Ashton	Dublin, Ireland	EX 4
Dec 13	Jack Ashton	Waterford, Ireland	EX
Dec 14	Jack Ashton	Cork, Ireland	EX
Dec 15	Jack Ashton	Limerick, Ireland	EX 4
Dec 16	Jack Ashton	Dublin, Ireland	EX 4
Dec 17	Jack Ashton	Belfast, Ireland	EX

Sullivan also exhibited in Edinburgh, Scotland.

1888

Jan 5	Jack Ashton	Cardiff, Wales	EX
Jan 5	William Samuells	Cardiff, Wales	KO 3

Sullivan gave boxing exhibitions in Portsmouth, England.

Mar 10	Charley Mitchell	Chantilly, France	D 39

London Prize Ring Rules bout lasting 3 hours, 10 minutes, and 55 seconds.

May 15	Jack Ashton	Boston, MA	EX 4
Jun 4	Mike Donovan	New York, NY	EX
Jun 4	Jack Ashton	New York, NY	EX

1889

Apr 24	Jack Ashton	Brooklyn, NY	EX 3

In May, Sullivan began training with William Muldoon in preparation for the Kilrain fight. They visited Detroit, Cincinnati, New Jersey, and New York giving wrestling exhibitions. Mike Cleary was also brought in to spar with John.

May 6	Jack Ashton	Tarrytown, NY	EX
May 28	Billy Madden	Cincinnati, OH	EX
Jul 8	Jake Kilrain	Richburg, MS	KO 75

London Prize Ring Rules, lasting either 2 hours, 13 minutes, 2 hours, 16 minutes, or 2 hours, 18 minutes.

Sep 9	Mike Cleary	New York, NY	EX 3

1890

Peter Jackson and Sullivan gave separate sparring exhibitions the same week in February at the same place in Hoboken, but on different nights.

Feb 7	Joe Lannon	Newark, NJ	EX 3
Feb 12	Joe Lannon	Hoboken, NJ	EX 3

Another report said Sullivan sparred Lannon in Hoboken again on the 13th. Sullivan was scheduled to give an exhibition in Troy, and was set to proceed to Mississippi.

In May in New York, Sullivan and Lannon appeared, giving light friendly exhibitions as part of a play called *The Paymaster*. In late August, Sullivan began performing in the play *Honest Hearts and Willing Hands*.

1891

Jun 26	James J. Corbett	San Francisco, CA	EX 4

Sullivan took a trip to Australia with Jack Ashton, arriving there on July 21, 1891. On the way, they visited Honolulu and gave an exhibition there. In Australia, they would give frequent 3-round exhibitions. They left on October 5, 1891.

Nov 25	Paddy Ryan	San Francisco, CA	EX 3
Dec 20	Joe Choynski	San Francisco, CA	EX 3

1892

Sullivan arranged a sparring company and showed in the West, British Columbia, and Manitoba. They appeared in Philadelphia for a week, Brooklyn for a week, and closed in Boston on June 4, 1892. Sullivan sparred Ashton and Lannon in preparation for the Corbett bout.

Sep 7	James J. Corbett	New Orleans, LA	LKO by 21
Sep 17	James J. Corbett	New York, NY	EX 3

1894

May 21	Paddy Ryan	Boston, MA	EX 3
Jun 26	Paddy Ryan	Boston, MA	EX 3

1895

Jun 8	Jack Dempsey	New York, NY	EX
Jun 27	James J. Corbett	New York, NY	EX 3
Jul 23	Paddy Ryan	Bangor, ME	EX 3
Jul 25	Paddy Ryan	Bar Harbor, ME	EX
Oct 14	Paddy Ryan	Jersey City, NJ	EX 3
Nov 18	Paddy Ryan	Buffalo, NY	EX 3

1896

Aug 31	Tom Sharkey	New York, NY	EX 3

1897

Feb 17	Paddy Ryan	Philadelphia, PA	EX 3
Jul 5	Bob Fitzsimmons	Brooklyn, NY	

The bout was scheduled for 6 rounds but the police prevented it from taking place.

1900

Aug 29	James J. Jeffries	New York, NY	EX 3

1905

Mar 1	Jim McCormick	Grand Rapids, MI	KO 2

Sullivan died on February 2, 1918, at age 59.

Notes

1—Understanding the System Under Which They Fought

1. John V. Grombach, *The Saga of the Fist* (New York: A.S. Barnes, 1949, 1977); *National Police Gazette*, January 21, 1882; Alexander Johnston, *Ten and Out!* (New York: Ives Washburn, 1927).

2—Sullivan's World

1. *Australian Sportsman*, January 10, 1883.
2. United States Civil War Center.
3. *People's Advocate* (Washington, D.C.), September 29, 1883.

3—The Local Rise of the Boston Strongboy

1. Early sources said that Sullivan's middle name was Longfellow, but later sources said that it was Lawrence.
2. *National Police Gazette*, November 5, 1881.
3. *Louisville Evening Post*, October 29, 1883.
4. *Saint Paul Daily Globe*, November 25, 1883; *New York Times*, October 21, 1883.
5. *Brooklyn Daily Eagle*, June 1, 1890.
6. *National Police Gazette*, March 24, 1888; *San Francisco Chronicle*, August 29, 1892.
7. *The Ring*, February 1926, page 24.
8. John L. Sullivan, *I Can Lick Any Sonofabitch in the House!* (Carson City: Proteus Publishing Co., 1979), a reprint of the 1892 autobiography by Sullivan called *Life and Reminiscences of a Nineteenth Century Gladiator*. In an editor's note at 7, Gilbert Odd observed, "This autobiography does not give detailed accounts of his great ring battles simply because to the author they were foregone conclusions.... Thus the fistic purist may be a little frustrated and will have to look elsewhere for punch for punch details." This book will provide those details, and correct Sullivan's inaccuracies.
9. *Rochester Daily Union and Advertiser*, April 20, 1882.
10. Michael T. Isenberg, *John L. Sullivan and His America* (Chicago: University of Illinois Press, 1988), 35–36. Isenberg's book is amongst the better researched and documented books available regarding Sullivan, but Isenberg's greatest strength is his sociological analysis and discussion of events outside the ring. The book you are now reading is more detailed and thorough in regards to Sullivan's fights; Sullivan in *Reminisces* incorrectly claimed that the Woods bout took place in 1878.

11. *Boston Daily Globe*, March 15, 1879.
12. *National Police Gazette*, September 23, 1882.
13. *Boston Daily Globe*, March 15, 1879.
14. *Boston Daily Globe*, March 15, 1879.
15. Cyberboxingzone.com; Sullivan at 23.
16. Cyberboxingzone.com.
17. Sullivan at 23.
18. *National Police Gazette*, April 26, 1884.
19. *Times-Democrat* (New Orleans), February 8, 1882.
20. *National Police Gazette*, March 12, 1881; William Burns, *Incidents in the Life of John L. Sullivan and Other Famous People of Fifty Years Ago* (1928), 46. One caveat is that Burns appears to write the book from memory and has many factual inaccuracies throughout.
21. *National Police Gazette*, December 31, 1881.
22. Sullivan at 23–24; Mike Donovan, *The Roosevelt That I Know* (New York: B.W. Dodge and Co., 1909), 37–43, 121.
23. *Times-Democrat* (New Orleans), February 8, 1882.
24. *New York Clipper*, March 13, 1880.
25. *National Police Gazette*, April 26, 1884.

4—The World's Best ... but with Gloves

1. *National Police Gazette*, May 22, 1880, January 20, 1883, January 27, 1883; *New York Clipper*, March 28, 1885.
2. *New York Clipper*, April 3, 1880.
3. *National Police Gazette*, May 22, 1880.
4. *National Police Gazette*, April 16, 1881; Sullivan at 24.
5. *National Police Gazette*, May 7, 1904.
6. *Boston Daily Globe*, April 7, 1880.
7. *New York Times*, February 8, 1882.
8. *New York Clipper*, March 27, April 3, 1880.
9. *National Police Gazette*, June 26, 1880.
10. *National Police Gazette*, December 17, 1881, May 15, 1880.
11. *Boston Daily Globe*, June 28, 1880.
12. *National Police Gazette*, April 16, 1881, July 17, 1880.
13. *Boston Daily Globe*, June 29, 1880. Sullivan at 29 claimed it was a 2 rounder, but he was incorrect, for Rooke was taken out in the 3rd round. John L. said that Rooke was down seven times.
14. Sullivan at 30.
15. Isenberg at 87.
16. Sullivan at 30.
17. *Cincinnati Commercial*, December 5, 1880; *National Police Gazette*, April 16, 1881; Sullivan at 31.
18. *Cincinnati Commercial*, December 5, 1880.
19. *Cincinnati Commercial*, December 12, 1880.

20. *National Police Gazette*, January 8, 1881.
21. *Cincinnati Daily Enquirer*, December 24, 25, 1880; *Cincinnati Commercial*, December 25, 1880.
22. *National Police Gazette*, January 8, 1881, April 16, 1881.
23. *Minneapolis Tribune*, January 25, 1887.
24. Sullivan at 32; Isenberg at 87–89; Cyberboxingzone.com.
25. *Australian Sportsman*, May 28, 1881.
26. *National Police Gazette*, January 1, 1881, September 8, 1883; *Australian Sportsman*, May 28, 1881.
27. *New York Clipper*, March 27, April 3, 1880.
28. *New York Clipper*, March 20, 1880.
29. Sullivan at 33; Isenberg at 89.
30. *Boston Herald*, January 4, 1881.
31. *Boston Daily Globe*, January 4, 1881.
32. *Australian Sportsman*, February 12, 1881.
33. *New York Clipper*, April 2, 1881.
34. *Boston Daily Globe*, March 22, 1881, March 20, 1881.
35. Sullivan at 33.
36. Cyberboxingzone.com.
37. *Seattle Daily Post-Intelligencer*, February 5, 1884; *Galveston Daily News*, April 10, 1884.
38. Sullivan at 34.
39. *New York Clipper*, April 9, 1881.
40. *New York Herald*, April 1, 1881; *National Police Gazette*, April 16, 1881; *New York Clipper*, April 9, 1881.
41. Isenberg at 8.
42. Sullivan at 34.
43. *National Police Gazette*, February 18, 1882.
44. *New York Herald*, May 17, 1881; *New York Clipper*, May 21, 1881.
45. *New York Clipper*, June 18, 1881.
46. *Australian Sportsman*, May 28, 1881.
47. *Philadelphia Press*, July 12, 1881.
48. *Philadelphia Record*, July 12, 1881.
49. *New York Clipper*, July 16, 1881.
50. *New York Clipper*, July 30, 1881.
51. Isenberg at 98–100. Isenberg cites primary sources for this fight, but not local ones.
52. *New York Clipper*, July 30, 1881; *National Police Gazette*, August 13, 1881.
53. *Philadelphia Press*, July 22, 1881.
54. *Philadelphia Record*, July 22, 1881.
55. *Daily Arkansas Gazette* (Little Rock), April 29, 1884, quoting the *Pittsburgh Times*.
56. Sullivan at 38.
57. *New York Clipper*, July 30, 1881.
58. *National Police Gazette*, September 3, 1881, November 12, 1881; *Chicago Daily News*, August 13, 1881; *Chicago Herald*, August 13, 1881; Sullivan at 39.
59. *National Police Gazette*, September 3, 1881, November 12, 1881.
60. *Chicago Times*, August 14, 1881; *Chicago Herald*, August 15, 1881.
61. *Chicago Tribune*, August 14, 1881.
62. *Chicago Herald*, August 15, 1881.
63. *Chicago Times*, August 14, 1881.
64. *National Police Gazette*, September 3, 1881.
65. *Chicago Tribune*, September 3, 1881; *Daily Inter Ocean* (Chicago), September 3, 1881; *Chicago Herald*, September 5, 1881; *Chicago Times*, September 4, 1881. Some sources list Burns as taller and larger, but this is what the local newspapers of the day indicated. Sullivan at 39 claimed Burns was 6'6½".
66. *Chicago Tribune*, September 4, 1881; *Boston Daily Globe*, September 5, 1881.

67. *Chicago Herald*, September 5, 1881.
68. *Chicago Times*, September 4, 1881.
69. *Daily Inter Ocean*, September 5, 1881.
70. Isenberg at 223.
71. *National Police Gazette*, October 29, 1881.
72. *New York Clipper*, November 12, 1881.
73. *Cincinnati Commercial*, November 28, 29, 1881.

5—A "Real" Fight

1. Sullivan at 40.
2. *National Police Gazette*, October 29, 1881, February 18, 1882.
3. *New York Herald*, February 8, 1882.
4. *Times-Democrat* (New Orleans), February 2, 4, 6, 1882.
5. *Times-Democrat*, February 2, 4, 6, 1882.
6. *Daily Picayune* (New Orleans), February 3, 1882, February 8, 1882.
7. *Times-Democrat* (New Orleans), February 3, 1882.
8. *Times-Democrat* (New Orleans), February 4, 1882.
9. *Times-Democrat* (New Orleans), February 7, 1882.
10. *Daily Democrat* (Natchez), February 8, 1882.
11. Throughout this book, weight ranges will be provided because quite often multiple accounts will have many different reports of the fighters' weights. Thus, often a low and high will be presented to provide a range potential. Fighters' weights for early bouts have had great inconsistency from one source to another and are notoriously unreliable. They were often self-reported by the fighters themselves or their seconds, as an official weigh-in was not usually required for heavyweight fights. The other inconsistent aspect of early reporting was the spelling of names. Quite often, no two sources could agree on the names or spelling of them.
12. *National Police Gazette*, November 5, 1881, February 18, 1882.
13. *Times-Democrat* (New Orleans), February 2, 1882.
14. *Boston Daily Globe*, February 2, 1882.
15. *National Police Gazette*, October 29, 1881, February 18, 1882.
16. *New York Herald*, February 8, 1882.
17. *Daily Picayune*, February 8, 1882; *Daily Democrat* (Natchez), February 8, 1882.
18. John J. McCusker, "Comparing the Purchasing Power of Money in the U.S. from 1665 to Any Other Year, Including the Present," from Economic History Services, <http://www.eh.net/hmit/ppowerusd/>; <http://eh.net/hmit/gdp/>.
19. *New York Herald*; *Daily Picayune*; *Times-Democrat*; *New York Times*; *Boston Herald*; *Boston Daily Globe*, all February 8, 1882; *National Police Gazette*, March 11, 1882.
20. *National Police Gazette*, February 25, 1882.
21. *Boston Daily Globe*, February 9, 1882.
22. *New York Herald*, February 8, 1882.
23. *Times-Democrat*, February 8, 1882.
24. Sullivan at 64–65.
25. *Boston Daily Globe*, February 9, 1882.
26. *National Police Gazette*, March 18, 1882.

6—Now They'll Have to Do It My Fashion

1. *National Police Gazette*, March 11, 1882.
2. *National Police Gazette*, September 24, 1904.

3. Sullivan at 71–72.
4. *New York Clipper*, April 1, 1882; Sullivan at 72.
5. *New York Clipper*, April 1, 1882.
6. Sullivan at 72.
7. Cyberboxingzone.com.
8. *New York Clipper*, April 22, 1882.
9. *Rochester Daily Union and Advertiser*, April 20, 1882.
10. *New York Herald*, April 21, 1882.
11. *New York Clipper*, April 29, 1882.
12. *Rochester Morning Herald; Rochester Democrat and Chronicle; Rochester Daily Union and Advertiser*, all April 21, 1882.
13. *National Police Gazette*, December 25, 1880, September 23, 1882, October 7, 1882, October 14, 1882.
14. Cyberboxingzone.com.
15. *National Police Gazette*, December 25, 1880, April 15, 1882, March 17, 1883; *Times-Democrat*, February 8, 1882.
16. *Boston Daily Globe*, April 6, 1879.
17. Cyberboxingzone.com.
18. *National Police Gazette*, October 7, 1882, October 14, 1882; *New York Daily Tribune*, July 5, 1882.
19. *New York Herald*, July 5, 1882.
20. Sullivan at 74; *Boston Daily Globe*, July 5, 1882, confirmed that the crowd numbered about 5,000.
21. Isenberg at 119–120.
22. *New York Times*, July 5, 1882; *New York Daily Tribune*, July 5, 1882; *New York Herald*, July 5, 1882.
23. *National Police Gazette*, October 14, 1882.
24. *Brooklyn Daily Eagle*, July 1, 1882.
25. *New York Times*, June 29, 1882, July 18, 1882.
26. *National Police Gazette*, July 8, 1882.
27. *New York Times*, June 29, 1882.
28. *New York Times*, July 18, 1882.
29. *New York Daily Tribune*, July 18, 1882; *New York Times*, July 18, 1882. The *Times* said the gloves were 2 ounces, but *The Tribune* said they were 4 ounces.
30. *New York Herald*, July 18, 1882.
31. *New York Times*, July 18, 1882.
32. *New York Daily Tribune*, July 18, 1882.
33. Isenberg at 120–122; Cyberboxingzone.com.
34. Sullivan at 75, 77.
35. *New York Times*, July 28, 1882.
36. *National Police Gazette*, October 14, 1882.
37. *Boston Herald*, August 20, 1882; *Boston Daily Globe*, August 20, 1882.
38. Sullivan at 78.
39. *National Police Gazette*, September 23, 1882.
40. Sullivan at 78–79.
41. *National Police Gazette*, October 7, 1882.
42. *Buffalo Courier*, September 23, 1882.
43. *New York Tribune*, September 24, 1882; *New York Herald*, September 24, 1882.
44. *New York Clipper*, October 7, 1882.
45. *National Police Gazette*, October 14, 1882.
46. *Buffalo Courier*, September 24, 1882.
47. *National Police Gazette*, November 4, 1882.
48. *Indianapolis Sentinel*, October 17, 1882.
49. *Chicago Daily News*, October 31, 1882.
50. *Chicago Herald*, October 31, 1882; *Daily Inter Ocean*, October 31, 1882.
51. *Chicago Herald*, November 1, 1882; *Daily Inter Ocean*, November 1, 1882.
52. *New York Clipper*, November 25, 1882.
53. *Washington Post*, November 18, 1882; *Washington Evening Star*, November 18, 1882.

54. Sullivan at 83; *National Police Gazette*, February 10, 1883.
55. *National Police Gazette*, February 10, 1883, September 20, 1884.
56. *National Police Gazette*, February 10, 1883; Cyberboxingzone.com.
57. *New York Herald*, December 28, 1882.
58. *New York Herald*, December 29, 1882.
59. *National Police Gazette*, February 10, 1883.
60. *Toronto Globe*, January 24, 1883; see also *Toronto Evening Telegram*, January 24, 1883.
61. *National Police Gazette*, January 27, 1883.
62. Isenberg at 126. Isenberg only cites *The National Police Gazette* for the Gilman fight, but a review of the dates cited, February 10 and 17, 1883, do not reveal the fight.
63. Burns at 47.
64. *Toronto Globe*, January 26, 1883; *Toronto Evening Telegram*, January 26, 1883.
65. Sullivan at 85.
66. *Toronto Globe*, January 31, 1883.
67. *Billings Herald*, January 18, 1883.
68. *Toronto Globe*, January 31, 1883.
69. *National Police Gazette*, February 17, 1883.
70. *National Police Gazette*, February 17, 1883.
71. *Boston Herald*, February 23, 1883.
72. *New York Daily Tribune*, March 2, 1883; *New York Times*, March 2, 1883.
73. *New York Times*, March 2, 1883.
74. *National Police Gazette*, November 4, 1882.
75. *Boston Herald*, March 20, 1883; *New York Clipper*, March 24, 1883.
76. Isenberg at 128.

7—The Game Little Englishman and the Maori

1. *National Police Gazette*, February 10, 1883, April 14, 1883, April 21, 1883; *Australian Sportsman*, May 9, 1883; Isenberg at 133.
2. *New York Times*, May 15, 1883; *New York Tribune*, May 15, 1883; *New York Herald*, May 15, 1883; *New York Clipper*, May 19, 1883; *Boston Herald*, May 15, 1883.
3. *National Police Gazette*, May 26, 1883.
4. Against Mitchell, some say Sullivan was dropped by a right (John Durant, *The Heavyweight Champions* (New York: Hastings House, 1960, 1976), 23–24; Rex Lardner, *The Legendary Champions* (New York: American Heritage Press, 1972), 49; while others say it was a left (Isenberg, *John L. Sullivan and His America*, 135). Most accounts say this was the first time Sullivan was dropped, such as Isenberg at 135, but the Cyberboxingzone.com lists Sullivan as being decked by John Hogan in 1879, a bout Sullivan won in 4 rounds. However, this author has not reviewed any primary source supporting that assertion. William Inglis, *Champions Off Guard* (New York: Vanguard Press, 1932), 25–28, claimed that Ramon Guiteras dropped Sullivan with an uppercut in one of John's first bouts (a 4-round draw), but this author has found no confirming primary source for this claim or for the fight.
5. Sullivan at 86, 178.
6. *New York Times*, May 15, 1883; *New York Tribune*, May 15, 1883; *New York Herald*, May 15, 1883; *New York Clipper*, May 19, 1883; *National Police Gazette*, May 26, 1883, July 12, 1884.

7. Although Isenberg at 135 used this version, the majority of primary sources reviewed here did not mention Sullivan falling on Mitchell.

8. *Brooklyn Daily Eagle*, May 15, 1883.

9. *Boston Herald*, May 15, 1883, May 16, 1883.

10. Ibid.; see also *Boston Globe Supplement*, May 17, 1883.

11. *National Police Gazette*, May 26, 1883, July 12, 1884.

12. Sullivan at 86–87.

13. *National Police Gazette*, August 4, 1883.

14. *National Police Gazette*, September 8, 1883.

15. *National Police Gazette*, January 27, 1883, February 24, 1883.

16. *National Police Gazette*, August 18, 1883.

17. Sullivan at 94–95, quoting *Cincinnati Enquirer* (no date provided); *National Police Gazette*, January 2, 1883.

18. *New York Clipper*, January 27, 1883.

19. *New York Clipper*, February 3, 1883.

20. Congressional Quarterly's Guide to the Presidency; senate.gov.

21. *New York Times*, August 7, 1883; *New York Herald*, August 7, 1883; *National Police Gazette*, August 18, 1883; *New York Clipper*, August 11, 1883.

22. *Brooklyn Daily Eagle*, August 6, 1883, August 7, 1883.

23. Sullivan at 98–99.

8—The Tour: 1883

1. Isenberg at 209.

2. Sullivan at 95.

3. *New York Clipper*, September 22, 1883.

4. Sullivan at 96.

5. *Baltimore Sun*, September 29, 1883; *Baltimore American*, September 29, 1883.

6. *Baltimore Sun*, September 29, 1883; *Baltimore American*, September 30, 1883.

7. *People's Advocate*, September 29, 1883.

8. *Baltimore Sun*, September 29, 1883; *Baltimore American*, September 30, 1883.

9. *New York Clipper*, October 6, 1883.

10. Sullivan at 96.

11. *New York Clipper*, October 20, 1883.

12. Sullivan at 96.

13. Isenberg at 149, 151; Sullivan at 104 claimed it took place on October 17, 1883. His itinerary on page 96 indicated that they were in Youngstown, Ohio, on the 18th.

14. *Seattle Daily Post-Intelligencer*, February 5, 1884.

15. *New York Clipper*, October 27, 1883.

16. *Daily Arkansas Gazette*, April 30, 1884, quoting *The Pittsburgh Times*.

17. *National Police Gazette*, December 22, 1883; *Seattle Daily Post-Intelligencer*, February 5, 1884.

18. *Pittsburg Dispatch*, October 20, 1883; *Pittsburgh Daily Post*, October 20, 1883.

19. *New York Clipper*, October 27, 1883.

20. *New York Times*, October 21, 1883; *Saint Paul Daily Globe*, November 25, 1883.

21. *New York Times*, October 21, 1883.

22. Sullivan at 96.

23. *New York Clipper*, November 17, 1883.

24. *Louisville Evening Post*, October 29, 1883.

25. *Louisville Courier-Journal*, October 30, 1883.

26. *Chicago Herald*, November 4, 1883.

27. *National Police Gazette*, November 24, 1883.

28. *Louisville Evening Post*, October 29, 1883.

29. Sullivan at 96; *The Chicago Herald*, November 4, 1883, confirmed that the Sullivan combination had previously been in Danville, Illinois.

30. *Missouri Republican* (St. Louis), November 3, 1883.

31. *Missouri Republican* (St. Louis), November 4, 1883.

32. *St. Louis Daily Globe-Democrat*, November 4, 1883.

33. *Missouri Republican* (St. Louis), November 4, 1883; *St. Louis Daily Globe-Democrat*, November 4, 1883.

34. *St. Louis Daily Globe-Democrat*, November 4, 1883.

35. *National Police Gazette*, November 24, 1883.

36. *Missouri Republican* (St. Louis), November 5, 1883; *St. Louis Daily Globe-Democrat*, November 5, 1883.

37. *Missouri Republican* (St. Louis), November 6, 1883; *St. Louis Daily Globe-Democrat*, November 6, 1883.

38. *St. Louis Daily Globe-Democrat*, November 7, 1883.

39. *New York Clipper*, November 17, 1883.

40. *Chicago Herald*, November 4, 1883.

41. Sullivan at 96.

42. Sullivan at 96, 107.

43. *Chicago Herald*, November 16, 1883, November 17, 1883.

44. *New York Clipper*, November 24, 1883.

45. Sullivan at 108.

46. *National Police Gazette*, November 24, 1883.

47. Sullivan at 96.

48. *Eau Claire Daily Leader*, November 24, 1883.

49. *Eau Claire News*, December 8, 1883.

50. Sullivan at 96.

51. *Saint Paul and Minneapolis Pioneer Press*, November 24, 1883; *St. Paul Daily Globe*, November 25, 1883.

52. *Saint Paul and Minneapolis Pioneer Press*, November 26, 1883.

53. *Saint Paul Daily Globe*, November 26, 1883.

54. *Saint Paul Daily Globe*, November 27, 1883; *Saint Paul and Minneapolis Pioneer Press*, November 27, 1883.

55. *Saint Paul and Minneapolis Pioneer Press*, November 26, 1883.

56. *Saint Paul and Minneapolis Pioneer Press*, November 28, 1883.

57. Sullivan at 96; *Eau Claire News*, December 1, 1883.

58. *National Police Gazette*, December 29, 1883.

59. *Davenport Daily Gazette*, December 5, 1883.

60. *Davenport Democrat*, December 5, 1883.

61. *Davenport Democrat*, December 6, 1883.

62. *New York Clipper*, December 22, 1883.

63. Sullivan at 96.

64. *New York Clipper*, January 5, 1884.

65. Sullivan at 96, 112.

66. *New York Clipper*, January 5, 1884.

67. *Helena Independent*, January 3, 1884.

68. *Butte Daily Miner*, January 5, 1884.

69. Sullivan at 111.

9—The Tour Continues: 1884

1. Sullivan at 96. While the tour was in Montana, a local paper said that the combination had been in Salt Lake.

2. *Helena Daily Herald*, January 8, 1884.

3. *Helena Daily Herald*, January 9, 1884.

4. *Butte Daily Miner*, January 8, 1884, January 9, 1884.

5. *Helena Independent*, January 8, 1884; *Helena Daily Herald*, January 8, 1884.

6. *Helena Daily Independent*, January 11, 1884; *Helena Daily Herald*, January 11, 1884.

7. *Helena Daily Independent*, January 12, 1884.

8. *National Police Gazette*, February 9, 1884.
9. *Butte Daily Miner*, January 9, 1884, January 13, 1884.
10. *Butte Daily Miner*, January 13, 1884, January 15, 1884.
11. *National Police Gazette*, February 9, 1884.
12. Sullivan at 97.
13. *San Francisco Daily Examiner*, January 25, 1884.
14. *San Francisco Daily Examiner*, January 26, 1884; *San Francisco Chronicle*, January 26, 1884.
15. *San Francisco Daily Examiner*, January 27, 1884; *San Francisco Chronicle*, January 27, 1884; *New York Clipper*, February 9, 1884, quoting a report out of *The Alta-Californian*.
16. *San Francisco Daily Examiner*, January 26, 1884; *San Francisco Chronicle*, January 26, 1884.
17. *San Francisco Chronicle*, January 29, 1884.
18. *New York Clipper*, February 2, 1884.
19. *Daily Astorian*, February 1, 1884.
20. *Daily Astorian*, February 1, 1884.
21. *National Police Gazette*, March 1, 1884; *New York Clipper*, February 16, 1884.
22. *Daily Astorian*, February 2, 1884.
23. *San Francisco Examiner*, September 3, 1892.
24. Sullivan at 114; *National Police Gazette*, April 15, 1905.
25. *New York Clipper*, February 16, 1884.
26. Sullivan at 97.
27. *Seattle Daily Post-Intelligencer*, February 5, 1884.
28. *Seattle Daily Post-Intelligencer*, February 7, 1884.
29. *New York Clipper*, February 23, 1884.
30. *Seattle Daily Post-Intelligencer*, February 8, 1884.
31. *Seattle Daily Post-Intelligencer*, February 10, 1884.
32. Sullivan at 97.
33. *San Francisco Daily Examiner*, February 19, 1884.
34. *New York Clipper*, March 8, 1884.
35. *New York Clipper*, March 8, 1884.
36. *National Police Gazette*, March 15, 1884.
37. *National Police Gazette*, February 10, 1883.
38. *San Francisco Daily Examiner*, March 3, 1884.
39. *National Police Gazette*, March 22, 1884, April 5, 1884.
40. *New York Clipper*, March 15, 1884.
41. Isenberg at 161 incorrectly asserted that Robinson lasted the distance.
42. *San Francisco Chronicle*, March 7, 1884.
43. *San Francisco Daily Examiner*, March 7, 1884.
44. *Daily Picayune*, April 12, 1884, citing a San Francisco newspaper report.
45. *Arizona Weekly Citizen*, March 22, 1884.
46. Joe Chisholm, *Brewery Gulch: Frontier Days of Old Arizona* (San Antonio: The Naylor Company, 1949), 41–46.
47. *Arizona Weekly Citizen*, March 29, 1884.
48. Sullivan at 96–97.
49. *National Police Gazette*, March 22, 1884.
50. *New York Clipper*, April 5, 1884.
51. *New York Clipper*, April 5, 1884.
52. *Galveston Daily News*, April 10, 1884.
53. *Galveston Daily News*, April 10, 1884.
54. *Galveston Daily News*, April 11, 1884; *Daily Picayune*, April 11, 1884.
55. *Daily Picayune*, April 28, 1884; *National Police Gazette*, May 24, 1884.
56. *Daily Picayune*, April 13, 1884.
57. *New York Clipper*, April 19, 1884.
58. Cyberboxingzone.com.
59. *Daily Picayune*, April 14, 1884.
60. *Daily Picayune*, April 15, 1884.
61. Sullivan at 97.
62. *Daily Picayune*, April 28, 1884.
63. *Memphis Daily Appeal*, April 29, 1884.
64. *Daily Arkansas Gazette* (Little Rock), April 29, 1884.
65. *Daily Arkansas Gazette* (Little Rock), April 29, 1884, quoting *The Pittsburg Times*.
66. *National Police Gazette*, May 24, 1884.
67. *Daily Arkansas Gazette* (Little Rock), May 1, 1884.
68. *Daily Arkansas Gazette* (Little Rock), April 29, 1884, April 30, 1884.
69. *Daily Arkansas Gazette* (Little Rock), May 1, 1884.
70. *Memphis Daily Appeal*, May 2, 1884; *Daily Memphis Avalanche*, May 1, 1884, May 2, 1884.
71. Sullivan at 117.
72. *Daily Memphis Avalanche*, May 3, 1884.
73. Isenberg at 166–167.
74. *Nashville Daily American*, May 3, 1884.
75. Sullivan at 118.
76. *Nashville Banner*, May 3, 1884.
77. *Nashville Daily American*, May 3, 1884.
78. *Nashville Banner*, May 3, 1884.
79. *Nashville Banner*, May 3, 1884.
80. *Nashville Banner*, May 3, 1884.
81. *National Police Gazette*, May 24, 1884.
82. Sullivan at 97.
83. *National Police Gazette*, May 31, 1884.
84. *New York Clipper*, May 10, 1884.
85. *Vincennes Daily Commercial*, May 6, 7, 1884.
86. *Missouri Republican* (St. Louis), May 7, 8, 1884.
87. *Missouri Republican*, May 9, 1884.
88. Sullivan at 97, 118.
89. *National Police Gazette*, April 15, 1905.
90. Isenberg at 166–170.
91. *National Police Gazette*, April 15, 1905.
92. Sullivan at 118.
93. *Louisville Courier-Journal*, December 24, 1899.
94. *National Police Gazette*, April 15, 1905.
95. senate.gov; Isenberg at 169–170.

10—Unfinished Business and Prelude to a Grudge Match

1. *New York Clipper*, May 31, 1884.
2. *New York Clipper*, June 14, 1884.
3. *New York Clipper*, June 28, 1884.
4. *National Police Gazette*, July 12, 1884.
5. *Brooklyn Daily Eagle*, July 1, 1884.
6. *New York Clipper*, July 5, 1884.
7. *Boston Herald*, August 15, 1884.
8. Sullivan at 119–120.
9. *Boston Herald*, August 14, 1884.
10. *Boston Daily Globe*, August 14, 1884.
11. *Boston Herald*, August 14, 1884.
12. *New York Clipper*, August 30, 1884, September 6, 1884, March 22, 1884, June 7, 1884, September 20, 1884; *National Police Gazette*, September 13, 1884.
13. *New York Clipper*, October 18, 1884.
14. Cyberboxingzone.com.

11—Accepted, but Not Quite

1. *National Police Gazette*, November 29, 1884.
2. *New York Times*, November 11, 1884.
3. *New York Herald*, November 11, 1884.
4. *New York Clipper*, November 15, 1884.

5. Donovan at 104. He incorrectly called this the 3rd round.

6. *National Police Gazette*, September 9, 1882; *New York Clipper*, March 20, 1880.

7. *New York Clipper*, November 8, 1884; *National Police Gazette*, June 28, 1884, July 5, 1884.

8. *New York Herald*, November 18, 1884; Isenberg at 176–178.

9. *New York Herald*, November 19, 1884; *New York Times*, November 19, 1884.

10. *New York Clipper*, November 29, 1884.

11. Donovan at 106.

12. *Brooklyn Daily Eagle*, December 17, 1884.

13. Isenberg at 178–181; Sullivan at 126.

14. *Boston Herald*, January 13, 1885; Sullivan at 126.

15. *Boston Daily Globe*, January 13, 1885.

16. *Boston Daily Globe*, January 19, 1885.

17. *Brooklyn Daily Eagle*, January 19, 1885.

18. *Brooklyn Daily Eagle*, January 19, 1885.

19. *New York Times*, January 20, 1885.

20. *New York Herald*, January 20, 1885.

21. *New York Clipper*, January 24, 1885.

22. *Boston Daily Globe*, January 19, 1885.

23. *Brooklyn Daily Eagle*, April 2, 1885; *New York Clipper*, April 11, 1885.

24. *National Police Gazette*, June 28, 1884, July 5, 1884; Donovan at 102.

25. *New York Clipper*, October 11, 1884.

26. *National Police Gazette*, November 8, 1884.

27. Boxrec.com; *Boston Daily Globe*, March 11, 1888.

28. Boxrec.com.

29. *New York Clipper*, March 7, 1885.

30. *San Francisco Daily Examiner*, July 25, 1887; *National Police Gazette*, December 4, 1886; Boxrec.com.

31. *Philadelphia Inquirer*, June 15, 1885, said Sullivan weighed 237 pounds.

32. *Chicago Daily News*, June 12, 1885; *Chicago Herald*, June 13, 1885.

33. *Chicago Tribune*, June 14, 1885.

34. *Chicago Herald*, June 14, 1885.

35. *Chicago Tribune*, June 14, 1885.

36. *National Police Gazette*, June 27, 1886; *Brooklyn Daily Eagle*, June 14, 1885; *New York Clipper*, June 20, 1885; *Boston Herald*, June 14, 1885.

37. Sullivan at 127.

38. Donovan at 102.

12—Mystery of the Seven-Round Decision

1. *Chicago Herald*, June 14, 1885.

2. *National Police Gazette*, March 1, 1884, August 16, 1884, September 13, 20, 27, 1884, October 24, 1885, December 4, 1886; *Cincinnati Commercial Gazette*, August 29, 1885.

3. *Cincinnati Enquirer*, August 29, 1885.

4. Grombach, *The Saga of the Fist*, 44; Johnston, *Ten and Out!*, 65–66; Lardner, *The Legendary Champions*, 50.

5. Isenberg at 190 incorrectly asserted that the bout was stopped after 6 rounds when Sullivan wrestled McCaffrey to the ground and pinned him.

6. *National Police Gazette*, September 12, 1885.

7. *New York Times*, August 30, 31, 1885.

8. *Brooklyn Daily Eagle*, August 13, 1885.

9. *New York Clipper*, August 22, 1885.

10. *Brooklyn Daily Eagle*, August 29, 1885.

11. *National Police Gazette*, September 19, 1885.

12. *Boston Daily Globe*, August 30, 1885, August 31, 1885; *Boston Herald*, August 30, 1885; *National Police Gazette*, September 12, 1885.

13. *National Police Gazette*, September 19, 1885; *Cincinnati Enquirer*, September 4, 1885.

14. Sullivan at 128.

15. *Brooklyn Daily Eagle*, August 16, 1885.

16. *Cincinnati Commercial Gazette*, August 17, 23, 24, 1885.

17. *Cincinnati Evening Post*, August 25, 28, 1885.

18. *Cincinnati Commercial Gazette*, August 28, 1885.

19. *Philadelphia Press*, August 29, 1885.

20. *Cincinnati Commercial Gazette*, August 29, 1885.

21. *Cincinnati Enquirer*, August 30, 1885.

22. *Cincinnati Evening Post*, August 25, 1885.

23. *Cincinnati Commercial Gazette*, August 26, 1885.

24. *Cincinnati Evening Post*, August 27, 1885.

25. *Cincinnati Evening Post*, August 27, 1885.

26. *Cincinnati Evening Post*, August 28, 1885.

27. *Cincinnati Commercial Gazette*, August 29, 1885.

28. *Cincinnati Commercial Gazette*, August 28, 1885.

29. *Cincinnati Commercial Gazette*, August 29, 1885.

30. *Cincinnati Evening Post*, August 29, 1885.

31. *Cincinnati Enquirer*, August 30, 1885.

32. *Cincinnati Evening Post*, August 31, 1885; Sullivan at 128.

33. *Cincinnati Commercial Gazette*, August 26, 31, 1885.

34. *Cincinnati Enquirer*, September 4, 1885.

35. *Cincinnati Commercial Gazette*, August 31, 1885.

36. *National Police Gazette*, March 19, 1887.

13—The Plateau and the Break

1. *Referee* (Sydney), October 26, 1892; Sullivan at 130.

2. Sullivan at 130; Isenberg at 195–196.

3. *National Police Gazette*, July 10, 1886, August 28, 1886.

4. *Pittsburg Dispatch*, September 16, 1886.

5. *Philadelphia Press*, September 18, 1886; *Pittsburg Dispatch*, September 16, 1886.

6. *Pittsburg Dispatch*, September 17, 19, 1886.

7. *Denver Daily News*, September 20, 1886.

8. *Philadelphia Press*, September 19, 1886; *Philadelphia Inquirer*, September 20, 1886; *Pittsburg Dispatch*, September 19, 20, 1886; *Pittsburgh Daily Post*, September 20, 1886; *New York Clipper*, September 25, 1886; *National Police Gazette*, October 2, 1886.

9. *Pittsburg Dispatch*, September 19, 1886.

10. *Pittsburg Dispatch*, September 20, 1886.

11. *New York Clipper*, October 16, 1886.

12. Sullivan at 131.

13. *New York Clipper*, November 6, 1886.

14. *Minneapolis Tribune*, October 25, 1886.

15. La Blanche would go on to score an 1889 KO32 over Dempsey in a non–title bout rematch.

16. *New York Clipper*, November 6, 1886; *Minneapolis Tribune*, October 30, 1886.

17. *St. Paul and Minneapolis Pioneer Press*, October 30, 1886.

18. *Minneapolis Tribune*, October 31, 1886; *St. Paul and Minneapolis Pioneer Press*, October 31, 1886.

19. *St. Paul and Minneapolis Pioneer Press*, October 31, 1886, November 1, 3, 1886.

20. *National Police Gazette*, November 27, 1886.

21. *Rocky Mountain News*, November 14, 1886; *Helena Independent*, November 14, 1886; *Desert Evening News*, November 15, 1886. This is the version also put forth by *The National Police Gazette*, November 27, 1886.

22. *San Francisco Examiner*, November 14, 1886.

23. *San Francisco Chronicle*, November 14, 1886.

24. *Denver Tribune-Republican*, December 26, 28, 1886.

25. *Denver Daily News*, December 27, 1886.

26. *New York Clipper*, May 24, 1884. Some say it was the 34th round. *Denver Daily News*, December 29, 1886.

27. *National Police Gazette*, November 15, 1884, October 16, 1886; *Salt Lake Daily Tribune*, August 29, 1886.

28. Johnston, *Ten and Out!*, at 67 said Sullivan stopped McDonald, but this is likely inaccurate; *The Referee* (Sydney), October 26, 1892, said that Sullivan fought McDonald to a 4-round draw. Isenberg at 194 said they sparred a relaxed 4 rounds, but called it a draw. For whatever reason, most Sullivan records list the Sullivan-McDonald sparring exhibition as a D4.

29. *Denver Daily News*, December 28, 1886.

30. *Denver Tribune-Republican*, December 28, 1886; *Denver Daily News*, December 29, 1886.

31. *Denver Tribune-Republican*, December 26, 1886; *Denver Tribune-Republican*, December 28, 1886.

32. *Denver Daily News*, December 29, 1886.

33. *Denver Tribune-Republican*, December 29, 1886.

34. *Denver Tribune-Republican*, December 30, 1886.

35. *Colorado Miner* (Georgetown), January 1, 1887.

36. *Denver Republican*, January 2, 1887.

37. *San Francisco Examiner*, July 18, 1887.

38. *National Police Gazette*, January 8, 1887.

39. *Denver Republican*, January 1, 1887.

40. *National Police Gazette*, January 15, 1887; *Denver Daily News*, January 3, 1887.

41. *National Police Gazette*, January 22, 1887.

42. *Helena Independent*, January 19, 1887, listed Sullivan as 215 pounds and Cardiff as 185.

43. Cyberboxingzone.com; *Minneapolis Tribune*, January 19, 1887; *National Police Gazette*, July 14, 1888; *Chicago Herald*, June 15, 1885.

44. *Minneapolis Tribune*, October 26, 1886.

45. *Minneapolis Tribune*, January 17, 1887, January 19, 1887.

46. *National Police Gazette*, January 29, 1887.

47. *Helena Independent*, January 19, 1887.

48. *Minneapolis Tribune*, January 19, 1887.

49. *National Police Gazette*, February 12, 1887.

50. *Minneapolis Tribune*, January 19, 1887.

51. *Saint Paul and Minneapolis Pioneer Press*, January 19, 1887.

52. *Saint Paul and Minneapolis Pioneer Press*, January 20, 1887.

53. *Irish Standard*, January 22, 1887.

54. *National Police Gazette*, January 29, 1887.

55. *Helena Independent*, January 20, 1887.

56. Ibid.; *National Police Gazette*, February 12, 1887.

57. *Minneapolis Tribune*, January 25, 1887.

58. Sullivan at 131.

59. *Referee* (Sydney), June 16, 1887.

60. *San Francisco Examiner*, December 28, 1891.

61. Donovan at 108. He like Sullivan incorrectly claimed that Sullivan got the decision.

62. *Minneapolis Tribune*, January 25, 1887.

63. *National Police Gazette*, July 14, 1888; *The Morning Oregonian*, July 27, 1889, said Killen stopped him in the 5th round.

64. *National Police Gazette*, March 28, 1887.

65. *National Police Gazette*, April 16, 1887.

66. *Referee* (Sydney), June 16, 1887.

67. *National Police Gazette*, April 16, 1887.

68. *Boston Daily Globe*, July 8, 1889; *The San Francisco Daily Examiner*, July 8, 1889.

69. *Daily Alta California*, December 31, 1888.

70. *National Police Gazette*, November 15, 1884. Kilrain and Godfrey met again many years later, in 1891, and Kilrain scored a 44th-round knockout.

71. *National Police Gazette*, April 12, 1884; *New York Clipper*, April 5, 1884.

72. *National Police Gazette*, March 29, 1884.

73. *New York Clipper*, May 17, 1884.

74. *National Police Gazette*, April 12, 1884, July 12, 1884, November 15, 1884, November 27, 1886, November 5, 1887; *Boston Daily Globe*, July 8, 1889; *San Francisco Daily Examiner*, July 8, 1889.

75. *New York Clipper*, June 11, 1887.

76. *Referee* (Sydney), August 4, 1887.

77. Sullivan at 133.

78. *Referee* (Sydney), October 26, 1892; Sullivan at 133 claimed it was worth $8,000.

79. *New York Clipper*, August 13, 1887.

14—The European Tour

1. *San Francisco Daily Examiner*, August 8, 1887.

2. *New York Clipper*, November 5, 1887.

3. Sullivan at 138, 148.

4. *Referee* (Sydney), October 26, 1892.

5. *New York Clipper*, November 19, 1887.

6. Sullivan at 137.

7. *New York Clipper*, November 19, 1887.

8. *New York Clipper*, December 3, 1887, quoting *London Sportsman*, *Birmingham Gazette*, and *Sporting Life*.

9. Sullivan at 138.

10. *New York Clipper*, December 3, 1887, quoting *London Sportsman*, *Birmingham Gazette*, and *Sporting Life*.

11. *New York Clipper*, December 10, 1887.

12. *New York Clipper*, December 10, 1887.

13. *New York Clipper*, December 17, 1887.

14. Sullivan at 144.

15. Sullivan at 146–148.

16. *National Police Gazette*, March 6, 1886; *Referee* (Sydney), December 18, 1889.

17. *Brooklyn Daily Eagle*, March 14, 1886.

18. *National Police Gazette*, January 21, 1888.

19. *Brooklyn Daily Eagle*, December 23, 1887.

20. Sullivan at 148.

21. *New York Clipper*, January 14, 1888.

22. Sullivan at 148.

23. *New York Clipper*, February 4, 1888.

24. *New York Clipper*, February 25, 1888.

25. *Boston Daily Globe*, March 11, 1888.

26. Sullivan at 149.

27. Sullivan at 187–188.

28. *New York Times*, March 11, 1888.

29. *National Police Gazette*, March 24, 1888.

30. *San Francisco Chronicle*, March 11, 1888.

31. Sullivan at 151–154, 178.

32. *Boston Herald*, March 11, 1888; *Boston Daily Globe*,

March 11, 1888; *Referee* (Sydney), April 19, 1888, quoting *Sporting Life*, an English paper.
33. *San Francisco Chronicle*, March 11, 1888.
34. *San Francisco Examiner*, March 12, 1888.
35. *National Police Gazette*, September 1, 1888.
36. *San Francisco Chronicle*, March 26, 1888.
37. *San Francisco Chronicle*, April 9, 1888.
38. *Boston Daily Globe*, March 12, 1888.

15—The Color Line

1. *Police Gazette*, June 3, 1905; Cyberboxingzone.com; *Ring*, June 1926, page 9; *Referee* (Sydney), April 27, 1892; Burns at 31; *Referee* (Sydney), September 26, 1888.
2. *Daily Alta Californian*, December 31, 1888.
3. *National Police Gazette*, March 17, 1883.
4. Nat Fleischer, *Black Dynamite*, vol. 1 (New York: Nat Fleischer, 1938), 116.
5. *National Police Gazette*, November 15, 1884, November 5, 1887
6. *Referee* (Sydney), September 26, 1888.
7. *New York Clipper*, May 26, 1888.
8. In November 1889, Godfrey would score a KO14 over Ashton (Boxrec.com).
9. *Boston Herald*, May 16, 1888.
10. *New York Clipper*, June 9, 1888.
11. *Toronto Evening Telegram*, January 26, 1883.
12. *Philadelphia Press*, October 16, 17, 1883. The decision was not applicable to the District of Columbia, but affected all of the states.
13. *National Police Gazette*, August 30, 1884.
14. *New York Clipper*, September 27, 1884, quoting *Australian Sportsman*.
15. *Australian Sportsman*, June 25, 1884.
16. *New York Clipper*, November 15, 1884, quoting *Sydney Bulletin*, October 4, 1884.
17. *New York Clipper*, January 17, 1885, quoting *Sydney Bulletin*.
18. *San Francisco Daily Examiner*, December 29, 1888; *Australian Sporting Celebrities* (Melbourne: A.H. Massina and Co., 1887), 64; Boxrec.com.
19. *San Francisco Daily Examiner*, June 5, 1888. Jackson said that Riordan was the first boxer that he sparred with in America. *Referee* (Sydney), April 20, 1892.
20. *National Police Gazette*, June 9, 1888.
21. *San Francisco Daily Examiner*, August 25, 1888.
22. *San Francisco Daily Examiner*, December 28, 1888.
23. *National Police Gazette*, January 19, 1889.
24. *San Francisco Daily Examiner*, June 12, 1888.
25. *San Francisco Daily Examiner*, June 27, 1888.
26. *San Francisco Daily Examiner*, July 2, 1888.
27. *Referee* (Sydney), August 2, 1888.
28. *San Francisco Daily Examiner*, August 25, 1888.
29. *San Francisco Daily Examiner*, August 25, 1888.
30. *San Francisco Daily Examiner*, August 26, 1888.
31. *San Francisco Daily Examiner*, August 27, 1888.
32. *San Francisco Daily Examiner*, July 8, 1889; *Referee* (Sydney), October 26, 1892.
33. Sullivan at 154–155.
34. Donovan at 110.
35. *San Francisco Daily Examiner*, December 24, 1888; *Boston Daily Globe*, July 8, 1889; *Referee* (Sydney), October 26, 1892; Isenberg at 263.
36. *Brooklyn Daily Eagle*, December 9, 1888, quoting *London Sporting Life*.

37. *San Francisco Daily Examiner*, August 26, 1888.
38. *San Francisco Daily Examiner*, December 24, 1888, December 28, 1888; *San Francisco Chronicle*, December 29, 1888.
39. *San Francisco Daily Examiner*, December 28, 1888, December 29, 1888.
40. *San Francisco Daily Examiner*, December 29, 1888; *San Francisco Chronicle*, December 29, 1888.
41. *San Francisco Daily Examiner*, December 30, 1888.
42. *San Francisco Daily Examiner*, December 31, 1888.
43. *San Francisco Daily Examiner*, July 30, 1889.
44. *Police Gazette*, June 3, 1905; Cyberboxingzone.com; *Ring*, June 1926, page 9; *Referee* (Sydney), April 27, 1892; Burns at 31.
45. *Referee* (Sydney), September 26, 1888.
46. *Daily Alta California*, December 31, 1888.
47. *New York Clipper*, April 29, 1882.
48. *National Police Gazette*; August 4, 1883; *San Francisco Daily Examiner*, January 26, 1884.
49. *Daily Picayune*, April 15, 1884.
50. *New York Clipper*, May 26, 1888; *Boston Herald*, May 16, 1888.
51. *National Police Gazette*, February 23, 1889.
52. *Referee* (Sydney), February 27, 1889, quoting *London Sporting Life*.
53. *Brooklyn Daily Eagle*, April 25, 1889.
54. *New York Clipper*, May 4, 1889.
55. *San Francisco Daily Examiner*, April 26, 1889.
56. *San Francisco Chronicle*, April 27, 1889; *San Francisco Daily Examiner*, April 27, 1889; *National Police Gazette*, May 11, 1889.
57. *Daily Picayune*, July 7, 1889.

16—End of an Era

1. *New York Clipper*, May 18, 1889.
2. *Daily Alta California*, May 27, 1889, quoting the *St. Louis Republican*.
3. *New York Clipper*, June 8, 1889.
4. *San Francisco Evening Post*, June 10, 1889.
5. *San Francisco Chronicle*, June 10, 1889.
6. *Times-Democrat*, July 3–6, 1889; *Daily Picayune*, July 7, 1889.
7. *Times-Democrat*, July 7, 1889.
8. *Times-Democrat*, July 3–8, 1889.
9. *Times-Democrat*, July 8, 1889.
10. *San Francisco Examiner*, July 10, 1889.
11. *Brooklyn Daily Eagle*, July 8, 1889.
12. *Daily Picayune*, July 10, 1889.
13. *San Francisco Examiner*, July 10, 1889.
14. *Daily Picayune*, July 10, 1889.
15. Donovan at 125–128.
16. *Daily Picayune*, July 9, 1889; *Times-Democrat*, July 9, 10, 1889; *Boston Herald*, July 9, 1889; *New York Daily Tribune*, July 9, 1889; *New York Times*, July 9, 1889; *National Police Gazette*, July 20, 1889, July 27, 1889; *Boston Daily Globe*, July 9, 1889.
17. *Brooklyn Daily Eagle*, July 9, 1889.
18. *Daily Picayune*, July 9, 1889, July 10, 1889, July 24, 1889.
19. *Brooklyn Daily Eagle*, July 9, 1889.
20. *Boston Herald*, July 10, 1889; *Boston Daily Globe*, July 9, 1889; *Daily Picayune*, July 10, 1889.
21. *Brooklyn Daily Eagle*, July 8, 1889.
22. *Times-Democrat*, July 11, 1889.

23. Ibid.
24. *Brooklyn Daily Eagle*, July 9, 1889; *Times-Democrat*, July 9, 1889.
25. *The Boston Herald*, July 30, 1889.
26. *Times-Democrat*, July 9, 1889.
27. *Boston Daily Globe*, July 9, 1889.
28. *Daily Picayune*, July 10, 1889.
29. *Times-Democrat*, July 10, 1889.
30. *Daily Picayune*, July 10, 1889.
31. *Times-Democrat*, July 9–11, 1889.
32. *Brooklyn Daily Eagle*, July 9, 1889.
33. *Times-Democrat*, July 11, 1889.
34. *San Francisco Daily Examiner*, July 29, 1889.
35. *San Francisco Examiner*, July 10, 1889.
36. *Brooklyn Daily Eagle*, July 9, 1889.
37. *San Francisco Examiner*, July 10, 1889.
38. *San Francisco Examiner*, July 10, 1889.
39. *Boston Daily Globe*, July 9, 1889.
40. *Times-Democrat* (New Orleans), July 10, 1889.
41. *Clarion-Ledger*, July 11, 1889.
42. *Brooklyn Daily Eagle*, July 11, 1889; *Times-Democrat*, July 12, 13, 1889.
43. *Times-Democrat*, July 13, 1889.
44. *Clarion-Ledger*, July 18, 1889.
45. *Times-Democrat*, July 20, 1889.
46. *Times-Democrat*, August 1, 1889; *Clarion-Ledger*, August 8, 1889.
47. *Clarion-Ledger*, August 22, 1889; *Brooklyn Daily Eagle*, March 18, 1890.
48. *Clarion-Ledger*, September 29, 1889.
49. *Clarion-Ledger*, August 29, 1889.
50. *Clarion-Ledger*, March 27, 1890; Rex Lardner, *The Legendary Champions*, 55; Isenberg at 278–279; *San Francisco Examiner*, December 15, 1889.
51. Sullivan at 166.
52. *Brooklyn Daily Eagle*, March 18, 1890.
53. *Clarion-Ledger*, June 26, 1890; *New York Clipper*, July 5, 1890.
54. Sullivan at 167.
55. Sullivan at 182–184.

17—Retired?

1. *New York Daily Tribune*, July 10, 1889; *Boston Daily Globe*, July 9, 1889.
2. *Boston Herald*, July 10, 1889.
3. *San Francisco Examiner*, July 10, 1889.
4. *New York Clipper*, September 14, 1889.
5. *Referee* (Sydney), September 11, 1889.
6. *Clarion-Ledger*, September 29, 1889.
7. *New York Times*, November 11, 1889; *San Francisco Examiner*, December 2, 1889.
8. *Referee* (Sydney), November 20, 1889.
9. *Times-Democrat*, July 1889; *Clarion-Ledger*, July 18, 1889, quoting *Houston Free South* and *Williamsburg Journal*.
10. *Times-Democrat*, July 22, 1889.
11. *San Francisco Examiner*, December 2, 1889.
12. *Referee* (Sydney), December 4, 1889.
13. Fleischer, *Black Dynamite*, vol. 1 at 152, quoting the *London Sportsman*, December 26, 1889.
14. *San Francisco Examiner*, December 17, 1889.
15. *San Francisco Examiner*, December 24, 1889; *National Police Gazette*, January 4, 1890.
16. *Brooklyn Daily Eagle*, February 10, 1890.
17. *New York Clipper*, February 15, 1890.
18. *New York Clipper*, February 22, 1890.
19. *Referee* (Sydney), April 16, 1890.
20. *New York Clipper*, February 15, 1890.
21. *San Francisco Examiner*, February 8, 1890.
22. *National Police Gazette*, March 8, 1890.
23. *Referee* (Sydney), March 6, 1890.
24. *National Police Gazette*, March 18, 1892.
25. *New York Clipper*, May 24, 1890.
26. *San Francisco Examiner*, May 20, 1890.
27. *Chicago Tribune*, May 20, 1890.
28. *National Police Gazette*, December 13, 1890; Fleischer, *Black Dynamite*, vol. 1, at 114.
29. *New York Clipper*, May 24, 31, 1890.
30. *San Francisco Chronicle*, July 8, 1890.
31. *Referee* (Sydney), October 22, 1890, October 26, 1892. The first performance might have been August 27, 1890; Sullivan at 167.
32. *Minneapolis Tribune*, May 3, 1891.
33. *Referee* (Sydney), October 22, 1890; *National Police Gazette*, December 6, 1890, December 13, 1890.
34. *Referee* (Sydney), December 17, 1890.
35. *Referee* (Sydney), December 24, 1890.
36. *Referee* (Sydney), February 11, 1891, quoting *The New York Herald*.
37. *San Francisco Examiner*, April 28, 1891.
38. *Referee* (Sydney), March 4, 1891.
39. The Corbett-Jackson bout will be thoroughly discussed in the Corbett volume.
40. *Referee* (Sydney), May 27, 1891.
41. *Referee* (Sydney), June 3, 1891, quoting *The San Francisco Daily Report*.

18—Changing His Tune

1. *San Francisco Examiner*, June 27, 1891.
2. *Referee* (Sydney), July 22, 1891; Sullivan at 173.
3. *Referee* (Sydney), July 29, 1891.
4. Sullivan at 174.
5. *Referee* (Sydney), August 5, 1891.
6. *Referee* (Sydney), August 12, 1891.
7. *Referee* (Sydney), September 30, 1891.
8. *Referee* (Sydney), August 19, 1891.
9. *Referee* (Sydney), September 9, 1891.
10. *Referee* (Sydney), September 23, 1891.
11. Boxrec.com.
12. *Referee* (Sydney), October 7, 1891.
13. *Referee* (Sydney), November 4, 1891, November 18, 1891; *Clarion-Ledger*, November 19, 1891.
14. *San Francisco Chronicle*, November 26, 1891.
15. *Referee* (Sydney), December 23, 1891.
16. *San Francisco Examiner*, December 21, 1891.
17. *San Francisco Examiner*, December 21, 1891.
18. *Philadelphia Inquirer*, March 6, 1892; James J. Corbett, *The Roar of the Crowd* (New York: G.P. Putnam's Sons, 1925), 164–165. Corbett claimed the challenge was issued March 5, 1892, given to the Associated Press.
19. *Clarion-Ledger*, January 9, 1890.
20. *Daily Picayune*, September 4, 1892.
21. Robert L. Zangrando, "About Lynching," from *The Reader's Companion to American History*, editors Eric Foner and John A. Garraty, Houghton Mifflin Co., 1991.
22. *Clarion-Ledger*, January 9, 1890.
23. Sullivan at 176.
24. The Jackson-Slavin bout will be further discussed in the Corbett volume.

25. The Corbett-Sullivan bout will be fully discussed in the Corbett volume.

19—The Legacy

1. Sullivan at 179–180.
2. Sullivan at 179.
3. *Times-Democrat*, September 8, 1892.

4. *Times-Democrat*, September 1, 1892.
5. Richard K. Fox, *The Life and Battles of James J. Corbett, The Champion Pugilist of the World* (New York: Richard Fox, 1892, 1895), 39–40.
6. Sullivan at 179.
7. Sullivan at 181.
8. Burns at 25–28.
9. Corbett at 117–122.
10. *Daily Picayune*, September 8–13, 1892.

Bibliography

Primary Sources

Alta-Californian. 1884.
Australian Sportsman. 1881–1884.
Baltimore American. 1883 .
Baltimore Sun. 1883.
Billings Herald. 1883–1885.
Birmingham Gazette (England). 1887.
Boston Daily Globe. 1879–1889.
Boston Herald. 1881–1889.
Brooklyn Daily Eagle. 1882–1890.
Buffalo Courier. 1882.
Butte Daily Miner. 1884.
Chicago Daily News. 1881–1885.
Chicago Herald. 1881–1885.
Chicago Times. 1881.
Chicago Tribune. 1881–1890.
Cincinnati Commercial. 1880–1881.
Cincinnati Commercial Gazette. 1885.
Cincinnati Daily Enquirer. 1880.
Cincinnati Enquirer. 1885.
Cincinnati Evening Post. 1885.
Clarion-Ledger. 1889–1891.
Colorado Miner (Georgetown). 1887.
Daily Arkansas Gazette (Little Rock). 1884.
Daily Astorian. 1884.
Daily Democrat (Natchez). 1882.
Daily Inter Ocean (Chicago). 1881–1882.
Daily Memphis Avalanche. 1884.
Daily Picayune (New Orleans). 1882–1892.
Davenport Daily Gazette. 1883.
Davenport Democrat. 1883.
Denver Daily News. 1886–1887.
Denver Tribune-Republican. 1886.
Denver Republican. 1887.
Desert Evening News. 1886.
Eau Claire Daily Leader. 1883.
Eau Claire News. 1883.
Galveston Daily News. 1884.
Helena Daily Herald. 1884.
Helena Independent. 1884–1887.
Houston Free South. 1889.
Indianapolis Sentinel. 1882.
Irish Standard (Minneapolis). 1887.

London Sporting Life. 1887–1889.
London Sportsman. 1887–1889.
Louisville Courier-Journal. 1883–1899.
Louisville Evening Post. 1883.
Memphis Daily Appeal. 1884.
Minneapolis Tribune. 1886–1891.
Missouri Republican (St. Louis). 1883–1884.
Morning Oregonian. 1889.
Nashville Banner. 1884.
Nashville Daily American. 1884.
National Police Gazette (New York). 1880–1905.
New York Clipper. 1880–1890.
New York Daily Tribune. 1882–1889.
New York Herald. 1881–1891.
New York Times. 1882–1889.
People's Advocate (Washington, D.C.). 1883.
Philadelphia Inquirer. 1885–1892.
Philadelphia Press. 1881–1886.
Philadelphia Record. 1881.
Pittsburg Dispatch. 1883–1886.
Pittsburgh Daily Post. 1886.
Pittsburgh Times. 1884.
Referee (Sydney). 1887–1892.
Rochester Daily Union and Advertiser. 1882.
Rochester Democrat and Chronicle. 1882.
Rochester Morning Herald. 1882.
Rocky Mountain News. 1886.
St. Louis Daily Globe-Democrat. 1883.
Saint Paul and Minneapolis Pioneer Press. 1883–1887.
Saint Paul Daily Globe. 1883.
Salt Lake Daily Tribune. 1886.
San Francisco Chronicle. 1884–1892.
San Francisco Daily Examiner. 1884–1892.
San Francisco Daily Report. 1891.
Seattle Daily Post-Intelligencer. 1884.
Sydney Bulletin. 1884–1885.
Times-Democrat (New Orleans). 1882–1889.
Toronto Evening Telegram. 1883.
Toronto Globe. 1883.
Vincennes Daily Commercial. 1884.
Washington Evening Star. 1882.
Washington Post. 1882.
Williamsburg Journal. 1889.

Additional Sources, Including Secondary Sources

Australian Sporting Celebrities. Melbourne: A.H. Massina, 1887.

Boxrec.com.

Burns, William. *Incidents in the Life of John L. Sullivan and Other Famous People of Fifty Years Ago.* 1928.

Corbett, James J. *The Roar of the Crowd.* New York: G.P. Putnam's Sons, 1925.

Cyberboxingzone.com.

Donovan, Mike. *The Roosevelt That I Know.* New York: B.W. Dodge and Co., 1909.

Durant, John. *The Heavyweight Champions.* New York: Hastings House, 1960, 1976.

Fleischer, Nat. *Black Dynamite.* Vol. 1. New York: Nat Fleischer, 1938.

Grombach, John V. *The Saga of the Fist.* New York: A.S. Barnes, 1949, 1977.

Inglis, William. *Champions Off Guard.* New York: Vanguard Press, 1932.

Isenberg, Michael T. *John L. Sullivan and His America.* Chicago: University of Illinois Press, 1988.

Johnston, Alexander. *Ten and Out!* New York: Ives Washburn, 1927.

Lardner, Rex. *The Legendary Champions.* New York: American Heritage Press, 1972.

McCusker, John J. "Comparing the Purchasing Power of Money in the U.S. from 1665 to Any Other Year, Including the Present." Economic History Services. <http://www.eh.net/hmit/ppowerusd/>.

The Ring. 1926.

Senate.gov.

Sullivan, John L. *I Can Lick Any Sonofabitch in the House!* Carson City: Proteus Publishing Co., 1979. A reprint of the 1892 autobiography by Sullivan called *Life and Reminiscences of a Nineteenth Century Gladiator.*

Zangrando, Robert L. "About Lynching." In *The Reader's Companion to American History*, editors Eric Foner and John A. Garraty. Houghton Mifflin Co., 1991.

Index